SHIFTING SANDS

LATERAL EXCHANGES: ARCHITECTURE, URBAN DEVELOPMENT,
AND TRANSNATIONAL PRACTICES

A series edited by Felipe Correa, Bruno Carvalho, and Alison Isenberg

Also in the series

Tara Dudley, *Building Antebellum New Orleans:*
Free People of Color and Their Influence

Ana María León, *Modernity for the Masses:*
Antonio Bonet's Dreams for Buenos Aires

Burak Erdim, *Landed Internationals:*
Planning Cultures, the Academy, and the Making of the Modern Middle East

Mary P. Ryan, *Taking the Land to Make the City:*
A Bicoastal History of North America

Fabiola López-Durán, *Eugenics in the Garden:*
Transatlantic Architecture and the Crafting of Modernity

SHIFTING SANDS

Landscape, Memory, and Commodities in China's Contemporary Borderlands

XIAOXUAN LU

University of Texas Press

Austin

All maps, diagrams, and photos are by the author, unless otherwise noted. All translations are the author's own, unless otherwise indicated.

An earlier version of the essay titled "Silk Road Urbanism" was published as Xiaoxuan Lu, "Re-territorializing Mengla: From 'Backwater' to 'Bridgehead' of China's Socio-economic Development," *Cities* 117 (2021): 103311. An earlier version of the essay titled "*Shan-shui* Memory" was published as Xiaoxuan Lu, "My Love from the Mountain: Contingent Bordering Processes at Mount Changbai/ Baekdu," *Area* 53 (2021): 511–521.

Requests for permission to reproduce material from this work should be sent to:
    Permissions
    University of Texas Press
    P.O. Box 7819
    Austin, TX 78713-7819
    utpress.utexas.edu/rp-form

♾ The paper used in this book meets the minimum requirements of ANSI/NISO Z39.48-1992 (R1997) (Permanence of Paper).

Library of Congress Cataloging-in-Publication Data

Names: Lu, Xiaoxuan, author.
Title: Shifting sands : landscape, memory, and commodities in China's contemporary borderlands / Xiaoxuan Lu.
Description: First edition. | Austin : University of Texas Press, 2023. | Series: Lateral exchanges: architecture, urban development, and transnational practices | Includes index.
Identifiers: LCCN 2022042456
    ISBN 978-1-4773-2755-5 (hardcover)
    ISBN 978-1-4773-2756-2 (PDF)
Subjects: LCSH: Borderlands—China—Economic conditions—20th century. | Borderlands—China— Economic conditions—21st century. | Borderlands—China—Social conditions. | Borderlands— China—Civilization. | Economic development—China—History—20th century. | Economic development—China—History—21st century. | Infrastructure (Economics)—China—History—20th century. | Infrastructure (Economics)—China—History—21st century.
Classification: LCC HC428.B67 L8 2023 | DDC 330.951—dc23/eng/20230317
LC record available at https://lccn.loc.gov/2022042456

doi:10.7560/327555

CONTENTS

PART III. SETTLEMENTS AND MEMORIES

Additional maps, timelines, and other resources may be found at
https://www.shiftingsandsproject.com.

ABBREVIATIONS

ADB   Asian Development Bank
AJK   Azad Jammu and Kashmir
ASEAN   Association of Southeast Asian Nations
AVG   American Volunteer Group
BRI   Belt and Road Initiative
CAREC   Central Asia Regional Economic Cooperation
CCTV   China Central Television
CDB   China Development Bank
CER   Chinese Eastern Railway
CGGC   China Gezhouba Group Corporation
CIMC   China International Marine Containers Corporation
CMG   China Merchants Group
COCZ   Chinese Overseas Economic and Trade Cooperation Zone
COFCO   China Oil and Foodstuffs Corporation
COSCO   China Ocean Shipping Company
CPC   Communist Party of China
CRBC   China Road and Bridge Corporation
CRCT   China Railway Container Transport Corporation
DSSC   Danube Shipping and Stevedoring Company
EU   European Union
GEACPS   Greater East Asia Co-Prosperity Sphere
GMO   genetically modified organism
GMS   Greater Mekong Subregion
GSCS   Greater Southeast China Subregion
GSIP   Great Stone Industrial Park
GTI   Greater Tumen Initiative
GTS   Greater Tumen Subregion
IMF   International Monetary Fund
IT   information technology

JAO   Jewish Autonomous Oblast
KBE   Kunming–Bangkok Expressway
KBS   Korean Broadcasting System
KKH   Karakoram Highway
KMT   Chinese Nationalist Party (Kuomintang)
KTZ   Kazakhstan Temir Zholy
LPH   Lianyungang Port Holdings
MASL   meters above sea level
MFA   Ministry of Foreign Affairs (China)
MOC   Ministry of Commerce (China)
MOF   Ministry of Finance (China)
MW   megawatt
NDRC   National Development and Reform Commission (China)
NEA   National Energy Administration (China)
NJHP   Neelum Jhelum Hydroelectric Project
NRC   National Resources Commission (China)
OFDI   outward foreign direct investment
PCT   Piraeus Container Terminal
PLA   People's Liberation Army
PRC   People's Republic of China
RMB   Chinese yuan (Renminbi)
ROC   Republic of China
RZD   Russian Railways Logistics (Rossiyskie Zheleznye Dorogi)
SASAC   State-Owned Assets Supervision and Administration
        Commission (China)
SEZ   special economic zone
SINOMACH China National Machinery Industry Corporation
SMR   South Manchuria Railway
SOB   state-owned bank
SOE   state-owned enterprise
TEU   twenty-foot equivalent units
TRADP   Tumen River Area Development Program
TSR   Trans-Siberian Railway
UN   United Nations
UNDP   United Nations Development Programme
UNESCO United Nations Educational, Scientific and Cultural Organization
USSR   Union of Soviet Socialist Republics
WAPDA   Water and Power Development Authority (Pakistan)
WTO   World Trade Organization
XBRBGC Xinjiang Beixin Road & Bridge Group Corporation
XUAR   Xinjiang Uygur Autonomous Region

PREFACE

On my way from Urumqi to Khorgas on July 12, 2015, I had to make an unscheduled overnight stop at Alashankou. The next day I planned to cross the China-Kazakhstan border at Khorgas, a major trade and transport hub, before heading west to Almaty, the former capital of Kazakhstan. Knowing that the Central Asia–China gas pipeline enters China at Alashankou, I decided to take an early morning walk around the small border city before embarking on another four-hour drive to Khorgas. Just as my car was about to leave Alashankou, however, I was apprehended by local border police, taken to a police station, and interrogated for six hours. When asked why I had come to Alashankou and was "wandering around the city," I explained that I majored in landscape studies and was curious to see how Alashankou and the region had recently been transformed by massive transnational infrastructure development. "What is landscape?" demanded the interrogator, probably unaware that his question would trigger a four-hour explanation of my understanding of "landscape," the different types of landscape design, and the various research projects I had worked on so far. Every single word was dutifully jotted down in a notebook, which was practically full by the end of the process. Finally, the interrogator seemed satisfied with my explanations and ended the cross-examination by saying, "Everything you said is quite interesting. However, in future you'd better not be so curious about these kinds of projects in the border regions. The governments have them all under control; anyway, as a landscape architect, these projects are none of your business."

My interrogator would probably be dismayed to learn that my curiosity about China's borderlands intensified and persists unabated. Indeed, some of the ideas I shared about "landscape" during that six-hour detention at Alashankou are further elaborated in these pages and helped shape the overall conceptualization of this book. My knowledge of and interest in the history and historical geography of China's borderlands are synthesized and communicated by using the methodological approach, conceptual framing, and representational techniques inherent in landscape studies. Hence, this wider "landscape approach" aims to distinguish this book from other borderland scholarship as well as contributing to the field of landscape studies itself by presenting the unique research subject of China's borderland landscapes in all their geological, cultural, and political diversity. Over the years, especially when carrying out fieldwork in the often politically sensitive and geographically demanding border regions, I have profited greatly from the friendship and support of Zhuldyz Bakytzhan, Benny Shaffer, Justin Stern, Ashley Scott Kelly, Sandor Scheeres, Deang Souliya, Bo Wang, Yammi Yik Ming Tsang, and Robert Winstanley-Chesters. Thanks are due to Aristo Xubin Chen, the research assistant for this project, for his indispensable assistance in revising and formatting the illustrations that grace this book. Special thanks go to Gavin Coates for his invaluable support, both emotional and editorial, as the book chapters developed and evolved. I am grateful to the University of Hong Kong (HKU) Fund for Basic Research 2018/20 (Project No. 201807159002) and 2019/20 (Project No. 201910159296) for partially supporting this project and to the HKU Department of Architecture's Fund for Design Publishing for making it possible to publish the book in color.

SHIFTING SANDS

STRATIGRAPHY OF CHINA'S BORDERLANDS

China's strengthening of transport infrastructure as part of its Belt and Road Initiative (BRI) is revealed by the extensive road widening from two to four lanes on Chinese Provincial Road 201 going east toward Quanhe-Wonjeong, the last China–North Korea border port along the Tumen River before it empties into the Sea of Japan. As a contested multicultural region at the intersection of the boundaries of China, North Korea, and Russia, the Tumen River borderland displays a dizzying array of contemporary economic and political paradoxes and historical legacies. The river's historic role as an important Chinese trade route between northeastern China and the Sea of Japan was greatly impaired after Russia's annexation of Outer Manchuria in the late 1850s, resulting in the border between the Russian Empire and Joseon Korea, running 15 kilometers along the lowest reaches of the Tumen River and its estuary. Although China retained navigation rights along the final stretch of the river under the terms of the 1886 Sino-Russian Border Treaty, China's access to the sea was completely cut off after construction of the Korea-Russia Friendship Bridge in the 1950s. To transport military supplies to support the Korean People's Army during the Korean War (1950–1953), the Soviet Union built a temporary wooden bridge 500 meters downstream from the China-Korea-Russia border intersection, upgrading it to a railway bridge in 1959. Providing a critical connection between the Vladivostok branch of the Russian Far Eastern Railway at Khasan railway station and the Hongui Line of the Korean State Railway at Tumangang Station, the railway bridge with its 11-meter clearance effectively blocks oceangoing vessels from accessing the sea by the Tumen River.

Five decades of fruitless negotiation with Russia and North Korea left China with little hope of regaining navigation rights to the lowest 15 kilometers of the

FIGURE 0.1
The Korea-Russia Friendship Bridge spanning the Tumen River, looking toward the river estuary and Sea of Japan in the far distance, June 2018.

FIGURE 0.2
A construction site safety warning sign standing at the edge of Chinese Provincial Road 201 during road widening near Quanhe Port, Hunchun City, Yanbian Korean Autonomous Prefecture, June 2018.

Tumen River in the foreseeable future. Recently, the Chinese central government and the administration of landlocked Yanbian Korean Autonomous Prefecture have pursued a new strategy called *jiegang chuhai* (literally, "borrowing a foreign port to gain access to the sea").[1] Expanding and upgrading railways and roads is considered vital to improving connections between Yanbian and the Russian ports of Zarubino and

Vladivostok and the North Korean port of Rason (formerly Rajin-Sonbong). Enormous billboards mounted above the portals of a tunnel on Provincial Road 201 near the Quanhe-Wonjeong port reveal ambiguities between the region's current obsession with infrastructure expansion and China's mourning of the loss of coastal territory in the late nineteenth century and shipping access to the sea in the mid-twentieth century. Chinese characters reading "Constructing a sea-access corridor, promoting development, and opening up" tower above a computer-rendered collage with one tree in the foreground, one road leading to the ocean, and a cargo vessel flying the Chinese flag. The retaining walls of both tunnel portals are also bedecked with bilingual signs in Chinese and Korean: "The prosperity of the region depends on the protection of its road" and "A smooth road connection leads to a thriving revolutionary frontier." All these signs trumpet the critical role that roads play in boosting the economic vitality of the borderland area lacking direct access to the sea.

The Tumen River border is typical of many examples examined in this book, where the materiality and narratives of infrastructure are foundational to a broader investigation that seeks to understand the contemporary development and urbanization of China's borderlands as transnational, nonlinear, and contingent processes driven by historical and multilateral influences. The investigation is based on the following three premises. First, beyond a China-centric narrative, this book highlights the transnational nature of borderlands, whose physical and socioeconomic landscapes have long been shaped by multidirectional flows of materials and ideas. Second, focusing beyond the changes initiated by the Belt and Road Initiative, this book recognizes the significance of borderlands in various manifestations and visions of Silk Roads promoted by a multiplicity of agents who have been striving to integrate borderlands into their respective spheres of influence since the nineteenth century. Third, beyond a purely historical investigation, this book foregrounds the contemporary socioeconomic implications of the complex intertwining of history, memory, and identity in borderlands, in the context of surging domestic and foreign capital now flooding into these resource-rich far-flung regions.

Inevitably, this book draws insights from a rich seam of classical and contemporary studies on the subject of borderlands and frontiers, which has been mined by scholars for more than a century. Scholarly discourse started to focus on this field of interest in the late nineteenth century, exemplified by the writings of Frederick Jackson Turner on the American frontier.[2] Turner conceptualized the frontier as an uninhabited wilderness over which civilization marched inexorably from the eastern core areas westward, ruthlessly incorporating the frontier into the nation. Although this narrative has been criticized on several fronts, such as ignoring the fact that the American West was not a wilderness but a homeland from the perspective of Native Americans, Turner's frontier thesis exerted an enormous influence over scholarship on the frontiers of the American West and elsewhere in the world. Critiques of and debates about Turner's frontier thesis have fueled the development of a growing body of scholarship on comparative frontiers that seeks to explain common fundamentals and unique distinctions while encouraging interdisciplinary approaches that increasingly blur the boundaries of history, anthropology, sociology, and geography.[3]

Notably, literature on Chinese frontiers has played a significant role in the field of frontier studies, though small in scope. One of the great seminal works on this subject, Owen Lattimore's 1940 book *Inner Asian Frontiers of China*, revolutionized the field of international frontier studies by moving away from the nationalistic US model toward a more intercultural and flexible model of interactions between peoples on the frontier.[4] Lattimore conceptualized frontiers as inhabited areas and described a cyclic process in which Chinese frontiers were alternately more or less integrated with the national core without ever being completely integrated into the nation proper. He focused on the landscape and environmental characteristics of the transfrontier regions (Manchuria, Mongolia, Chinese Turkestan, and Tibet), including their original forms, the historical and societal processes influencing them, the types and styles of interactions between them and China itself, and how all these factors combined to shape various sectors of the frontier and the frontier as a whole.

Despite occasional attempts, this all-encompassing and audacious approach to examining the entire Chinese frontier area as a research topic has not been emulated since the publication of Lattimore's book, partly due to the Chinese frontier areas being inaccessible and consigned to obscurity for most of the second half of the twentieth century. After a series of frontier development initiatives launched by successive Chinese governments since the early 2000s, the past two decades have witnessed a resurgence of scholarly interest in China's borderlands. These scholarly works are mostly journal articles with a strong regional focus and do not take on the subject of the entire frontier region.[5]

Eight decades after the first publication of *Inner Asian Frontiers of China*, this book refocuses Lattimore's wide-angle lens, including all of China's frontier areas as a research topic and reasserting the critical significance of Inner Asia in world history.[6] Since the age of Christopher Columbus, the cyclical rise and fall of Inner Asian powers has been subject to the political tectonic shifts between land-based and seafaring powers. During the first era of globalization born of Western imperial adventurism and industrial prowess in the middle of the nineteenth century, Inner Asia became the focus of various power struggles and attempts to form land and sea connections, exemplified by the rapid inroads made by European colonial powers from the coasts of Eurasia deep into the Asian heartland. The remainder of this introduction contextualizes the historical transformation of China's borderlands in the context of the development and modernization of Inner Asia since the nineteenth-century advent of globalization. It examines the transition from imperial frontiers to national borderlands since the mid-nineteenth century, a process coauthored by Chinese anti-imperialist revolutionaries and foreign powers within the context of a burgeoning new global economy driven by the Second Industrial

Revolution. Two infrastructural initiatives that may be seen as precursors to China's current Belt and Road Initiative are juxtaposed: first, the 1920 plan developed by Sun Yat-sen, the father of modern China, and, second, a range of plans proposed by Russia, Japan, and several European colonial powers. The BRI launched by Beijing in 2013, combining land-based "belt" with marine "road" projects, can be understood as the latest stratum of development overlaid on multiple previous layers of multinational built and unbuilt projects, spanning the centuries and vast distances between Eurasia's coastlands and Asia's heartlands.

FROM IMPERIAL FRONTIERS TO NATIONAL BORDERLANDS

China's contemporary borderlands are inherited from the Inner Asian frontiers of the Great Qing, the last imperial Chinese dynasty founded by the Manchu Aisin Gioro clan of Manchuria, which ruled China proper from 1644 to 1912. During the Qing dynasty, Yunnan and Tibet in the southwest, East Turkestan (Xinjiang) in the northwest, and Mongolia and Manchuria in the north and northeast were all incorporated into a China-centered empire. Following military conquest and annexation of these frontier dependencies (*fanshu*), the Qing court maintained a light grip on its Inner Asian frontiers until the mid-nineteenth century. Qing military officials oversaw these far-flung ethnically and culturally diverse frontiers with the cooperation of a network of indigenous local headmen.[7] Some scholars, particularly those associated with New Qing History, saw this hands-off approach as symptomatic of the pluralistic view of empire held by the ruling Manchu minority.[8] Others point out the practical challenges the Qing court faced concerning the cost and difficulty of undertaking programs of settlement and administrative expansion over its vast Inner Asian territory.[9]

The Qing dynasty's frontier policy started to evolve during and after the First Opium War (1839–1842) in response to the dramatic expansion of Western imperialism in Asia, fueled by the industrial revolutions of Europe and the United States and their rapacious demands for raw materials. Influenced by Western "statecraft" (*jingshi*), a new generation of Chinese thinkers called on the Qing court to abandon pluralism in the empire's frontier regions in favor of an integrationist policy.[10] For example, noted statesman Gong Zizhen advocated a new frontier policy of accelerated investment in agricultural expansion in the frontier dependencies, encouraging migration from China proper, thereby raising their status to official provinces of the empire.[11]

Stable populations of taxpaying immigrants under the administration of Qing-controlled provincial governments eased the fiscal burden of managing the frontier areas. Integration of the frontiers had been ratcheted up further by the late nineteenth century, prompted by reformist Qing officials who had adopted the Western notion

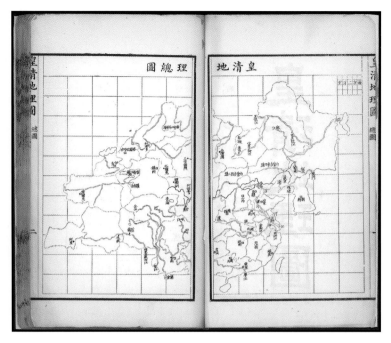

FIGURE 0.3

Dong Youcheng, *Overview Map*, in *Geographical Map of the Qing Empire* (Guangzhou: Yifangzhai, 1856). World Digital Library, https://www.loc.gov/item/2021668287.

of the "nation-state" (*minzu guojia*).[12] Consequently, the turn of the twentieth century saw a new phase of frontier integration, transforming traditional imperial frontiers into modern national borderlands. The Qing reformists believed more fundamental changes were required beyond agricultural expansion, migration, and administrative reform. They promoted integrationist strategies such as political reform, education and cultural campaigns, and investment in transportation infrastructure.[13]

These initiatives were perpetuated well into the Republic of China (1912–1949) era, after the overthrow of Qing imperial rule in 1911. After 1912, these integrationist strategies were instigated under new social and political circumstances. After 268 years under Manchu rule, China transitioned from a Manchu-ruled empire to a Han Chinese–ruled nation-state. The Qing dynasty's pluralistic vision of empire that had been crumbling since the mid-nineteenth century ended and was abruptly replaced by a new Chinese nationalism: *minzu zhuyi* (literally, "the doctrine of the people's lineage"). Sun Yat-sen, the Republic's first president, proclaimed *minzu zhuyi*, *minquan zhuyi* (literally, "the doctrine of the people's sovereignty"), and *minsheng zhuyi* (literally, "the doctrine of the people's livelihood") to be the three evolutionary stages that China needed to pass through to ensure its survival in the modern world.[14] China's frontier policy entered a new era of national unity, whereby the integration of frontier populations as part of the Chinese nation (*zhonghua minzu*) and the

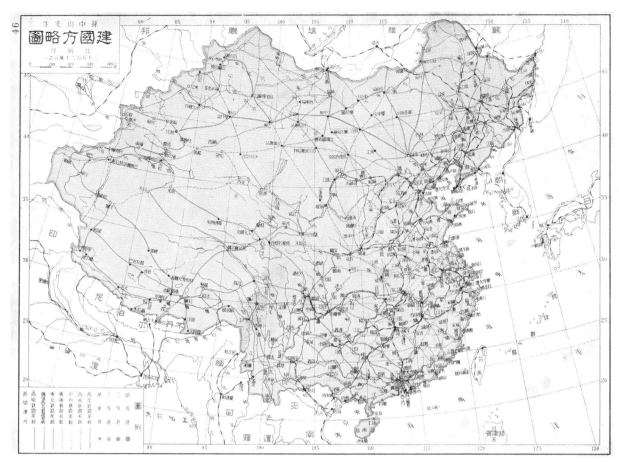

FIGURE 0.4
Map of Dr. Sun Yat-sen's Plan for National Reconstruction (1929). Wikimedia Commons.

integration of frontier territories became indispensable cornerstones of the newly established Chinese nation-state.

Unlike most of his nationalist peers, who adopted a definition of the Chinese nation based exclusively on homogeneous Han ethnicity (Hanzu), Sun Yat-sen developed his own distinct nonethnic interpretation.[15] To him, it was important to move away from a Han ethnic notion of China toward a more inclusive definition grounded in a shared culture, language, and territory. Even in 1900, when Sun spatially mapped the future nation-state of China, he categorically drew its boundaries to include the existing frontier regions of the Qing Empire. Sun believed in the importance of preserving the Chinese nation as "a bounded territory" including all the peoples of the Qing Empire, even after the Manchu dynasty itself was extinguished.[16] In the years following the establishment of the Republic of China in 1912, Sun actively promoted improvements in education and communication as ways of reining in frontier regions seeking to break away from the new Republic, rather than the violent confrontation advocated by militarists. Sun believed that education and communication would help develop a shared language and culture throughout the Chinese nation and "gradually help" frontier populations understand the benefits of Chinese nationhood.[17]

Along with other republican reformists, Sun recognized that industrialization and modernization need to go hand in hand with nationalist efforts to transform frontier areas into territorially "integrated cornerstones" of a modern Republic.[18] After 1912, Sun spent much of his time developing a detailed plan for China's national development, first published in English in 1920 under the title *The International Development of China* (hereinafter referred to as the "1920 plan").[19] It was published in Chinese in 1921 under the title *Shiye Jihua* (literally, "plan for industry and commerce").[20] The plan outlined several massive infrastructure development projects intended to link China proper with its remote borderlands, including nearly 100,000 miles of railway, 1 million miles of tarmacadam roads, dozens of ports and transportation corridors, and an ambitious telephone and telegraph system.[21]

The former imperial frontiers, now national borderlands, featured prominently in the 1920 plan not only because Sun and other republican reformists realized the significance of borders in defining the nation-state but also because of the importance of the resource-rich borderlands in the context of an increasingly integrated global resource market. The first chapter of the 1920 plan entitled "A Project to Assist the Readjustment of Postbellum Industries" emphasized the importance of resource development after World War I (1914–1918), to balance China's trade deficit with other commercial nations. Sun declared:

> All the commercial nations are looking to China as the only "dumping ground" for their over-production. The pre-war condition of trade was unfavorable to China. The balance of imports over exports was something over one hundred million dollars gold annually. The market of China under this condition could not expand much for soon after there will be no more money or commodities left for exchanging goods with foreign countries. Fortunately, the natural resources of China are great and their proper development would create an unlimited market for the whole world and would utilize the greater part, if not all of the billions of dollars' worth of war industries soon to be turned into peace Industries.[22]

Despite this clear vision for the future held by Sun and other republican reformists, hardly any of the railway lines and trade corridors that were included in the 1920 plan and intended to strengthen the borderlands' connections to central China, regional neighbors, and even the world were implemented during China's republican era due to the lack of political and economic capital. The People's Republic established in 1949 soon shelved the 1920 plan because the focus of development shifted to central China during the leadership of Mao Zedong (1949–1976) and the coastal regions during the leadership of Deng Xiaoping (1978–1997).

China's state-sponsored development of its Inner Asian borderlands only gathered momentum at the beginning of the new millennium. In response to increasing inequality between coastal and inland regions since the commencement of the Reform and Opening Up policy (*gaige kaifang*) in the late 1970s, the central government launched a broad change to its regional development strategy at the end of the twentieth century. Nine provinces bordering fourteen countries along a land boundary 22,117 kilometers long are covered by the Western Development Strategy (*xibu da kaifa*) promulgated in 2000 and the Northeast China Revitalization Strategy (*zhenxing dongbei jihua*) in 2003. These border regions have since strengthened connections with other Chinese metropoles as well as the world market following China's admission to the World Trade Organization (WTO) in 2001. The state-driven development of China's Inner Asian borderlands moved full steam ahead after President Xi Jinping announced the Silk Road Economic Belt strategy in September 2013, referred to in English as the Belt and Road Initiative (*yidai yilu*). Many scholars claim that Sun Yat-sen's 1920 plan, particularly his vision for opening China up by sea and rail to the international community, was the precursor of the contemporary BRI. These scholars note that the 1920 plan to build tens of thousands of kilometers of railways and roads as well as dozens of ports and transportation corridors has finally been revived after lying idle for almost a century, and it now serves as a guiding principle behind the BRI.[23]

The BRI launched in 2013 does echo the 1920 plan, although another side of the story outside the state-centered narrative of integration is frequently overlooked. In fact, a myriad of Chinese and transnational actors participated in the transition from imperial frontiers to national borderlands. The current rapid transformation of China's Inner Asian borderlands is rooted in a complex conceptual and material stratigraphy of development. In discussing the idea of the "region," Chinese scholar Hui Wang placed the ambiguity, fluidity, hybridity, and overlapping of regions at the center of our reflection of history and introduced a temporal dimension that he called "horizontal time." It draws less from linear theological time than from the classical Chinese notion of "time and circumstances" (*shi shi*) and secular time as defined in modern European thought. According to Wang, time and circumstances and secular time picture us in a horizontal world, where "new collective organizations and activities revolve around the axis of horizontal time."[24]

Wang's idea of horizontal time offers a conceptual lens through which to examine the multilevel and multinational stratigraphic layering beneath the landscape of China's border regions, understanding the 1920 plan as a historical product of a multitude of conditions and interactions within the context of global capitalism's influence in Inner Asia since the mid-nineteenth century. The 1920 plan and earlier development plans envisioned by late Qing reformists collectively represented a response to the existing and planned development concessions and trade corridors affecting the border regions of the Qing Empire before 1911 and later the Republic. Initiated by Western powers, and the two non-Western imperialist powers Russia and Japan, these layers of development were driven by the rise of transnational flows of capital, technology, materials, and people.

BEYOND THE 1920 PLAN: THE MANY SILK ROADS

Late Qing and early republican leaders' development plans were rarely implemented successfully due to a lack of political and economic capital. In contrast, the Western and non-Western colonial powers were active in China's border regions for over a hundred years since the mid-nineteenth century. This period, during which the Western colonial powers diplomatically and militarily dominated China, became known by the Chinese as the Century of Humiliation (*bainian guochi*). Each colonial power planned and built infrastructure for its own political, military, and economic benefit. British and French influence in the southwest, Russian and German in the northwest, and Russian and Japanese in the northeast resulted in China inheriting a mishmash of disjointed infrastructure. On the basis of their experience at home as well as in other colonies established around China, the colonial powers were well aware of the impact of transport and other infrastructural networks on economic and political integration. While Sun and other Chinese reformists envisioned further integration of borderlands into China proper, the colonial powers took full advantage of the fact that China's power weakened at the peripheries of the country, actively integrating the various border regions into their respective spheres of influence. These manifold versions of integration are displayed in the heterogeneous forms of imagined and built modern transportation corridors that echo the Silk Road, an ancient transcontinental network of trade routes. The colonial powers rushed to send survey expeditions to establish the best possible river and land routes. This section examines the stratigraphy of China's borderlands in terms of horizontal time, focusing on the southwest, northwest, and northeast borderlands, which were all subject to distinct imperial influences in the late nineteenth and early twentieth century. Three modern Silk Roads promoted by France, Germany, and Japan to strengthen their respective spheres of influence in China are spotlighted. The 1920 plan and these colonial visions of modern trading corridors have had long-term impacts that haunt the contemporary transformation and urbanization of China's borderlands to this day.

From Saigon to Kunming: A Southwest Corridor

Within the context of nineteenth-century Anglo-French geostrategic rivalry in Southeast Asia, especially the race to control China's markets, the Mekong River was soon seen as a natural divide between British and French spheres of influence.

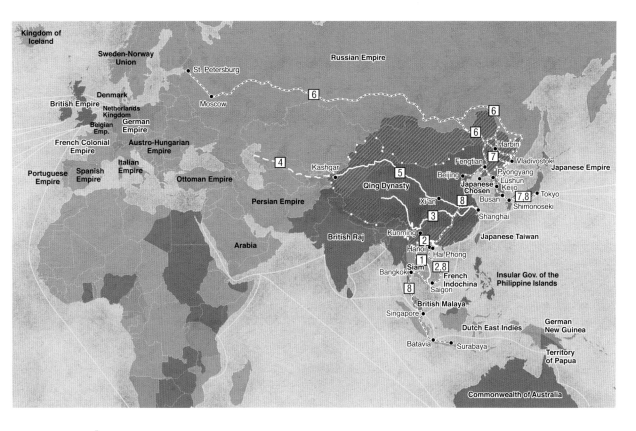

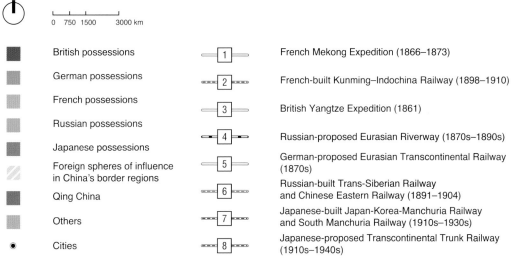

British possessions   [1] French Mekong Expedition (1866–1873)

German possessions   [2] French-built Kunming–Indochina Railway (1898–1910)

French possessions   [3] British Yangtze Expedition (1861)

Russian possessions

Japanese possessions   [4] Russian-proposed Eurasian Riverway (1870s–1890s)

Foreign spheres of influence in China's border regions   [5] German-proposed Eurasian Transcontinental Railway (1870s)

Qing China   [6] Russian-built Trans-Siberian Railway and Chinese Eastern Railway (1891–1904)

Others   [7] Japanese-built Japan-Korea-Manchuria Railway and South Manchuria Railway (1910s–1930s)

Cities   [8] Japanese-proposed Transcontinental Trunk Railway (1910s–1940s)

FIGURE 0.5

Planned modern transportation corridors reviewed in this chapter, overlaid on a map showing foreign spheres of influence in China's border regions in the last years of the Qing dynasty, in a world dominated by European colonialism (particularly the British Empire).

Colonial boundaries were gradually established along the Mekong River and in the upper Mekong Basin. After Napoleon III came to power in 1852, France perceived a pressing need to counter British influence in East Asia. France's strategic priorities were the consolidation and expansion of French colonial possessions, the containment of Britain's colonization of Upper Burma, and the suppression of British economic interference across the Southeast Asian subcontinent.[25] In the 1860s attention turned to the question of who would control the Mekong once the French had consolidated their presence in Cochinchina (the southern regions of modern-day Vietnam). Inspired by the way Britain took control of Shanghai at the mouth of the Yangtze, France believed that Saigon, the capital of Cochinchina, east of the Mekong Delta, could become an equally successful commercial center and that the Mekong River could provide access to the fabled riches of the largest potential market in the world: imperial China.

At the time, the Mekong River was largely unknown to modern Western cartography. The best available regional maps showed much of the Mekong with little if any degree of accuracy, leaving large stretches of the river to the imagination of early cartographers.[26] The French Mekong Expedition of 1866–1868 demystified the Mekong and accurately mapped the river from Saigon in Cochinchina to Dali in Yunnan for the first time. Unfortunately, the discovery of impassable rapids, waterfalls, treacherous shoals, and sandbanks shattered French hopes that the Mekong would immediately open a great new trade route to China. The dream would not be abandoned so quickly, however, and questions were repeatedly asked as to whether the rapids were truly impassable and whether the islands of Khone were really an insurmountable barrier.[27] The French undertook more surveys, military missions, and expeditions throughout the late nineteenth century, notably four missions led by the French explorer and diplomat Auguste Pavie, between 1879 and 1895. The Pavie Mission covered 676,000 square kilometers and led to the production of the first atlas of the Mekong and at least six volumes of observations.[28]

These cartographic advances and persistent hopes that the Mekong might become a significant trade route between Saigon and southern China rationalized the French strategic annexation of protectorates east of the Mekong and the adoption of the river as a colonial boundary throughout the last two decades of the nineteenth century. The French acquired Tonkin and Annam (parts of modern-day Vietnam) in 1884, established the Indochinese Union in 1887, and turned Laos and Cambodia into protectorates of French Indochina after the French victory in the Franco-Siamese War of 1893. Under the 1893 Treaty of Bangkok, Siam (now Thailand) was obliged to renounce its claims to the Shan region of northeastern Burma to Britain and give up control of the Lao principalities on the east bank of the Mekong to France. To consolidate their interests in the region, the French claimed that the Mekong was the obvious boundary of these colonial possessions. To ensure control over any future Mekong navigation, most of the demarcation line was along the deepest sections of the main river channel, allocating river islands to French Laos.[29] After securing the Mekong River as the colonial boundary at the turn of the twentieth century, the French proceeded to implement road and rail infrastructure projects in Indochina, particularly Laos, in the years preceding World War II. These

FIGURE 0.6

Jacques Nicolas Bellin, *Carte des royaumes de Siam, de Tunquin, Pegu, Ava Aracan, &c.* (Map of the kingdoms of Siam, Tunquin, Pegu, Ava Aracan, etc.) (Paris: Bellin, 1764). Library of Congress, https://www.loc.gov/item/2008621653.

infrastructure projects served the colonial government's goal to connect Laos with the rest of French Indochina on the other side of the Annamite Mountains and remove it as much as possible from the cultural and economic influence of Greater Siam on the other side of the Mekong River.[30]

Newly created Laos on the east banks of the Mekong was important for French colonial strategic ambitions to connect southern China and the rest of Indochina.

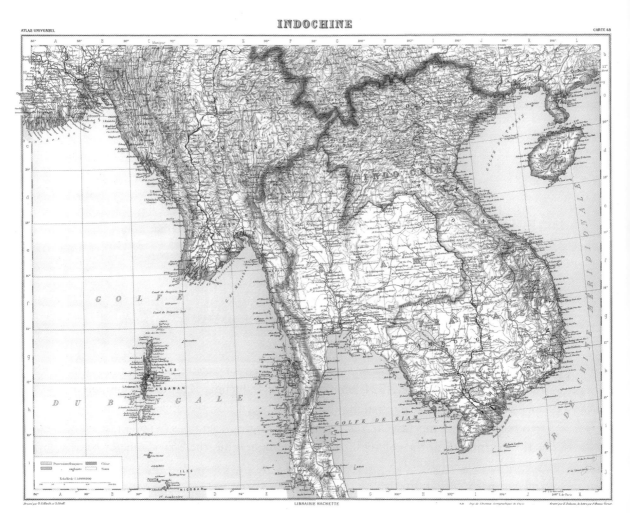

FIGURE 0.7

Louis Vivien de Saint-Martin and Franz Schrader, *Indochine* (Indochina), in *Atlas universel de géographie* (Atlas of universal geography) (Paris: Librairie Hachette, 1936). David Rumsey Map Collection, https://www.davidrumsey.com/luna/servlet/s/15eovz.

Laos safeguarded a potential French-controlled river route along the Mekong River and a land route along the Himalayan foothills linking China, Burma, Siam, and Laos to the Indochinese coast. The French colonial government was well aware of the existing southern Silk Road linking southern China with Southeast Asia. Nineteenth-century French Mekong explorers (including Auguste Pavie, who became the first governor-general of the French colony of Laos in 1894) had noted that Yunnanese muleteers carried Chinese products, such as salt, tea, opium, silk, furs, and metal goods, on their southward journeys, selling them in villages along the traditional trade route that ran across northern Siam to the Burmese coast. The muleteers carried local produce and British manufactured goods on their return trip to

Yunnan.[31] The French made use of these observations when demarcating the border between French Laos and China in the late 1890s, exemplified by French insistence that Boten be situated within Laotian territory. Boten, famed for its salt wells, was a well-established caravan stop on a major trade route. The significance of the French acquisition of Boten was not territorial; rather, it guaranteed French access to commercially important areas in southern China.[32] China, distracted by Japanese aggression in the First Sino-Japanese War (1894–1895), signed an agreement with the French in 1895, handing over control of Boten and granting preferential terms for French goods entering Yunnan.[33]

Despite various plans and vocal commitments to implement them on the part of French Indochina (1887–1954), a river route along the Mekong west of French Laos to China was never established. In contrast, the development of land routes progressed steadily during the first two decades of the twentieth century. Railway construction in particular proceeded apace, as the French colonial government saw it as an effective way to set up a basic infrastructural network across French Indochina while simultaneously diverting trade to and from southwestern China away from British Burma (now Myanmar) and Siam. In 1896 Paul Doumer, the recently appointed governor-general of French Indochina and later president of France (1931–1932), convinced the French parliament to pass a franc-loan for construction of a railway in Indochina.[34] In 1898 the 2,524-kilometer Trans-Indochina Railway was proposed: one line running north-south along the coast between Hanoi and Saigon connected to other lines running east-west across the Annamite Mountains, linking the coast with "the interior of the colony."[35] Around the same time, the 865-kilometer Kunming–Hai Phong Railway was proposed to connect southern Yunnan in China and northern Tonkin in Vietnam, further strengthening links between China and Indochina. Among many other financial privileges, the governor-general of French Indochina guaranteed a loan to the Lao Cai–Yunnan Railway Company (Société Concessionnaire du Chemin de Fer de Laokay à Yunnansen) for a 75-year term.[36]

The Kunming–Hai Phong Railway was constructed in two sections: the 466-kilometer China section from Kunming to Hekou/Lao Cai along the Yunnan-Tonkin border and the 389-kilometer Indochina section along the Red River from Hekou/Lao Cai to Hai Phong through Hanoi, to meet the north end of the Trans-Indochina Railway. The Indochina section was completed in 1906, with the entire line beginning commercial operation in 1910.[37] With more than 3,000 bridges and tunnels, the railway was widely praised as symbolic of France's advanced engineering and transportation technology. A promotional brochure published by the Touring Club of France (Touring-Club de France) in 1910 proclaimed the Kunming–Hai Phong Railway "one of the boldest and most extraordinary in the world."[38] Despite the repeated challenges and turbulence affecting Yunnan and Tonkin since completion of the railway in 1910, including World War I and World War II, the Kunming–Hai Phong Railway was financially solvent between 1910 and 1945. In addition to its role

FIGURE 0.8

A page about the Kunming–Hai Phong Railway from Touring-Club De France's guidebook: "The Yunan and Yunanfou Railway," in *Indo-Chine* (Indochina) (Paris: Touring-Club de France, 1910), 18. Library of Congress, https://www.loc.gov/item/2008625105.

as a trade corridor, the railway carried armaments and military supplies to Chinese forces resisting Japanese occupation. The volume of goods transported on this line increased dramatically, from 6,000 tons per year on average during the first years of the 1930s to 18,000 tons in 1939. The railway played a key role in French efforts to curtail Japanese influence in Southeast Asia. One French writer declared that "the best solution to protect Indochina would be to support the Republic of China using the Hai Phong–Kunming Railway line."[39]

From Berlin to Xi'an: A Northwest Corridor

The Tarim Basin region between the Tianshan Mountains, Kunlun Mountains, and Arjin Mountains in Central Asia was a significant theater for competing British, Russian, and Qing imperial ambitions during the Great Game rivalry (1813–1907), particularly during the last four decades of the nineteenth century. British expansion into Peshawar (1849) and Gilgit (1877) to the south and southwest of the Tarim Basin was driven by anxiety about Russia's designs on British India following Britain's defeats in the First Anglo-Afghan War (1839–1842). Russian advances into Central Asia west and northwest of the Tarim Basin throughout the nineteenth

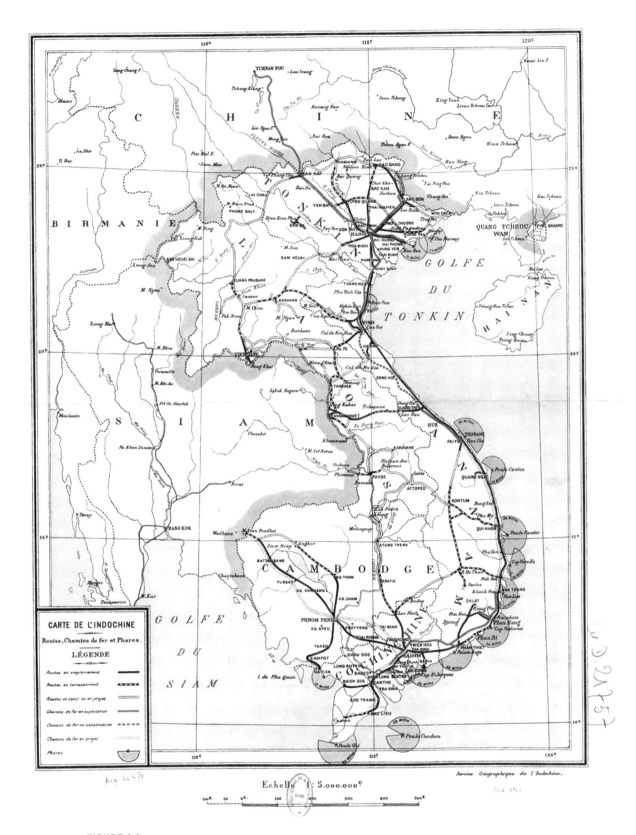

Indochine Française Service Géographique, *Carte de l'Indochine: Routes, chemins de fer et phares In-dochine française* (Map of Indochina: Roads, railways, and lighthouses in French Indochina) (Hanoi: Service Géographique de l'Indochine, 1933). Bibliothèque Nationale de France, Département Cartes et Plans, GE D-21757, https://gallica.bnf.fr/ark:/12148/btv1b530574891.

century—particularly the annexations of Tashkent (1865), Samarkand (1868), and Osh (1876)—were intended to stymie British efforts to impose self-advantageous trade terms on China.[40] Trade between Russia and China increased rapidly after Qing China and the Russian Empire signed the Treaty of Kuldja in 1851, an unequal treaty in Russia's favor that opened Kuldja and Chuguchak in the Kuldja/Ili River region to Sino-Russian trade. Russian influence intensified during the Dungan Revolt (*tongzhi huiluan*) when Yaqub Beg, who had fled from the Kokand Khanate after losing Tashkent to the Russians, established an Islamic state (1864–1877) in the Tarim Basin region.[41]

British and Russian occupation and annexation were spearheaded by exhaustive expeditions seeking ways to draw Central Asia into their respective spheres of influence. Two of the most ambitious of the numerous schemes for routes proposed in the latter half of the nineteenth century involved river routes: one between the Russian Central Asian colonies westward to Europe and the other connecting British India to China's Pacific coast. In a quest for cheaper and quicker trade routes to export raw materials from and import manufactured goods to Central Asia, Tsar Alexander II appointed Russian military officer A. I. Glukhovskoy to lead several expeditions to Central Asia between 1879 and 1883.[42] Glukhovskoy argued that Russia should build a canal connecting the Amu Daria River and the Caspian Sea as part of a Great Eurasian Waterway. This plan was intended to revive the fabled Central Asian trade routes between Asia and Europe, which had fallen into disuse after the British established a maritime connection between British India and Europe via the Cape of Good Hope. Glukhovskoy's expedition surveyed more than 36,000 square kilometers, confirming the feasibility of a river trade route across Central Asia.[43] British efforts to find a route between India and China's Pacific coast were set in motion immediately after the end of the Second Opium War (1856–1860). A Royal Navy expedition in 1861 led by Admiral James Hope established the first British treaty ports between Shanghai and Hankou on the mighty Yangtze River. The expedition advanced 246 kilometers beyond Hankou to Yuezhou (now Yueyang), where a party led by Captain Thomas Wright Blakiston transferred to local boats to continue upstream. Blakiston's survey team intended to follow the Yangtze to its source in Tibet then cross the Himalayas into India. However, due to regional political strife, he had to abandon the expedition at Pingshan, approximately 2,900 kilometers from the ocean.[44]

Although the visions of the Russian Great Eurasian Waterway and the British Great Yangtze Riverway were actively pursued for the rest of the nineteenth century, both were eventually shelved due to the rapid railway expansion in Central Asia and China. Russia completed the Trans-Caspian Railway in Central Asia in 1886, successfully connecting the Caspian Sea to Charjui on the Amu Daria. In 1875 Jardine, Matheson, and Company of Britain built the Shanghai–Woosung Line, the first railway in China. It was surreptitiously conceived and implemented without permission from the Qing authorities, and the regional official Shen Baozheng bought up and

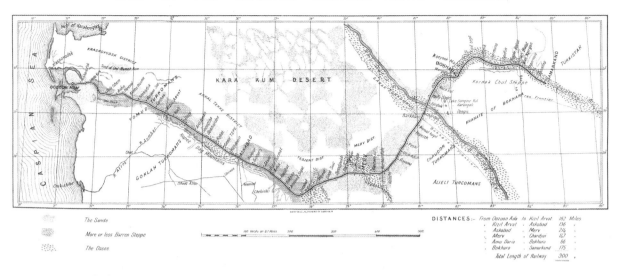

FIGURE 0.10

George Dobson, *Map of the Russian Central Asian Railway, in Russia's Railway Advance into Central Asia: Notes of a Journey from St. Petersburg to Samarkand* (London: W. H. Allen, 1890), 110. World Digital Library, https://www.loc.gov/resource/gdclccn.01001556/?sp=141.

dismantled the railway in 1877, less than a year after it opened.[45] However, Qing government opposition to foreign railway construction did little to curb its subsequent expansion, especially after China's defeat in the First Sino-Japanese War. Although they always required Chinese partners, foreign governments and companies routinely devised railway treaties to facilitate territorial encroachment for their own benefit. Projects were underwritten by loan agreements that denied the Chinese government the right to repurchase the lines until decades after construction.[46] According to a map produced by German diplomat Max von Brandt in 1899, more than 800 kilometers of railroad had been laid in China by that time: the map clearly outlined Russian, British, French, Japanese, German, Belgian, and American "conceded or projected railroads," "territories," and "spheres of interest."[47]

One railway not marked on Max von Brandt's 1899 map was a Eurasian transcontinental railway between Europe and China envisioned by German geographer Ferdinand von Richthofen. Around the same time that the Russian and British expeditions set out to investigate the feasibility of their respective river routes, Richthofen embarked on a series of geological surveys of China between 1868 and 1872. He reported on China's commercial mining and railway projects to the European-American Chamber of Commerce in Shanghai between 1870 and 1872 and published his findings in a five-volume work between 1877 and 1912.[48] At the time, Richthofen was inspired by the completion of the transcontinental railway in the United States in 1869 and the intensifying international competition for railway concessions in

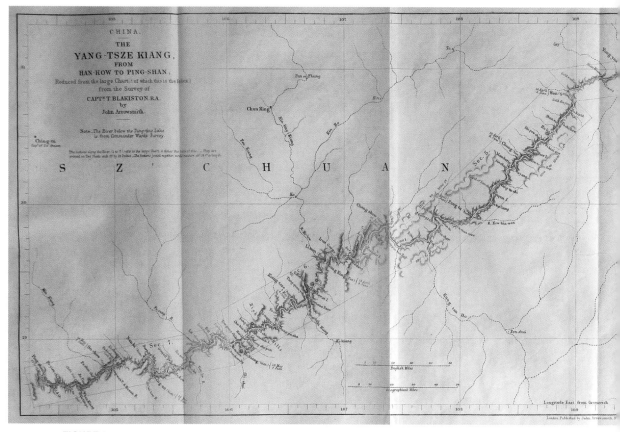

FIGURE 0.11

John Arrowsmith, *The Yang-tsze Kiang, from Hankow to Pingshan, from the Survey of Captain Blakiston,*
in Thomas W. Blakiston, *Five Months on The Yang-Tsze,* appendix X (London: John Murray, 1862).
Internet Archive, https://archive.org/details/b24865953/page/380/mode/2up.

China by foreign governments and private corporations.[49] His surveys aimed to map
the best possible routes for his sponsors to introduce railways to China to connect
Europe and China directly: "In 1861, following Blakiston's journey on the Yangtze,
came the era of the development of China for science and thus also for her full
practical exploitation through world-traffic, and we face the great task of exploring,
according to the views of our times, this country."[50]

Although they did not possess extensive colonies or trading concessions in
the region like their Russian and British counterparts, Richthofen's European and
American sponsors believed that geological surveys and transcontinental railways
would secure their interests in China and greater Eurasia.[51] Combining his geological
surveys of China, cartographic studies of ancient caravan routes between Europe and
China, and up-to-date information from international exploration and surveys of
Central Asia, Richthofen highlighted the potential of future rail links running west
from Xi'an. The Tarim Basin region in particular took pride of place in Richthofen's
vision of a transcontinental railway:

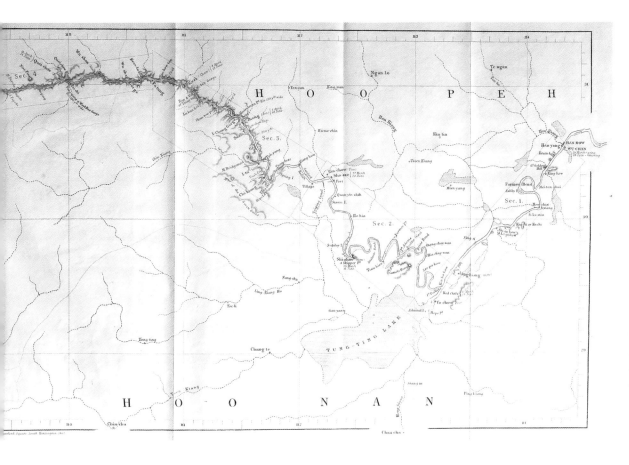

Little doubt can exist that, eventually, China will be connected with Europe by rail. . . . As regards natural facilities, and the supply, at both ends of the line, of the populous, productive and large commercial countries, the only line which ever can come into consideration is that by Si-ngan-fu [Xi'an], Lan-chau-fu [Lanzhou], Su-chau [Suzhou] and Hami. It is a remarkable coincidence that this whole road, including the Pelu [Beilu, the "northern route" around the Tarim Basin], is well provided with coal. . . . There is scarcely an instance on record, where so many favorable and essential conditions co-operate to concentrate all future intercourse on so long a line upon one single and definite channel.[52]

Richthofen's blueprint for a Eurasian transcontinental railway never materialized due to the international scramble for railway concessions in China, but it had a profound influence on the planning and construction of roads in China's northwest borderlands in the early twentieth century. The geographer Sven Hedin, Richthofen's Swedish student, inherited and further developed Richthofen's late nineteenth-century vision, leading the Sino-Swedish Expedition from 1927 to 1935 to carry out scientific research in north and northwest China.[53] The first

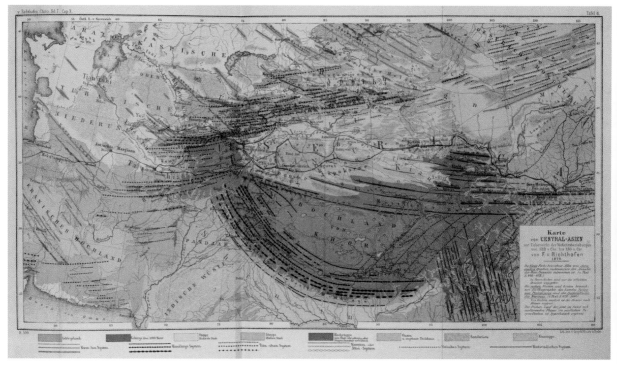

FIGURE 0.12

Ferdinand von Richthofen, *Karte von Central-Asien: Zur Übersicht der Verkehrsbeziehungen von 128 v. Chr. bis 150 n. Chr.* (Map of Central Asia: Overview of transport-connections from 128 BC to 150 AD), in *China: Ergebnisse eigener Reisen und darauf gegründeter Studien* (China: The results of my travels and the studies based thereon), vol. 1 (Berlin: Verlag von Dietrich Reimer, 1877), 500. Digital Silk Road Project, Toyo Bunko, http://dsr.nii.ac.jp/toyobunko/viewer/index.html?pages=III-2-A-19 /V-1&pos=550&lang=en.

period of the Sino-Swedish Expedition (February 1927–May 1928), which sought an optimal airline route between Berlin and Peking (now Beijing), was carried out on behalf of the German government and Deutsche Luft Hansa AG. The expenses of the second period of the Sino-Swedish Expedition (summer 1928 to autumn 1933) were paid by the Swedish state and others. The working program included only scientific tasks. The Chinese Nationalist government financed the third period of the Sino-Swedish Expedition (autumn 1933 to spring 1935) to plan a road for motor vehicles between Europe and China. A map was included in Hedin's *The Silk Road*, showing a road connecting Shanghai, Xi'an, Kashgar, Istanbul, and Vienna. From there, one road reached Hamburg through Berlin and another reached Boulogne through Paris.[54] Unlike its predecessors, the Grand Eurasia Roadway envisioned by Hedin was partially implemented: the section built between Xi'an and Urumqi became a logistical lifeline for the Chinese armed forces during the Second Sino-Japanese War (1937–1945), particularly after the Japanese took control of the China coast. The 719-kilometer Xi'an–Lanzhou Road was completed in 1935, and the 2,925-kilometer Lanzhou–Urumqi Road was constructed during

FIGURE 0.13
Sven Hedin, *Map of the Grand Eurasia Roadway*, in *The Silk Road* (London: George Routledge, 1938), 231. Internet Archive, https://archive.org/details/in.ernet.dli.2015.79991/page/n271/mode/2up.

the war between 1937 and 1939. Soviet supplies delivered to Sary-Ozek Station on the Turkestan–Siberian Railway were then transported eastward by motor vehicle, entering Xinjiang through Khorgas-Khorgos on the Sino-Soviet border before finally reaching Urumqi and Lanzhou.[55]

From Tokyo to Harbin: A Northeast Corridor

Manchuria saw the rapid expansion of its modern infrastructure after the 1880s, resulting from vigorous competition between Russia and Japan for commercial and military influence in Northeast Asia. Japan's influence predominated after its victory in the Russo-Japanese War in 1905, despite Russia having secured favorable trading conditions with China since its rapid expansion into Siberia during the sixteenth and seventeenth centuries. Soon after the northeastern Qing Chinese–Russian border was agreed upon, along the Stanovoy Range under the 1689 Treaty of Nerchinsk, Peter the Great initiated state-operated caravans from Moscow to Peking. The 1727 Treaty of Kyakhta formalized the northern Qing Chinese-Russian border (now Mongolian-Russian border) west of the Argun/Amur River and dictated that trading caravans had to cross at the border town of Kyakhta south of Lake Baikal.[56] This caravan route fell into decline during the second half of the nineteenth century, outcompeted by a new sea route between Russian Odessa and China via the Suez Canal (which opened in 1869) and the new Trans-Siberian Railway (TSR) from Moscow to Vladivostok in the Russian Far East.[57]

The Chinese branch of the Trans-Siberian Railway was constructed in the 1890s.

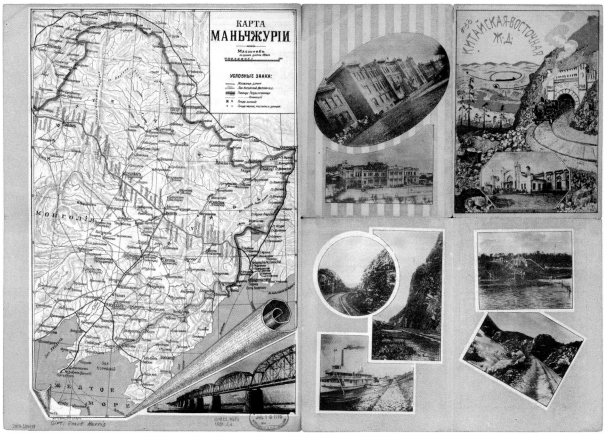

FIGURE 0.14

Railway map of Manchuria with the Chinese Eastern Railway emphasized. *Karta Manchzhurii* (Map of Manchuria) (Russia, 1903). Library of Congress, https://www.loc.gov/item/2019585139.

Known as the Chinese Eastern Railway (CER; *dongqing tielu*), it played a key role in international affairs because it formed a critical link for two transcontinental corridors: one planned by Russia to link "Greater Asia" with Europe and one planned by Japan to connect regions within its Greater East Asia Co-Prosperity Sphere (GEACPS). Although the Trans-Siberian Railway cemented Russia's connection to the Far East, Vladivostok's port was operational only in the summer. Thus, Russia was determined to establish a year-round Pacific port on China's Liaodong Peninsula. Together with Germany and France, Russia objected to the terms of the Treaty of Shimonoseki (or Treaty of Bakan, 1895) imposed by Japan on a defeated China in the First Sino-Japanese War, requiring the Liaodong Peninsula and the islands of Taiwan and Penghu to be ceded to Japan.[58] After Japan reluctantly renounced its claim on the Liaodong Peninsula under diplomatic pressure, Tsar Nicholas II negotiated an agreement with the Qing court in 1896 to construct a branch of the Trans-Siberian Railway through Manchuria, some 800 kilometers shorter than the all-Russian route. Construction of the CER started in summer 1897 and proceeded in earnest after Russia negotiated a 25-year lease of the Liaodong Peninsula, including the ice-free Port Arthur (now Port Lüshun) in 1898.[59]

During its five-year construction until its completion in 1902, the CER was the focus of Russian disputes with other imperialist powers and was a major factor in provoking the Russo-Japanese War (1904–1905). The Qing Chinese–Russian agreement concerning the CER was one of the main sparks that ignited the Boxer Rebellion (*yihetuan yundong*), an uprising against the spread of Western and Japanese influence in northern China between 1899 and 1901. In response to the Boxer Rebellion, the Eight-Nation Alliance (a multinational military coalition including Russia) raised a force of some 45,000 troops in 1900. In addition, Russia sent a separate force of approximately 200,000 troops to Manchuria, ostensibly to protect the CER, which was under construction at the time.[60] Under diplomatic pressure from the other Eight-Nation Alliance members, who saw their own interests threatened by the Russian invasion of Manchuria, Russia reluctantly signed a three-stage troop-withdrawal agreement with Qing China in 1902. Russia had fulfilled only the first stage of withdrawal by 1903, thereby violating the agreement, so Japan opened negotiations with Russia in the hope of clarifying their respective areas of control in the region. After several rounds of bilateral negotiations, diplomacy failed. Japan declared war in April 1904. The war formally ended with the signing of the Treaty of Portsmouth in September 1905, under which the Russians were obliged to leave Manchuria and recognize Japanese control of the Korean Peninsula.[61]

Seizure of the Korean Peninsula provided Japan with a land bridge between Japan proper and the continent, enabling Japanese territorial expansion through Manchuria to the rest of China and even farther into Central Asia.[62] Ironically, the CER, originally built to integrate northern China into the Russian sphere of influence, became a critical component of Japanese regional integration through infrastructure construction after falling into Japanese hands. The southern branch of the CER (Harbin to Shenyang to Dalian) became the Japanese South Manchuria Railway (SMR) under the South Manchuria Railway Company (Mantetsu), established in 1906.[63] Mantetsu drove the rapid expansion of the railway network in both Manchuria and Korea and soon grew into an industrial conglomerate managing mines, ironworks, harbors, and other industries. Largely based on their experience developing infrastructure at home in the early years of the Meiji (1868–1912), the Japanese government and business leaders set great store by transportation and communication infrastructure in their blueprint for imperial expansion.[64]

Between the annexation of Korea in 1910 and the surrender of Japan in 1945, the Japanese adopted a two-stage blueprint for regional integration. Stage one (from 1910 to the outbreak of the Second Sino-Japanese War in 1937) was characterized by a policy of detaching north China from Chinese central government control, to economically integrate north China and Korea with Japan. Railway construction in Korea gradually increased after 1910, accelerating dramatically under an ambitious

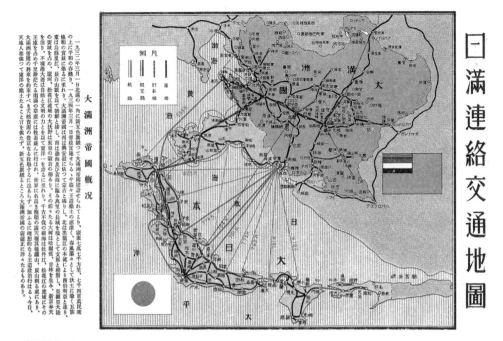

FIGURE 0.15
Japan-Manchukuo Transport Connections (1930s). This sketch map (oriented with north to the right) depicts planned and built railways as well as air and shipping routes between Japan and Manchukuo. Manchukuo and China Puppet Government Collection, Japan War Art, https://japanwarart.ocnk.net /product/6326.

twelve-year expansion plan (1921–1933) that oversaw the building of 1,400 kilometers of railways.[65] After the Japanese invasion of northeastern China in 1931 and the establishment of the state of Manchukuo (1932–1945), a Northern Development strategy was launched in Manchuria, leading to extensive infrastructure construction in its thinly populated northern parts through the 1930s. Manchuria boasted 11,000 kilometers of railways by 1939, equivalent to half of the national railway within Japan itself.[66] Additional infrastructure was built to strengthen connections between Manchuria and the Korean Peninsula, across the Yalu/Amnok and Tumen/Tuman Rivers, and between the Korean Peninsula and mainland Japan, separated by the Sea of Japan/East Sea. Japanese officials from Korea and officials of the newly established Manchukuo signed an agreement in 1932 to construct six highway bridges over the two rivers by 1939. Completion of the bridge at Tumen joining the Harbin to Tumen and Tumen to Rajin railway lines was credited with revolutionizing transportation in East Asia. Mantetsu started the construction of a new port in Rajin in 1933 to serve the shortest shipping distance between the heart of Manchukuo and Japan.[67]

Stage two of Japanese regional integration spanned a shorter period, from 1937 to 1945, during which much of the infrastructure proposed was so ambitious as to be

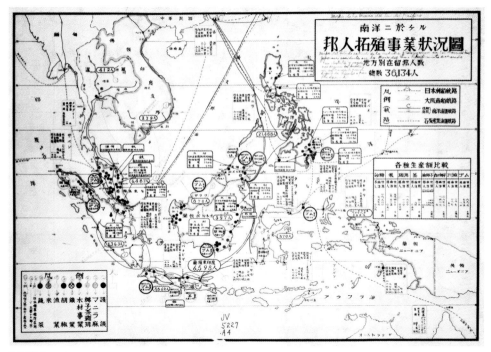

FIGURE 0.16

Japanese Enterprises in the South Seas and the Distribution of Japanese Nationals (1935) depicts locations and numbers of Japanese nationals as well as Japanese commercial interests, consulates, resources, and rail and sea routes. In *Japanese Pre-War Colonization* (Washington, DC: Federal Bureau of Investigation, 1935) , 1. Library of Congress, https://www.loc.gov/resource/g3201em.gct00493/?sp=2.

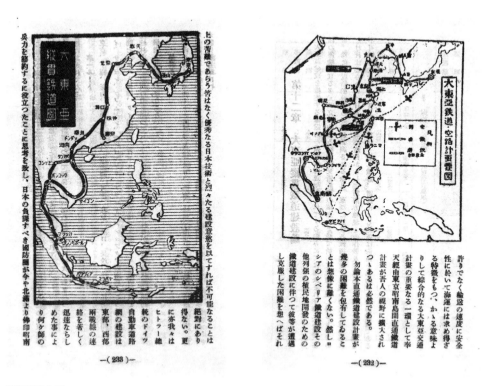

FIGURE 0.17

Sketch maps of the Greater East Asian Transcontinental Trunk Railway connecting Tokyo and Surabaya, in Manchurian Information Center, *Manchuria and the South Sea: Northbound and Southward* (Hsinking/Changchun: Manchurian Information Center, 1943), 232–233. National Diet Library, Japan, https://dl.ndl.go.jp/info:ndljp/pid/1445352.

delusional. Much more grandiose infrastructure plans were drawn up in the context of Japanese imperial ambitions encompassing Northeast Asia and the imagined geography of the Greater East Asia Co-Prosperity Sphere, which envisioned the cultural and economic unity of Northeast Asians, Southeast Asians, South Asians, and Oceanians.[68] In addition to ferries linking Japan with the continent, a trans–Korean Strait undersea tunnel was proposed by a Japanese railway official, Yumoto Noboru. Originally put forward in 1939, the plan was seriously considered after the outbreak of the Pacific war in 1941. A 3.6-kilometer prototype section of the underwater tunnel was built in the early 1940s.[69]

In terms of railway development, a Japanese-controlled Transcontinental Trunk Railway in Asia was promoted. The implementation of such a plan would have required a herculean effort to expand railways and unify operations across the GEACPS, notably coordinating land, port, and maritime systems and eliminating railway gauge differences. Among numerous iterations of this transcontinental railway was a grandiose plan for a Trans-Greater East Asian Railway drawn up by Mantetsu in 1942, enabling a seven-day journey across a total distance of some 8,000 kilometers between Manchukuo and Singapore.[70] Yumoto, the instigator of the trans–Korea Strait undersea tunnel, later proposed to extend the Trans-Greater East Asian Railway across the Strait of Malacca to the island of Java. According to Yumoto, undersea tunnels and high-speed trains would make it possible to travel the 11,618 kilometers between Tokyo and Batavia (now Jakarta) in four and a half days.[71] Most of these ambitious plans for future infrastructure in the GEACPS remained pipe dreams, with the war turning against Japan in the Pacific after 1943 and ending in defeat in 1945.

ORGANIZATION OF THE BOOK

The preceding narrative examines many versions of integration as revealed in the heterogeneous forms of imagined and actual modern transportation corridors built to achieve political control, bolster military strategy, and smooth the way for economic activity. Transportation infrastructure construction played a central role in China—together with political reform, education, and cultural campaigns—to promote Sun Yat-sen's nonethnic definition of the Chinese nation, defined by a bounded territory integrating the ethnically diverse frontier regions of the former Qing Empire into the Chinese nation-state. Simultaneously, foreign powers planned and built a disjointed hodgepodge of infrastructure, often in opposition to Chinese state interests, to integrate border regions into their specific spheres of influence: notably the British and French in the southwest, the Russians and Germans in the northwest, and the Russians and Japanese in the northeast. Chinese and foreign planning and implementation of these respective visions for infrastructure development and regional transformation were highly contingent on the availability of political and economic capital, expertise and technological know-how, and patterns of political and military power-relations within specific "time and circumstances."

The heterogeneous integration strategies examined in this overview help ground the investigation of contemporary urbanization in China's borderlands, where the stratifications underlying its landscape not only have tangible, material manifestations but also have very real socioeconomic and political resonances. Three key insights drawn from this overview set the scene for the overall structure of this book. First, China's borderlands can be understood through the lens of "Exchanges and Flows" on a global scale. This framework refers not only to the transportation of large volumes of processed products or raw materials through the borderlands but also to the circulation of ideology, expertise, and technology, which enables and is facilitated by the planning and construction of specific development projects. Second, China's borderlands can be understood through the lens of "Corridors and Concessions" on a regional scale. The transformation of far-flung "wasteland" into valuable resources is made possible by demarcating specific routes to maximize efficacy and profit and/or by delineating zones of resource development, be they agriculture, forestry, energy production, or mineral extraction. Third, China's borderlands can be understood through the lens of "Settlements and Memories" on a local scale. The implementation of specific development projects reconfigures the spatial and ecological landscape as well as sociocultural practices, given that these projects often involve immigration driven by labor demand and/or emigration caused by disruption of livelihoods.

Accordingly, this book is structured by a multiscale framework and divided into three parts. Part I focuses on the key agents that play a major role in controlling the quantities and types of exchanges and flows between China and the rest of the world. Specifically, it focuses on the role of state-owned enterprises (SOEs) in integrating China's borderlands into the national and international network of material and knowledge transfer in the People's Republic of China era. Part I maps out the spatial and temporal patterns of China's rapid integration into the world market system facilitated by the SOEs, providing fine-grained case studies of connections between key agents and four aspects of exchanges and flows: infrastructure, logistics, expertise, and resources.

Following part I's examination of the global patterns of exchanges and flows that integrate China into the global knowledge and economic systems, part II investigates the social and spatial implications of this integration for China's borderlands. Specifically, it focuses on the heterogeneous forms of resource commodification within the context of the rapid transition of the borderlands from economic backwaters in the twentieth century into hotbeds of frenetic resource exploitation and development in the twenty-first century. Part II includes essays on three differing types of corridors and concessions within the geographically and socioculturally distinct regions of the China-Laos, China-Kyrgyzstan, and China-Korea borderlands.

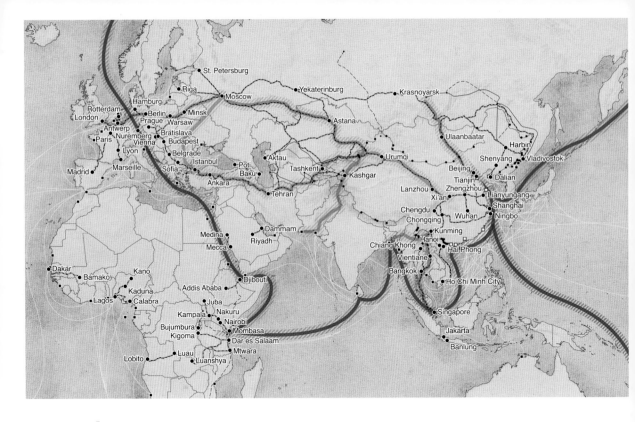

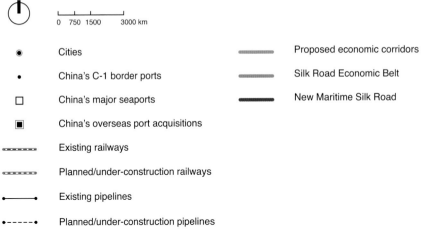

● Cities	▭▭▭▭ Proposed economic corridors
• China's C-1 border ports	▭▭▭▭ Silk Road Economic Belt
▢ China's major seaports	▬▬▬▬ New Maritime Silk Road
■ China's overseas port acquisitions	
▭▭▭▭ Existing railways	
▭▭▭▭ Planned/under-construction railways	
•————• Existing pipelines	
•-----• Planned/under-construction pipelines	

FIGURE 0.18

China's category-one (C-1) border ports, overlaid on a map showing existing and planned projects promulgated under China's Belt and Road Initiative.

Part III investigates the dynamism of border ports and settlements on a local scale in the global and regional contexts of the transformation of China's borderlands examined in parts I and II, respectively. Specifically, it focuses on how natural, technological, and social contingencies define the spatial and temporal patterns of specific border port and settlement agglomerations. Part III is effectively an atlas, featuring thirty-six border port-settlement agglomerations in China's southwest, northwest, and northeast borderlands that are most representational in terms of illustrating the tensions and connections between past and present. This atlas showcases the diversity of port-settlement agglomerations along China's borderlands and enables comparisons among the various sites on spatial and temporal scales.

Collectively, these three parts offer fresh perspectives on these poorly understood areas in China's borderlands that stand at the vanguard of global urbanization while still being haunted by their tangled legacy of socioecological systems, diverse traditions of territorial governance, and convoluted histories of internal and international armed conflicts. French infrastructure built to transport goods from Indochina to the Chinese market has been revamped by China to access the resource-abundant economies of lower Mekong countries. A road project initiated by the European-American Chamber of Commerce built during the Sino-Japanese War now leads to the massive dry port of Khorgos, which is sometimes called the Rotterdam of Central Asia. The Hunchun Museum of History just outside the Hunchun Sino-Russian Trade Zone displays panels and videos showing how northeastern China lost access to the Sea of Japan after Russia annexed Outer Manchuria. The significance of contemporary developments, particularly those driven by China's reglobalization ambitions as manifested in the BRI, cannot be denied. However, understanding how these ongoing transformations are enabled and constrained by past and present perceptions and practices allows us to critically evaluate them through a wide-angle conceptual lens and with historical depth.

NOTES

1. Yanbian is an autonomous prefecture in Jilin Province, in northeastern China bordering North Korea and Russia, home to a large population of Chinese Koreans (*chaoxianzu*).

2. Turner's 1893 essay "The Significance of the Frontier in American History" and the twelve other essays or papers in this field were collected and republished under the title *The Frontier in American History* (New York: H. Holt, 1920).

3. See, for example, Dietrich Gerhard, "The Frontier in Comparative View," *Comparative Studies in Society and History* 1, no. 3 (1959), 205–229; Martin T. Katzman, "The Brazilian Frontier in Comparative Perspective," *Comparative Studies in Society and History* 17, no. 3 (1975), 266–285; Howard R. Lamar and Leonard Thompson (eds.), *The Frontier in History: North America and Southern Africa Compared* (New Haven: Yale University Press, 1981); William Cronon, *Nature's Metropolis: Chicago and the Great West* (New York: W. W. Norton, 1991); and William Cronon, George A. Miles, and Jay Gitlin (eds.), *Under an Open Sky: Rethinking America's Western Past* (New York: W. W. Norton, 1993).

4. Owen Lattimore, *Inner Asian Frontiers of China* (New York: American Geographical Society, 1940). Lattimore brings together concepts that he previously presented in several books and scores of articles published through the early twentieth century, weaving a slew of old facts and new interpretations into a comprehensible pattern.

5. Two representative examples of recently published books on China's borderlands are Nianshen Song's *Making Borders in Modern East Asia: The Tumen River Demarcation,*

1881–1919 (Cambridge: Cambridge University Press, 2018), and Judd C. Kinzley's *Natural Resources and the New Frontier: Constructing Modern China's Borderlands* (Chicago: University of Chicago Press, 2018).

6. "Inner Asia" has been defined differently in different periods. It overlaps with some definitions of "Central Asia," but some other parts of Inner Asia are never considered to be part of Central Asia in any definition. In its broadest sense, Inner Asia can be considered to be the frontier of China and is sometimes contrasted with China proper, the original core provinces mostly occupied by Han Chinese populations.

7. Kinzley, *Natural Resources and the New Frontier*, 3.

8. See, for example, Pamela Crossley, *A Translucent Mirror: History and Identity in Qing Imperial Ideology* (Berkeley: University of California Press, 1999), and Mark C. Elliott, *The Manchu Way: The Eight Banners and Ethnic Identity in Late Imperial China* (Palo Alto, CA: Stanford University Press, 2001).

9. See, for example, Kinzley, *Natural Resources and the New Frontier*, and Dittmar Schorkowitz and Ning Chia (eds.), *Managing Frontiers in Qing China: The Lifanyuan and Libu Revisited* (Leiden: Brill, 2016).

10. Stephen R. Halsey, "Introduction: State-Making and Empire in a World-Historical Context," in *Quest for Power: European Imperialism and the Making of Chinese Statecraft* (Cambridge, MA: Harvard University Press, 2015), 6.

11. Richard S. Horowitz, "Qing Officials, Extraterritoriality, and Global Integration in Nineteenth-Century China," in Daniel S. Margolies, Umut Özsu, Maïa Pal, and Ntina Tzouvala (eds.), *The Extraterritoriality of Law: History, Theory, Politics* (Abingdon, UK: Routledge, 2019), 75–90.

12. Halsey, "Introduction: State-Making and Empire in a World-Historical Context," 11.

13. For more on Qing and early republican reformists' integrationist strategies, see Michael E. Clarke, *Xinjiang and China's Rise in Central Asia: A History* (Abingdon, UK: Routledge, 2011), and Edward J. M. Rhoads, *Manchus and Han: Ethnic Relations and Political Power in Late Qing and Early Republican China, 1861–1928* (Seattle: University of Washington Press, 2000).

14. Sun Yat-sen, "Three Principles of the People [三民主義]," in *Complete Works of Sun Yat-sen* [孫中山全集], vol. 5 (Beijing: Zhonghua Shuju, 1981), 36.

15. Han or Hanzu is a term translated in English as "ethnic Chinese" or "Chinese of native stock." Despite the existence of many cultural, linguistic, and regional differences in China, Han is the dominant ethnic group in China and outnumbers the minority groups.

16. James Leibold, "Positioning 'Minzu' within Sun Yat-Sen's Discourse of Minzuzhuyi," *Journal of Asian History* 38, no. 2 (2004), 163–213, 172, 173.

17. Sun Yat-sen, "Discussion with a Reporter from Hong Kong Telegraph, May 20, 1912 [在香港與(士蔑西報)記者的談話, 1912年5月20日]," in *Complete Works of Sun Yat-sen* [孫中山全集], vol. 2 (Beijing: Zhonghua Shuju, 1981), 185.

18. Kinzley, *Natural Resources and the New Frontier*, 4.

19. Sun Yat-sen, *The International Development of China* (Shanghai: Commercial Press, 1920).

20. "Sun Wen Theory [孫文學說]," "Plan for Industry and Commerce [實業計劃]," and "Parliamentary Law [民權初步]," written between 1917 and 1920, constitute Sun Yat-sen's "Plan for National Reconstruction [建國方略]."

21. Sun, *The International Development of China*, iii.

22. Sun, *The International Development of China*, ii.

23. See, for example, Andrew Grant, "China's Double Body: Infrastructure Routes and the Mapping of China's Nation-State and Civilization-State," *Eurasian Geography and Economics* 59, no. 3-4 (2018), 378–407, and Tjio Kayloe, *The Unfinished Revolution: Sun Yat-Sen and the Struggle for Modern China* (Singapore: Marshall Cavendish International, 2017).

24. Hui Wang, "Trans-systemic Society and Regional Perspective in Chinese Studies," *Boundary 2* 38, no. 1 (2011), 165–201, 193, 194.

25. John Keay, "The Mekong Exploration Commission, 1866–68: Anglo-French Rivalry in South East Asia," *Asian Affairs* 36, no. 3 (2005), 289–312.

26. Milton E. Osborne, *River Road to China: The Mekong River Expedition, 1866-1873* (New York: Liveright, 1975), 14.

27. Louis-Joseph-Marie de Carne, *Travels in Indo-China and the Chinese Empire* (London: Chapman and Hall, 1872), 36.

28. Auguste Pavie, *Mission Pavie Indo-Chine: Atlas, notices et cartes* (Paris: Augustin Challamel, 1903).

29. Andrew Walker, *The Legend of the Golden Boat: Regulation, Trade and Traders in the Borderlands of Laos, Thailand, China, and Burma* (Honolulu: University of Hawaii Press, 1999), 45.

30. For more on infrastructure development in French Indochina, see Søren Ivarsson, "Roads, History, Religion and Language, 1893–1940," in *Creating Laos: The Making of a Lao Space between Indochina and Siam, 1860–1945* (Copenhagen: NIAS Press, 2008), 93–144.

31. See, for example, Louis de Carne, *Voyage en Indo-Chine et dans l'Empire Chinois* (Paris: Edouard Dentu, 1872); Francis Garnier, *Voyage d'Exploration en Indo-Chine* (Paris: Hachette, 1885); and Auguste Pavie, *Exposé des travaux de la mission, Mission Pavie Indo-Chine 1879-1895: Géographie et voyages* (Paris: Ernest Leroux, 1906).

32. Walker, *The Legend of the Golden Boat*, 57.

33. John Robert Victor Prescott, *Map of Mainland Asia by Treaty* (Melbourne: Melbourne University Press, 1975), 450.

34. Cam Anh Tuan, "Vietnam-Indochina-Japan Relations during the Second World War: Documents and Interpretations," in Masaya Shiraishi, Nguyễn Văn Khánh, and Bruce McFarland Lockhart (eds.), *Vietnam-Indochina-Japan Relations during the Second World War: Documents and Interpretations* (Tokyo: Waseda University Institute of Asia-Pacific Studies, 2017), 252.

35. Aline Demay, *Tourism and Colonization in Indochina, 1898–1939* (Newcastle upon Tyne, UK: Cambridge Scholars Publishing, 2015), 7.

36. Tuan, "Vietnam-Indochina-Japan Relations during the Second World War," 252.

37. Tuan, "Vietnam-Indochina-Japan Relations during the Second World War," 252.

38. Touring-Club de France, *Indo-Chine* (Paris: Touring-Club de France, 1910), 11.

39. Tuan, "Vietnam-Indochina-Japan Relations during the Second World War," 254, 255.

40. Gerald Morgan, *Anglo-Russian Rivalry in Central Asia, 1810–1895* (Hove, UK: Psychology Press, 1981).

41. Tsing Yuan, "Yakub Beg (1820–1877) and the Moslem Rebellion in Chinese Turkestan," *Central Asiatic Journal* (1961), 134–167.

42. Prince Kropotkin, "The Old Beds of the Amu-Daria," *Geographical Journal* 12, no. 3 (1898), 306–310.

43. Maya K. Peterson, *Pipe Dreams: Water and Empire in Central Asia's Aral Sea Basin* (Cambridge: Cambridge University Press, 2019), 45.

44. A. D. Blue, "Land and River Routes to West China (With Especial Reference to

the Upper Yangtze)," *Journal of the Hong Kong Branch of the Royal Asiatic Society* 16 (1976), 162–178, 165.

45. Hsien-Chun Wang, "Merchants, Mandarins, and the Railway: Institutional Failure and the Wusong Railway, 1874–1877," *International Journal of Asian Studies* 12, no. 1 (2015), 31–53.

46. Chi-ming Hou, *Foreign Investment and Economic Development in China, 1840-1937*, Harvard East Asian Series 21 (Cambridge, MA: Harvard University Press, 2013), 70.

47. Tamara Chin, "The Invention of the Silk Road, 1877," *Critical Inquiry* 40, no. 1 (2013), 194–219, 214.

48. Ferdinand von Richthofen, *China: The Results of My Travels and the Studies Based Thereon* [*China: Ergebnisse eigener Reisen und darauf gegründeter Studien*], 5 vols. (Berlin: Verlag von Dietrich Reimer, 1877–1912).

49. Chin, "The Invention of the Silk Road," 210.

50. Richthofen, *China*, vol. 1, 729, translated and quoted in Chin, "The Invention of the Silk Road," 209.

51. For more on Richthofen's field expedition in China, see Chin, "The Invention of the Silk Road," and Shellen Wu, "The Search for Coal in the Age of Empires: Ferdinand von Richthofen's Odyssey in China, 1860–1920," *American Historical Review* 119, no. 2 (2014), 339–363.

52. Ferdinand von Richthofen, *Baron Richthofen's Letters, 1870–1872* (Shanghai: North China Herald, 1903), 151–152, quoted in Chin, "The Invention of the Silk Road," 210.

53. A voluminous series of reports from the Sino-Swedish Expedition was published: Sven Hedin and Folke Bergman (eds.), *History of the Expedition in Asia, 1927-1935: Reports from the Scientific Expedition to the North-Western Provinces of China under the Leadership of Dr. Sven Hedin*, 3 vols. (Stockholm: Elanders Boktryckeri Aktiebolag, 1943–1944).

54. Sven Hedin, *Sidenvägen: En bilfärd genom Centralasien* (Stockholm: Albert Bonnier, 1936); Sven Hedin, *The Silk Road: Ten Thousand Miles through Central Asia*, translated from the Swedish by F. H. Lyon (London: George Routledge & Sons, 1938).

55. Jonathan Haslam, "The Sino-Japanese War and Soviet Aid to China, 1937-38," in *The Soviet Union and the Threat from the East, 1933–41* (London: Macmillan, 1992), 88–111.

56. Mia Bennett, "The Silk Road Goes North: Russia's Role within China's Belt and Road Initiative," *Area Development and Policy* 1, no. 3 (2016), 341–351, 343.

57. Mark Mancall, "The Kiakhta Trade," in Charles Donald Cowan (ed.), *The Economic Development of China and Japan* (Abingdon, UK: Routledge, 1964), 19–48.

58. Sarah C. M. Paine, "The Triple Intervention and the Termination of the First Sino-Japanese War," in Bruce A. Elleman and Sarah C. M. Paine (eds.), *Naval Coalition Warfare: From the Napoleonic War to Operation Iraqi Freedom* (London: Routledge, 2008), 75–85.

59. Stephen Kotkin, "Preface," in Bruce A. Elleman and Stephen Kotkin (eds.), *Manchurian Railways and the Opening of China: An International History* (London: Routledge, 2010), xiii–xvi.

60. Paine, "The Triple Intervention and the Termination of the First Sino-Japanese War."

61. John V. A. MacMurray (ed.), *Treaties and Agreements with and concerning China 1894–1919*, vol. 1 (New York: Oxford University Press, 1921), 523.

62. For a detailed examination of Japan's infrastructure expansion in Korea and Manchuria, see Daqing Yang, "Japanese Colonial Infrastructure in Northeast Asia: Realities, Fantasies,

Legacies," in Charles K. Armstrong, Gilbert Rozman, Samuel S. Kim, and Stephen Kotkin (eds.), *Korea at the Center: Dynamics of Regionalism in Northeast Asia* (New York: Routledge, 2005), 92–109.

63. For more on the South Manchuria Railway Company, see Emer O'Dwyer, "Japanese Empire in Manchuria," in *Oxford Research Encyclopedia of Asian History* (online, 2017), http://asianhistory.oxfordre.com/view/10.1093/acrefore/9780190277727.001.0001/acrefore -9780190277727-e-78?rskey=AQ9aDc&result=1 (accessed November 14, 2020; the web pages cited in the notes were still available on the access dates); and Louise Young, "Manchukuo and Japan," in *Japan's Total Empire: Manchuria and the Culture of Wartime* (Berkeley: University of California Press, 1998), 3–20.

64. Yang, "Japanese Colonial Infrastructure in Northeast Asia," 94.

65. Yang, "Japanese Colonial Infrastructure in Northeast Asia," 94. For more on this subject, see Takahashi Yasuyaka, *History of Japanese Colonial Railways* [日本植民地鉄道史論] (Tokyo: Nihon Keizai Hyoronsha, 1990).

66. Yang, "Japanese Colonial Infrastructure in Northeast Asia," 95.

67. Yang, "Japanese Colonial Infrastructure in Northeast Asia," 96. For more on this subject, see Kobayashi Hideo (ed.), *A Historical Survey of Japanese Activities Overseas: Korea 8* [日本人の海外活動に関する歴史的調査：朝鮮篇 8] (Tokyo: Okurasho Kanrikyoku, 1950).

68. For more on the Greater East Asia Co-Prosperity Sphere, see Peter Duus, "Imperialism without Colonies: The Vision of a Greater East Asia Co-prosperity Sphere," *Diplomacy and Statecraft* 7, no. 1 (1996), 54–72, and Janis Mimura, "Japan's New Order and Greater East Asia Co-Prosperity Sphere: Planning for Empire," *Asia-Pacific Journal* 9, no. 49 (2011), 1–12.

69. Yang, "Japanese Colonial Infrastructure in Northeast Asia," 103. For more on this subject, see Harada Katsumasa, *Railway* [鉄道] (Tokyo: Nihon Keizai Hyoronsha, 1988), 202–209.

70. Yang, "Japanese Colonial Infrastructure in Northeast Asia," 103.

71. Yang, "Japanese Colonial Infrastructure in Northeast Asia," 104. For a detailed overview of Yumoto's plan, see Yumoto Noboru, "On Building a Trans-Greater East Asian Railway [大東亞縱貫鐵道建設論]," *Kagakushugi Kogyo* [科学主義工業] 6, no. 3 (March 1942), 36–43.

PART I

EXCHANGES AND FLOWS

THE INTERNATIONAL DEVELOPMENT OF CHINA

At its inauguration in 1912, the Republic of China (ROC) heralded a "new China," whose inheritance was not so much a "historical China" as it was the Qing Empire. No Chinese empire had ever been as extensive geographically or as long-lived as that of the Qing dynasty, which ruled over a multiethnic and multicultural expanse including such far-flung areas as Manchuria, Mongolia, Xinjiang, and Tibet. Many scholars have pointed out that one of the most remarkable feats of the Republic was to redefine this vast territory as "Chinese" despite the numerous crises that threatened its dissolution during the first decade of the twentieth century. The state diplomatically defended it so successfully that (with the exception of Outer Mongolia) the borders of today's People's Republic of China (PRC) are essentially the same as the borders of the Qing Empire.[1] Moreover, the Republic won back for China what it had almost lost under the late Qing: the capacity to reassert itself on the international stage and orchestrate relationships with foreign powers in the service of the state.[2]

The expansion of foreign trade as much as diplomacy played a critical role in the development of republican China's foreign relationships and undergirded the sustained economic expansion of the national economy. Despite simmering antiforeign and anti-imperialist resentments in the context of China's Century of Humiliation (1839–1949), dominated by unequal treaties and political weakness, internationalism peaked during the republican era, when the country embraced an unprecedented surge of international economic influences. For Sun Yat-sen and other republican reformists, industrialization and modernization went hand in hand with the efforts to achieve national unity, and industrialization was inseparable from internationalization. As the English title of his 1920 plan (*The International Development of China*) declared, it was Sun's intention that international capital should come to China for developing railways, highways, water conservation and irrigation, modern ports and cities, and basic industries and public utilities.[3]

Many scholars have commented on Sun's ambiguous attitude toward foreign capital in his Three Principles of Nationalism, Democracy, and Livelihood. While Sun expressed deep concern over the self-interest of Western capitalists and advocated protective tariffs when talking about nationalism (*minzu*), he simultaneously strove to attract foreign investment into China with the promise of greater profits when talking about livelihood (*minsheng*).[4] Such seemingly contradictory claims need to be understood within the international context at that time. The unity of the Western powers (including Japan after 1900) in their dealings with the Qing authorities had seriously hampered the Qing Empire's trade advantages and diplomatic room for maneuver. However, this changed dramatically after World War I, when the Western powers no longer operated as a distinct entity and the Republic of China started to emerge as a player in a multipolar international system.

Sun believed that opening China to foreign capitalism could benefit all parties. The industries of the Western powers victorious in World War I could more easily capitalize on pursuing peacetime business opportunities in wider and more diverse markets, while foreign capital would allow China to overcome its lack of technological wherewithal on its path to a modern and more economically just society. Unlike the Qing dynasty, which embarked on foreign trade under unequal terms, Sun insisted that the Republic would only accept foreign capital on equitable and businesslike terms: "The Chinese people will welcome the development of our country's resources provided that it can be kept out of Mandarin corruption and ensure the mutual benefit of China and the countries cooperating with us."[5]

Sun's 1920 plan highlighted China's trade deficit with other nations and promoted Sino-foreign economic cooperation in the fields of infrastructure construction and resource development as a means to reverse the transnational flows that had depleted Chinese state interests and prevent China from becoming a "dumping ground for commercial nations' over-production."[6] He believed it was necessary to welcome international capital, technology, equipment, and talent into China to establish commerce and industry, gradually modernize the Chinese economy, and ultimately catch up with and outpace the advanced Western capitalist economies.[7] *The International Development of China* ended with Sun's proposition that foreign capitalism could be used to build socialism in China: "In a nutshell, it is my idea to make capitalism create socialism in China so that these two economic forces of human evolution will work side by side in future civilization."[8] Throughout his life, Sun never abandoned hope that China would one day devise a way to harness the energy of capitalism to serve the justice of socialism.[9]

Some scholars of modern Chinese history have pointed out that there is no such thing as a "China-centered" historical narrative, given that everything important for modern China had an international dimension.[10] The remainder of this opening essay outlines the long-lasting impacts of Sun Yat-sen's plan and different approaches to state-building and internationalization within the ever-changing national and international contexts. It focuses on the formation and restructuring of China's state-owned enterprises over the past century and the significant roles they have played in the various stages of the country's development and international relationships. These stages include China's enthusiastic opening up to international economic influences during the Nationalist era and early years of the PRC (1928–1958), the drastic fluctuations in the country's attitudes toward global market integration over the last four decades of the twentieth century (1959–1999), and the gradual formation of an "economic diplomacy" since the start of the new millennium (2000–present).

FROM SINO-WEST ALLIANCE TO SINO-SOVIET ALLIANCE (1928–1958)

Sun Yat-sen died in 1925, just as the Nationalist movement he had helped initiate was gaining momentum. His vision continued to guide the social and economic development of China, particularly the dramatic integration with global markets during the Nationalist era (1928–1949). The economy was largely militarized due to the Chinese Civil War (which erupted intermittently between 1927 and 1949) and increasing tensions with Japan, which culminated in the Second Sino-Japanese War. The Nationalist government moved rapidly after 1927 to form important economic and strategic ties with three of the world's most powerful nations at the time—Germany, the United States, and the Soviet Union—in order to defend itself against Japan. Modern China's first cooperative international relationship based on the principles and practice of equality and mutual benefit was made between the Republic of China's Nanjing government and Germany in the late 1920s.[11] Alliances with the Soviet Union in the late 1930s and the United States in the early 1940s were responses to the rising Japanese threat. These partnerships with foreign firms and governments played a critical role in the expansion of the national rail network, the introduction of civil aviation to China, the establishment of the country's first automotive manufacturing company, and, most important, the formation of the state industrial sector that would become the economic foundation of the late Nationalist and early Communist regimes.[12]

Most studies of twentieth-century China identify the year 1949 (the founding of the PRC) as the pivotal point in history where the establishment of a Communist system and the influence of the Soviet Union on the Chinese Communist Party her-alded a centrally planned economy. In fact, the Nationalist government's substantial expansion of the state sector of the economy through the 1930s and 1940s set in place a strong foundation for the PRC's initiatives in the 1950s. In *The International*

Development of China Sun Yat-sen emphasized the importance of both harnessing the energy of capitalism and strengthening state influence to achieve socialism in China. Sun's vision was deemed acceptable by his successors within the specific national and international context of the time. The global crisis of capitalism in the 1930s and the evident achievements of Soviet planning demonstrated the transforming power of the state and the increased role that state planning could play in the future.[13] Nationalist economic bureaucrats considered central planning and state ownership crucial for national defense at a time of crisis. After the Japanese invasion of Manchuria in 1931, modern development bureaucracies were rapidly established and planning personnel significantly expanded. The most notable progress in this regard was made under the National Resources Commission (NRC; *ziyuan weiyuanhui*), the technical and managerial institution formed in 1932 that soon dominated state industries.[14]

The formation of a state-controlled economy was accelerated after the outbreak of the Second Sino-Japanese War in 1937. The NRC expanded from 23 mining and industrial units and 2,000 staff members in 1937 to 103 mining, manufacturing, and electrical enterprises, 12,000 staff members, and 160,000 workers by 1944.[15] In addition to planning and managing the war economy, the NRC played a central role in formulating plans for the postwar economic development of the whole country. The first national plan for the postwar period prepared by the NRC in 1943 made it explicit that the expansion of government controls and growth of the state industrial sector would continue apace in peacetime.[16] The twenty-volume national plan included detailed schedules for the development of key industrial sectors, including over 300 heavy industrial enterprises and 3,000 light industrial units, many of which had been independent of the government before 1937.[17]

After the end of the Second Sino-Japanese War, the *Three-Year Construction Plan for State Industry* was released in 1946.[18] This plan expanded the scope of government control beyond industry to include agriculture, forestry, fisheries, livestock production, and water conservation.[19] This intensification of government monopolies and the socialization of a planned industrial economy was the Nationalist government's response to the many challenges it faced in the late 1940s, especially given the resumption of the Chinese Civil War following Japan's defeat, the industrial plunder of Manchuria by the Soviet Union, and American pressure to privatize Chinese industry. The NRC was further expanded during this period, becoming the largest civilian government agency and controlling the rapidly growing state industrial sector as well as Chinese foreign trade agreements and economic cooperation. Indeed, by the end of the republican era, the NRC accounted for two-thirds of China's total industrial capital and employed more than 500,000 staff and workers.[20] Many NRC engineers and planners were trained abroad and then brought experience from the world's most advanced industrial economies to bear on China's challenging local circumstances.[21]

At the end of the Civil War in 1949, the Communist Party took control of mainland China and established the PRC, while the Nationalist Party retreated to Taiwan. The transition from ROC to PRC governance was one of continuity rather than disruption for the state industrial economy, particularly in terms of the Chinese approach to technology transfer and foreign economic cooperation. The formation of a state-controlled industrial sector during the Nationalist era had set the stage for the PRC's even more extensive state monopoly. Enterprises under NRC management were classified by the PRC government as state-operated enterprises and were allowed to continue operating as they had before the establishment of the PRC. Priorities set out in the PRC's First Five-Year Plan (1953–1957) were similar to those of the 1946 plan for China's postwar economic reconstruction.[22]

The decade between the founding of the PRC and the end of the First Five-Year Plan witnessed the unprecedentedly rapid integration of China into the international economy. The human and industrial capital accumulated during the Nationalist era made possible the rapid growth of the socialist state sector of the PRC. This process was accelerated by the Sino-Soviet alliance forged in the tensest years of the Cold War against the United States and its allies.[23] What started as an alliance based on shared ideology after decades of Soviet mentoring of the Chinese Communist Party since its founding in 1921 soon evolved into a multifaceted alliance embracing military, cultural, educational, and economic cooperation. Notably, the "156 technology transfer projects" program that operated from 1950 until the abrupt end of the alliance in 1957 because of unanticipated Sino-Soviet political tensions was vital in transplanting a 1930s Soviet development model in China.[24] During this project, large capital-intensive heavy industrial plants were constructed and state-of-the-art Soviet machinery and equipment were moved to China. Technical assistance and know-how were spread throughout China by thousands of Soviet experts who came to teach and the thousands of Chinese who studied in the Union of Soviet Socialist Republics (USSR). During the early years of the People's Republic, industrialization proceeded hand in hand with internationalization just as it had under the Republic of China.

FROM SELF-RELIANCE TO SOCIALIST MARKET ECONOMY (1959–1999)

The rush to open the economy to international influences and integrate it with global markets that characterized China's modern history since the beginning of the Republican era ended abruptly after the end of the First Five-Year Plan. The pro-Soviet foreign policy of the 1950s was replaced by an anti-Soviet and anti-American stance, leaving China in a state of diplomatic isolation and economic limbo.[25] Toward the end of the 1950s Chinese leaders started to reevaluate the long-term impact of the Sino-Soviet alliance. Soviet support came with a series of unreasonable demands, such as the permanent stationing of Soviet forces at strategic ports in northeastern China and the establishment of a Soviet-controlled longwave radio station for naval communication.[26] Technology transfers and aid were also leading to China's increased economic dependency on the Soviet Union. Ideological and political differences between the two countries, serious concerns about unreasonable demands, and the fear that economic dependence would threaten China's national independence all contributed to the Sino-Soviet split of the early 1960s.

From the early 1960s until the country's return to an Opening Up policy in 1978, China adopted a different strategy of state-building and practice of internationalism, both tailored to meet the goal of promoting and preserving national independence. Believing that China could never achieve complete national independence without economic independence, Mao Zedong advocated the economic strategy of "self-reliance" with economic development reliant on domestic resources. Mao explicitly rejected the concepts of international division of labor promoted by Western theorists of interdependent development, stating that "the correct method is each [country] doing the utmost for itself as a means toward self-reliance for new growth. . . . Reliance on other countries . . . is most dangerous."[27] Notably, the strategy of self-reliance did not eliminate all exchanges between China and foreign countries. Just as China withdrew from Soviet- and Western-aided cooperative projects, it sought cooperation with Third World countries through an extensive aid program. According to Mao, in addition to maintaining its own self-reliance and independence, a truly socialist state is obligated to help countries in the developing world "towards escaping or limiting the consequences of the international capitalist division of labor."[28]

Despite its own underdeveloped economy, China lent large amounts of aid to the Third World on generous terms, with much of its foreign assistance in the form of gifts.[29] Chinese aid tended to concentrate on certain types of projects, particularly highly visible infrastructure that could come into operation quickly, resulting in a good deal of publicity. Infrastructure projects such as roads, railways, ports, factories, and sport stadiums made up 67 percent of China's economic aid programs by the mid-1970s in terms of the number of contracts.[30] Sometimes projects were chosen to demonstrate that China was a strong power despite high costs and technical challenges. For example, the Tanzania–Zambia Railway built between 1970 and 1975 was the largest single foreign-aid project undertaken by China at that time. China decided to finance and support the project largely because the Soviet Union and the West had declined to support it because of practical difficulties.[31] In addition to preferring certain types of projects, Chinese aid was clearly concentrated geographically, with most allocated to neighboring countries with an eye to reinforcing China's own national security. Although Chinese aid had been extended to more than seventy countries on five continents by the end of the 1970s, North Korea, North Vietnam, and Pakistan were the three largest recipients in response to the Korean War, the Vietnam War, and the threat of India along China's southern border.[32]

In the 1960s and 1970s state-owned enterprises (SOEs) not only undertook the full gamut of state-building tasks guided by the principle of self-reliance but also played a critical role in facilitating and implementing projects carried out under China's aid programs. Originally formed during the Nationalist era under the NRC, many SOEs were renamed and reorganized after the NRC was incorporated into the First Ministry of Machine Industry in 1952. Consequently, while some SOEs were run as government units under the direct control of line ministries, others came under the control of the Engineering Corps of the People's Liberation Army (PLA). For example, Chinese assistance on the Tanzania–Zambia Railway was provided in large part by the Railway Engineering Corps of the PLA (predecessor of the China Railway Construction Corporation formed in 1982) and the foreign aid department of the Ministry of Railways (predecessor of China Civil Engineering Construction Corporation established in 1979).[33] If the establishment and development of the SOEs during the Nationalist era and early years of the People's Republic were dominated by the transfer of capital and knowledge from the industrialized powers to China, the two decades following the Sino-Soviet split were characterized by the outflow of Chinese aid and expertise to economically underdeveloped countries. While the former phase was mostly driven by economic incentives, the latter phase would appear to be more politically inspired.

At the end of the 1970s, China went through a sea change in its domestic politics and foreign relations. The end of the Cultural Revolution, a sociopolitical movement that ran from 1966 until Mao Zedong's death in 1976, marked the beginning of the post-Mao era in the PRC and the country's reintegration into the international system. In 1978, under the leadership of Deng Xiaoping, China adopted the Reform and Opening Up policy that replaced the Mao-era principles of self-reliance and aid-oriented international trade. The Bank of China started to solicit overseas deposits in 1978. China joined the International Monetary Fund (IMF) and the World Bank in 1980.[34] Notably, many pro-Deng commentators used ideas included in Sun Yat-sen's *The International Development of China* to support Deng's Reform and Opening Up policy. They argued that foreign participation could not benefit the country when Sun was alive due to the Western powers' aggressive posture; however, Sun's proposals, particularly his advocacy of harnessing the energy of capitalism to achieve the justice of socialism, could be of service to the nation once China had become strong enough to control its own destiny and security.[35] Sun's idea of combining the best features of capitalism and socialism found new expression in the term "socialism with Chinese characteristics," which stood for Deng's overall program of adopting some elements of the market economy to foster growth by using foreign investment while acknowledging that the Chinese Communist Party retained its formal commitment to achieve communism and maintained its monopoly on political power.

Reform of the SOEs, which had been charged with nation-building tasks for three decades since the founding of the PRC, was an important component of a nationwide economic and political reform program. As previously mentioned, under the centrally planned economy, fully state-owned SOEs were often referred to as state-operated enterprises (*guoying qiye*). It was estimated in 1976 that over one-third of all SOEs were running at a loss and were draining fiscal and quasi-fiscal government resources as a result of multiple factors inherent in a centrally planned economy, such as poor incentive systems for labor and management, rigid economic planning, and serious challenges in fostering technological innovation.[36] Prices were increasingly determined by market forces and competition in the Chinese economy after the implementation of the Opening Up policy, so SOEs had to undergo a long process of reformation to become incorporated business entities competing with one another in domestic and global markets. China decided to reform SOEs by establishing a modern enterprise system separating ownership and management. The corporatization of SOEs gave increased autonomy to SOE managers to run the businesses while the state retained ownership or majority control, resulting in the more common use of the description "state-owned enterprises" (*guoyou qiye*).

FROM ECONOMIC DEVELOPMENT TO STRATEGIC INTEGRATION (2000–PRESENT)

China's SOE reform entered a new stage in 2003, guided by the principle of "grasping the big, letting go of the small" (*zhuada fangxiao*) that defined the roles of the central and local governments in managing different types of SOEs. According to this principle, local governments should be the owners of smaller and less important SOEs and accelerate their restructuring through employee buyouts, open sales, leasing, joint ventures, mergers, or bankruptcy. Meanwhile, the central government should be the owners of large SOEs and facilitate improvement of their efficiency and competitiveness, particularly in the case of industries that are essential to the nation's economy and homeland security. Major efforts were initiated to make large SOEs globally competitive, particularly in the key strategic sectors of energy, telecoms, aviation, railways, and defense. To this end, the State-Owned Assets Supervision and Administration Commission (SASAC) of the State Council and Central Huijin Investment Co., Ltd., were set up as investors acting on behalf of the state. Under this framework, major industrial SOEs are owned for the state by SASAC, while state-owned financial institutions are owned by Central Huijin, which became part of the China Investment Corporation in 2007.[37]

This new phase of SOE reform took place in the context of the fourth generation of PRC leadership's ascent to power in November 2002, assessment of the achievements of the two decades of Reform and Opening Up policy launched by Deng

Xiaoping in the late 1970s, and new challenges that needed to be addressed in light of rapidly changing domestic and international realities. At the domestic level, there was an urgent need to reconsider the coastal-inland relationship and expand the Reform and Opening Up policy to inland regions. Rapid growth of export-oriented manufacturing in the coastal regions since 1978 had led to a huge disparity of wealth between coastal and inland regions, posing a threat to China's political and economic stability. Consequently, the central government initiated a number of strategies to reduce inequality, including the promulgation of the Western Development Strategy in 2000 and the Northeast China Revitalization Strategy in 2003. At the international level, it became increasingly clear that China needed to balance the inflow and outflow of capital and technology and enhance its strategic position in the world economically and politically. The first two decades of the Chinese Reform and Opening Up policy were dominated by the Bring In policy (*yinjinlai*) that made China one of the most important recipients of foreign capital and technology. In anticipation of China's further integration into the global economy and its expected entry into the World Trade Organization in December 2001, a Go Out policy (*zouchuqu*) was initiated in 1999 to tackle the lack of competitiveness of Chinese enterprises.

SOEs have always been the main implementors at the forefront of China's reforms. The new phase of SOE reform after 2003 facilitated these national efforts to achieve balanced development between coastal and inland regions and an equitable inflow and outflow of capital and technology. Together, these efforts at the domestic and international levels led to the optimization of China's overall industrial structure and a dramatic increase in foreign trade. The average annual growth rate of China's exports and imports reached 17.4 percent and 16.3 percent, respectively, between 1978 and 2001.[38] These figures leapt even higher between 2001 and 2008, reaching 27.6 percent and 24.8 percent, far higher than the global average.[39] Meanwhile, China's total value of imports and exports, estimated at US$14.4 billion in 1978, surged to US$516.1 billion in 2001 and US$2.6 trillion in 2008, ranking third after the United States and Germany. Despite a temporary decrease in export and import value between 2008 and 2009 due to the global financial crisis, China's foreign trade quickly recovered. China surpassed Germany in 2009 and the United States in 2013 to become the world's largest trading nation.[40]

As noted, Sun Yat-sen's 1920 plan highlighted China's trade deficit with other commercial nations and promoted a series of projects to stop China from becoming a "dumping ground for commercial nations' over-production." Since the reforms of 1978, particularly after its accession to the WTO in 2001, China has rapidly developed into a global manufacturing and trading giant, redrawing the map of global trade and political influence and resulting in new collaborations and conflicts. Although China's foreign exports and imports have increased at similar rates since 1978, trade balances between China and other countries are uneven geographically and temporally. For example, among China's top trading partners, Germany has long enjoyed a trade surplus with China, Russia has moved from a trade-surplus to a trade-deficit with China since 2007, and the United States has a long-standing trade deficit with China. The US trade shortfall rose from US$83.0 billion in 2001 to US$375.6 billion in 2017, eventually leading to open trade conflict between the two countries in 2018.[41]

In this new era of internationalization, SOEs are the key agents controlling the quantities and types of exchanges and flows crossing China's borders. Their domestic and global economic footprints have expanded along with the increasing volume and value of Chinese foreign trade. As the gateways of these transnational exchanges and flows, existing ports are upgraded and new ones are developed at both the inland and marine frontiers of the nation. A century ago, the blueprints of transcontinental corridors drawn up by the colonial powers emphasized the coordination of land, port, and maritime capacity to better connect marine and land-based trade routes. For the majority of the twentieth century, even after 1978, the opening and development of the inland border ports lagged well behind the coastal ports. SOEs with long-established operations at coastal ports have been actively setting up at inland border ports as well since the early 2000s. The inland border ports, particularly those with category-one status, are now better connected to China's coastal areas and regional neighbors, and, internationally, to land, marine, and air transport.

These ambitious frontier developments are facilitated by the sociopolitical realities of the new millennium, whereby the central government puts equal emphasis on development and security and sets the goal of making China a composite land-sea power by using soft initiatives such as economic diplomacy. The development of China's inland frontier was deemed impractical during the twentieth century, partly due to its largely undefined borders with neighboring new and newly liberated states in Asia. After a half-century of diplomatic negotiations since 1949, the development of inland frontiers became more achievable, as China entered the twenty-first century having settled all its land boundaries except with India and Bhutan.[42] Similarly, the accelerated development of China's marine frontier and its ever-closer collaborative relationship with the inland frontiers are driven by new circumstances. The two-decade rapid development of China's coastal regions after 1978 was motivated primarily by an economic impetus. China's maritime frontier assumed greater strategic importance when the fourth generation of PRC leadership came to power in late 2002 and kick-started a maritime renaissance program that set the goal of China becoming a strong global sea power by the middle of the twenty-first century, marking 200 years since the outbreak of the First Opium War.[43]

The soft diplomatic approach to making China a composite land-sea power culminated in the launch of the Belt and Road Initiative by Xi Jinping in 2013, a year after he became the paramount leader of the fifth generation of the PRC leadership. Through the land-based Silk Road Economic Belt and the ocean-based Twenty-First Century Maritime Silk Road, China's marine and inland frontiers are further integrated with international production networks and global value chains. Rather than being an economic-centered project, the BRI combines strategic and economic objectives and is largely an economic diplomacy strategy supporting the building of "a community of shared interest, shared responsibility and common destiny."[44] SOEs are the primary representatives of the state in China's economic diplomatic strategy, which aims to *yijing cuzheng* (literally, "use economics to promote politics") and *zhengjing jiehe* (literally, "combine politics and economics").[45] The consolidation and restructuring process since 2013 has further intensified to promote the competitiveness of SOEs that both influence China's policy-making on the BRI and receive policy guidance from the state. As a result of mergers, the number of SOEs owned on behalf of the state by SASAC dropped from 189 in 2002 to 150 at the dawn of the global financial crisis in 2008 and then to 96 in 2018.[46] Meanwhile, through a wide range of projects (especially in the key connectivity sectors of transportation, energy, water, and telecommunications), SOEs have gained a wealth of experience carrying out economic activities abroad. By the end of 2018 Chinese SOEs were responsible for about half of BRI projects by number and more than 70 percent by project value.[47]

As this opening essay shows, the form, speed, and direction of exchanges and flows are highly dynamic and subject to the intricate relationships between trade and diplomacy on one hand and economy and security on the other. The following four detailed contemporary case studies explore these relationships further, including the connections between key agents and various aspects of exchanges and flows, which are examined within their specific geophysical, ecological, socioeconomic, and geopolitical contexts at both the national and international levels. Collectively, they highlight the correlations between present and past, local and global, inflows and outflows, and inland and coastal. Case 1 focuses on infrastructure and examines how the country's largest shipping company, the China Ocean Shipping Company (COSCO), is rearranging global transportation routes through its rapid acquisition of overseas seaports in the Indian Ocean, the Mediterranean, and the Atlantic rim as well as dry ports in Europe and Asia. Case 2 focuses on logistics and examines how the China Railway Container Transport Corporation (CRCT), the country's largest container operator, is increasing the competitiveness and diversifying the types of goods transported along Eurasian land-based routes through the optimization of direct freight services, known as CR express trains, between China and Europe. Case 3 focuses on expertise and examines how the country's largest international engineering contractor, the China National Machinery Industry Corporation (SINOMACH), is reshaping regional and global knowledge networks and power dynamics through joint venture projects, such as overseas infrastructure and industrial park construction. Case 4 focuses on resources and examines how the China Oil and Foodstuffs Corporation (COFCO), the country's largest food processor, is playing an increasingly important role in China's transition from fossil fuels to biofuels, creating novel forms of global bioenergy resource networks and transforming the domestic biophysical landscape through grain-based and nongrain-based ethanol fuel production.

NOTES

1. See, for example, James Leibold, "From Empire to Nation: The Bounding of the Chinese Geo-body," in *Reconfiguring Chinese Nationalism: How the Qing Frontier and Its Indigenes Became Chinese* (New York: Palgrave Macmillan, 2007), 17–47, and Hsiao-ting Lin, "Frontier Politics in Metropolitan China," in *Modern China's Ethnic Frontiers: A Journey to the West* (Abingdon, UK: Routledge, 2010), 47–63.

2. William C. Kirby, "The Internationalization of China: Foreign Relations at Home and Abroad in the Republican Era," *China Quarterly* 150 (1997), 433–458, 433.

3. Sun Fo, "Preface to Second Edition," in Sun Yat-sen, *The International Development of China*, 2nd ed. (London: Hutchinson, 1928), 3–5.

4. Michael R. Godley, "Socialism with Chinese Characteristics: Sun Yatsen and the International Development of China," *Australian Journal of Chinese Affairs* 18 (1987), 109–125, 117.

5. Sun Yat-sen, *The International Development of China* (Shanghai: Commercial Press, 1920), iii.

6. Sun, *The International Development of China*, ii.

7. Godley, "Socialism with Chinese Characteristics," 111.

8. Sun, *The International Development of China*, 165.

9. Godley, "Socialism with Chinese Characteristics," 113.

10. See, for example, Guoqi Xu, *China and the Great War: China's Pursuit of a New National Identity and Internationalization* (Cambridge: Cambridge University Press, 2005), and David Scott, *China and the International System, 1840-1949: Power, Presence, and Perceptions in a Century of Humiliation* (New York: Suny Press, 2008).

11. Kirby, "The Internationalization of China," 443. For more on this subject, see William C. Kirby, *Germany and Republican China* (Stanford, CA: Stanford University Press, 1984).

12. Kirby, "The Internationalization of China," 457.

13. William C. Kirby, "Continuity and Change in Modern China: Economic Planning on the Mainland and on Taiwan, 1943–1958," *Australian Journal of Chinese Affairs* 24 (1990), 121–141, 126.

14. Kirby, "Continuity and Change in Modern China," 125. For more on the establishment and development of the National Resources Commission, see William C. Kirby, "Technocratic Organization and Technological Development in China: The Nationalist Experience and Legacy, 1928–1953," in Denis Fred Simon and Merle Goldman (eds.), *Science and Technology in Post-Mao China* (Cambridge, MA: Harvard University Asia Center, 1989), 23–44, and William C. Kirby, "Traditions of Centrality, Authority and Management in Modern China's Foreign Relations," in Thomas W. Robinson and David L. Shambaugh (eds.), *Chinese Foreign Policy: Theory and Practice* (Oxford: Clarendon Press 1994), 13–29.

15. Kirby, "Continuity and Change in Modern China," 128.

16. NRC, *Preliminary Enforcement Plan for Postwar Industrial Construction* [戰後工業建設實施計劃] (Nanjing: National Resources Commission, 1943).

17. Kirby, "Continuity and Change in Modern China," 130.

18. NRC, *Three-Year Construction Plan for State Industry* [國營工業三年建設計劃] (Nanjing: National Resources Commission, 1946).

19. Linsun Cheng, "The Origin of China's Planned Economy and the National Resources

Commission [中國計劃經濟的起源與資源委員會]," *Twentieth Century Bimonthly* (online), August 31, 2007, https://www.cuhk.edu.hk/ics/21c/media/articles/c082-200307109.pdf (accessed September 4, 2020).

20. Kirby, "Continuity and Change in Modern China," 132.

21. Cheng, "The Origin of China's Planned Economy and the National Resources Commission."

22. Kirby, "Continuity and Change in Modern China," 133.

23. For more on this subject, see Shuguang Zhang, *Economic Cold War: America's Embargo against China and the Sino-Soviet Alliance, 1949–1963* (Palo Alto, CA: Stanford University Press, 2001), and Austin Jersild, *Sino-Soviet Alliance: An International History* (Chapel Hill: University of North Carolina Press, 2014).

24. For more on this subject, see Baichun Zhang, Jiuchun Zhang, and Fang Yao, "Technology Transfer from the Soviet Union to the People's Republic of China: 1949–1966," *Comparative Technology Transfer and Society* 4, no. 2 (2006), 105–167.

25. For more on the evolution of China's foreign policy since 1949, see Tianbiao Zhu, "Nationalism and Chinese Foreign Policy," *China Review* 1, no. 1 (2001), 1–27, and Chen Zhimin, "Nationalism, Internationalism and Chinese Foreign Policy," *Journal of Contemporary China* 14, no. 42 (2005), 35–53.

26. Chun-Tu Hsueh, "Introduction," in Chun-Tu Hsueh (ed.), *China's Foreign Relations: New Perspective* (New York: Praeger, 1982), 2–3.

27. Mao Zedong, *A Critique of Soviet Economy*, translated by Moss Roberts (New York: Monthly Review Press), 103, quoted in Friedrich W. Y. Wu, "From Self-Reliance to Interdependence? Developmental Strategy and Foreign Economic Policy in Post-Mao China," *Modern China* 7, no. 4 (1981), 445–482, 456.

28. Edward Friedman, "On Maoist Conceptualizations of the Capitalist World System," *China Quarterly* 80 (1979), 806–837, 822.

29. Wolfgang Bartke, *China's Economic Aid* (London: C. Hurst, 1975), 20.

30. Janos Horvath, *Chinese Technology Transfer to the Third World* (New York: Praeger, 1976), 84.

31. George T. Yu, "Working on the Railroad: China and the Tanzania-Zambia Railway," *Asian Survey* 11, no. 11 (1971), 1101–1117.

32. John Copper, *China's Foreign Aid* (London: Lexington Books, 1976), 24, 45, 134.

33. Wei Song, "Seeking New Allies in Africa: China's Policy towards Africa during the Cold War as Reflected in the Construction of the Tanzania–Zambia Railway," *Journal of Modern Chinese History* 9, no. 1 (2015), 46–65.

34. Godley, "Socialism with Chinese Characteristics," 115.

35. Cai Shan, "On Sun Yat-sen's Ideas about Opening the Country [論孫中山的對外開放思想]," *Huanan Shifan Daxue Xuebao* [華南師範大學學報] 3 (1985), 21–26, 21, cited in Godley, "Socialism with Chinese Characteristics," 113.

36. Elizabeth J. Perry and Christine Wong, "Introduction," in Elizabeth J. Perry and Christine Wong (eds.), *The Political Economy of Reform in Post-Mao China* (Cambridge, MA: Council on East Asian Studies, Harvard University, 1985), 4.

37. Gang Fan and Nicholas C. Hope, "The Role of State-Owned Enterprises in the Chinese Economy," in *US China 2022 Economic Relations in the Next Ten Years* (Hong Kong: China–United States Exchange Foundation, 2013), 5, 6.

38. Calculations are based on the *China Statistical Yearbooks* for 1982 and 2002, both edited by the National Bureau of Statistics and published by China Statistics Press.

39. Calculations are based on the *China Statistical Yearbooks* for 2002 and 2009, both edited by the National Bureau of Statistics and published by China Statistics Press.

40. Kunwang Li and Wei Jiang, "China's Foreign Trade: Reform, Performance and Contribution to Economic Growth," in Ross Garnaut, Ligang Song, and Cai Fang (eds.), *China's 40 Years of Reform and Development: 1978–2018* (Singapore: ANU Press, 2018), 575–594.

41. "What Is the US-China Trade War?" *South China Morning Post*, April 13, 2020, https://www.scmp.com/economy/china-economy/article/3078745/what-us-china-trade-war-how-it-started-and-what-inside-phase (accessed June 8, 2020).

42. Even today, Bhutan and India are the only two countries with which China has an unsettled land border. Bhutan is China's only neighbor that does not have official diplomatic ties with Beijing.

43. Hu Jintao's administration (2002–2012) was pivotal in the development of China's maritime strategy on the ideological, military, and government-planning fronts.

44. NDRC, MFA, and MOC, "Vision and Proposed Actions Outlined on Jointly Building Silk Road Economic Belt and 21st-Century Maritime Silk Road," *China Daily*, March 30, 2015, https://language.chinadaily.com.cn/2015-03/30/content_19950951.htm (accessed June 25, 2020).

45. Denghua Zhang and Jianwen Yin, "China's Belt and Road Initiative, from the Inside Looking Out," *Interpreter*, July 2, 2019, https://www.lowyinstitute.org/the-interpreter/china-s-belt-and-road-initiative-inside-looking-out (accessed June 24, 2020).

46. Karen Jingrong Lin, Xiaoyan Lu, Junsheng Zhang, and Ying Zheng, "State-Owned Enterprises in China: A Review of 40 Years of Research and Practice," *China Journal of Accounting Research* 13, no. 1 (2020), 31–55, 39.

47. Xinwei Zhen, "The High-Quality Participation of State-Owned Enterprises in the Belt and Road Initiative [央企高質量參加一帶一路建設意義重大]," *Belt and Road Portal*, April 22, 2019, https://www.yidaiyilu.gov.cn/xwzx/roll/86585.htm (accessed June 25, 2020).

CHINA OCEAN SHIPPING COMPANY

Transnational shipping corporations, such as the Chinese-Polish Joint Stock Shipping Company and the Czechoslovakia International Ocean Shipping Company, were founded in the late 1950s, when measures to revitalize the shipping industry and reestablish the global shipping connectivity of the People's Republic of China were put in place after two decades of disruption and decline during the Civil War and subsequent political transition. Building on these first steps, the China Ocean Shipping Company (COSCO) was established in 1961 as the PRC's first international overseas shipping company headquartered in Beijing. Five branches of COSCO were created over the next two decades in the country's long-established port cities: Guangzhou (1961), Shanghai (1964), Tianjin (1970), Qingdao (1976), and Dalian (1980). In the 1960s the development of international shipping routes was relatively slow. The China to North Korea and China to Japan shipping routes were set up in 1964, and the first international shipping service between China and Western Europe, in 1967. Following the admission of the PRC as a permanent member of the United Nations (UN) in 1971 and China's adoption of its Reform and Opening Up policy in 1978, the number of sea routes between China and other countries and regions around the world gradually increased. Milestone events of the 1970s include the visit of COSCO's motor vessel *Xiong Yue Cheng* from the Port of Shanghai to Australia in 1978, marking the establishment of the PRC's first international container shipping business, and the visit of COSCO's motor vessel *Liu Lin Hai* to Seattle, heralding the first time in thirty years that a Chinese ship berthed in the United States.[1]

As a central government SOE, COSCO has undergone several reforms over the four decades since 1978. Measures to redefine the market positioning of the

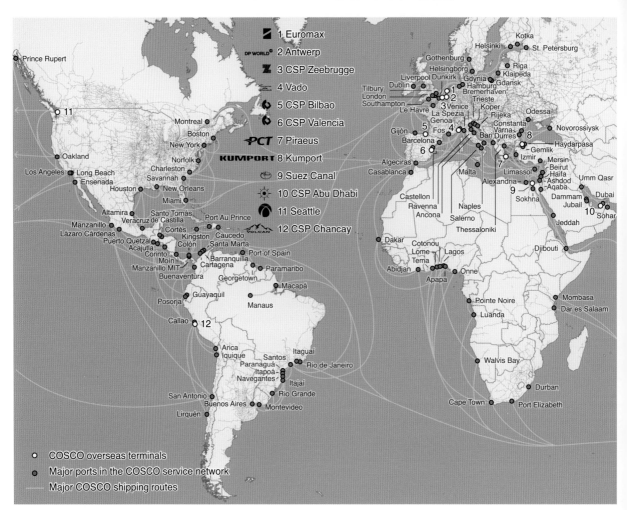

FIGURE I.1.1A
Ports managed and/or invested in by COSCO in Europe, the Middle East, Africa, and the Americas.

conglomerate's five branches were initiated through the 1980s. The pace of COSCO's business diversification had picked up significantly by the end of that decade. Following the acquisition of the China Marine Bunker Supply Company in 1988 and the China Road Transport Company in 1992 as subsidiaries, the conglomerate became a holding company and was renamed the COSCO Group in 1993. After the national Go Out policy was launched in 1999, the COSCO Group entered a period of rapid growth and global expansion featuring major transformations described by the company as "Two Shifts": a "shift from a global shipping operator to a shipping-based logistics operator" and a "shift from a transnational operator to a multinational corporation."[2] The most recent company restructuring took place in 2016 when the Chinese State Council approved the merger of the COSCO Group and China Shipping, forming COSCO Shipping, which now accounts for 80 percent of China's international merchant fleet and is the world's second-largest shipping company by twenty-foot equivalent units (TEU) capacity.[3] This case study focuses on COSCO's international port investments, one of the key components of

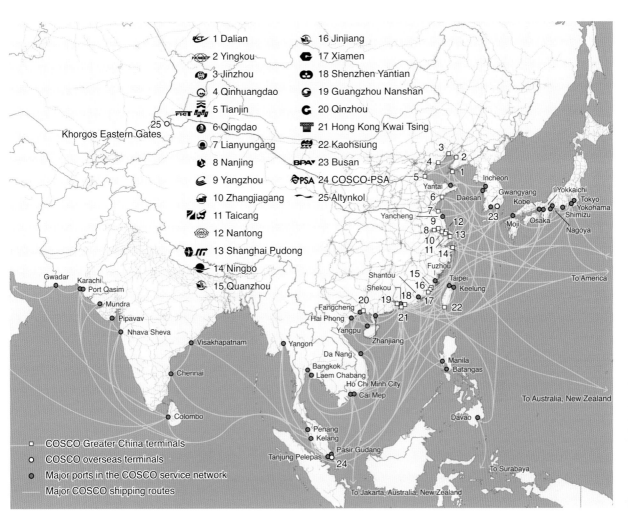

FIGURE I.1.1B
Ports managed and/or invested in by COSCO in Asia.

its global expansion since the early 2000s. First it contextualizes COSCO's overseas port investments within China's maritime renaissance of the early 2000s. Then it investigates how new forms of land-sea trade corridors are taking shape across the landmass of Eurasia, by examining the seaport of Piraeus in Greece, one of the fastest-growing ports in the world, and the Khorgos Gateway dry port in Kazakhstan, the world's largest dry port.

OVERSEAS PORTS AND CHINA'S MARITIME RENAISSANCE

From a Chinese viewpoint, the First Opium War (1839–1842) represents the beginning of both its modern history and the Century of Humiliation that ended in 1949 with the founding of the PRC. That century witnessed the rapid development of ports along China's coastline, mainly developed by the European colonial powers of the late nineteenth century during and following the Treaty Ports era when China was obliged to lease territories or concessions to Germany, the United Kingdom, France, Russia, and Japan up to the late 1920s. During the five decades after 1949, China predominantly pursued a land-focused approach to economic development, even after adopting its Reform and Opening Up policy in 1978. China did not fully turn its attention back to the potential of the ocean until the late 1990s, when the productivity of its earlier economic reforms began to wane. China's embrace of a maritime renaissance was announced at the 16th National Party Congress of November 2002, when the fourth generation of the PRC's leadership came to power. The national congress dubbed the twenty-first century the "ocean century" and predicted that China would become a strong Pacific sea power between 2010 and 2030, eventually taking its place as a strong global sea power between 2030 and 2050.[4] Since then, China's aim of becoming a strong global sea power by the middle of the twenty-first century, which marks the 200th anniversary of the outbreak of the First Opium War, has been promoted as a political objective of the highest priority.

China's maritime renaissance is demonstrated by the transformation of its navy from a traditionally brown-water inshore defense force to a regional blue-water force capable of carrying out offshore defensive operations, the unprecedented expansion of its merchant fleet, the increasing dominance of the global shipbuilding market, and its construction and management of overseas ports and port facilities. Ports are geopolitical assets that form crucial links in sea lines of communication, stimulate industrial development, address trade and energy needs, and enhance naval capabilities. Overseas ports in particular are critical investments offering economic, political, and diplomatic advantages that promote the investing country's national interests by expanding its economic presence and political influence in the host country.[5] COSCO is at the forefront of state-led efforts to expand the geographic range of China's worldwide investments in overseas ports and related infrastructure and has been busy acquiring overseas seaports in the Indian Ocean, the Mediterranean, and the Atlantic rim since the mid-2000s. By the 19th National Party Congress, held in October 2017, COSCO owned more than forty-six container terminals worldwide, processing 90 million TEU, the second-largest volume of trade of any company in the world.[6] That same year, COSCO was awarded $26.1 billion by the China Development Bank to participate in the Belt and Road Initiative, specifically to invest in ports and infrastructure projects.[7] COSCO's ports, which vary in geography, capacity, and functionality, are mostly located in secondary and tertiary powers that face structural constraints by the other dominant world powers: the United States, the European Union (EU), and Russia. In addition to its investments in seaports, COSCO has been increasingly engaged in the development of dry ports in Europe and Asia, dramatically expanding its sea-rail and sea-truck intermodal transport capacity.

SEAPORTS AND DRY PORTS

Piraeus Seaport

Piraeus, the most important port in Greece, is an exemplary case study of COSCO's overseas port investments in regions experiencing EU structural constraints and occupies an important place in COSCO's global expansion plan, which has gained momentum since the early 2000s. Piraeus is the nearest major port capable of handling the largest container ships after they enter the Mediterranean from the Suez Canal. China's interest in Piraeus can be traced back to the 1990s, when a subsidiary of China Shipping signed a contract to use Piraeus for transshipment with the Greek state-owned Piraeus Port Authority (PPA), which operates the entire container terminal. When the China Shipping contract was approaching its expiration date in 2001, COSCO expressed an interest in developing and enlarging Piraeus as a transshipment hub. In November 2008, after an extended tendering process, COSCO signed a 35-year concession agreement with the PPA to operate and develop Terminals 2 and 3, with Terminal 1 remaining under the management of the PPA.[8] Given the significance of the arrangement for both Greece and China, the agreement was signed in Athens in the presence of China's president, Hu Jintao, and Greece's prime minister, Kostas Karamanlis. COSCO established Piraeus Container Terminal (PCT) to operate Terminals 2 and 3, the company's first wholly owned terminal subsidiary outside of China, which commenced operations in October 2009.[9]

China's entry into Greece under the 2008 Piraeus port agreement was reached within the specific context of the Greek government-debt crisis triggered by the financial crisis of 2007–2008 and ushered in a new kind of business relationship with the European geopolitical structure overall. In fact, before that financial crisis, which hit those economies already suffering internal economic weaknesses particularly hard, the Chinese-Greek economic relationship was of little significance. The deterioration of the Greek economy since 2008 along with the policies enforced by the EU and its partners induced Greece to seek help from alternative sources, notably China, which perceived opportunities to bolster its regional and global influence after the financial crisis.[10] At the G20 Summit on Financial Markets and the World Economy held in November 2008, China's president, Hu Jintao, proposed that affected countries work together to tackle their immediate financial challenges while addressing their long-term needs. In the same month, President Hu made a state visit to Greece, during which the PPA-COSCO concession agreement was signed.[11]

The 2008 agreement obliged COSCO to make substantial investments in Terminal 2 to speed up the handling of containers and to complete a new section of Terminal 3. In order to sustain its investment in Piraeus, COSCO had taken several bank loans from one of its principal bankers, the China Development Bank (CDB), a Chinese state-owned bank responsible for raising funds for large infrastructure

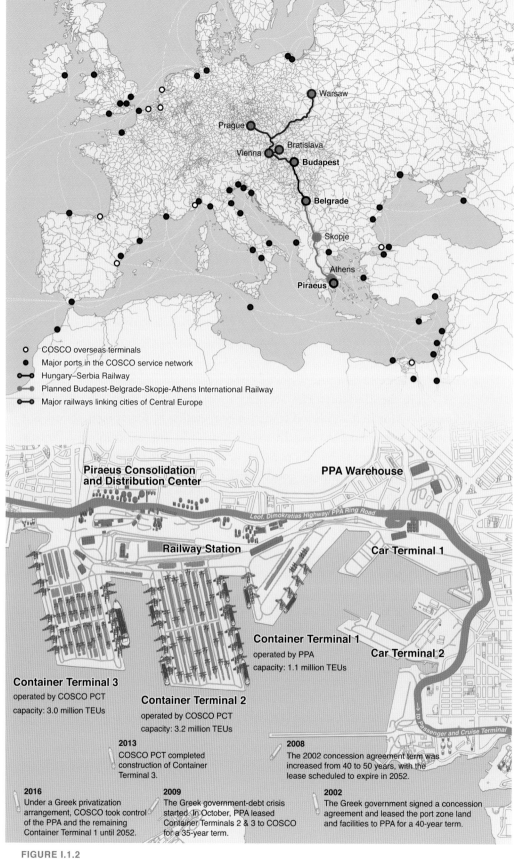

COSCO overseas terminals
Major ports in the COSCO service network
Hungary–Serbia Railway
Planned Budapest-Belgrade-Skopje-Athens International Railway
Major railways linking cities of Central Europe

Piraeus Consolidation and Distribution Center

PPA Warehouse

Leof. Dimokratias Highway/ PPA Ring Road

Railway Station

Car Terminal 1

Container Terminal 1
operated by PPA
capacity: 1.1 million TEUs

Car Terminal 2

Container Terminal 3
operated by COSCO PCT
capacity: 3.0 million TEUs

Container Terminal 2
operated by COSCO PCT
capacity: 3.2 million TEUs

To Passenger and Cruise Terminal

2013
COSCO PCT completed construction of Container Terminal 3.

2008
The 2002 concession agreement term was increased from 40 to 50 years, with the lease scheduled to expire in 2052.

2016
Under a Greek privatization arrangement, COSCO took control of the PPA and the remaining Container Terminal 1 until 2052.

2009
The Greek government-debt crisis started. In October, PPA leased Container Terminals 2 & 3 to COSCO for a 35-year term.

2002
The Greek government signed a concession agreement and leased the port zone land and facilities to PPA for a 40-year term.

FIGURE I.1.2
Piraeus Seaport, Greece.

projects in China and abroad. COSCO borrowed 215 million euros from CDB in 2009 for the sole purpose of investing in Piraeus, and another 120 million euros from CDB in 2012 to finance construction work at Terminal 3.[12] Since COSCO's 2008 intervention, Piraeus has become one of the fastest-growing ports in the world: its container throughput increased from 433,000 TEU in 2008 to 3.7 million TEU in 2016, making it the eighth-busiest port in Europe.[13] The Greek government sold its majority stake in the PPA to COSCO in 2016 in order to repay its debt to the IMF and the EU. A deal was struck between COSCO and the Hellenic Republic Asset Development Fund (Greece's privatization agency), under which COSCO agreed to buy 51 percent of the Port of Piraeus for 280.5 million euros (US$312.5 million). This agreement enabled COSCO to take over the PPA and the remaining container Terminal 1 until 2052.[14] The Port of Piraeus became the first instance where COSCO acquired the dominant stake of an entire port in the EU rather than partial control of component container terminals.

During the final stage of the 2016 acquisition process, Greek prime minister Alexis Tsipras went on a state visit to Beijing, where he was received by Xi Jinping. During the meeting, President Xi stressed that China would be willing to continue to work with Greece to build the Port of Piraeus into "the biggest container transshipment port in the Mediterranean Sea, a bridgehead of land-ocean transportation, and a major pivot for Belt and Road Initiative cooperation by fostering practical and wide-ranging cooperation between the two countries."[15] The acquisition of Piraeus is part of COSCO's plan to build a network of ports, logistic centers, and transport systems for distributing Chinese goods across Europe. COSCO is increasingly focused on developing Piraeus from a major transshipment hub into a significant entry and exit point for overland trade between the Mediterranean and Central Europe, stressing the development of sea-rail intermodal transport services. Immediately upon arrival of a container ship at the Port of Piraeus, its cargo can rapidly be transported to Austria, the Czech Republic, Poland, and other Central European countries via the Budapest–Belgrade Railway (the Hungary–Serbia Railway). This railway is the first stage of the planned Budapest-Belgrade-Skopje-Athens railway, connecting central and southeastern Europe, carried out under the umbrella of the BRI. COSCO's ultimate ambition is to establish the so-called China-Europe Land-Sea Express Route as a north-south transport corridor linking Piraeus and Hamburg via the Balkans, Hungary, Austria, the Czech Republic, Poland, and Germany.[16]

Khorgos Dry Port

COSCO has been expanding its investments in port and logistics projects in an ever-greater range of maritime nations since the mid-2000s. COSCO had thirteen overseas subsidiaries and interests in terminals by early 2020, with combined shipments of 28.4 million TEU accounting for 22.9 percent of the company's global throughput.[17] While these investments in maritime nations clearly demonstrate

COSCO's commitment to realizing China's maritime renaissance, the location of one of the company's 2017 foreign investment projects almost at the Eurasian pole of inaccessibility in landlocked Kazakhstan adds a novel twist to COSCO's international ambitions. COSCO Shipping, China's Lianyungang Port Holdings Group (LPH), and Kazakhstan Temir Zholy (KTZ), the national railway operator of Kazakhstan and the original owner of the Khorgos dry port in the Khorgos Eastern Gates SEZ, officially signed a three-party share transfer agreement in May 2017 in Beijing. Under the agreed terms, COSCO and LPH both acquired 24.5 percent of the shares: a combined 49 percent stake in the Khorgos dry port, the world's largest dry port, located only 15 kilometers from the Chinese border. In return, KTZ will acquire a 49 percent stake in a container-handling terminal in the Chinese seaport of Lianyungang, one of the ten largest ports in China, situated some 4,200 kilometers east of the Khorgos dry port. Such an arrangement facilitates high operational efficiency, with the same company loading containers in China and unloading them at Khorgos in Kazakhstan.[18]

The reality of Chinese groups acquiring a stake in the Khorgos dry port does more than reconfigure global transport routes: it reshapes the Kazakh and Eurasian geopolitical landscape, as China consolidates its influence in a region that Russia long considered its own backyard. During most of the Cold War era, the border area between Kazakhstan and China was a sealed military zone. There was even a brief border conflict between Soviet border guards and the Chinese military in 1969 just north of Khorgos. Kazakhstan, the geographically largest and most economically developed post-Soviet state, has tried to keep on friendly terms with Russia since the disintegration of the USSR, while intentionally distancing itself from the "Russian world" by expanding ties with China. From a Chinese perspective, Kazakhstan is of particular geostrategic importance, given its central Eurasian location. Compared to Russia, which has long served as China's land link to Europe, Kazakhstan is unconditionally enthusiastic about establishing itself as a transit hub for trade between Europe and Asia. In addition, Kazakhstan's relatively high political stability compared to other countries in the region makes it an appealing gateway for China to access the burgeoning Central Asian markets, where millions of aspiring middle-class consumers are hungry for European and Chinese manufactured goods delivered at the cheapest possible prices. The Sino-Kazakhstan strategic partnership was raised to a new level in 2013, when Xi Jinping visited Astana and announced China's Silk Road Economic Belt, the land-based component of the BRI.

In fact, Kazakhstan articulated its national strategic development objective of becoming the principal bridge between East and West very early after independence from the former USSR, and cooperation between Kazakhstan and China considerably predates the BRI. For example, the development of the Khorgos dry port, now branded as a BRI project, began in the late 2000s and was kick-started by Nurly Zhol, a government investment program launched by Kazakhstan's president

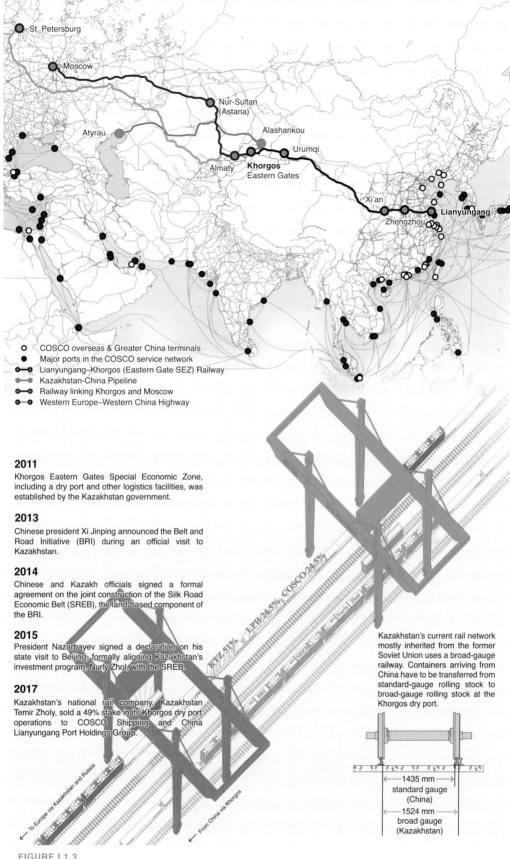

COSCO overseas & Greater China terminals
Major ports in the COSCO service network
Lianyungang–Khorgos (Eastern Gate SEZ) Railway
Kazakhstan-China Pipeline
Railway linking Khorgos and Moscow
Western Europe–Western China Highway

2011

Khorgos Eastern Gates Special Economic Zone, including a dry port and other logistics facilities, was established by the Kazakhstan government.

2013

Chinese president Xi Jinping announced the Belt and Road Initiative (BRI) during an official visit to Kazakhstan.

2014

Chinese and Kazakh officials signed a formal agreement on the joint construction of the Silk Road Economic Belt (SREB), the land-based component of the BRI.

2015

President Nazarbayev signed a declaration on his state visit to Beijing, formally aligning Kazakhstan's investment program, Nurly Zhol, with the SREB.

2017

Kazakhstan's national rail company, Kazakhstan Temir Zholy, sold a 49% stake in its Khorgos dry port operations to COSCO Shipping and China Lianyungang Port Holdings Group.

Kazakhstan's current rail network mostly inherited from the former Soviet Union uses a broad-gauge railway. Containers arriving from China have to be transferred from standard-gauge rolling stock to broad-gauge rolling stock at the Khorgos dry port.

1435 mm
standard gauge
(China)

1524 mm
broad gauge
(Kazakhstan)

FIGURE I.1.3

Khorgos dry port, Kazakhstan.

Nursultan Nazarbayev after the financial crisis of 2007–2008. Nurly Zhol (meaning "path to the future") includes a major component related to logistics and transportation that aims to transform landlocked Kazakhstan into a land-linked Eurasian crossroads. Kazakhstan started construction of the Western Europe–Western China Highway in 2008, which was planned to link Lianyungang port on the Yellow Sea to St. Petersburg on the Baltic. An oil pipeline connecting Kazakhstan and China was completed in 2009, which broke a pipeline export monopoly previously held by Russia's state-owned pipeline company, Transneft. The Khorgos Eastern Gates was established by the Kazakhstan government in 2011 to boost the country's exports. The facility covers 600 hectares, including a dry port and logistic and production zones.[19] Soon after the launch of the BRI in 2013, Chinese and Kazakh officials synergized these developments and signed a formal agreement on the Joint Construction of the Silk Road Economic Belt in December 2014. On his state visit to Beijing in September 2015, President Nazarbayev formally aligned Nurly Zhol with the Silk Road Economic Belt by signing a declaration coordinating the two initiatives.[20]

The Khorgos dry port is a crucial project, taking advantage of the synergies between the Nurly Zhol and the BRI. The announcement of the BRI means an additional boost for the Khorgos dry port: COSCO and LPH's 2017 acquisition of part ownership of the dry port leveraged the efficiencies of cooperative decision-making. The dry port provides transit for containers by freight train, logistics, multimodal transport, warehousing, and storage. It is also the point where Chinese-made cranes transfer cargo between the different rail gauges of China (1,435 mm) and Kazakhstan (1,520 mm). Occupying one of the points on earth farthest from any ocean, the Khorgos dry port links Western Europe and China by railway and highway, being nine to ten days from Europe by rail and five days from Lianyungang. Despite being 4,200 kilometers east of the Khorgos dry port, the Lianyungang seaport is described by landlocked Kazakhstan as its "window to the sea," enhancing the country's transit potential.[21] Investing in and acquiring ownership of the Khorgos dry port allowed COSCO to further expand its international sea-rail and sea-truck intermodal transportation network. COSCO handles the logistics of goods transported between Khorgos and Lianyungang, adaptively catering to customers' ever-changing requirements as the dynamic China-Kazakhstan-Europe value chain evolves.

NOTES

1. COSCO, "COSCO History [發展沿革]," http://www.coscoshipping.com/col/col6862/index.html (accessed April 15, 2021).

2. COSCO, "COSCO History."

3. COSCO, "Group Profile [集團概況]," http://www.coscoshipping.com/col/col6858/index.html (accessed April 15, 2021).

4. Zhiguo Gao, "Embracing the Blue Ocean [擁抱藍色的海洋]," in Gao Zhiguo and Zhang Haiwen (eds.), *Essays on Chinese Ocean Policy* [海洋國策研究文集] (Beijing: Ocean Publishing House, 2007), 4.

5. Frans-Paul van der Putten, *European Seaports and Chinese Strategic Influence* (Clingendael: Netherlands Institute of International Relations, 2019).

6. Zhong Nan, "Full Steam Ahead for Shipping Giant," *China Daily*, June 22, 2017, http://www.chinadaily.com.cn/business/2017-06/22/content_29838514.htm (accessed May 12, 2021).

7. COSCO, "COSCO Shipping Pens Financing Cooperation with China Development Bank [中遠海運集團與國家開發銀行簽署《開發性金融合作協議》]," January 11, 2017, http://www.coscoshipping.com/art/2017/1/11/art_6864_54526.html (accessed May 12, 2021).

8. Harilaos N. Psaraftis and Athanasios A. Pallis, "Concession of the Piraeus Container Terminal: Turbulent Times and the Quest for Competitiveness," *Maritime Policy & Management* 39, no. 1 (2012), 27–43, 30, 31.

9. Frans-Paul van der Putten, *Chinese Investment in the Port of Piraeus, Greece* (Clingendael: Netherlands Institute of International Relations, 2014), 10.

10. EU financial assistance came with stringent requirements for Greece to restructure its economy and raise capital by privatizing state assets and enterprises. See Symeon Mavridis, "Greece's Economic and Social Transformation 2008–2017," *Social Sciences* 7, no. 1 (2018), 1–14.

11. "COSCO Signs Deal with Greek Port," *China Daily*, November 27, 2008, http://www.chinadaily.com.cn/china/2008-11/27/content_7244698.htm (accessed October 4, 2020).

12. Keith Wallis, "Expansion at Greek Container Terminal," *South China Morning Post*, May 18, 2012, https://www.scmp.com/article/1001299/expansion-greek-container-terminal (accessed May 12, 2021).

13. The container throughput at Piraeus reached 5.4 million TEU in 2020, making it the fourth-busiest port in Europe. See COSCO, "COSCO SHIPPING Ports Limited Container Throughput 2020," https://ports.coscoshipping.com/en/Businesses/MonthlyThroughput/pdf/2020.pdf (accessed May 12, 2021).

14. Maria Petrakis, "COSCO Agrees to Pay 368.5m Euros for Control of Key Greek Port," *China Daily*, January 21, 2016, https://www.chinadaily.com.cn/business/2016-01/21/content_23175889.htm (accessed May 14, 2021).

15. MFA, "Xi Jinping Meets with Prime Minister Alexis Tsipras of Greece," July 6, 2016, https://www.fmprc.gov.cn/mfa_eng/zxxx_662805/t1378515.shtml (accessed May 14, 2021).

16. van der Putten, *Chinese Investment in the Port of Piraeus, Greece*, 13.

17. COSCO, "Sustainability Report 2020," https://doc.irasia.com/listco/hk/coscoship/annual/2020/esr.pdf (accessed May 14, 2021), 14.

18. "Chinese Companies Buy Stake in Dry Port in Kazakhstan," *Xinhua News*, May 15, 2017, http://www.xinhuanet.com//english/2017-05/15/c_136285595.htm (accessed 2021).

19. Nargis Kassenova, "China's Silk Road and Kazakhstan's Bright Path: Linking Dreams of Prosperity," *Asia Policy* 24, no. 1 (2017), 110–116.

20. National People's Congress of the People's Republic of China, "China's Top Legislator Meets Kazakh President," September 7, 2015, http://www.npc.gov.cn/englishnpc/c2762/201509/d4aafcdd98d5449cbcf744d10bc14515.shtml (accessed May 14, 2021).

21. Kassenova, "China's Silk Road and Kazakhstan's Bright Path," 111.

CHINA RAILWAY CONTAINER TRANSPORT CORPORATION

Founded in 2003 as part of the China Railway Corporation, the China Railway Container Transport Corporation (CRCT) was established in the context of the Chinese central government's promotion of railway container transportation. Early container systems had been developed in Europe in the early nineteenth century but were only applied internationally during and after World War II. The rise of container shipping from the 1950s coincided with the strong growth of postwar international trade and became a major element in subsequent globalization, as it dramatically reduced transportation costs. Test runs of domestic container transport systems started in China in the mid-1950s, but the progress of containerization for rail and water transportation was slow.[1] Over the two decades following the Reform and Opening Up policy of the late 1970s, containerization in marine shipping increased dramatically. The China International Marine Containers Corporation (CIMC) was founded in Shenzhen in 1980.[2] The 1990s witnessed even more rapid growth in the container shipping industry. China's throughput of containers, including Hong Kong, increased from 6.2 million TEUs in 1990 to over 36.5 million TEUs in 2002, accounting for over 14 percent of the global total, which resulted in China overtaking the United States as the world's top handler of container traffic.[3] The Tenth Five-Year Plan (2001–2005) launched a national effort to improve rail transportation for domestic and international trade, which included prioritizing containerization. A network of eighteen major and forty minor inland container depots connected by regular rail services had been established by 2006.[4]

Before 2010, the central government promoted railway container transportation mainly as an alternative to road haulage to link manufacturing bases and major

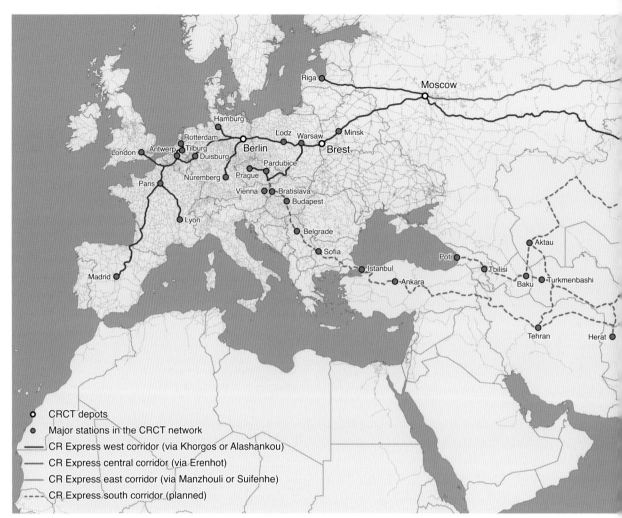

FIGURE I.2.1
Major corridors of the China Railway Express (CR Express).

seaports. The advantages of road haulage, long the dominant transport mode for freight due to its reliability and flexibility, started to be questioned in the face of increasing congestion around seaports, concerns over air pollution from vehicle emissions, and the increasing number of manufacturers relocating inland in search of cheaper labor.[5] The Twelfth Five-Year Plan (2011–2015) launched ambitious plans to further expand the role of rail transport, with the objective of making railway container transportation an increasingly important component of China's international trade as compared to seaborne container shipping. The milestone event of this plan was the establishment of the China Railway Express (CR Express) in 2011, consisting of international container rail services with fixed train numbers, routes, schedules, and timetables between China and Europe.[6] CRCT plays a vital role in facilitating the establishment of overland transport corridors between China and Europe, being the sole operating and service platform for the CR Express. While information technology (IT) products produced in China's inland manufacturing bases have long been the dominant products transported by the CR Express since its

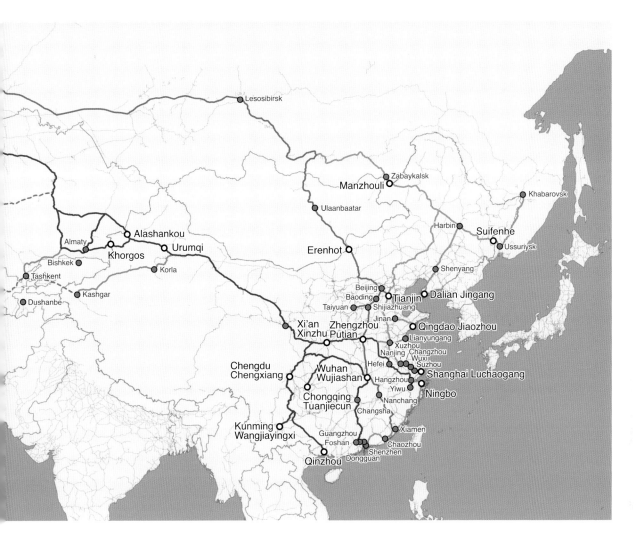

operation, this case study focuses on plants and timber, two novel types of products reflecting the CR Express's increasingly diversified cargo. It first positions the launch of the CR Express within the context of China's Western Development program formally inaugurated in early 2000. It then analyzes how the CR Express is reconfiguring the pattern, speed, and volume of the global botanical and timber trade by examining the export of plants from inland China on the Chengdu–Europe Railway and the import of timber into China on the Russia–China Railway.

THE CR EXPRESS AND CHINA WESTERN DEVELOPMENT

The central government had already identified the imbalance in the development of coastal and inland provinces as an important issue to be resolved in the 1950s, but the disparity had become exacerbated by the last two decades of the twentieth century. China's Reform and Opening Up policy of the late 1970s prioritized

China's coastal provinces, which witnessed the rapid development of export-oriented manufacturing and assembly within a wider transformation of global supply chains and business models. The Western Development program was launched in March 2000 to mediate the growing economic disparity between China's coastal and inland regions, together with such related issues as burgeoning migration from inland to coastal areas and surging labor and land prices in the coastal regions. Although not descriptive of a specific geographical area, the concept of the "west" is understood to mean the country's remote frontier areas that actually cover culturally diverse and geographically vast territories. The Western Development program offers incentives including state-led subsidies, contracts, and infrastructural development to encourage manufacturers to relocate or expand into less-developed inland areas. The IT industry pioneered this process with well-known international firms, such as Hewlett-Packard, Acer, and Asus, relocating their production bases from coastal areas to the upper Yangzi River region, notably Chongqing, Wuhan, and Chengdu, to take advantage of these policies.[7] This kind of relocation, however, necessitates the establishment of alternatives to container shipping by sea, to export IT products particularly to European countries. It was in this context that China's Europe-bound freight-train service, now formally named the CR Express, was conceived.

The first CR Express route, known as the Yu-Xin-Ou (Chongqing-Xinjiang-Europe) route, began operating in early 2011, running from Chongqing Municipality through Alashankou in Xinjiang to Duisburg in Germany. The travel time for this 11,179-kilometer route is seventeen days, twenty-three days less than the rail and sea route via the Chongqing–Shenzhen Railway and then by sea to Europe or the river and sea route via the Yangtze River to Shanghai and then by sea to Europe.[8] CR Express routes and train services have proliferated since the launch of the BRI, with inbound services commencing in 2014. The number of CR express train services has grown from 17 in 2011 to 815 in 2015 to 8,225 in 2019, reaching a cumulative total of 20,000 trains by the end of 2019. To date, fifty-nine Chinese cities are served by sixty-five CR Express lines, connecting to forty-nine cities in fifteen European countries.[9] The CR Express runs along three major overland corridors, two via the Siberian Land Bridge and one via the New Eurasian Land Bridge. The west corridor carries the largest freight volume and offers the highest benefits of the three routes, delivering goods from the central region of China to Europe via Khorgas-Khorgos or Alashankou-Dostyk on the Chinese-Kazakh border; the central corridor connects central and north China with Europe via Erenhot–Zamyn-Uud on the Chinese Mongolian border; and the east corridor connects southeast China with Europe via Manzhouli-Zabaykalsk or Suifenhe-Pogranichny, both on the Chinese Russian border. CR Express generally can transport cargo from inland regions of China to European destinations by rail three times faster than shipping by sea and at one-fifth of the cost of transport by air. Technological and logistical innovations by CR

Express are constantly improving the speed and range of connections between the sources of products and their destinations.[10]

PLANTS AND TIMBER

Export of Plants

CR Express container transport by rail is more advantageous than shipping by sea for inland regions far from seaports when exporting high-value-added products. Since CR Express commenced operations in 2011, the frequency and capacity of China's freight trains have increased and the cargo they carry has diversified. The 9,826-kilometer Rong-Ou (Chengdu-Europe) route, for example, is one of the busiest routes, currently accounting for 16.5 percent of CR Express annual freight traffic. It now includes domestic household products, auto accessories, and even flowers and plants as well as China-made IT products, such as laptops and cell phones.[11] The transport of 19,140 Chinese banyans (*Ficus microcarpa*) from Chengdu (the capital of the Chinese province of Sichuan) to the Dutch city of Tilburg via the Rong-Ou route over a thirteen-day period kick-started the export of Chinese flowers and plants to Europe via the CR Express in December 2016. By comparison, shipping plants from Chengdu by sea to their destinations in Europe normally takes up to thirty-five days. The plants must be taken 2,000 kilometers by road from Chengdu to Xiamen Port on China's southeast coast. They are loaded aboard a container ship, which then has to cross the Indian Ocean and Red Sea to eventually reach European seaports.[12]

Transporting plants by CR Express cuts travel time and significantly reduces wastage. In fact, ever since British and European botanists and commercial nurseries began actively prospecting the world for new plants at the end of the sixteenth century, transnational transportation of the plants has been a major challenge. Before the mid-nineteenth century, plants had to be transported as seeds or corms or as dry rhizomes and roots because of lengthy sailing times and changes in climate en route. In the 1830s the invention of the Wardian case, a sealed protective container that greatly enhanced the chances of successfully shipping live plants, revolutionized the process. The Wardian case and successive technologies made long-distance plant shipments possible but were only applicable for small-scale commercial consignments, limiting the range of species and numbers of plants available to the international nursery trade. Horticultural trade between Sichuan and Europe was possible by sea only until 2016, so plants routinely experienced considerable damage, such as loss of foliage caused by salt-laden air, lack of light, lack of fresh water, and insufficient care during the journey. Consequently, the plants normally required expensive recuperative care for half a year or more at local plant nurseries in Europe before being salable on the market. By contrast, CRCT has developed specially designed climate-controlled containers, so that moisture content, oxygen level, temperature, and other critical factors can be remotely monitored and controlled. As a result, CR Express can improve the plant survival rate by 10 percent in comparison to the seaborne container shipping option, decreasing the cost of postshipment plant recuperation and ensuring the plants can be sold on the market much sooner and at higher prices.[13]

Southwestern China is one of the most botanically species-rich terrestrial regions on earth, with a high level of species endemism. The region has been a hot spot for scientific and commercially motivated botanical exploration by Western missionaries and explorers since the early nineteenth century. Today its botanical wealth is playing an increasingly important role in the context of China's Western Development program. Although the nursery industry in southwestern China has a relatively long history, it was at a disadvantage compared to coastal regions in terms of exporting flowers and plants, as the only transport option available before 2016 was by sea. The option of transporting plants by the CR Express is rejuvenating the nursery industry in southwestern China, reconfiguring the distribution of the Chinese nursery industry, and diversifying the range of species on offer by the international nursery trade. For example, China's largest flower and plant import and export distribution center is under construction in Wenjiang City in Sichuan Province, one of China's four major nursery bases.[14] The establishment of the Wenjiang distribution center resulted from a trade agreement made in November 2017 between Coloríginz, a Dutch import and export company, and two Sichuan-based companies: ARP Joint Greening and HSD Trade. Under this agreement, flowers and plants valued at 300 million euros will be exported from Wenjiang to the Netherlands between 2017 and 2022.[15]

With ARP Joint Greening as the project's primary investor, the 550,000-square-meter Wenjiang distribution center will be implemented in two phases. Phase one, completed at the end of 2019, includes a business administration center, logistics and supporting facilities, greenhouses, a controlled atmosphere warehouse, and the first and only Entry-Exit Inspection and Quarantine Zone in Sichuan Province. The designated quarantine facility will process all flowers and plants exported from Sichuan to Europe via the Rong-Ou route of the CR Express, including required decontamination, fumigation, disinfection, and quarantine functions. Phase two of the project will include a trading center and a convention and exhibition center. The CR Express and the Wenjiang distribution center together facilitate the rapid development of the export-oriented nursery industry in Sichuan Province. In addition, increasing numbers of nurseries from China's southeastern coastal regions such as Guangdong and Fujian are relocating to Sichuan Province because of the cheaper operational costs and the advantages of exporting by the CR Express rather than by conventional seaborne transport. Currently, Chinese banyans (*Ficus microcarpa*), silver willows (*Salix argyracea*), bamboo palms (*Rhapis excelsa*), moth orchids (*Phalaenopsis amabilis*), and various types of Sichuan bonsai dominate the range of flowers and plants exported to Europe via the CR Express.[16] A number of transnational collaboration projects have been established between Chinese and European companies and research organizations with a view to diversifying the range of species for export. For example, ARP Joint Greening has announced an ambitious plan to produce six to eight new export-oriented species per year, to be supported by projects carried out under collaborative research agreements with the Dutch company Coloríginz, the French company Delbard Nursery, and the European Plant Science Organization.[17]

Import of Timber

Although the volume of cargo transported by the CR Express has grown exponentially since its launch in 2011, the imbalance of inbound and outbound trade is a persistent issue.[18] One of the earlier ways to avoid sending empty containers back to China was to fill the containers with timber from Europe. Originally this was a mitigation measure to increase the container utilization rate, but this timber trade has gradually evolved into a major business facilitated by the CR Express, particularly between Russia and China. Over the course of fourteen days in March 2018, the first batch of customized CR Express trains carrying 1,740 tons of timber traveled from Krasnoyarsk in eastern Siberia to Chengdu, the capital of Sichuan Province in southwestern China.[19] Transporting timber via customized CR Express trains is a joint initiative by CRCT and Russian Railways Logistics (Rossiyskie Zheleznye Dorogi: RZD), the largest multimodal logistics operator in Russia, Commonwealth of Independent States countries, and the Baltic states. The Krasnoyarsk to Chengdu timber transport is carried out under the scheduled container train service on the CR Express Russia to China route, branded by the RZD as the Panda Land Bridge project, in reference to the trains' destination: Sichuan, home of giant pandas.[20] The Panda Land Bridge is considered a strategic project by the Russian Export Center to support Russian non-energy-related export-oriented companies to transport their goods to China.

Timber occupies an important place in Sino-Russian trade. Since China began restricting commercial logging in its own natural forests two decades ago, the country has experienced an increasingly significant timber deficit, with domestic supplies now meeting only 50 percent of demand. China is the largest timber importer in the world, with Russia the top supplier, contributing 30 percent of China's timber imports.[21] Since the launch of the Western Development program, Sichuan's demand for timber has increased dramatically to serve its booming construction and furniture industries. Before the Krasnoyarsk to Chengdu timber transport via the CR Express was made possible in 2018, Sichuan-based companies could purchase timber only from cities in northeastern China, notably Manzhouli in the Inner Mongolia Autonomous Region and Suifenhe in Heilongjiang Province, where Russian timber arrives for customs clearance at the Chinese border. Timber destined for Sichuan then has to be transported another 3,800 kilometers by road or rail. The CR Express Russia to China route allows Sichuan-based companies to order timber directly from companies in Krasnoyarsk, decreasing the transport time for timber deliveries by about a month and reducing the total cost of logistics by up to 20 percent.[22] Krasnoyarsk, with its estimated timber reserves of 14 billion cubic meters, is also well connected with other timber-rich regions in Siberia via the Yenisei River and the Trans-Siberian Railway.

Various softwoods, notably white pine (*Pinus armandii*), Baltic pine (*Pinus sylvestris*), and Dahurian larch (*Larix gmelinii*), make up the majority of Sichuan's timber imports. Proper storage is crucial, given that most imported Russian timber is unprocessed or roughly processed, making it susceptible to decay, splitting, distortion, and discoloration. To minimize storage costs and damage, Chengdu International Railway Port in collaboration with the CRCT launched the Transport and Trade Integration project for the CR Express Russia to China route in 2019, to ensure timely and effective responses to changes in market supply and demand. The Qing-baijiang International Wood Trading Center in the Chengdu International Railway Port Economic Development Zone is a critical component of the Transport and Trade Integration project.[23] With a total planned area of 350,000 square meters, the Qingbaijiang Wood Trading Center is the largest CR Express timber distribution center in China and the largest Russian timber trading center in western China.[24] In addition to functions such as cargo handling, logistics and distribution, timber storage, timber identification, and wholesale transactions, the trading center offers an expanding range of other services, such as finance and loans, e-commerce, convention and exhibition facilities, and cross-border trade.

The transportation of timber along the CR Express Russia to China route has reconfigured patterns of imported timber distribution and manufacture of timber products in China. The majority of timber trade companies in the past set up branches in Manzhouli and Suifenhe in China's northeastern region bordering Russia. Russian timber was then transported from those border towns to timber-product manufacturers, mostly distributed throughout China's coastal regions. Since 2018 many timber trading companies have relocated or expanded their business to Chengdu, including more than 350 companies from nineteen provinces that have established their branches at the Qingbaijiang Trading Center to capitalize on its booming timber trade.[25] The increased availability of Russian timber has also facilitated the rapid development of timber-processing industries in China's inland regions under the Western Development program. Many companies have relocated their manufacturing bases from coastal to inland regions. There they manufacture high-quality and competitively priced value-added timber products, primarily plywood and furniture, China's main timber-related exports. An increasing volume of imported timber is transported from Chengdu to cities in western and northwestern provinces or province-level autonomous regions, such as Ningxia, Gansu, Inner Mongolia, and even Tibet, regions with the lowest forest coverage rates in the country and far away from traditional timber distribution centers.

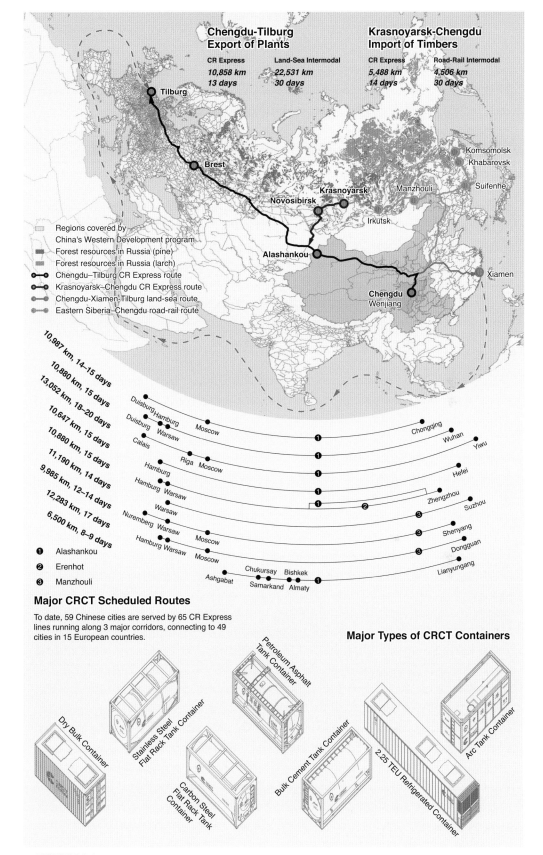

Chengdu-Tilburg Export of Plants

CR Express	Land-Sea Intermodal
10,858 km	22,531 km
13 days	30 days

Krasnoyarsk-Chengdu Import of Timbers

CR Express	Road-Rail Intermodal
5,488 km	4,506 km
14 days	30 days

Regions covered by China's Western Development program
Forest resources in Russia (pine)
Forest resources in Russia (larch)
Chengdu–Tilburg CR Express route
Krasnoyarsk–Chengdu CR Express route
Chengdu-Xiamen-Tilburg land-sea route
Eastern Siberia–Chengdu road-rail route

10,987 km, 14–15 days
10,880 km, 15 days
13,052 km, 18–20 days
10,647 km, 15 days
10,880 km, 15 days
11,190 km, 14 days
9,985 km, 12–14 days
12,283 km, 17 days
6,500 km, 8–9 days

❶ Alashankou
❷ Erenhot
❸ Manzhouli

Major CRCT Scheduled Routes

To date, 59 Chinese cities are served by 65 CR Express lines running along 3 major corridors, connecting to 49 cities in 15 European countries.

Major Types of CRCT Containers

Dry Bulk Container
Stainless Steel Flat Rack Tank Container
Petroleum Asphalt Tank Container
Carbon Steel Flat Rack Tank Container
Bulk Cement Tank Container
2.25 TEU Refrigerated Container
Arc Tank Container

FIGURE I.2.2

China's export of plants via the CR Express Rong-Ou (Chengdu-Europe) route and import of timber via the CR Express Russia to China route.

The 1830s invention of the Wardian case, a sealed protective container, greatly increased the success rate of shipping living plants and revolutionized their global distribution.

Wardian Case

Silver Willow

Bamboo Palm

Chinese Banyan

Moth Orchids

Export of Plants via CR Express

Chinese banyan, silver willow, bamboo palm, moth orchids, and various types of Sichuan bonsai dominate the range of flowers and plants exported to Europe via the CR Express.

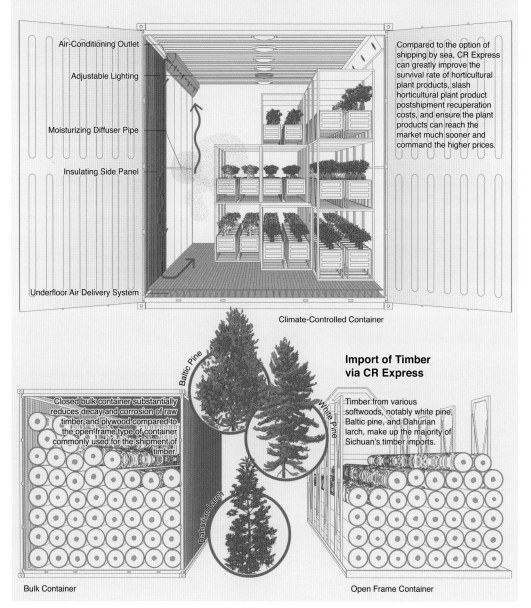

Air-Conditioning Outlet

Adjustable Lighting

Moisturizing Diffuser Pipe

Insulating Side Panel

Underfloor Air Delivery System

Compared to the option of shipping by sea, CR Express can greatly improve the survival rate of horticultural plant products, slash horticultural plant product postshipment recuperation costs, and ensure the plant products can reach the market much sooner and command the higher prices.

Climate-Controlled Container

Import of Timber via CR Express

Baltic Pine

White Pine

Dahurian Larch

Closed bulk container substantially reduces decay and corrosion of raw timber and plywood compared to the open frame type of container commonly used for the shipment of timber.

Timber from various softwoods, notably white pine, Baltic pine, and Dahurian larch, make up the majority of Sichuan's timber imports.

Bulk Container

Open Frame Container

FIGURE I.2.3

Technological innovations in the transnational transportation of horticultural plant products and timber.

NOTES

1. Zenglin Han, Chengjin Wang, and Fei You, "The Characteristics of the Development and Distribution about Chinese Logistics and the Discussion of the Developing Strategies [我國物流業發展與布局的特點及對策探討]," *Progress in Geography* [地理科學進展] 21, no. 1 (2002), 81–89.

2. CIMC, "Group Profile [集團概況]," http://www.cimc.com/index.php?m=content&c=index&a=lists&catid=5 (accessed October 23, 2020).

3. Peter J. Rimmer and Claude Comtois, "China's Container-Related Dynamics, 1990–2005," *GeoJournal* 74, no. 1 (2009), 35–50, 35.

4. ADB, *The Railways of the People's Republic of China* (Manila: Asian Development Bank, 2008), 10.

5. ADB, *People's Republic of China: Railway Container Transport Development* (Manila: Asian Development Bank, 2013), 1.

6. CRCT, "Company Profile [公司簡介]," http://www.crct.com/index.php?m=content&c=index&a=lists&catid=15 (accessed October 20, 2020).

7. Yonglei Jiang, Jiuh-Biing Sheu, Zixuan Peng, and Bin Yu, "Hinterland Patterns of China Railway (CR) Express in China under the Belt and Road Initiative: A Preliminary Analysis," *Transportation Research Part E: Logistics and Transportation Review* 119 (2018), 189–201, 192.

8. Jiang et al., "Hinterland Patterns of China Railway (CR) Express in China under the Belt and Road Initiative," 191.

9. CRCT, "International Transport [國際聯運]," http://www.crct.com/index.php?m=content&c=index&a=lists&catid=22 (accessed October 20, 2020).

10. Yitong Ma, Xianliang Shi, and Ying Qiu, "Hierarchical Multimodal Hub Location with Time Restriction for China Railway (CR) Express Network," *IEEE Access* 8 (2020), 61395–61404, 61396.

11. CRCT, "International Transport."

12. State Council Information Office, "CR Express: Opening up the Grand Channel to the West [中歐班列：向西拓展開放大通道]," May 3, 2017, http://www.scio.gov.cn/31773/35507/35513/35521/Document/1550432/1550432.htm (accessed October 14, 2020).

13. Wangshu Luo, "CR Express Carries Weight of Expectations," *China Daily*, May 8, 2017, https://www.chinadaily.com.cn/world/2017-05/08/content_29245849.htm (accessed October 14, 2020).

14. Jianguo Zhang, "The Ongoing Upgrading of Wenjiang's Nursery Industry [溫江花木產業轉型升級在路上]," *China Flowers and Horticulture* [中國花卉園藝] 1 (2019), 52.

15. "Wenjiang Strives to Build China's Largest Distribution Center for Import and Export Plants [溫江努力打造全國最大花木進出口集散地]," *Sina News*, October 22, 2018, https://k.sina.cn/article_1700648435_655dd5f302000d0ws.html (accessed October 27, 2020).

16. "Wenjiang Strives to Build China's Largest Distribution Center for Import and Export Plants."

17. Chengdu Agricultural and Rural Bureau, "Spending 260 million RMB to Build the Largest Distribution Center for Import and Export Plant in China [2.6億打造國內最大花木進出口集散地]," November 1, 2018, http://cdagri.chengdu.gov.cn/nyxx/c109562/2018-11/01/content_361c60b6bf9543d89344f98c5aa31741.shtml (accessed June 14, 2021).

18. Jiang et al., "Hinterland Patterns of China Railway (CR) Express in China under the Belt and Road Initiative," 192.

19. MOC, "Integration of Transport and Trade along the CR Express Russia–China Route [中歐班列成都至俄羅斯專線運貿一體化班列]," June 10, 2019, http://tradeinservices .mofcom.gov.cn/article/lingyu/gjhdai/201906/84309.html (accessed October 28, 2020).

20. Ling Chen, "The Logistics of China's Open Market," *China Pictorial* 845 (2018), 49–51, 50.

21. Sepul Kanti Barua, Juho Penttilä, and Miika Malmström, *China as a Timber Consumer and Processing Country: An Analysis of China's Import and Export Statistics with In-Depth Focus on Trade with the EU* (Helsinki: Indufor Oy, 2017), 14.

22. MOC, "Integration of Transport and Trade along the CR Express Russia–China Route."

23. Ajiang Zou, "Qingbaijiang International Wood Trading Center [成都青白江國際木材交易中心]," *People.cn*, June 16, 2021, http://sc.people.com.cn/BIG5/n2/2021/0616 /c345167-34779266.html (accessed August 14, 2021).

24. Zou, "Qingbaijiang International Wood Trading Center."

25. MOC, "Integration of Transport and Trade along the CR Express Russia–China Route."

CHINA NATIONAL MACHINERY INDUSTRY CORPORATION

The origin of the China National Machinery Industry Corporation (SINOMACH; officially established in 1997 as a central government SOE) can be traced back to its predecessor, the First Ministry of Machine Industry. Both were intimately involved with the history of industrialization of the People's Republic of China.[1] Industrialization has been given extremely high priority for economic, political, and ideological reasons ever since the founding of the PRC in 1949. China's First Five-Year Plan (1953–1957) reestablished the former Ministry of Heavy Industry as the First Ministry of Machine Industry, which was charged with overseeing all sectors of industry except for the nuclear industry. With technical and economic support from the Soviet Union, the First Five-Year Plan witnessed the rapid development of industries particularly related to the defense sector, such as aviation, telecommunications, weaponry, and shipbuilding. After Sino-Soviet relations deteriorated in the 1960s, however, China sought out alternative technical exchange and industrial trade partnerships to sustain the momentum of the country's economic and social development. Industrial trade was dominated in the 1970s by imports of equipment to support the development of sea and air transportation.[2] Following implementation of the Reform and Opening Up policy in 1978, exports also grew rapidly through the 1980s, particularly equipment for hydroelectric and thermoelectric power plants sent to other developing countries, such as Indonesia, the Philippines, and Pakistan.[3]

The First Ministry of Machine Industry was consolidated with several other ministries in 1982 to form the Ministry of Machine Building, which was restructured and reestablished in 1997 as the China National Machinery Industry Corporation.[4] SINOMACH inherited over seventy research and design institutes, equipment-manufacturing companies, and industrial and trade enterprises from the

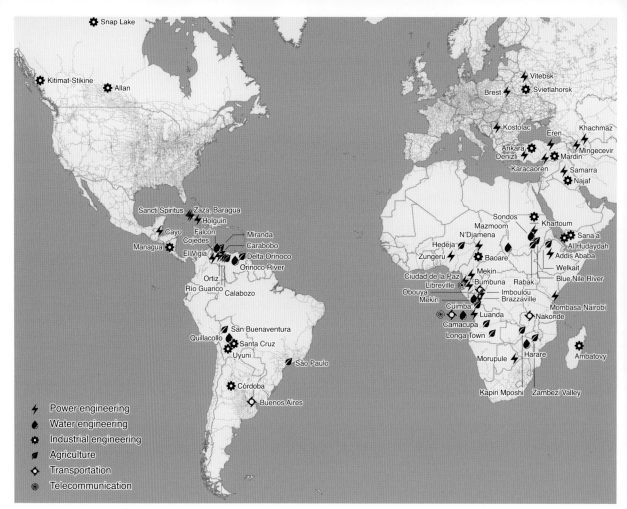

FIGURE I.3.1A

China overseas projects built by SINOMACH in Europe, the Middle East, Africa, and the Americas.

Ministry of Machine Building and has evolved into China's largest international engineering contractor since the country became a member of the World Trade Organization (WTO) in late 2001. By providing engineering and construction services to the global market, SINOMACH facilitates the outflow of technological know-how and labor through overseas projects in power engineering, water engineering, industrial engineering, transportation, telecommunications, and agriculture. This case study focuses on hydropower infrastructure projects and industrial parks, two distinct sectors of SINOMACH's overseas venture strategy. It first examines how SINOMACH has been actively establishing strategic partnerships with state-owned banks (SOBs) and other SOEs in the context of China's Go Out policy, formed in the late 1990s to promote Chinese investments abroad. It then investigates how SINOMACH's overseas projects are reshaping regional and global knowledge networks and power dynamics by analyzing its largest overseas hydropower project in Pakistan and its largest overseas industrial park project in Belarus.

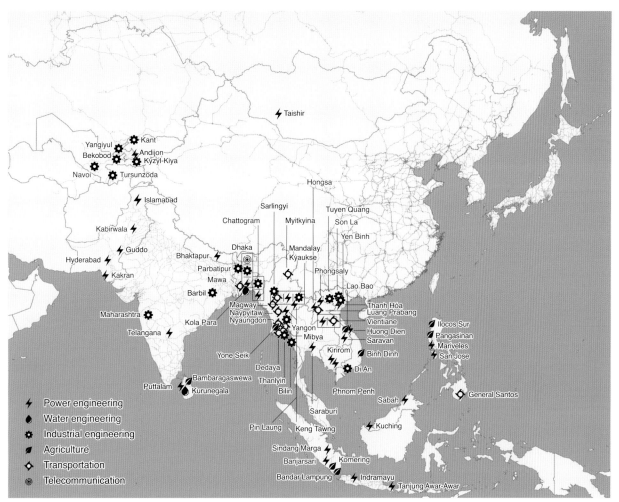

FIGURE I.3.1B

China overseas projects built by SINOMACH in Asia.

CHINESE EXPERIENCE AND GO OUT POLICY

The two decades following China's Reform and Opening Up policy of the late 1970s were dominated by the Bring In policy, characterized by the rapid inflow of foreign capital and expertise. More than 220,000 foreign-funded ventures had been approved in China by the late 1990s, and the country became the most important recipient of foreign direct investment in the developing world.[5] The objectives of the Go Out policy were formulated as a response to two major challenges associated with the Bring In policy. First, China faced increasing demands from the international community to float its currency, given that the buildup of very substantial foreign reserves had put upward pressure on the foreign exchange rate of the Chinese yuan (Renminbi: RMB). Second, given their lack of international experience, domestic firms struggled to compete for business in the Chinese market against world-class foreign competitors. The Go Out policy was initiated in 1999 in anticipation of

China's accession to the WTO, to facilitate using China's foreign reserves overseas and better prepare domestic firms to participate in international markets. As a result, China's outward foreign direct investment (OFDI) grew exponentially through the first decade of the twenty-first century, increasing from an average annual flow of US$2.69 billion between 1992 and 1999 (0.8 percent of total global investment) to US$56.53 billion in 2009 (5.4 percent of total global investment).[6]

Since the early 2000s SINOMACH has actively established strategic partnerships with SOBs and other SOEs in its role as one of the key implementers of China's Go Out policy and as the largest state-run industrial machinery manufacturer. For example, soon after China entered the WTO in December 2001, SINOMACH signed the "Bank-Enterprise Comprehensive Strategic Cooperation Agreement" with the Bank of China in early 2002. This agreement helped SINOMACH secure a credit line of 800 million RMB, or US$125 million, to expand its foreign trade and raise the status and quality of its overseas projects.[7] SINOMACH has reached similar agreements with other SOBs over the past two decades, notably the China Merchants Bank (2004), Export–Import Bank of China (2006), China Development Bank (2008), Industrial and Commercial Bank of China (2010), and China Construction Bank (2013).[8] Many of these cooperation agreements were expanded after the BRI was launched in late 2013, elevating the Go Out policy to the next level and encouraging the OFDI to prioritize high-value manufacturing and technology.

In addition to securing investment funds through cooperation with SOBs, SINOMACH's strengthened partnerships with other SOEs play an important role in realizing its global strategy. While SINOMACH specializes in equipment manufacturing and modern manufacturing services, it has long cooperated on projects with other companies covering other critical national economic fields, such as agriculture, energy, transportation, metallurgy, construction, and environmental engineering. To increase its chances of winning contracts and to enhance the attractiveness of the "Chinese experience" in the global market, SINOMACH typically forms consortiums with other SOEs, particularly those that have implemented world-renowned Chinese projects since the 1980s, to improve its international competitive bidding process. The following sections focus on SINOMACH's joint ventures with the China Gezhouba Group Corporation, set up to plan and construct China's first large-scale hydropower project, and with the China Merchants Group, set up to develop the first industrial zone in China.

HYDROPOWER PLANT AND INDUSTRIAL PARK

Neelum Jhelum Hydroelectric Project

In December 2007 the China Gezhouba Group Corporation (CGGC) and China Machinery Engineering Corporation (CMEC), a subsidiary of SINOMACH active in China's foreign aid program, successfully bid to construct the Neelum Jhelum Hydroelectric Project (NJHP) for the Pakistan Water and Power Development Authority (WAPDA).[9] As the largest overseas hydropower project ever undertaken by any Chinese company or joint venture, the NJHP is a milestone project for both SINOMACH and China, as the export of Chinese hydropower expertise is a relatively new phenomenon. Until the 1970s China's efforts to develop its domestic hydropower resources were hobbled by a combination of political instability and a lack of financing and technological capabilities. After that time, the urgent need to fuel economic growth that was being constrained by limited access to conventional energy sources spurred rapid development of China's hydropower capabilities. The quarter-century following the 1978 Reform and Opening Up policy saw the completion of two mega hydropower projects on the Yangtze River: China's second-largest, the 2,715 megawatt (MW) Gezhouba Water Control Project in 1988, and then the 22,500 MW Three Gorges Dam in 2003, now the largest hydropower project on earth.[10] The CGGC and the China Three Gorges Corporation were set up to plan and construct these projects and since then have led the way in exporting Chinese hydropower expertise abroad.

Since World War II, the United States has actively fostered its Cold War alliances through north-south development cooperation, particularly an international program of technical assistance. In its wake, China has taken on a role as a key player in south-south development cooperation since the 1980s, emerging as a new donor and technical assistance provider at the beginning of this millennium. Water management and development are central to both programs, with the US Tennessee Valley Authority and China's Yangtze River development symbolizing their respective overseas development initiatives. Pakistan occupies a strategic position in China's hydropower technical assistance program. Chinese companies' participation in Pakistan's river water projects can be traced back to the late 1980s.[11] Projects within the Indus River basin in Pakistan constitute an important part of China's balance-of-power approach in the context of uncertain Sino-India relations. Sharing a 592-kilometer border with southwestern China, Pakistan includes the majority of the Indus River downstream from its origin in China at Tibet's Lake Manasarovar, including its issue into the Arabian Sea. Although the extent of the Indus River basin is contested due to an unresolved territorial dispute between China and India in Kashmir, it is estimated that the annual flow within the Indus catchment area from Chinese territory into Indian territory is 181.62 cubic kilometers. Flow originating in Indian territory amounts to 50.86 cubic kilometers, resulting in a flow from Indian territory to Pakistani territory of 232.48 square kilometers.[12]

The NJHP was initiated in the mid-2000s in the context of an increasing energy deficit in Pakistan and uncertainty over the division of River Indus water resources between India and Pakistan. According to the 1960 Indus Waters Treaty, of the annual flow of 232.48 cubic kilometers flowing from India to Pakistan, 62.21 cubic kilometers are designated for India and 170.27 cubic kilometers for Pakistan.[13] However, population growth, agricultural development, rapid urbanization, and industrialization in both Pakistan and India have led to dissension over water allocation. Compared to the United States (where hydropower accounts for roughly 7 percent of total electricity generation) and China (where it accounts for 18 percent), in Pakistan hydropower is a primary domestic source of energy, providing 30 percent of the country's total power generation. Hydropower is believed to be essential for the socioeconomic uplift of the country. With a total generation capacity of 6,500 MW, accounting for 16 percent of a potential capacity of approximately 40,000 MW, there is considerable scope for further hydroelectric development.[14] According to WAPDA's "Vision" documents published in 2007, total installed hydropower capacity was expected to reach 20,000 MW by 2017 and 27,000 MW by 2025. Pakistan's northern frontier region bordering China and India, which has an estimated hydel (hydroelectric) potential of 15,000 MW, takes center stage in the country's ambitious hydropower development vision.[15] A number of new hydropower projects have been launched within Azad Jammu and Kashmir (AJK), the Pakistan-controlled portion of the disputed territory of Kashmir.

Many of these newly launched hydropower projects are being carried out in collaboration with Chinese contractors, including the NJHP, which features the diversion of water from one tributary of the Indus River to another via Pakistan's first major tunnel project. Situated in the vicinity of Muzaffarabad, the capital city of the AJK, the project diverts water from the Neelum River through a 32.5-kilometer-long tunnel system to a generating station and outfall into the Jhelum River. Described by WAPDA as a "strategically important" project, the NJHP will add 969 MW to Pakistan's hydroelectric generation capacity, while at the same time enabling the country to secure its claims over the Neelum-Jhelum waters within disputed Kashmir.[16] WAPDA awarded a US$1.5 billion NJHP contract to the Chinese CGGC and CMEC consortium in December 2007, with the CGGC responsible for civil engineering and construction and the CMEC responsible for the structural, mechanical, and electrical aspects of the project.[17] According to SINOMACH and mainstream media in China, the award of the contract and implementation of the NJHP, nicknamed Pakistan's Three Gorges Dam, was an important step toward establishing world-class Chinese companies with global competencies on the world stage, particularly within the international hydropower construction market previously dominated by European and American expertise. The NJHP project, situated in the Himalayas, the world's most tectonically active mountain range, also enhances Chinese hydropower expertise applicable to the Himalayan region of China itself, the nation's last frontier of hydropower expansion.

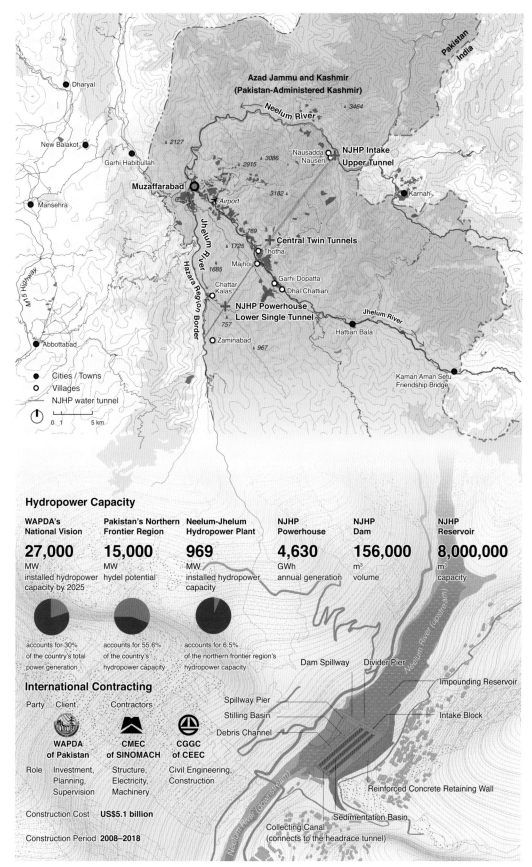

Hydropower Capacity

WAPDA's National Vision	Pakistan's Northern Frontier Region	Neelum-Jhelum Hydropower Plant	NJHP Powerhouse	NJHP Dam	NJHP Reservoir
27,000 MW installed hydropower capacity by 2025	**15,000** MW hydel potential	**969** MW installed hydropower capacity	**4,630** GWh annual generation	**156,000** m³ volume	**8,000,000** m³ capacity

accounts for 30% of the country's total power generation

accounts for 55.6% of the country's hydropower capacity

accounts for 6.5% of the northern frontier region's hydropower capacity

International Contracting

Party	Client	Contractors	
	WAPDA of Pakistan	**CMEC of SINOMACH**	**CGGC of CEEC**
Role	Investment, Planning, Supervision	Structure, Electricity, Machinery	Civil Engineering, Construction
Construction Cost	US$5.1 billion		
Construction Period	2008–2018		

FIGURE I.3.2

Neelum Jhelum Hydroelectric Project, Pakistan.

Great Stone Industrial Park

The president of Belarus, Alexander Lukashenko, proposed the idea of an industrial park to be jointly developed by China and Belarus in March 2010 during a state visit by Xi Jinping, vice president at the time. Shortly after Xi's visit, the Chinese Embassy in Belarus recommended SINOMACH, which already had operational experience in Belarus, to undertake the project. The Chinese Construction and Agricultural Machinery Engineering Corporation, a subsidiary of SINOMACH, signed a cooperation agreement with the Belarusian Ministry of Economy in October 2010 for the establishment of the Great Stone Industrial Park (GSIP) during Lukashenko's state visit to Beijing. An intergovernmental agreement on the participatory development of the park was signed a year later.[18]

Since the implementation of China's BRI, the GSIP has been rebranded as a landmark BRI project. To accelerate the project development, the China Merchants Group (CMG) joined SINOMACH in early 2015 as a key shareholder of the GSIP, participating in park development, especially investment promotion. Although China had established multiple overseas special zones and industrial parks prior to embarking on the GSIP, this project is the largest by far in terms of land area (112.5 square kilometers) and estimated project cost (US$6 billion). It signals a new era of transferring Chinese park development and management expertise to foreign countries.[19]

Like hydropower construction, the export of Chinese expertise in special zone development is a relatively new phenomenon. China is a latecomer when it comes to the establishment of special economic zones (SEZs) as an important national development instrument, compared with other Asian countries and regions, such as Singapore, the Republic of Korea, and Taiwan, all of which set up special zones in the 1960s and early 1970s to jump-start export-oriented industrialization. Nevertheless, since the establishment of the four SEZs (Shenzhen, Zhuhai, Shantou, and Xiamen) along its southeast coast in 1980, China has proved to be the world's leading success story when it comes to setting up various types of special zones to build up industrial capacity.[20] The idea of transferring China's special zone development success overseas emerged in the early 2000s in the context of China's Go Out policy. The establishment of special zones in other countries serves several new millennium strategic objectives for China itself, including consolidating its domestic restructuring, supporting the country's OFDI and market entry, and helping fulfill its "soft power" political goals by sharing the Chinese development model with friendly countries. In 2006 China's Ministry of Commerce indicated that the country would establish up to fifty Chinese Overseas Economic and Trade Cooperation Zones (COCZs), nineteen of which were officially approved by the end of 2007.[21] There are currently thirty-three COCZs: thirteen in Asia, nine in Europe and Central Asia, and eleven in Africa.[22]

As one of the first top-level Chinese industrial parks established abroad, the GSIP exemplifies how Belarusian state elites responded to the Chinese model of external engagement within specific geopolitical and geoeconomic circumstances. In fact, China originally considered Ukraine to be the front-runner as its future gateway to the European Union's market rather than Belarus. However, social unrest and political instability in Ukraine in the new millennium prompted China to search for alternative partnerships, with Belarus proving to be the only reliable land bridge in the region. Concurrently, Belarus was urgently trying to reduce its dependence on Russia and resist Moscow's demands for further integration between the two countries after Vladimir Putin's election as president of Russia in 2000. In this context, Belarus started to develop a closer relationship with China in the hope of diversifying and increasing the country's economic competitiveness. With easy access to Baltic seaports, and standing at the crossroads of major land transit routes between Europe and Asia, Belarus's geographical position is comparable to Ukraine's. In addition, from China's point of view, Belarus has the advantage of being the only country in Europe that has maintained an ideological "socialist choice," while having the economic advantage of being the westernmost member state of the Russian-led Eurasian Economic Union. During Xi Jinping's 2010 visit to Belarus, Xi and Lukashenko agreed to strengthen Sino-Belarusian economic, scientific, and military cooperation. The following decade saw a 200-fold increase in annual investments from China to Belarus.[23]

The GSIP conceived in 2010 was a milestone in the Sino-Belarus partnership. Located 25 kilometers east of Minsk, the Belarusian capital and largest city, the project stands in close proximity to major national and transnational transport routes, including Minsk International Airport, the Berlin–Moscow Highway, and several railways connecting Belarus with the Riga Free Port in Latvia and with the Port of Klaipeda in Lithuania. Given that Belarus is a member of the Eurasian Economic Union, the GSIP provides a duty-free entry into this market of 170 million people. Phase one of the project features the development of an 8.5-square-kilometer sparsely populated wooded area into an industrial park and rental residential complex. Given SINOMACH's lack of experience in industrial-zone development and industrial promotion, only two Chinese enterprises had invested in the park by early 2014. After the significance of the GSIP was increased by the launch of the BRI, the Chinese government arranged for CMG (which was responsible for establishing China's first industrial zone, the Shekou Industrial Zone in Shenzhen) to join SINOMACH to develop the park in April 2015. A month later, Xi and Lukashenko visited the GSIP, lavishing praise on the project as the "pearl" of the BRI. Since then, the number of enterprises in the park has grown rapidly, reaching a total of sixty by the end of 2019.[24] After starting to participate in the development of the GSIP in 2015, CMG has been actively modifying and restructuring the Chinese special zone

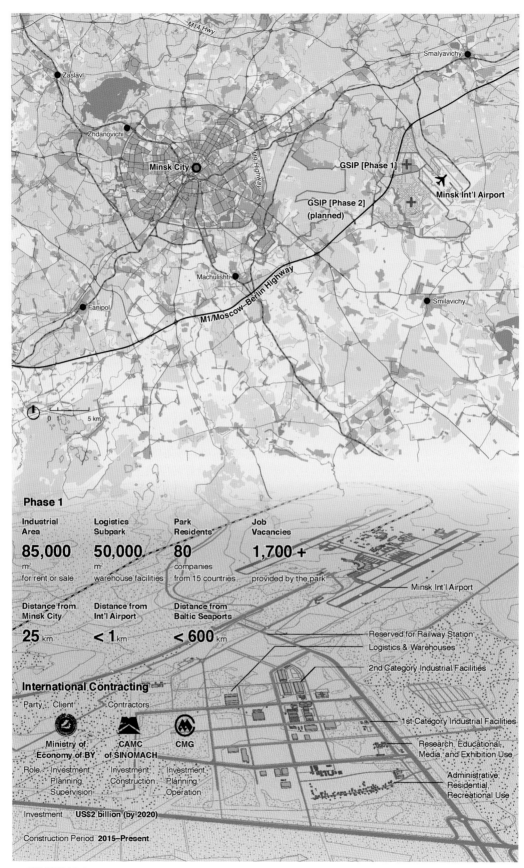

Phase 1

Industrial Area	Logistics Subpark	Park Residents*	Job Vacancies
85,000	**50,000**	**80**	**1,700 +**
m² for rent or sale	m² warehouse facilities	companies from 15 countries	provided by the park

Distance from Minsk City	Distance from Int'l Airport	Distance from Baltic Seaports
25 km	**< 1** km	**< 600** km

International Contracting

Party	Client	Contractors	
	Ministry of Economy of BY	CAMC of SINOMACH	CMG
Role	Investment Planning Supervision	Investment Construction	Investment Planning Operation

Investment **US$2 billion (by 2020)**

Construction Period **2015–Present**

Minsk Int'l Airport

Reserved for Railway Station

Logistics & Warehouses

2nd Category Industrial Facilities

1st Category Industrial Facilities

Research, Educational, Media, and Exhibition Use

Administrative, Residential, Recreational Use

FIGURE I.3.3

Great Stone Industrial Park, Belarus.

model to suit the sociopolitical context of Belarus. For example, the Shekou model is characterized by a Port/Park/City model (a port in front, an industrial zone in the middle, and a city at the back), whereas the GSIP has adopted an integrated Logistics/Production/Urban Services model in order to address the lack of sea access and adequate suburban facilities.

NOTES

1. SINOMACH, "Development Timelines [發展歷程]," http://www.sinomach.com.cn/gygj/gjgk/fzlc (accessed November 23, 2020).

2. This included importing ten Boeing 707 jet airliners from the United States and hundreds of dredging vessels from Japan and the Netherlands to increase the carrying capacity of the nation's seaports.

3. SINOMACH, "Development Timelines."

4. SINOMACH, "Development Timelines."

5. Stefan Kaiser, David A. Kirby, and Ying Fan, "Foreign Direct Investment in China: An Examination of the Literature," *Asia Pacific Business Review* 2, no. 3 (1996), 44–65, 44.

6. Bijun Wang and Kailin Gao, "Forty Years Development of China's Outward Foreign Direct Investment: Retrospect and the Challenges Ahead," *China & World Economy* 27, no. 3 (2019), 1–24, 5.

7. "Bank of China and SINOMACH Signed an 800-Million-Yuan Bank-Enterprise Cooperation Agreement [中行與中國機械裝備集團簽訂80億銀企合作協議]," *China News*, January 28, 2002, https://www.chinanews.com.cn/2002-01-28/26/158112.html (accessed November 12, 2020).

8. SINOMACH, "Development Timelines."

9. SASAC, "CMEC and Gezhouba Group Corporation Bid to Construct the Hydropower Project in Pakistan [國機與葛洲壩集團所屬公司聯合中標巴基斯坦水電站項目]," March 26, 2008, http://www.sasac.gov.cn/n2588025/n2588124/c3844512/content.html (accessed November 12, 2020).

10. Xiaolin Chang, Xinghong Liu, and Wei Zhou, "Hydropower in China at Present and Its Further Development," *Energy* 35, no. 11 (2010), 4400–4406, 4401.

11. Srikanth Kondapalli, "The Indus Basin: The Potential for Basin-Wide Management between China and Its Himalayan Neighbours India and Pakistan," in Zafar Adeel and Robert G. Wirsing (eds.), *Imagining Industan* (Singapore: Springer, 2017), 159–174.

12. Aaron T. Wolf, Jeffrey A. Natharius, Jeffrey J. Danielson, Brian S. Ward, and Jan K. Pender, "International Basins of the World," *Water Resources Development* 15, no. 4 (1999), 387–427, 401.

13. Food and Agriculture Organization of the United Nations, *Transboundary River Basin Overview: Indus* (Rome: Food and Agriculture Organization of the United Nations, 2011), 3.

14. Private Power & Infrastructure Board, *Pakistan Hydel Power Potential* (Islamabad: Ministry of Water and Power of Pakistan, 2003), 3.

15. Saad Ullah Khan, "Exploring the Effect of Political Risks in Large Infrastructure Projects in Politically Unstable Countries Using a Probabilistic Modelling Approach" (master's

thesis, Queensland University of Technology, 2014), 34.

16. WAPDA, "PM Inaugurates 969 MW Neelum Jhelum Power Project," April 13, 2008, http://www.wapda.gov.pk/index.php/newsmedia/news-views/307-pm-inaugurates-969-mw-neelum-jhelum-power-project (accessed November 12, 2020).

17. State Council Information Office, "Pakistan's 'Three Gorges Dam' Continues to Write Stories about Sino-Pakistani Friendship [巴基斯坦「三峽工程」續寫中巴友誼佳話]," October 31, 2016, http://www.scio.gov.cn/32621/32629/32754/Document/1514522/1514522.htm (accessed November 12, 2020).

18. SASAC, "China-Belarus Industrial Park: An International Cooperation Model Characterized by High-Efficiency and Environmentally Friendly [中白工業園：高效、環保、國際化的合作典範]," October 17, 2017, http://www.sasac.gov.cn/n2588030/n2588924/c8022963/content.html (accessed November 27, 2020).

19. SASAC, "China–Belarus Industrial Park."

20. Xiangming Chen, "Change and Continuity in Special Economic Zones: A Reassessment and Lessons from China," *Transnational Corporations Journal* 26, no. 2 (2019), 49–74.

21. Deborah Bräutigam and Xiaoyang Tang, "'Going Global in Groups': Structural Transformation and China's Special Economic Zones Overseas," *World Development* 63 (2014), 78–91, 82.

22. COCZ, "Overseas Economic and Trade Cooperation Zones [中國境外經貿合作區]," http://www.cocz.org/index.aspx (accessed March 4, 2021).

23. Warsaw Institute Foundation, "The Belarus Crisis Threatens China's Belt and Road Initiative," September 4, 2020, https://warsawinstitute.org/belarus-crisis-threatens-chinas-belt-road-initiative (accessed March 4, 2021).

24. Zhigao Liu, Michael Dunford, and Weidong Liu, "Coupling National Geo-political Economic Strategies and the Belt and Road Initiative: The China-Belarus Great Stone Industrial Park," *Political Geography* 84 (2021), 102296.

CHINA OIL AND FOODSTUFFS CORPORATION

First established in Tianjin as the North China Foreign Trade Company in February 1949, China Oil and Foodstuffs Corporation (COFCO) was reorganized into a national trading company and relocated to Beijing after the founding of the People's Republic of China in October 1949. Before the promulgation of the Reform and Opening Up policy in the late 1970s, COFCO played an important role in the PRC's socioeconomic development, establishing export and import businesses mostly with the former Soviet Union and other socialist countries. COFCO's export of raw agricultural products was of critical importance to building up China's foreign exchange reserves from the 1950s to the 1970s, strengthening the new regime's resilience in the face of domestic and global economic fluctuations. In the early 1960s COFCO was one of the leading state-owned SOEs implementing emergency remedial measures to rectify the devastating impact of the Great Chinese Famine and associated economic hardship. To meet domestic demand, COFCO imported grain from countries such as Canada, Australia, France, Argentina, and Mexico and raw sugar from Cuba. In the 1970s COFCO focused on increasing agricultural and other exports, establishing numerous agricultural production bases around the country with processing plants to ready the products for export.[1] These export-oriented schemes directly impacted national crop and livestock production systems and geographies and accelerated the advancement of the "one region, one product" model to increase the specializations and comparative advantages of different regions.

Like other SOEs, COFCO went through a long process of progressive reform beginning in the early 1980s, when China restructured its foreign trade systems. COFCO was transformed from a state-owned agency with exclusive focus on foreign trade into a state-owned enterprise characterized as "comprehensive, multifunctional,

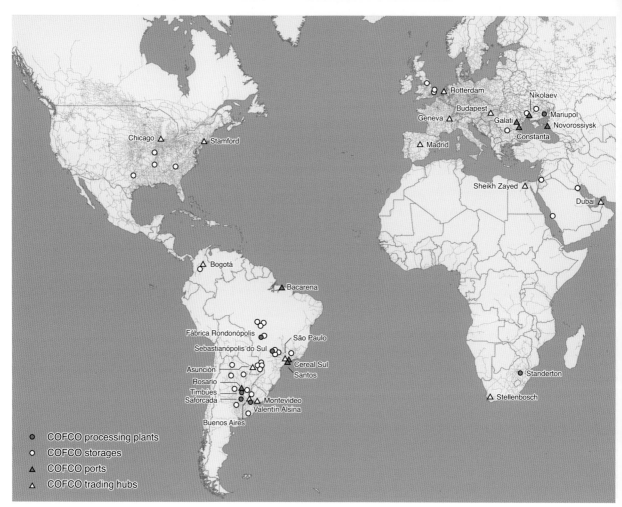

FIGURE I.4.1A
COFCO facilities in Europe, the Middle East, Africa, and the Americas.

and international."[2] By the early 2000s, after two decades of reform and development, COFCO had significantly scaled up its traditional production and processing businesses and expanded into real-estate development (such as COFCO Property Group Co., Ltd.), financial services (such as COFCO Capital Holdings Co., Ltd.), and insurance (such as Aviva-COFCO Life Insurance Co., Ltd.). This case study focuses specifically on COFCO's increasing expansion into the biomass energy industry since 2005, when COFCO acquired a 37 percent equity share of China Resources Biochemical, 100 percent of Heilongjiang China Resources Ethanol, and 20 percent of Jilin Fuel Ethanol, taking total control of Anhui BBCA Biochemical a year later.[3] This case study first outlines how COFCO's leading role in China's biomass energy industry development has been integrated with national energy policy since the mid-2000s. It then investigates how COFCO's biofuel projects are establishing new patterns of global connectivity and influencing the domestic biophysical landscape, by examining the production of two sources of ethanol fuel production: grain biofuel from corn and nongrain biofuel from cassava.

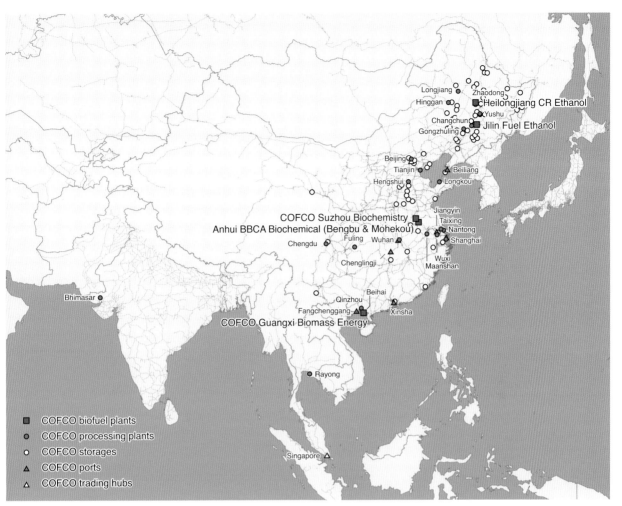

FIGURE I.4.1B
COFCO facilities in Asia.

BIOFUEL AND CHINA'S ENERGY POLICY REFORM

Several major policy reforms have gathered momentum since the mid-2000s in the lead-up to the thirtieth anniversary of China's Reform and Opening Up policy. The State Council elevated Energy Efficiency and Pollution Abatement to the status of a national policy in 2006, positioning it as a major pillar of Chinese domestic policy.[4] Energy insecurity and environmental degradation resulting from three decades of rapid industrial development were identified as major limits to the long-term economic and ecological well-being of the nation. A national biomass energy strategy was drawn up as an important element of China's long-running strategic energy plan first outlined in the 11th Five-Year Plan (2006–2010). It called for expanded use of biofuel to reduce the country's reliance on petroleum, thereby protecting the environment, preventing energy shortages, and reducing dependence on energy imports. The Medium and Long-Term Development Plan for Renewable Energy in China issued by the National Development and Reform Commission (NDRC) in 2007 (hereinafter referred to as the 2007 Renewable Energy Plan) outlined more details of the speed and scale of China's strategic energy plan. It put forward guidelines, objectives, priority sectors, policies, and measures for the development of renewable energy in China up to 2020, including a national biomass power capacity target of thirty gigawatts and annual production targets of 50 million tons of biomass pellets, 44 billion cubic meters of biogas, 10 million tons of ethanol fuel, and 2 million tons of biodiesel.[5]

With China facing growing international pressure to reduce greenhouse gas emissions, additional plans were launched during the Thirteenth Five-Year Plan (2016–2020) to reinforce the policies and measures set out in the 2007 Renewable Energy Plan. Six months after China signed the Paris Agreement on Climate Change in April 2016, the National Energy Administration (NEA) issued its Thirteenth Five-Year Plan for Biomass Energy in October, reaffirming the goals of reaching annual production of 10 million tons of fuel ethanol and 2 million tons of biodiesel by 2020.[6] A plan focused specifically on ethanol production and use was jointly announced by the NDRC, the NEA, the Ministry of Finance (MOF), and twelve other ministries in 2017, entitled the Implementation Plan concerning the Expansion of Ethanol Production and Promotion for Transportation Fuel (also commonly referred to as the E10 Ethanol Mandate Plan). The plan called for China to provide 10 percent of its energy demand from ethanol (E10) by 2020. COFCO is a leading contributor to the technological innovation and expansion of biomass energy production required to achieve the national targets described here. Since acquiring several major biomass energy enterprises in mid-2000, COFCO has become a major provider of China's biomass energy, particularly ethanol fuel, contributing more than 50 percent of the national ethanol fuel production capacity since 2009.[7] While COFCO has been using corn as its major source for ethanol production, ongoing initiatives are under way to expand the use of nongrain crops, such as cassava, particularly since the 2007 Renewable Energy Plan, which was released in the context of increasing concerns over domestic food security in a country where the area of arable land per capita is only 40 percent of the world's average.

CORN AND CASSAVA

Corn Ethanol

Although corn is still the primary crop for most Chinese biofuel, currently accounting for more than 80 percent of Chinese ethanol production, domestic attitudes toward the corn-based ethanol industry have fluctuated in response to the size of the national corn reserve and local and global corn prices.[8] The challenge of excess stock in the nation's grain reserve system provided the primary motivation for kick-starting China's ethanol fuel production in the early 2000s. China's national grain reserve system was established long ago for the purpose of national security, reserving 17 to 18 percent of annual grain production in case of harvest failures or natural disasters. Following four consecutive bumper grain harvests between 1996 and 1999, the country's reserves were virtually at capacity, grain prices plunged, and the price of corn, for example, fell to its lowest level since 1975.[9] Four ethanol plants were established in the early 2000s and authorized by the central government to produce ethanol fuel from grain in those regions worst affected by the price collapse, to remediate the economic losses in major grain-producing regions and provide alternative uses for moldy grain. The four ethanol plants are Jilin Fuel Ethanol, Heilongjiang China Resources Ethanol, and Anhui BBCA Biochemical, which all use corn as their energy source, and the Henan Tianguan Group, which uses wheat as its energy source.

In tandem with major national energy policy reforms inaugurated in the mid-2000s, COFCO strategically acquired interests in three ethanol plants using corn as their energy source between 2005 and 2008, establishing COFCO (Jilin) Biochemical, COFCO (Zhaodong) Biochemical, and COFCO (Anhui) Biochemical. Consequently, COFCO became China's largest domestic corn-processing enterprise, equipped with a National Engineering Research Center for Deep Processing of Corn, a National Energy Bio-Liquid Fuel R&D (Experimental) Center, and a National Enterprise Technology Center established in COFCO (Anhui) Biochemical.[10] China had become the world's third-largest producer and consumer of ethanol after Brazil and the United States by 2007. COFCO contributed 76.5 percent of the national capacity of 1.02 million tons of grain-based ethanol.[11] The COFCO ethanol-production facilities particularly strengthen the energy security of northeastern China, the center of Chinese corn production. The 300,000-ton COFCO (Jilin) Biochemical facility supplies ethanol in Liaoning Province and Jilin Province, and the 100,000-ton COFCO (Zhaodong) Biochemical facility supplies ethanol in Heilongjiang Province, both using corn mostly from the country's grain reserve system.[12] After the launch of the Renewable Energy Plan in 2007, which set a national ethanol fuel consumption target of 10 million tons annually by 2020, COSCO put plans in place to increase its ethanol production, including a project to expand the production capacity of COFCO (Zhaodong) Biochemical from 100,000 tons to 250,000 tons.[13]

Concurrently, COFCO's corn-sourcing network has undergone major restructuring since 2008 in the context of increasing concerns over national and international food security. The period 2005–2008 witnessed the first major global food crisis in thirty years, prompting a reexamination of the role of bioenergy and highlighting the industry's impact on agricultural production for food. China adopted a strategy to increase grain imports in 2008 and altered its biofuel subsidy policies to support non-grain-based biofuels, following a decline in grain stocks from 2000 to 2008.[14] China steadily increased its corn imports between 2008 and 2014. Its main overseas supplier was the United States, which accounted for 95 percent of China's corn imports in 2011.[15] Concerned about the US monopoly on corn supplies, China sought to diversify its sources. Ukraine Land Farming signed a corn supply agreement with COFCO in November 2012, and the first Ukrainian shipment to China was made the following month.[16] The percentage of China's total corn imports provided by Ukrainian corn increased dramatically after 2014 as a result of biotech-related trade disputes. China enforced a zero-tolerance policy of unapproved genetically modified organism (GMO) traits in imported corn in late 2013, resulting in several rejections of US corn imports due to detection of a genetically modified strain of corn, MIR 162.[17] As a result, the supply of non-GMO corn from Ukraine rapidly took over, accounting for over 75 percent of China's corn imports in 2015. Since then, Ukraine has remained China's primary corn supplier.[18]

Although the dramatic reconfiguration of China's global corn import strategy in 2014 was primarily driven by biotech-related trade disputes rather than by financial considerations, in retrospect the transition aligned well with the overall agenda of China's BRI first proposed in late 2013. In terms of the BRI, Ukraine is envisioned as a major logistics hub connecting Europe and Asia as well as a strategic supplier of agricultural products contributing to China's food and energy security. As a leading participant in the BRI's agricultural sector, COFCO has rapidly expanded into the business of international grain trading. The establishment of COFCO's subsidiary COFCO Agri Ukraine in 2014 included major investments made to upgrade existing facilities to expand trading capacity, particularly the enhancement of river navigation and logistics infrastructure, such as the commencement of construction in August 2014 of COFCO Agri Ukraine's US$75 million complex for transshipment of grain and oilseeds at the Danube Shipping and Stevedoring Company (DSSC) terminal of Nikolaev Merchant Seaport.[19] The complex has a daily auto-reception capacity of 120 road vehicles and 120 railway wagons. It is designed to receive up to 10 thousand tons of cargo per day and boasts a storage capacity of 140 thousand tons and an annual handling capacity of 2.5 million tons.[20] Since the terminal started operation in May 2016, shipping corn has been its main product-handling activity. The 1.62 million tons of corn exported through the DSSC terminal in 2017 accounted for some 50 percent of the value of all goods shipped overseas by COFCO Agri Ukraine.[21]

Cassava Ethanol

COFCO's expansion and reconfiguration of its global corn-sourcing network since the late 2000s hit the headlines worldwide thanks to its increasing BRI affiliation after 2013. Meanwhile, COFCO's efforts to expand China's domestic production of cassava and cassava-based ethanol, also kick-started in the late 2000s, is a lesser-known yet equally significant process in the context of China's fast-track development of its bioenergy sector. As noted, China shifted its policy to promote nongrain biofuel after 2008 in the face of increasing concerns over food security. Notably, the "Generation 1.5" biofuels produced from nongrain-based crops such cassava and sweet sorghum are seen as the solution to reconciling the conflicting demands between food production and bioenergy development in China, which has only 7 percent of the world's arable land to feed 19 percent of the world's population.[22] Unlike corn and wheat, cassava and sweet sorghum can be grown on marginal land and require much less water and fewer nutrients. The national plan to expand the production of Generation 1.5 biofuels is an opportunity for the country's primary regions producing cassava and sweet sorghum, including the Guangxi Zhuang Autonomous Region. Located in southern China on the border with Vietnam, Guangxi has long languished as one of China's poorest provinces, characterized by mountainous terrain, little agricultural land, and poor transportation. The development of nongrain biofuel helps lift Guangxi out of poverty while contributing to the energy and food security of the entire nation.

Guangxi was designated China's pilot province for the production of cassava-based ethanol in 2007.[23] The province was already the largest cassava-producing province in China, with an estimated planted area of 2.4 million hectares, mostly on sandy and hilly marginal agricultural land, producing 6.5 million tons of cassava a year, representing 70 percent of national production.[24] However, cassava deteriorates rapidly after harvesting, making it difficult to store and transport. As a result, the supply of cassava is limited to October to March the year after planting and is mostly used regionally. Cassava-based ethanol had long been manufactured locally to produce liquor, but the national plan to expand and industrialize the production of cassava-based ethanol for biofuel raises new hopes for this low-value crop. COFCO (Guangxi) Biomass Energy was established in 2007, and COFCO reached an agreement with the Guangxi government to construct the world's first cassava-ethanol fuel plant in Beihai City. With an initial design capacity of 200,000 tons, the plant started operation in late 2007 and maintained an annual production worth 600 million RMB, or US$94 million, before further expansion in 2012.[25] Just as COFCO's strategic acquisition of three corn-ethanol production facilities in northeastern China led to the company becoming China's largest domestic corn-processing enterprise, the construction of the cassava-ethanol production facility in Guangxi has enabled COFCO to establish a new stronghold in southwestern China and become China's largest domestic cassava-processing enterprise.

Construction of the second phase of the COFCO cassava-ethanol plant in Beihai City began in late 2012. When completed, it will double its annual production capacity to 400,000 tons, making it the largest bioenergy production base in southern China.[26] The increased cassava-ethanol production capacity led to an expansion of domestic cassava cultivation and imports from abroad. At the local level, COFCO applies an industrial model combining agriculture and industry to operate its cassava-ethanol venture. Since the establishment of its cassava-ethanol plant, COFCO has signed production contracts with local farmers to cultivate cassava in the surrounding regions. COFCO encourages the farmers to increase the acreage of cassava cultivation and provides them with technology and equipment to improve yields. According

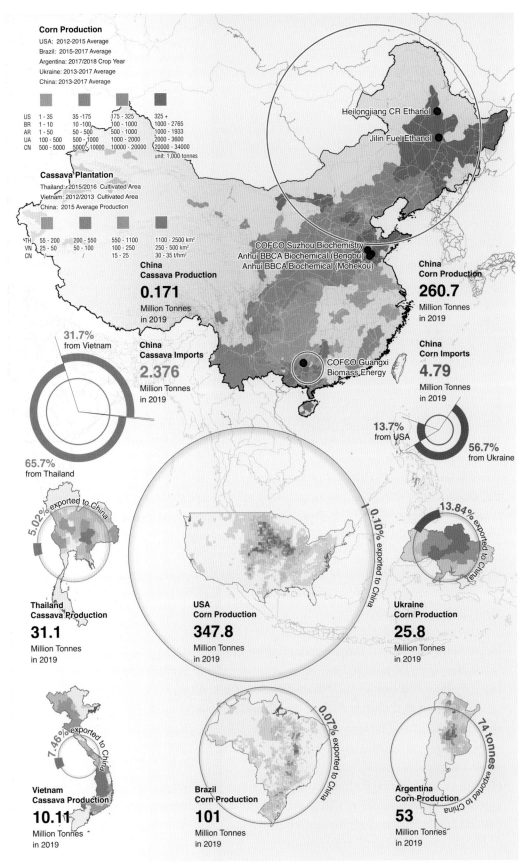

Corn Production

USA: 2012-2015 Average
Brazil: 2015-2017 Average
Argentina: 2017/2018 Crop Year
Ukraine: 2013-2017 Average
China: 2013-2017 Average

US	1 - 35	35 -175	175 - 325	325 +
BR	1 - 10	10 -100	100 - 1000	1000 - 2765
AR	1 - 50	50 - 500	500 - 1000	1000 - 1933
UA	100 - 500	500 - 1000	1000 - 2000	2000 - 3600
CN	500 - 5000	5000 - 10000	10000 - 20000	20000 - 34000

unit: 1,000 tonnes

Cassava Plantation

Thailand: 2015/2016 Cultivated Area
Vietnam: 2012/2013 Cultivated Area
China: 2015 Average Production

TH	55 - 200	200 - 550	550 - 1100	1100 - 2500 km²
VN	25 - 50	50 - 100	100 - 250	250 - 500 km²
CN			15 - 25	30 - 35 t/hm²

Heilongjiang CR Ethanol

Jilin Fuel Ethanol

COFCO Suzhou Biochemistry
Anhui BBCA Biochemical (Bengbu)
Anhui BBCA Biochemical (Mohekou)

China Cassava Production

0.171

Million Tonnes
in 2019

China Corn Production

260.7

Million Tonnes
in 2019

China Cassava Imports

2.376

Million Tonnes
in 2019

31.7%
from Vietnam

65.7%
from Thailand

COFCO Guangxi
Biomass Energy

China Corn Imports

4.79

Million Tonnes
in 2019

13.7%
from USA

56.7%
from Ukraine

5.02% exported to China

Thailand Cassava Production

31.1

Million Tonnes
in 2019

0.10% exported to China

USA Corn Production

347.8

Million Tonnes
in 2019

13.84% exported to China

Ukraine Corn Production

25.8

Million Tonnes
in 2019

7.46% exported to China

Vietnam Cassava Production

10.11

Million Tonnes
in 2019

0.07% exported to China

Brazil Corn Production

101

Million Tonnes
in 2019

74 tonnes exported to China

Argentina Corn Production

53

Million Tonnes
in 2019

FIGURE I.4.2

China's domestic production and importation of corn and cassava.

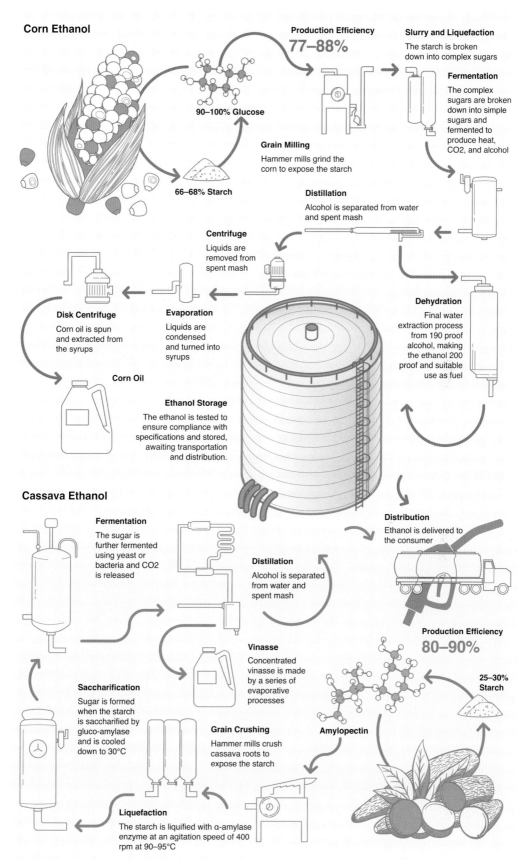

Corn Ethanol

90–100% Glucose

66–68% Starch

Production Efficiency
77–88%

Grain Milling
Hammer mills grind the corn to expose the starch

Slurry and Liquefaction
The starch is broken down into complex sugars

Fermentation
The complex sugars are broken down into simple sugars and fermented to produce heat, CO2, and alcohol

Distillation
Alcohol is separated from water and spent mash

Centrifuge
Liquids are removed from spent mash

Dehydration
Final water extraction process from 190 proof alcohol, making the ethanol 200 proof and suitable use as fuel

Disk Centrifuge
Corn oil is spun and extracted from the syrups

Evaporation
Liquids are condensed and turned into syrups

Corn Oil

Ethanol Storage
The ethanol is tested to ensure compliance with specifications and stored, awaiting transportation and distribution.

Cassava Ethanol

Fermentation
The sugar is further fermented using yeast or bacteria and CO2 is released

Distillation
Alcohol is separated from water and spent mash

Distribution
Ethanol is delivered to the consumer

Saccharification
Sugar is formed when the starch is saccharified by gluco-amylase and is cooled down to 30°C

Vinasse
Concentrated vinasse is made by a series of evaporative processes

Grain Crushing
Hammer mills crush cassava roots to expose the starch

Amylopectin

25–30% Starch

Production Efficiency
80–90%

Liquefaction
The starch is liquified with α-amylase enzyme at an agitation speed of 400 rpm at 90–95°C

FIGURE I.4.3
Corn and cassava-ethanol production processes.

to COFCO, a cassava-ethanol fuel-production enterprise yielding 100,000-tons per year can employ 300 workers and 11,362 farmers, supporting approximately 35,000 people based on the average family structure (a couple, two children, and two seniors) in the region.[27] At the transnational level, COFCO has been increasing imports of cassava starch and dried cassava chips from Association of Southeast Asian Nations (ASEAN) countries, notably neighboring Thailand and Vietnam, the world's top cassava producers. The imported cassava is particularly important to sustain a continuous year-round supply of raw material for ethanol production, especially from March to September between local harvests. Taking advantage of Guangxi's close geographical proximity to Southeast Asia's primary cassava producers, improved transnational transportation infrastructure, and preferential trade agreements enacted under the auspices of China's BRI, COFCO has led the way importing cassava into China, with the country's cassava imports growing at an average of 10.5 percent annually between 2007 and 2017.[28]

NOTES

1. COFCO, "History and Honor [歷史與榮譽]," http://www.cofco.com/cn/About-COFCO/HistoryandHonor (accessed August 3, 2021).

2. COFCO, "History and Honor."

3. Kai Cui, *Map of China's Biomass Industry* [中國生物質產業地圖] (Beijing: China Light Industry Press, 2007), 76.

4. Yoonhee Macke, *Biofuels Annual (China): Growing Interest for Ethanol Brightens Prospects* (Beijing: USDA Foreign Agricultural Service, 2017), 2.

5. NDRC, "Medium and Long-term Development Plan for Renewable Energy in China [可再生能源中長期發展規劃]," August 31, 2007, http://www.nea.gov.cn/131053171_15211696076951n.pdf (accessed September 20, 2020).

6. NEA, "China's 13th Five-Year Plan for Biomass Energy [生物質能發展十三五規劃]," October 28, 2016, http://www.gov.cn/xinwen/2016-12/06/content_5143612.htm (accessed September 20, 2020).

7. COFCO, "History and Honor."

8. Alfred Cang, "Corn Rally Sparks Green Fuel Rethink by Chinese Energy Giant," *Bloomberg News*, November 2, 2020, https://www.bloomberg.com/news/articles/2020-11-02/hungry-hogs-spark-a-green-fuel-rethink-by-chinese-energy-giant (accessed November 14, 2020).

9. Andrew Anderson-Sprecher and James Ji, *Biofuels Annual (China): Biofuel Industry Faces Uncertain Future* (Beijing: USDA Foreign Agricultural Service, 2015), 3.

10. COFCO, "COFCO Biochemical [中糧生物科技]," http://www.cofco.com/cn/BrandProduct/COFCOBiochemical (accessed August 3, 2021).

11. Weiguang Wu, Huanguang Qiu, and Jikun Huang, "Bio-ethanol Development: Current Status, Potential Impacts, and Policy Suggestions for China [全球生物乙醇發展現狀、

可能影響與我國的對策分析]," *China Soft Science* [中國軟科學] 3 (2009), 23–29, 24.

12. Mogens Slot Knudsen, Bo Andersen, and Claus Bo Larsen, *From Corn Waste to Green Energy in China* (Copenhagen: Danish Environmental Protection Agency, 2018), 4.

13. "Production of Fuel Ethanol Regains Momentum [燃料乙醇重現光明]," *Sina Finance*, December 19, 2010, http://finance.sina.com.cn/stock/t/20101219/16373554029.shtml (accessed October 23, 2020).

14. Anderson-Sprecher and Ji, *Biofuels Annual (China)*, 3.

15. Hao Guo and Xiaofeng Liu, "Retrospect of China's Corn Market in 2011 and Prospect of 2012 Market [2011 年中國玉米市場回顧及 2012 年展望]," *Chinese Journal of Animal Science* [中國畜牧雜誌] 48, no. 4 (2012), 8–12, 9.

16. Ke Wang, "The First Vessel of Ukrainian Corn Will Reach China by the End of the Year [首批烏克蘭玉米最快年底抵達中國]," *People.cn*, December 7, 2012, http://finance.people.com.cn/n/2012/1207/c1004-19827149.html (accessed October 23, 2020).

17. Andrew Anderson-Sprecher and Junyang Jiang, *Grain and Feed Annual (China)* (Beijing: USDA Foreign Agricultural Service, 2014), 5.

18. Valbona Zeneli and Nataliia Haluhan, "Why China Is Setting Its Sights on Ukraine," *Diplomat*, October 4, 2019, https://thediplomat.com/2019/10/why-china-is-setting-its-sights-on-ukraine (accessed October 24, 2020).

19. COFCO, "The DSSC Terminal Invested in and Constructed by COFCO in Ukraine Officially Started Operation [中糧集團在烏克蘭投資建設的DSSC碼頭正式投產]," May 25, 2016, http://www.cofco.com/cn/News/Allnews/Press/2016/0525/45551.html (accessed October 24, 2020).

20. COFCO, "The DSSC Terminal Invested in and Constructed by COFCO in Ukraine Officially Started Operation."

21. COFCO Agri Ukraine, "Business Profile COFCO Agri Ukraine," https://latifundist.com/kompanii/803-cofco-agri-ukraine (accessed October 24, 2020).

22. Aiqi Chen, Huaxiang He, Jin Wang, Mu Li, Qingchun Guan, and Jinmin Hao, "A Study on the Arable Land Demand for Food Security in China," *Sustainability* 11, no. 17 (2019), 4769.

23. Hongmei Li, "Guangxi Will Implement the Plan of Producing Ethanol Fuel from Cassava [廣西將實施木薯變汽油計劃]," *Sina Finance*, September 18, 2007, http://finance.sina.com.cn/china/dfjj/20070918/06583988098.shtml (accessed October 16, 2020).

24. Nao Nakanishi and Niu Shuping, "Ethanol Fires Hope for China's Poor Guangxi," *Reuters*, January 25, 2007, https://www.reuters.com/article/lifestyle-china-ethanol-guangxi-dc/ethanol-fires-hope-for-chinas-poor-guangxi-idUKT13856320070126 (accessed October 16, 2020).

25. Anderson-Sprecher and Ji, *Biofuels Annual (China)*, 7.

26. COFCO, "COFCO's 400,000-Ton Fuel Ethanol Project Breaks Ground in Guangxi," March 20, 2012, http://www.cofco.com/en/News/Allnews/2012/0320/46473.html (accessed October 24, 2020).

27. COFCO, "COFCO's 400,000-Ton Fuel Ethanol Project Breaks Ground in Guangxi."

28. Yanwen Tan, Congxi Li, and Huasheng Zeng, "Analysis of China's Cassava Production and Trade Development [中國木薯生產和貿易發展分析]," *World Agriculture* [世界農業] 10 (2018), 163–168, 167.

PART II

CORRIDORS AND CONCESSIONS

CHINA AND THE TRANSBORDER SUBREGIONS IN ASIA

When the Republic of China was established in 1912, it was burdened with the extraterritoriality of foreign concessions and settlements imposed on Chinese soil since the mid-nineteenth century, which were outside Chinese government control. One of the Republic of China's top diplomatic priorities was to extirpate these extraterritorial relics of imperialist politics as soon as possible. The watershed event in the tedious process of unraveling Western privileges was the Chinese forces overrunning the British concession at Hankou in 1927, which had been set up as a treaty port under the 1858 treaties of Tianjin and had served as the critical collection point for much of the vast inner regions of China. This event triggered the collapse of extraterritoriality generally. By the early 1930s the Nationalist regime (1928–1949) had regained control over customs, tariffs, postal communications, and around two-thirds of the country's foreign concessions.[1] All foreign concessions (with the exceptions of Hong Kong and Macau) were formally dissolved at the end of World War II, with the demise of the old treaty system permitting subsequent more equal legal, commercial, and cultural treaties to be negotiated with the West. Consequently, in 1949 the People's Republic of China inherited a state that no longer gave foreigners immunity to Chinese law. Mao Zedong announced that the Chinese people had finally "stood up."[2]

The dissolution of colonial-era concessions, particularly those located along China's frontier regions, called for new forms of agreements regarding connections between China and its newly independent Asian neighbors. The absence of subregional cross-border integration and the relatively closed borders between China and neighboring states between the end of World War II and 1980 stem from the broader Asian political economy shaped by the Cold War. Until the early 1960s, a bipolar geopolitical, strategic, and economic chasm divided Asia: the capitalist United States and Japan on one side facing the Communist Soviet Union and China on the other. This ideological chasm intensified the security and sovereignty concerns that bedeviled the national borders of states on both sides of the divide. Although Sino-Soviet, Sino-US, and Sino-Japanese relations fluctuated dramatically in the 1960s and 1970s, the power positions and norms of the regional international system and their associated development ideologies and strategies continued to define regionalism in Asia as an assemblage of bilateral state relations until the early 1980s.[3]

With the dissolution of the Soviet Union in the late 1980s and the end of the Cold War in 1991, existing preconceptions surrounding the economic climate, political sovereignty, and spatial boundaries of the nation-state were called into question. The bipolarized Asian political economy entered a period of transformation.[4] The collapse of the bipolar regional structure led to improved interstate relations and increasingly porous international boundaries, creating space and opportunities for nearby countries to develop more cooperative relationships. The changing relationships between the nation-state and global capital were manifested by the formation of transborder subregions in Asia, where geographic proximity and cultural affinity were major factors encouraging cross-national economic cooperation and integration. China stands at the center of these post–Cold War transborder subregional developments, with its long coastline accessible to overseas trade and even longer land boundary bordering more countries than any other country in the world.

Much scholarly attention has been given to the development of the Greater Southeast China Subregion (GSCS), which consists of southern coastal China (Guangdong Province and Fujian Province), Hong Kong, and Taiwan.[5] Beginning in the early 1980s, a number of neighboring economies—first Hong Kong and Japan and later Taiwan and Korea—began to invest heavily in China. Many scholars have pointed out the critical role played by Asia's Chinese diaspora in reestablishing connections with China after being cut off from the China mainland by political and military events before and after 1949. Given its competitive labor and land costs at the time, China focused initially on export-oriented industrialization. Its first special economic zones, strategically located on the southeast coast, were established around 1980 and were similar to the Export Processing Zones established in Taiwan and South Korea during the 1960s and 1970s. The SEZs were far enough away from China's existing political and economic centers to reduce the potential impact of failure, while being geographically close enough to Hong Kong and Taiwan to take advantage of their surplus capital and existing industries hungry for land and labor.[6]

The diversity of China's transborder subregions outside the GSCS and the multitude of factors other than Chinese diaspora capital investment that facilitated cross-border economic networks are largely unexamined and unexplained. This opening essay provides an overview of three subregional initiatives in which China is a major participant: the Greater Mekong Subregion (GMS) Economic Cooperation

on China's southwestern frontier, the Central Asia Regional Economic Cooperation (CAREC) on China's northwestern frontier, and the Greater Tumen Initiative
(GTI) on China's northeastern frontier. These transborder subregions were all designated in the 1990s and supported by various United Nations agencies, such as the
United Nations Development Programme (UNDP), and multilateral entities, such
as the US-led World Bank (established 1944) and the Japan-led Asian Development
Bank (ADB, established 1966). These new types of transborder subregions, corridors, and concessions are not established and operated under colonial domination
or to contain a perceived Communist threat. Rather, they are designed to facilitate
economic growth and development by encouraging adjoining countries to make best
use of their complementarities, with less-developed but resource- and/or labor-rich
countries working in tandem with the capital, technology, and infrastructure from
relatively developed countries.

GREATER MEKONG SUBREGION ECONOMIC COOPERATION

The Greater Mekong Subregion (GMS) is an economic area with unparalleled natural and cultural riches, following the Mekong River, which rises in the Himalayas in
China and runs south through Myanmar, Laos, Thailand, Cambodia, and Vietnam.
The GMS countries have been shaped by their various individual histories of colonialism and war, except Thailand, which was never a Western colony. Myanmar (then
called Burma) was part of the British Empire, and Vietnam, Laos, and Cambodia
made up French Indochina. Burma gained independence from Britain in 1947. Vietnam, Laos, and Cambodia gained independence from France after the 1954 Geneva
Conference. The Mekong Committee, a US- and UN-led development initiative,
was established in 1957 in the context of the intensification of the Cold War and the
newfound independence of Southeast Asian countries and was therefore linked to the
process of decolonialism and subsequent geopolitical developments in the Mekong
region. The committee used water resource development as an effective geopolitical
tool to modernize Southeast Asia in a way politically oriented toward the United
States rather than the USSR. Only Thailand, Laos, Cambodia, and South Vietnam,
which are GMS countries but had not been dominated by Communist influence,
were members of the committee. Most long-term transnational projects envisioned
by the Mekong Committee failed to materialize due to the political conflicts of the
ensuing decades, particularly the Vietnam War, which reduced Vietnam, Laos, and
Cambodia to war zones.[7]

The Mekong region stabilized in the 1980s, following the end of the Vietnam
War in 1975. The rising economic powers of Thailand and China started to change
their frontier policies within the new economic and sociopolitical context. Thailand
shifted its foreign policy toward former Indochina in the 1980s, with a view to turning

the region's "battlefields" into "marketplaces."[8] China similarly sought to fulfill its ambition to make Yunnan "a grand passageway to Southeast Asia" in the early 1990s, a significant about-turn for a government that had seen its southern border mostly as a security threat since World War II.[9] There was a growing consensus that regional cooperation could be the engine of peacetime reconstruction and development within the resource-rich GMS countries, aided by Thailand and China's increasing capital, technology, and infrastructure. The Greater Mekong Subregion economic cooperation program (GMS Program) was established in 1992 with the assistance of the ADB, bringing together all six Mekong riparian countries. At its launch, the program focused on identifying and implementing projects across a range of sectors, including transportation, energy, telecommunications, environment, human resources development, trade and investment, tourism, and drug control. After the Asian financial crisis in 1997–1998, transport projects took priority over other sectors of engagement.[10]

While some improvements have been made to regional airports and air services, road connectivity has led the way for economic integration, cross-border trade, and prosperity. Beyond the impact of transport infrastructure itself, economic corridors along major roadways and/or railways host a variety of economic and social activities, linking centers of production (including manufacturing hubs, industrial clusters, and economic zones) and centers of demand (such as national/provincial capitals and major cities).[11] A network of cross-border north–south and east–west economic corridors has become the dominant feature of program maps in the new millennium. Of these, the 1,750-kilometer North-South Economic Corridor has seen the most rapid growth over the past two decades and has been promoted as a reincarnation of the ancient Southern Silk Road that linked southern China with Southeast Asia as far back as China's Han dynasty 2,000 years ago. The North-South Economic Corridor now links the region's largest national markets (China and Thailand) by road and railway through Laos and Myanmar, while making seaports accessible to the only two landlocked GMS members, China's Yunnan Province and Laos.

Compared to CAREC and the GTI, the GMS is characterized by its large population and rapid urbanization. Although the GMS was one of the least urbanized regions in the world, with only 21 percent of the population living in urban areas in 1990, it is estimated that more than 40 percent will be living in cities by 2030, given the rapid 3–5 percent annual increase in the number of city dwellers.[12] Notably, the rapid urbanization of the GMS is justified by the overarching foundational objectives of poverty alleviation and sustainable development. According to the ADB and other GMS Program donors, resource-rich GMS countries are potential hotspots for a "poverty-environment nexus" in which poverty and environmental degradation are caught in a mutually destructive spiral.[13] Rural-urban transformation is touted as a way to better manage GMS resources by replacing "unsustainable" and "unproductive" rural land uses with productive and market-oriented land uses. The transition is facilitated by two major concurrent processes, infrastructure construction and land assessment. Infrastructure construction focuses on improving physical connectivity across the GMS's challenging terrain. Neoliberal development discourse considers "inaccessibility" due to a lack of infrastructure a proxy for poverty and vigorously promotes infrastructure development as a panacea that can alleviate poverty, boost incomes, and raise living standards. Land assessment facilitates the legal accessibility of the GMS's natural resources. With the support of development partners, GMS countries have been busy carrying out regional and countrywide assessments of their territory in order to identify areas suitable for mining, hydropower, plantation, and agribusiness concessions or for special economic zones and, more recently, real estate development.[14]

CENTRAL ASIA REGIONAL ECONOMIC COOPERATION

Central Asia, stretching from the Tianshan Mountains and Tamir Mountains in the east to the Caspian Sea in the west, has long been a crossroads for people, goods, and ideas between Europe and Asia, a vast territory where Iranian, Turkic, Russian, and Chinese empires have vied for influence throughout history. Central Asia entered a period of Islamic domination around the tenth century following Turkish expansion to the east. Central Asian territory occupied by Turkic people became known as Turkestan. Russians adopted the name of Turkestan for newly conquered territory as they extended their influence across Central Asia in the nineteenth century. Territory west of the Pamir Mountains became known as Russian Turkestan, while Xinjiang under the rule of Qing China to the east was referred to as East Turkestan. The incorporation of Central Asia into the Russian Empire in 1867 led to Russians and other Slavs migrating into the area. During the Soviet era, a highly integrated and centrally planned economic structure connected the five Soviet republics of Kazakhstan, Kyrgyzstan, Tajikistan, Turkmenistan, and Uzbekistan with each other and with the rest of the USSR. Notably, rail infrastructure (initiated by the Russian Empire) and later airways covering vast distances were heavily subsidized.[15]

After the fall of the USSR in 1991, the Soviet centralized economic system and transborder infrastructure system in Central Asia collapsed almost immediately. After independence, the Central Asian Republics fragmented and regional economic activity plummeted, partly due to infrastructure degradation after the removal of maintenance subsidies and partly due to barriers to transit introduced by the individual Central Asian Republics to strengthen national security along their borders in response to intraregional conflicts.[16] Various forms of regional cooperation have been proposed in post-Soviet Central Asia in recognition of the region's strategic importance, given its location at the crossroads of Eurasia; its rich natural resources, such as oil, natural gas, and minerals; and the similar cultures and social systems prevalent throughout the region. The Central Asia Regional Economic Cooperation (CAREC) Program is considered one of the most successful attempts at regional cooperation. Founded in 1997 by the Asian Development Bank (ADB), CAREC is a partnership of eight countries (Afghanistan, Azerbaijan, China, Kazakhstan, Kyrgyzstan, Mongolia, Tajikistan, and Uzbekistan) along with six multilateral institutions: the ADB, European Bank for Reconstruction and Development, IMF, Islamic Development Bank, UNDP, and World Bank. The program expanded further with the accession of Turkmenistan and Pakistan in 2010 and Georgia in 2016.

The main focus of the CAREC program is to integrate the landlocked countries of Central Asia through trade and infrastructure development, particularly in the transport and energy sector, as well as providing assistance for institutional reform, facilitating cross-border agreements, and promoting the private sector to aid and support the transition from centrally planned to market economies.[17] Like Southeast Asia's GMS Program, the CAREC program embraces several economic corridors. An Implementation Action Plan (2008–2017) was endorsed by the ADB in November 2008, set up under the CAREC Transport and Trade Facilitation Strategy in the aftermath of the global financial crisis of 2007–2008. Under this plan, six CAREC corridors were identified, including the Europe to East Asia Corridor (Corridor 1), the Mediterranean to East Asia Corridor (Corridor 2), the Russia to Middle East and South Asia Corridor (Corridor 3), the Russia to East Asia Corridor (Corridor 4), the East Asia to Middle East and South Asia Corridor (Corridor 5), and the Europe to Middle East and South Asia Corridor (Corridor 6). Each corridor aims to improve access for CAREC countries to at least two large Eurasian markets as well as ports on the Caspian Sea and Arabian Sea. Notably, four out of the six corridors (Corridors 1, 2, 4, and 5) were envisaged to pass through the Xinjiang Uygur Autonomous Region (XUAR) of China, one of the key members of CAREC.[18]

Compared to the GMS and GTS, CAREC includes countries that have a reputation for more political volatility. Due to its many historical complexities, post–Cold War Central Asia has been subject to persistent ethnic conflicts, boundary disputes, and an upsurge of religious and nationalist radicalization. These ethnic and related boundary disputes are largely the result of Soviet-era border delineations that ignored ethnic population distribution and historical traditions and often established administrative boundaries that divided tribal communities and created ethnic enclaves.[19] After independence, many of the Central Asian Republics inherited populations segregated by ethnicity or religion, which sometimes resulted in violent interethnic conflicts born of ethnocentric nationalism and aspirations. Religious and nationalist radicalization, particularly Islamist extremism and terrorism, can partly be attributed to the harsh anti-Islamic policies and practices of the former Soviet Union. After the collapse of the USSR, dissidents previously suppressed by the Soviets could express themselves culturally and religiously, quickly leading to a surge of Islamic and nationalistic activism rooted in a desire for national sovereignty and cultural rejuvenation. Islamic independence movements arose in China as well, where the nineteenth-century Russian name of East Turkestan has been readopted by Muslim separatists seeking independence from China for the present-day XUAR. Within this context, many CAREC development projects enshrine national security as much as economic objectives.[20] China plays a particularly important role promoting collaborative partnerships among CAREC countries to combat terrorism and Islamic activism throughout the region.

GREATER TUMEN INITIATIVE

Unlike the GMS, whose members share similar attitudes to their common colonial past, or the CAREC region, dominated by the political and economic legacies of the USSR, the Greater Tumen Subregion (GTS) has a long history of being split between diverse regional powers and is generally considered the least successful of the three regional initiatives here described. The GTS is physically defined by the Tumen River, which arises on the slopes of Mount Changbai (Mount Baekdu, as it is known in the Koreas) and flows into the Sea of Japan (also known as the East Sea). Ever since the 1860 Convention of Peking, when the Russian Empire acquired territory adjacent to the Tumen River estuary, the Tumen area has been at the intersection of the border areas of Russia, China, and Korea and consequently has often been the focus of seismic rifts between the international powers.[21] Violent conflict has erupted repeatedly, notably during the Russo-Japanese War of 1904 to 1905, the annexation of Korea by Japan in 1910, the establishment of Japanese-controlled Manchukuo in northeast China in 1932, the partition of the Korean Peninsula in 1945, and the outbreak of the Korean War in 1950, when China and Soviet-backed North Korean forces fought US-led United Nations forces. Although Russia, China, and North Korea were all Communist bloc countries during the Cold War, their relationships were fraught, especially after Sino-Soviet relations deteriorated and the resultant Sino-Soviet split in 1960.

When the trilateral border was eventually opened to the outside world in the early 1990s, it was initially thought to have great potential for regional development. The UNDP launched the Tumen River Area Development Program (TRADP) in 1991, envisioning it as a means of facilitating the postsocialist economic transition of Northeast Asia.[22] In contrast to the economic shock therapy that resulted in the chaotic deterioration of many of the countries of the former Soviet Union and Eastern bloc in Europe, the UNDP considered the TRADP to be a potential exemplar of international aid development, anticipating that the Tumen region would readily benefit from global capital investment and soon become a hub of prosperity for Northeast Asia in the new post–Cold War era.[23] The region's location sported many advantages, including access to deep-sea ports, the Trans-Siberian Railway, and the burgeoning markets of East Asia. The region seemed poised to take advantage of the complementarities of capital and know-how from Japan and South Korea, low-cost labor from China and North Korea, and the abundant natural resources of the Russian Far East and Mongolia. Initially, the five member countries (Russia, China, North Korea, South Korea, and Mongolia) shared enthusiasm for the future of the TRADP, signing agreements on the establishment of the TRADP Consultative Commission in 1995. Notably, both Koreas anticipated that TRADP initiatives would benefit the prospects for future unification by exchanging technological expertise and other sources of cooperation, thereby avoiding the costs and risks of sudden unification, while setting the scene for constructive development and future prosperity.[24]

Although the first stage of the TRADP project was intended to run from 1995 to 2005, in fact it ground to a halt in 1998 due to a lack of investment from Japan and South Korea. Japan was initially interested in taking part in the initiative and suggested extending its scope to form an economic region centered on the Sea of Japan instead of just the Tumen River. Disagreements over the geographical range of the project, along with the other parties' negative image of Japan over its colonial-era rule, led to Japan eventually backing out, leaving South Korea as the only viable investor among the TRADP participants.[25] However, South Korea failed to fulfill its role as major investor due to the complexity of the inter-Korean relationship amid heightened tensions over North Korea's nuclear weapons program.[26] In 2005 member countries agreed to extend the initial 1995 agreements for another ten years with the TRADP (renamed the GTI) and North Korea excluded. During the second stage, a newly economically powerful China was able to join South Korea as a major investor. However, like the TRADP, the GTI also made slow progress, this time with the contentious relationship between China and Russia being the limiting factor. In 2003, two years before the GTI was launched, China initiated its Northeast Revitalization Strategy, rekindling Russia's vivid memory of the Sino-Russian territorial disputes over the Russian Far East and raising suspicions in Russia that China's regional scheme might have some strategic ulterior motives.[27]

Compared to the GMS and CAREC programs, the GTI and its predecessor the TRADP have been relatively unsuccessful and have rarely lived up to expectations. External forces promoting transborder integration have been frustrated by the three former socialist countries' insistence on absolute sovereignty in their frontier regions, where an awkward tension exists between the interests of global capital and those of the centralized state. Nevertheless, the Tumen region does not exist entirely outside the influence of globalization and the market economy. Rather than following the model of trilateral integration envisioned by the UNDP, development has proceeded albeit in a piecemeal manner in response to each country's unique border conditions. Notably, just as the Asia-based Chinese diaspora played a major role in the development of the GSCS, the Northeast Asian Korean diaspora and its community networks have fostered cross-border economic activity, although in a rather more complex and contentious manner than the GSCS due to this area's special historical and political circumstances. For example, given the volatile relationship between the two Koreas, and after China and South Korea established diplomatic relations in 1992, South Korean investment in China's Yanbian Korean Autonomous Prefecture blossomed, demonstrating a positive synergy between the flow of economic capital and the availability of social capital.[28] South Korean investors are increasingly involved in the culture-related tourism industry in the Yanbian region as well as garment manufacturing, food processing, and construction-material production.

As this opening essay reveals, post–Cold War transborder subregions in Asia have evolved in diverse and uneven ways, with the development of each subregion determined by its specific cultural and sociopolitical legacy and contemporary geopolitical, technical, and ideological contexts. This is illustrated in more detail by the following three photo essays, which focus on the diverse forms of corridors and concessions within these three transborder subregions. Nineteenth-century colonialists' dreams of reaching imperial China's valuable markets and fabled riches by river or railway routes from French Indochina, British India, Russian Turkestan, and Japanese Korea and Manchuria have been replaced by contemporary Chinese visions of reaching out to neighboring countries with their resource-abundant economies and markets. The first essay investigates the development of the neighboring border cities of Nanla New Town in China and Laos's Boten SEZ in the upper-Mekong borderlands. It reveals the increasing overlap between poverty reduction programs and the BRI in China's southwestern borderlands through a detailed examination of the Silk Road urbanism envisaged by the Haicheng Group, a real estate titan. The second essay investigates the development of North-South Road Projects in both Kyrgyzstan and China in the Tianshan Mountains borderlands. It highlights how the North-South Road Projects have been used to strengthen collaboration between CAREC and the BRI and to counterbalance the Muslim-dominated east-west connections in the socioeconomic and political interests of both the Kyrgyz and Chinese governments. The third essay investigates the burgeoning mineral-water industry funded by Chinese and South Korean investments in the upper reaches of the Tumen River in the Mount Changbai/Baekdu borderlands. It illustrates that the divergent *shan-shui* (akin to *genius loci*) memories harbored by Chinese and Koreans are still alive and that the commodification of borderland resources can be a touchstone for cultural and political identities.

NOTES

1. William C. Kirby, "The Internationalization of China: Foreign Relations at Home and Abroad in the Republican Era," *China Quarterly* 150 (1997), 433–458, 441.

2. Mao Zedong, Opening Address at the First Plenary Session of the Chinese People's Political Consultative Conference on September 21, 1949.

3. Xiangming Chen, "The Asia-Pacific Transborder Subregions: The Phenomenon, Historical Backdrop, and Conceptualization," in *As Borders Bend: Transnational Spaces on the Pacific Rim* (Lanham, MD: Rowman & Littlefield, 2005), 28, 29.

4. Xiangming Chen, "The Evolution of Free Economic Zones and the Recent Development of Cross-National Growth Zones," *International Journal of Urban and Regional Research* 19, no. 4 (1995), 593–621, 594.

5. See, for example, Robert F. Ash and Y. Y. Kueh, "Economic Integration within Greater China: Trade and Investment Flows between China, Hong Kong and Taiwan," *China Quarterly* 136 (1993), 711–745; Yun-Wing Sung, *The Emergence of Greater China: The Economic Integration of Mainland China, Taiwan, and Hong Kong* (New York: Palgrave Macmillan, 2004); and Barry Naughton (ed.), *The China Circle: Economics and Technology in the PRC, Taiwan, and Hong Kong* (Washington, DC: Brookings Institution Press, 2012).

6. Xiangming Chen, "Globalisation Redux: Can China's Inside-Out Strategy Catalyse Economic Development and Integration across Its Asian Borderlands and Beyond?," *Cambridge Journal of Regions, Economy and Society* 11, no. 1 (2018), 35–58, 41.

7. Chris Sneddon, "The 'Sinew of Development': Cold War Geopolitics, Technical Expertise, and Water Resource Development in Southeast Asia, 1954–1975," *Social Studies of Science* 42, no. 4 (2012), 564–590.

8. Piya Pangsapa, "When Battlefields Become Marketplaces: Migrant Workers and the Role of Civil Society and NGO Activism in Thailand," *International Migration* 53, no. 3 (2015), 124–149.

9. Ingrid d'Hooghe, "Regional Economic Integration in Yunnan," in David S. G. Goodman and Gerald Segal (eds.), *China Deconstructs* (London: Routledge, 2002), 286–321.

10. Xiangming Chen, "Four Cases across Southeast Asia," in *As Borders Bend: Transnational Spaces on the Pacific Rim* (Lanham, MD: Rowman & Littlefield, 2005), 195.

11. GMS, "Economic Corridors in the Greater Mekong Subregion," August 25, 2017, https://greatermekong.org/content/economic-corridors-in-the-greater-mekong-subregion (accessed January 15, 2021).

12. GMS, "The Greater Mekong Subregion: Rural No More," October 23, 2017, https://www.greatermekong.org/greater-mekong-subregion-rural-no-more (accessed January 15, 2021).

13. Susmita Dasgupta, Uwe Deichmann, Craig Meisner, and David Wheeler, "Where Is the Poverty–Environment Nexus? Evidence from Cambodia, Lao PDR, and Vietnam," *World Development* 33, no. 4 (2005), 617–638.

14. Ashley Scott Kelly and Xiaoxuan Lu, "From Land-Locked to Land-Linked?," in *Critical Landscape Planning during the Belt and Road Initiative* (Singapore: Springer, 2021), 50, 51.

15. Shubha Chatterjee, "Revisiting CAREC: A New Approach to Regional Economic Integration in Central Asia," *Himalayan and Central Asian Studies* 22, no. 1/2 (2018), 138–187, 140.

16. Chatterjee, "Revisiting CAREC," 141.

17. Chatterjee, "Revisiting CAREC," 155.

18. CAREC, "Implementation Action Plan for the Transport and Trade Facilitation Strategy (2008–2017)," January 1, 2008, https://www.carecprogram.org/?publication=implementation-action-plan-for-the-transport-and-trade-facilitation-strategy (accessed January 15, 2021).

19. Shahram Akbarzadeh, "Keeping Central Asia Stable," *Third World Quarterly* 25, no. 4 (2004), 689–705.

20. Chatterjee, "Revisiting CAREC," 141.

21. Hyun-Gwi Park, "One River and Three States: The Tumen River Triangle and the Legacy of the Postsocialist Transition," *Asian Perspective* 40, no. 3 (2016), 369–392, 370.

22. Park, "One River and Three States," 371.

23. First implemented in Eastern Europe in Poland, on January 1, 1990, shock therapy is an economic program that transforms a planned economy or developmentalist economy to a free market economy through sudden and dramatic neoliberal reform.

24. Batzorigt Uyanga, "Understanding the Stunted Progress of the Northeast Asian Regional Cooperation" (master's thesis, Seoul National University, 2016), 8.

25. Christopher W. Hughes, "Tumen River Area Development Program (TRADP): Frustrated Micro-Regionalism as a Microcosm of Political Rivalries," in Shaun Breslin and Glenn D. Hook (eds.), *Microregionalism and World Order* (London: Palgrave Macmillan, 2000), 115–143.

26. Park, "One River and Three States," 373.

27. Uyanga, "Understanding the Stunted Progress of the Northeast Asian Regional Cooperation," 34.

28. Xiangming Chen, "Spanning Socialist and Post-Socialist Borders," in *As Borders Bend: Transnational Spaces on the Pacific Rim* (Lanham, MD: Rowman & Littlefield, 2005), 165.

SILK ROAD URBANISM

New Town Development in the China–Laos Borderlands

The Xiaomo Highway running south toward Mengla Town is flanked by countless billboards, stretching for miles along both sides of the highway. Most of them are red propaganda banners bearing a variety of proclamations, extolling the virtues of the national campaign of poverty alleviation. Messages such as "Moving Full Steam Ahead to Implement Targeted Poverty Reduction, Speeding Up the Process of Becoming a Moderately Prosperous Society" and "Implementing Targeted Poverty Reduction to End the Cause of Deficiency, Entering the Moderately Prosperous Society Together to Create a New Symphony of Life" are trumpeted in giant white or gold Chinese characters.

Although China's help-the-poor program was initiated following the inauguration of the Reform and Opening Up policy of the late 1970s, it was not until the mid-1980s that a Development-Oriented Poverty Reduction program was implemented, which then truly gathered steam after the launch of the Seven-Year Priority Poverty Reduction Program (1994–2000).[1] Poverty alleviation with a particular focus on the western half of China entered a new stage at the beginning of the millennium as part of a broader change in China's regional development approach, specifically the launch of the Western Development Strategy.[2] The concept of a "moderately prosperous society" (*xiaokang shehui*) originated in the Confucian classics, describing a society where poverty is eliminated and inequality is reduced. It started to be emphasized in new iterations of the poverty alleviation campaign, partly in response to the increasing inequality between inland and coastal regions in the 1990s.[3] Two ten-year plans have been implemented since 2001, guided by the Outline for Poverty Reduction and Development of China's Rural Areas (2001–2010) and the Outline for Development-Oriented Poverty Reduction for China's Rural Areas (2011–2020,

FIGURE II.1.1
Propaganda billboard by the Xiaomo Highway, reading "Moving Full Steam Ahead to Implement Targeted Poverty Reduction, Speeding Up the Process of Becoming a Moderately Prosperous Society," March 2019.

hereinafter referred to as the 2011–2020 Poverty Reduction and Development Plan). The central government issued the Decision of the CPC Central Committee and the State Council on Winning the Battle against Poverty in 2015, setting 2020 as the year the country should have wiped out poverty and become a moderately prosperous society.[4]

The Western Yunnan Mountainous Border Area (*dianxi bianjing shanqu*; hereinafter referred to as the Dianxi Area) was selected as one of the fourteen "main battlefields" in the 2011–2020 Poverty Reduction and Development Plan.[5] According to the plan, the social and geographical conditions of this frontier area are characterized by poverty and ethnic diversity amid inaccessible and mountainous terrain. The Dianxi Area covers approximately 209,000 square kilometers, 53 percent of the total area of Yunnan Province, consisting of sixty-one districts classified as "extremely poor" in ten contiguous cities and autonomous prefectures.[6] Abutting Vietnam, Laos, and Myanmar, the Dianxi Area comprises twenty-two border counties and forty-eight ethnic regional autonomous counties. It is a hotbed of ethnic cultural diversity, home to an extraordinary number of ethnic minorities and cross-border ethnic groups. This mountainous area is celebrated for its biodiversity and ecological significance and includes the famous water source protection areas of the Yangtze, Lancang/Mekong, and Nu/Salween Rivers.

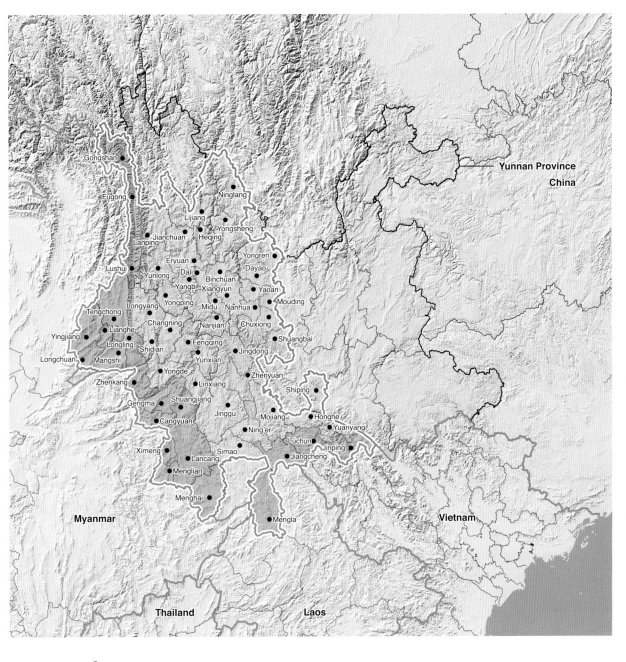

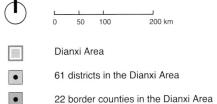

	Dianxi Area
	61 districts in the Dianxi Area
	22 border counties in the Dianxi Area

FIGURE II.1.2
Map of the Western Yunnan Mountainous Border Area (Dianxi Area), one of the fourteen main areas identified in China's 2011–2020 Poverty Reduction and Development Plan.

The 2011–2020 Poverty Reduction and Development Plan describes Dianxi, like all the main battlefields of poverty reduction in western China, as having "adverse natural conditions, underdeveloped infrastructure, and a largely impoverished population."[7] Infrastructure construction and urbanization are critical tools deployed by the Development-Oriented Poverty Reduction program in response to these natural and social challenges, in the belief that quality of life is dependent on how well the population is connected to markets. First, "inaccessibility" in terms of infrastructure is seen as an accurate proxy for poverty in rural developing economies. The argument is that poor infrastructure is a "problem" because it stymies trade for rural communities, raising the costs of inputs and lowering the value of outputs, thereby undermining livelihoods. According to this rationale, these areas require development intervention: highways have been built as a matter of urgency to connect the poorest counties with national and provincial trunk roads.[8]

Second, urbanization is considered an engine of economic growth, thereby reducing rural poverty. The argument is that the combination of poverty-relief relocation and new town construction will provide employment for impoverished farmers in urban areas and sectors outside agriculture while simultaneously protecting the endangered ecological environment.[9] Allowing former cultivated land to regenerate to forest and grassland is in line with the Grain for Green (*tuigeng huanlin*) policy, a major part of the West China Development program that promotes turning low-yielding farmland back into forest and pasture.[10]

Mengla County, located in the extreme south of Yunnan Province under the jurisdiction of the Xishuangbanna Dai Autonomous Prefecture, took on unprecedented significance within the broader poverty reduction and development plan of the Dianxi Area after 2013. In anticipation of the thirty-fifth anniversary of the country's Reform and Opening Up policy, the Decision on Major Issues concerning Comprehensively Deepening Reforms (hereinafter referred to as Decision on Deepening Reform) was issued at the Third Plenary Session of the 18th CPC Central Committee in November 2013. The decision included a special section on "Further Opening Up," advocating wider investment access (key point 24), speedier construction of free-trade zones (key point 25), and further opening up of inland and border areas (key point 26). Key point 26 declared the need to "quicken the pace of opening up in border areas and allow key ports, border cities, and economic cooperation zones in the border areas to have special methods and policies with regard to personnel exchange, processing and logistics, tourism, and some other areas" and to "accelerate the construction of infrastructure connecting China with neighboring countries and regions and work hard to build a Silk Road Economic Belt and a Maritime Silk Road, to form a new pattern of all-round opening."[11] Since then, a number of "key development and opening up experimental zones" have been established along major economic corridors under the Chinese Belt and Road Initiative. The State Council approved the establishment of a new experimental zone in Mengla County in July

2015: Mengla (Mohan) Key Development and Opening Up Experimental Zones (hereinafter referred to as the Mengla Experimental Zone).[12]

Mengla's current status as "one of the poverty-stricken counties in the Dianxi Area" and its historical role as "an important caravan stop along the old Southern Silk Road" heralded the inspiring narrative of an impoverished county's transformation to "the bridgehead of China's opening up to South and Southeast Asia through the Belt and Road Initiative."[13] Before European colonization (in particular of French Indochina east of the Mekong in the nineteenth century), various overland caravan routes and river-based routes in the upper Mekong together formed an important part of the Southern Silk Road between China and Southeast Asia. Sip Song Pan Na (modern Xishuangbanna) in southern Yunnan and Lan Na in northern Siam (modern Thailand) were key centers controlling the regulation and facilitation of trade in the upper-Mekong borderlands.[14] Both were celebrated as regional rice bowls (*na* means "rice paddies"; thus "Sip Song Pan Na" means "land of twelve thousand rice fields," and "Lan Na" means "land of a million rice fields" in the Dai language).[15] One of the main trade routes linked Mengla in Sip Song Pan Na to Luang Namtha, Viang Phoukha, and Houay Xay in Lan Na. From Houay Xay (on the east bank of the Mekong), trading caravans could cross the river to Chiang Khong to trade with Chiang Rai and Chiang Mai in Greater Siam or follow the river itself to Luang Prabang, the royal capital of the Lao Kingdom, also known as Mang Luang, meaning "principal city."[16]

Mengla's historical significance along the Southern Silk Road holds promise for its development future as envisaged by the BRI. Mengla has the longest national borderline (740.8 kilometers) of any county in Yunnan Province, sharing a 63-kilometer border with Myanmar in the west and a 677.8-kilometer border with Laos in the south.[17] Advocating the Development and Opening Up in Border Areas policy is a significant about-turn for a government that had seen its southern border as a security threat for most of the time since World War II.[18] Likewise, the exceedingly long national border of Mengla, formerly seen as a contributor to the county's "poverty" and "backwardness," has metamorphosed into a critical asset, endowing the county with unprecedented development opportunities. "One Artery and Three Windows" is the description of the organizational structure of the Mengla Experimental Zone, which boasts of being China's bridgehead along the revitalized Southern Silk Road. "Three Windows" refers to the three border ports: the provincial-level Guanlei Mekong River Port along the China-Myanmar border, the local-level Mengman-Pangthong Port, and the national-level Mohan-Boten Port along the China-Laos border. "One Artery" refers to the vision of a transportation corridor passing through Mohan-Boten Port, which consists of two major transportation infrastructures: the 1,900-kilometer Kunming–Bangkok Expressway and the 3,000-kilometer Kunming–Singapore Railway, now more often known as the Pan-Asia Railway.[19]

The renovation and upgrading of the 167-kilometer Xiaomo Highway, the southernmost section of the 730-kilometer China part of the Kunming–Bangkok

FIGURE II.1.3
Official map of the Mengla (Mohan) Key Development and Opening Up Experimental Zone, featuring five function zones, two logistic corridors, and two key nodes. *Yunnan Xinxi Bao.*

Expressway (KBE), was completed in September 2017, cutting the travel time between Xiaomengyang Town and Mohan Port in half, from 3 to 1.5 hours. Considered the most challenging section of the Chinese part of the KBE, the Xiaomo Highway passes through mountainous terrain clad in lush, tropical jungle. Of particular note in this regard is the Tengmie mountain range that runs north to south

FIGURE II.1.4
China–Laos Railway concrete viaduct columns under construction, as seen from the Xiaomo Highway near Mansan Village in the Nanla River valley, March 2019.

between the gorges of the Nanban River and Nanla River, two level-1 tributaries of the Mekong River. To negotiate this formidable terrain, the Xiaomo Highway is mostly built on elevated structures or tunnels, including two especially long tunnels: the 3.39-kilometer Tengmie Mountain Tunnel, which reaches an elevation of 934.6–1412.5 meters above sea level (MASL), and the 3.73-kilometer Nangong Mountain Tunnel, which reaches an elevation of 878.1–1409.2 MASL.[20] The China section of the 414-kilometer China–Laos Railway is the northernmost part of the Pan-Asia Railway linking Kunming and Mohan, mostly running immediately west of the Xiaomo Highway between Xiaomengyang Town and Mengla Town. On a recent visit, construction of the concrete railway viaduct columns was clearly visible from elevated sections of the highway. The terrain gradually becomes more accommodating as the Xiaomo Highway approaches Mengla Town in the Nanla River valley, and the railway finally bridges over the highway near Mansan Village in the south of Mengla Town just before entering Mengla Railway Station.

Transport infrastructure was not the only manifestation of rapid urbanization to be seen from the Xiaomo Highway, particularly on the approaches to Mengla Town, where newly cleared land and construction sites proliferated. Advertisements for Nanla New Town were conspicuous on highway structures, with the developer's name and investment hotline prominently displayed beneath catchy taglines, such as "Nanla New Town, Brightening Mengla" and "Embracing Five Countries, Walking

Up to the World." After leaving the Xiaomo Highway and following Mengla Center Road south through Mengla Town, visitors are led by a newly constructed six-lane road east across the Nanla River. A gigantic Water Splashing Square designed to host 6,000 people was recently completed on the east bank of the Nanla River at the main entrance of the new town, together with a two-story Nanla New Town Planning Exhibition Center, which, with its pitched roof, is a replica of the traditional Dai-style architecture, only ten times the scale. Surrounded by a sea of building sites littered with cranes and other construction paraphernalia, the entrance square and exhibition center seem to be almost the only features to have been completed within the 6-square-kilometer pilot zone of Nanla New Town. However, a 100-square-kilometer medium-term development zone and a 200-square-kilometer long-term control zone are projected for the future.[21]

Nanla New Town is being developed by Yunnan Haicheng Industrial Group Holdings Company, Ltd., a Yunnan-based conglomerate that was founded in 2000 and is headquartered in the provincial capital, Kunming.[22] Being one of the largest three real estate developers in Yunnan, the Haicheng Group mainly focused on land development and management during its first decade of operation. The company has a reputation particularly for tourism-related real estate development across Yunnan, notably the 4 billion RMB Gaozhuang Xishuangjing project situated along the Lancang/Mekong River in Jinghong City, the seat of the Xishuangbanna Dai Autonomous Prefecture. The project's name means "nine towers and twelve stockaded villages" in the Dai language. It is branded as "a new cultural city within Jinghong City" and has a gross floor area of 1.1 million square meters.[23] Rated as a national AAAA (4A)-level tourist attraction in 2018, the project has become one of the most sought-after residential properties in Jinghong City since phase 1 hit the market in 2009.[24] Another project, which earned national-level recognition for the Haicheng Group, is the development of the Boten Beautiful Land Special Economic Zone just across the border in northern Laos, the first SEZ in the country.[25] This special zone was formerly known as Golden Boten City, a casino boomtown with a salacious reputation, developed and operated by Fokhing, a Hong Kong–registered company, in the late 2000s. Following a Chinese government crackdown on just-over-the-border gambling and other licentious activities, the special zone was reinvented in the early 2010s. The Haicheng Group signed a 90-year concession agreement with the government of Laos in 2016 to redevelop the Boten SEZ.[26]

Although tourism-related real estate is a key component of both Nanla New Town and the Boten SEZ, seen together they represent a new genre of development for the Haicheng Group in the context of the BRI's social and economic geography. The twin cities located on either side of the China-Laos border represent the real estate giant's grandiose ambition to be "a pioneer implementer of China's BRI development strategy" enabling Silk Road urbanism. Silk Road urbanism is a new urbanism that blends the protection of supply chains and the security of nation-states, the result of a marriage between self-interested government policy and the private sector's irrepressible hunger for investment. The twin cities are the bridging point of a transnational corridor, strategically acquired by the Haicheng Group to be exploited for economic interests, including real estate, tourism, and logistics. The company launched a business diversification strategy in 2013 in the context of a nationwide Further Opening Up policy pursued by the central government and the legitimization of the BRI as a national development strategy. Since then, the company has rapidly expanded, establishing three subgroups: the Haicheng Real Estate Development Group, the Haicheng Jingland Cultural Tourism Group, and the Haicheng International Logistics Group.[27]

Following the promulgation of the experimental zone in Mengla County in 2015 and the inauguration of the construction of the China–Laos Railway in 2016, planning and development of both Nanla New Town and the Boten SEZ have proceeded apace. The mission statement "forging the China-Indochina Peninsula Economic Corridor and increasing the regional industrial value of the China-Laos-Myanmar-Thailand-Vietnam economic circle" features prominently on the homepage of the Haicheng Group's website. The twin cities play a central role in the imagined geography of regional integration.

COMMODIFICATION OF NATURE AND CULTURE IN THE BORDERLANDS

The Nanla New Town Planning Exhibition Center provides a glimpse into the narrative that conflates the area's impoverished past as a remote borderland and its promising future as a new hub of regional integration. A grandiose exhibition organized by the Mengla County Committee of the Communist Party of China (CPC) and the Mengla County People's Government is prominently displayed at the entrance of the exhibition center. Its title, "No One Must Be Left Behind: Witnessing the Battle against Poverty in Mengla County," draws on a quotation from the speech delivered by Chinese president Xi Jinping at the launch of the Battle against Poverty in 2015. President Xi declared that "we will establish a moderately prosperous society to be enjoyed by each and every one of us; on the march toward common prosperity, no one must be left behind."[28] The preface of the exhibition consists of five paragraphs articulating the geographical uniqueness, wealth of flora and fauna, cultural and ethnic diversity, logistical advantage, and unprecedented development potential under the umbrella of the BRI. The exhibition celebrates the transformation of Mengla from a lowly county struggling with "adverse natural conditions, underdeveloped infrastructure, and a large impoverished population," in the words of the 2011–2020 Poverty Reduction and Development Plan, into a bridgehead of China's embrace of South and Southeast Asia. Mengla has been reinvented as a forward-looking county

FIGURE II.1.5
The recently completed Water Splashing Square and two-story Nanla New Town Planning Exhibition Center at the main entrance of Nanla New Town, March 2019.

"endowed with rich natural and cultural resources ripe for improved management, regulation, and development."[29]

Despite being branded primitive (*yuanshi*), remote (*pianyuan*), and mountainous (*qiqu*) in most government reports, Mengla's natural and cultural attributes have long been prized. Also, as part of the broader Xishuangbann area, the county has been subject to radical changes through "socialist modernization" since the establishment of the People's Republic of China in 1949. In the early 1950s China's new regime launched the first wave of "socialist modernity" based on a political ideology that prioritized military security and national unification. Mengla, which means "Place of Tea" (*meng* means "place" and *la* means "tea" in the Dai language), has traditionally been acclaimed for its high-quality tea, especially Pu-er tea. The town had long been the northern gateway to the old Southern Silk Road (also known as the Ancient Tea Horse Road).[30] The Place of Tea witnessed a boom in rubber production in the 1950s when the central government designated natural rubber as a strategic industrial product during the Korean War in response to a US trade embargo.[31] Tropical rain forest across the lowlands of Jinghong and Mengla County formerly used by Dai farmers was cleared to make way for eight state rubber plantations in the 1950s.[32] At the same time, dramatic changes were imposed on the cultural and physical landscape. The new regime sent teams of scholars to carry out ethnic identification in Xishuangbanna to classify peoples "scientifically" into "minority nationalities" (*shaoshu minzu*). Just as in other regions of China populated by ethnic minorities, people in Xishuangbanna were classified and ranked according to a Stalinist model of social development based on modes of production along a continuum from primitive production through slavery, to feudalism, to early capitalism. State research teams identified thirteen minority nationalities in Xishuangbanna, the largest indigenous group being the Dai (one-third of the total population), ranked as feudal (wet rice farmers).[33]

A second wave of socialist modernity was inaugurated in the late 1990s, based on an environmental ideology formed after the catastrophic floods of 1998, the worst China had suffered since the 1954 Yangtze floods.[34] The central government deemed the flooding a national environmental catastrophe partly natural and partly human-made and initiated programs to tackle local land degradation and negative off-site environmental impact through water and soil conservation measures, including afforestation in upstream areas. Policy changes were implemented to recentralize state control over natural forests, including those in Xishuangbanna. The Natural Forest Protection Plan made illegal the cultivation of any land steeper than 25 degrees gradient and obliged farmers to plant trees or allow natural forest regeneration to rehabilitate any such sloping land lacking existing forest cover.[35] In addition, the Grain for Green or Returning Farmland to Forest Program granted farmers tree seedlings and eight years of grain and cash subsidies if they agreed to undertake reforestation of their sloping lands.[36] These policies and regulations were imposed on shifting cultivation and village and household forests, thereby resulting in huge losses of agricultural land for upland farmers. The Akhas, an indigenous group rated as primitive (shifting cultivators) by the ethnic identification program of the 1950s, now found themselves defined as environmentally destructive due to their traditional farming practices.[37]

After the adoption of the Decision on Deepening Reform by the CPC Central Committee in late 2013, a third wave of socialist modernity primarily based on an economic ideology has been promulgated, incorporating the environmental ideology dominant since the late 1990s. The latest rationale behind the governance of nature and culture emphasizes their economic value to attract investment capital and to enable a twenty-first-century urbanism that advocates "human–nature harmony." This is epitomized in the preface of the Mengla antipoverty exhibition, which gushes that "Mengla is the southernmost spring city [*chuncheng*] in China thanks to its monthly average temperature of 22 degrees C and year-round beauty. Mengla is the southernmost green city [*lücheng*] in China, thanks to its rich rain-forest resources. Known as the Kingdom of Plants and Animals, Mengla is situated within national key ecological function zones and national ecological demonstration zones."[38] The preface continues: "Mengla is also a green ecotourism city [*lüse shengtailüyou chengshi*] characterized by diverse ethnic customs and is a provincial-level model county for ethnic unity and progress. Accounting for 74.3 percent of the total county population, the minority population of 182,200 comprises 26 ethnic minorities."[39] The mountainous terrain and extensive rain forests account for the county's exceptional diversity of flora and fauna and its ethnic and cultural diversity, a key component of the flourishing ecotourism industry.

The last two paragraphs of the exhibition preface articulate Mengla's logistical advantages and unprecedented development opportunities under the BRI. The county is described as being at the vanguard of various national policies, "a strategic location where the Battle against Poverty, the Development and Opening Up in Border Areas, the Western Development Strategy, and the Belt and Road Initiative overlap, with poverty reduction being the overarching structure that guides the socio-economic development of Mengla." According to the preface, the BRI elevates the Development-Oriented Poverty Reduction to a higher level, and "One Artery and Three Windows," the organizational structure of the Mengla Experimental Zone designated in 2015, will optimize the county's logistical advantages. "Mengla," the preface continues, "provides the most convenient land and river-based routes linking China to the South and Southeast Asian countries."[40]

Against the background of a potential trade war with the United States, strengthening China–ASEAN trade and connectivity is a higher priority than ever.[41] Yunnan Province is at the forefront of regional integration plans, and Mengla County is a critical bridgehead for Yunnan's increasing engagement with regional Lancang-Mekong Cooperation and the ASEAN–China Free Trade Area. Locally, infrastructure construction and urbanization are finally opening the door to long-anticipated domestic and international capital investment in this remote border county, transforming Mengla's unique geography, wealth of flora and fauna, and cultural and ethnic diversity into resources that can be exploited for profit to be "enjoyed by each and every one of us regardless of ethnicity."[42]

Among the exhibition's main features are panels of photographs juxtaposing Mengla County's impoverished past with its prosperous future in the making.[43] Photographs of clearance of areas of shifting cultivation and shattered bamboo buildings perched on slopes are shown side by side with captions describing the region's past, characterized by adverse natural conditions, underdeveloped infrastructure, and a large impoverished population. By contrast, aerial views of newly completed highways and railways, ranks of brand new condominiums, and photographs of ethnic folk villages accompany the narratives of how the logistics, real estate, and tourism industries form the major pillars of a moderately prosperous society. The exhibition stresses the importance of urban and rural planning for Mengla County's development. In addition to the Mengla County Urban and Rural Master Plan, which has undergone four revisions since its conception in 2009, more than ten town-level urban and rural master plans have been drawn up over the past decade.[44] Collectively, these master plans guide Mengla's urbanization, which has increased from 36.0 percent of

FIGURE II.1.6

An exhibition panel with photographs of recently launched or completed infrastructure projects in Mengla County: notably the Xiaomo Highway, the China–Laos Railway, the Mengla–Mengman Highway, the Mengman Port, the Guanlei Mekong River Port, and the Mohan-Boten Port, March 2019.

the total county area in 2010 to 43.6 percent in 2017, projected to reach 47.6 percent by 2021.[45] In particular, the exhibition emphasizes how the real estate and tourism industries, guided by the master plans, attract ever-greater capital inflows, visibly transforming the situation on the ground. "Since 2010," the exhibition narrative declares, "with a favorable investment environment enabled by national macro-control policies, many well-known real estate development companies have shifted their attention from the first- and second-tier cities to Mengla County." While real estate developments reinvent towns along national and provincial-level roads as "towns of modern development," smaller towns and villages along county-level roads, particularly those inhabited by ethnic minorities, are envisaged to be revamped as "towns (villages) of tourism attraction."[46]

The first, second, and third waves of socialist modernity are essentially territorialization projects driven by distinct ideologies. By means of planning practices, national, provincial, and local authorities "divide their territories into complex and overlapping political and economic zones, rearrange people and resources within these units, and create regulations delineating how and by whom these areas can be used."[47] These territorialization projects produce and reproduce social power relationships, creating plans that serve the dominant political economy as much as they challenge existing social configurations. During the first wave of socialist modernity that started in the early 1950s, zoning was carried out based on the suitability of land for rubber plantations. As the traditional "low-efficiency" modes of agricultural production were replaced by the modern industrial mode of production in the valley floors, the patchwork of small paddy fields was swept away to be replaced by large state-run rubber plantations. Lowland farmers (predominantly Dai people) were cast out of their land in favor of "efficient" state farmworkers (almost exclusively Han people). During the second wave of socialist modernity that started in the late 1990s, zoning was carried out based on the suitability of land for forest protection and reestablishment. Environmentalists and authorities considered the uplands a "poverty-environment nexus" where poverty and environmental damage were locked in a mutually degrading vicious circle.[48] Traditional "environmentally destructive" modes of subsistence agriculture were replaced by forest conservation and afforestation initiatives. Upland farmers (predominantly Akha people), along with their traditional shifting agriculture and forest management practices, were evicted from the newly designated forest protection and conservation zones.

A substantial proportion of the "impoverished population" in the region consisted of people evicted from their lands, which had been reappropriated as rubber plantations and protected forests. Yet their impoverished status is itself appropriated by the third wave of socialist modernity driven by Development-Oriented Poverty Reduction, with land being zoned according to its suitability for natural and cultural resource commodification. Thus, the Mengla County Urban and Rural Master Plan (2016–2030) states:

> Of Mengla County's 6,860.8 square kilometers land area, the mountainous areas make up 96.1 percent of the total while the *bazi* [valley floors] constitute only 3.9 percent of the total. The geographical configuration and topography of a given area determine its socioeconomic development pattern. The mountainous areas characterized by ecological and cultural wealth bequeath to Mengla County tourism resources yet to be exploited. Meanwhile, the *bazi* areas provide Mengla County with precious land suitable for urban development. Urbanization must shift from an extensive to an intensive growth model to use limited land resources with maximum efficiency and optimize service provision.[49]

The county-level and town-level master plans support the efforts of governments and development agencies to facilitate the implementation of preferred socioenvironmental development patterns and projects, assigning people and human activities to their "right places." Towns in the *bazi* areas are expected to take on a contemporary urban outlook with multilane roads and high-rise condominiums. By contrast, towns and villages inhabited by ethnic minorities, who in many cases had been forced to relocate during the first and second waves of socialist modernity, are now expected to actively engage in the tourism industry, turning their traditions and customs into touristic commodities to graduate from their impoverished status.

NANLA AND BOTEN: TWIN CITIES WITHIN A REIMAGINED REGIONAL GEOGRAPHY

The interior of the Nanla New Town Planning Exhibition Center is decorated with shiny marble tiled floors and walls, as one would expect of a real estate sales office. The reception desk on the left-hand side of the main entrance displays brochures of the Nanla Bay project located in Nanla New Town and other Haicheng Group projects, such as the Friendship Avenue project in Boten, the Gaozhuang Xishuangjing project in Jinghong, and the Fuxian Lake project in Kunming. The exhibition space is a grand atrium with two smaller galleries along its south side, and the second floor is designated as office space. The gallery closest to the entrance is dedicated to the Haicheng Group, showcasing the company's mission statement, a timeline of major development milestones, and, most importantly, its role as "a pioneer implementer" of China's BRI development strategy. The second gallery is dedicated to "The Belt and Road," featuring a simplified timeline of the vast trade network connecting Eurasia and North Africa via land and sea starting from the second century BCE and continuing into the future. This gallery also highlights Nanla's strategic importance in Yunnan and globally, summarized in hyped-up titles such as "Opening up the Border Area to Build an Attractive Yunnan" and "Reviving the Historic Silk Road to Build a Better-Connected World."

The cartographic representation of the imagined geography of a reincarnated Silk Road and regional integration is installed on the wall just left of the "Belt and Road" gallery exit. The backlit engraved steel map highlights Yunnan's strategic location in an increasingly integrated Asia well placed to "Embrace Two Oceans (Pacific Ocean and Indian Ocean) and the Neighboring Three Asias (East Asia, South Asia, and Southeast Asia)," in the words of the guide. The map is covered with extensive captions for existing places and natural features, as well as regional and transnational infrastructure connections either under construction or planned. In addition to the Mekong River, which has defined the region's connectivity since time immemorial and is in the process of being transformed into an important river-based trade route, an octopus-like form crisscrosses the landmass of South and Southeast Asia. With its blue LED backlights twinkling, it sends four tentacles in different directions. One linking Mengla and Kunming is labeled "heading north through Central Yunnan to

FIGURE II.1.7
A backlit map at the Nanla New Town Planning Exhibition Center, indicating Mengla's strategic location in an increasingly integrated Southeast Asia, March 2019.

reach Chuanyu Region (Chongqing and Sichuan)." One linking Mengla and Bangkok is labeled "heading south through mainland Southeast Asia to reach the Malay Peninsula." One linking Mengla and Kyaukpyu is labeled "heading west through Myanmar to reach the Indian Ocean." Finally, one linking Mengla and Hai Phong is labeled "heading east through Vietnam to reach the Pacific Ocean."

Yunnan Province is depicted in the upper and upper-right part of the map linked to BRI-related economic regions in South and Southeast Asia. The Bangladesh-China-India-Myanmar Economic Area is shown in the upper-left part of the map, and the Greater Mekong Subregion Economic Cooperation Area and ASEAN Free Trade Area is shown in the lower part. The guide elaborated on the economic integration between China and neighboring countries: "If you draw a circle of 250 kilometers radius that passes through China, Myanmar, Thailand, Laos, and Vietnam, you will notice that Mengla County is at the very center of this circle." Mengla is represented on the map by a large red spot in the middle of the blue octopus-like form already described. Two dashed circles are centered on the red dot, one labeled "1h" and one "5h."

The guide continued:

Major border cities such as Tachileik in Myanmar, Luang Namtha and Phongsali in Laos, and Pu'er and Jinghong in Yunnan are located within the 1-hour [1h] Economic Circle centered on Mengla. The 5-hour [5h] Economic Circle centered on Mengla extends as far as Lashio (the largest town in northern Myanmar's Shan State), Chiang Mai (the largest city in northern Thailand), Vientiane (the capital and largest city of Laos), Hanoi (the capital and the second-largest city of Vietnam), and Kunming (the capital and largest city of Yunnan Province). As you can see, Mengla County is indeed at the "Golden Crossroads of Five-Country Collaboration."

The imagined geography of regional integration as represented in the 1:500,000-scale map with its diagrammatic blue octopus cross and red circles overlaid on a vast territory of over 3 million square kilometers might take a long time to materialize in reality. However, the actual situation on the ground is being transformed in and around the central red dot, with Nanla New Town clearly marked just to its north and Boten to its south. According to the guide, "in 2015 a 4,500-square-kilometer key development and opening up experimental zone was established in Mengla County. More than 240 major construction projects representing an investment of 200 billion RMB are planned, and many are currently under construction." Indicating the big red spot with a green laser pointer, he continued: "The spatial development of the experimental zone can be summarized as 'Five Function Zones, Two Logistic Corridors, and Two Key Nodes.'" The five function zones are the River Port Economic Function Zone, the Import and Export Processing Function Zone, the Cultural Tourism Function Zone, the Characteristic Agriculture Function Zone, and the Ecological Barrier Function Zone. The two logistic corridors are the Menglun-Mohan Land-Route Economic Corridor and the Jinghong-Guanlei River-Route Economic Corridor. The two key nodes are the Mengla-Nanla Modern Service Accumulation Area and the Mohan-Boten Economic Cooperation Area.[50] Both are located along the Menglun-Mohan Land-Route Economic Corridor adjacent to the ecological barrier function zone. "Nanla New Town and Boten SEZ," the guide said, "are endowed with logistical and ecological advantages and will together form the central hub of an integrated regional economy."

The geographical vision of Nanla and Boten curated by Haicheng defines their booming future and promising investment opportunities on two distinct scales. On the regional scale, the twin cities have shifted from the far periphery of China to the center of the whole of South and Southeast Asia, becoming the hub of a network of "Modern Silk Roads" consisting of numerous highways and railways linking China with the four neighboring countries. On the local scale, the twin cities metamorphosed from sparsely populated villages to new towns that could accommodate

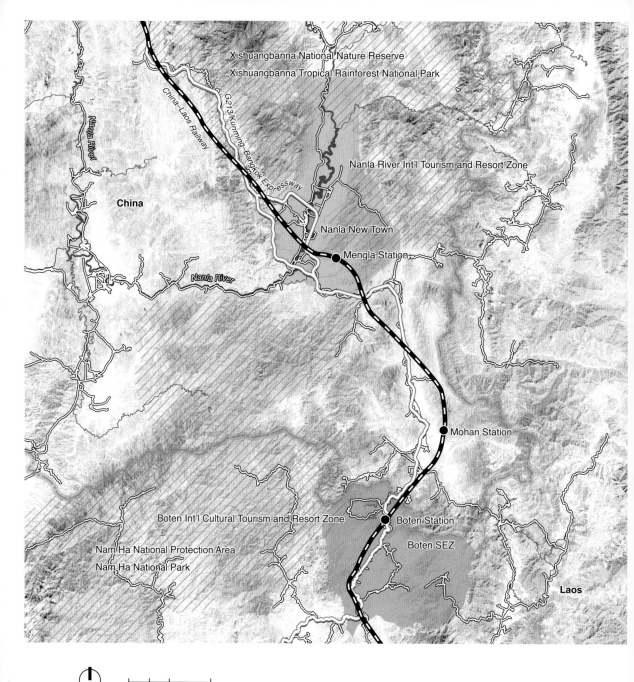

FIGURE II.1.8

Map showing the development enclaves in the China-Laos borderland, including Nanla New Town in China and the Boten Special Economic Zone in Laos. Both areas were acquired and developed by the Haicheng Group for real estate, tourism, and logistics.

millions of residents and attract large numbers of tourists to their well-forested tropical landscape by means of modern transport infrastructure. The promotional brochures of Nanla and Boten illustrate how these two distinct scales intersect, with the regional maps showing either Nanla or Boten at the center of the five surrounding countries. The brochure front covers are dedicated to the narratives of the twin cities' international status, sporting catchy taglines such as "Oriental Meeting Room," "Embracing Five Countries, Walking Up to the World," and "The Engine of the BRI China-Indochina Economic Corridor." Detailed breakdowns of travel times and distances between Nanla/Boten and other cities along the Pan-Asia Railway are sometimes provided. The brochure's back covers are adorned with floor plans of real-estate projects in the new towns, with jaunty taglines extolling the livability and ecological wealth of the twin cities, such as "Mysterious Tropical Rainforests," "Staying Green All Year Round, Warm and Humid All Four Seasons," and "Natural Gene Banks of Flora and Fauna Kingdoms."

The promotional brochures for Nanla New Town and Boten SEZ are highly similar and their showrooms almost identical. The Boten Special Economic Zone Planning Exhibition Center is approximately 200 meters from the Mohan (China)/Boten (Laos) checkpoint on the Lao side and 50 kilometers south of the Nanla New Town Planning Exhibition Center. Although the Boten showroom and exhibition center is much smaller than its Nanla counterpart, both feature central halls with a large LED facade display, a giant panorama of the new town, and an architectural model of the associated real estate project within the new town at 1:100 scale. Facing the main entrance, a dynamic promotional video featuring the local natural and cultural riches and urban and infrastructure progress in the region loops on the LED display. The videos portray the new town simultaneously as a paradise of elephants strolling through rain forests and villagers in ethnic costume picking Pu-er tea leaves, and as a modern metropolis with glistening high-rise buildings under construction and containers being uploaded onto freight trains and trucks. The video narrations describe Nanla/Boten as "international modern new towns with outstanding natural and cultural landscapes," master-planned under the auspices of "Prioritizing Environmental Protection, Integrating Industries and City." The Nanla and Boten master plans both contain four zones, corresponding to the four key industries of urban development, logistics, tourism, and ecological protection.

Large panoramic models take pride of place in the exhibition spaces in Nanla and Boten, featuring modern urban areas surrounded by lush tropical jungles connected to major transnational infrastructure, a twenty-first-century urban utopia celebrating ecology and modernity. While promotional videos play in the background, guides at both exhibition centers walk visitors through the interactive panorama model, announcing key elements of the new town as they are illuminated at the touch of a button. The 1:500 panoramic model in Nanla represents an area of 10 square kilometers, including the 6-square-kilometer pilot zone of Nanla New Town, which has

FIGURE II.1.9
Satellite image of Mengla Town and Nanla New Town in the Nanla River valley, with the Nanla River, the planned urban grid of the Nanla New Town pilot zone, and major transportation infrastructure highlighted.

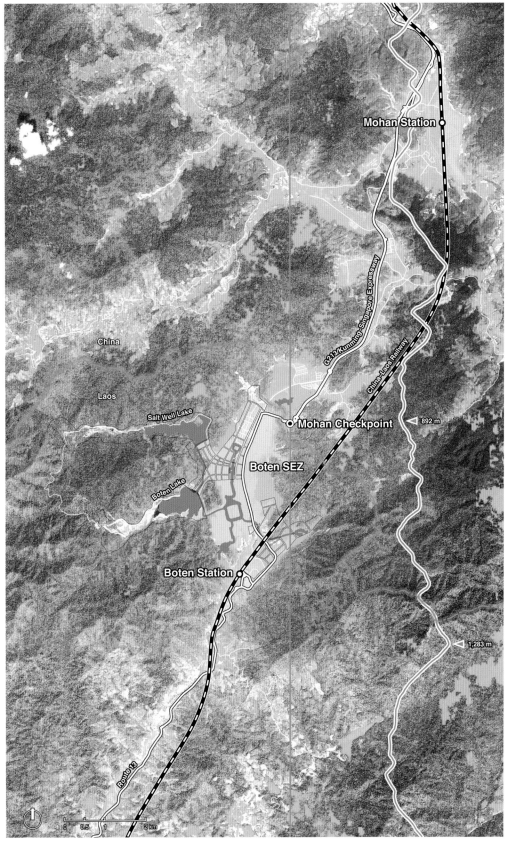

FIGURE II.1.10

Satellite image of the Boten SEZ, with the China-Laos border, artificial water features, the planned urban grid of the Boten SEZ core zone, and major transportation infrastructure highlighted.

a medium-term development zone of 100 square kilometers and a long-term control zone of 200 square kilometers. Nanla River, Guangbayin Mountain, and Nanla Avenue (which links the two) make up the main structure of the pilot zone.

While brand-new high-rise buildings line up on both sides of Nanla Avenue in the urban zone, existing traditional settlements are incorporated into two major areas of tourist attractions. The Nanla River International Tourism and Resort Zone—branded as "One River, Seven Villages, and Numerous Farms"—incorporates seven villages clustered along the Nanla River: Manhe, Mangangna, Manlong, Mannuanjiao, Manlongdai, Manlongle, and Manyong. Five Dai villages located on the slopes of Guangbayin Mountain within the Tropical Rainforest and Ecological Protection Zone are scheduled to be upgraded and collectively rebranded as the Traditional Dai Stockaded Villages Complex. This complex will include four major areas: the Comprehensive Service Area (Manling), the Ecological Waterscape Resort (Mandan), the Rainforest Art Exhibition Area (Manlang), and the Rainforest Restoration Experimental Area (Nanlang and Nanbang). According to the guide at the Nanla Exhibition Center, Nanla New Town will help make Xishuangbanna "one of the most popular tourist destinations in the world, boosting the annual tourism carrying capacity of Mengla County to 10 million people once the China–Laos Railway is completed."

The 1:1,000 panoramic model of Boten represents 20 square kilometers of the 34.3-square-kilometer Boten SEZ, expected to become the second-largest city in Laos, with a planned development area of 16.4 square kilometers and a forest protection area of 17.9 square kilometers. Route 13 in the urban zone, the Laos section of the Kunming–Bangkok Expressway, is flanked by new high-rises. Just as in Nanla, extensive areas in the new town are set aside for tourism. However, these tourist attractions are mostly created from scratch in Boten because it was originally less populated than Nanla. They involve significant earthworks, including excavation of a central canal in the urban zone, and dams built to create two artificial lakes in the tourism zone: Salt Well Lake and Boten Lake.[51] Five tourist attractions' themes borrow from Chinese and Laotian cultures. An ASEAN Traditional Architecture Complex with Southeast Asian (mainly Dai/Thai and Lao-style) buildings is located south of the central business district. A Lancang–Mekong Kingdom Wonder Park modeled after legends of rain-forest exploration in the fourteenth century during the reigns of the first and second Lan Xang kings (Fa Ngum and Oun Huan) will be constructed along the west bank of the Salt Well Lake. An Ancient Lao City modeled after the seventeenth-century Setthathirath Kingdom of Lan Xang will be constructed along the west bank of Boten Lake. The Gold Temple and Silver Temple located at the north and south ends of the Waterfront Park that runs alongside the central canal will become part of the larger International Buddhist Tourism Area. A folk village named One Garden, Two Countries (*yiyuan liangguo*) south of the central business district will showcase traditional culture from China and Laos. According to the guide at the Boten Exhibition Center, the Boten SEZ will become "a China-ASEAN tourist hub with sufficient capacity to cater for an expected 25 million people once the China–Laos Railway is complete."

The Nanla and Boten exhibition centers and their promotional videos and panoramic models illustrate the transformation of the region: from an impoverished past characterized by "adverse natural conditions, underdeveloped infrastructure, and a large impoverished population" into a brand new "Spring City," "Green City," and "Ecotourism City," as mentioned in the poverty-reduction exhibition outside the Nanla exhibition center. The forms and narratives applied to Nanla New Town and the Boten SEZ are clearly inspired by Gaozhuang Xishuangjing, inaugurated in 2009, one of the Haicheng Group's best-known tourism-related real-estate development projects situated in Jinghong City, the seat of the Xishuangbanna Dai Autonomous Prefecture.

Gaozhuang Xishuangjing occupies 0.8 square kilometers of riverside land and was carried out in three phases: Lan Xang Avenue, Bodhi Avenue, and Peacock Avenue, all three leading to a golden stupa built at the center of the project. The project commodified nature in the form of the Lancang/Mekong River and cultures in the form of Dai/Thai traditions. The project theme harked back to "the splendor of the heyday of the Kingdom in Sip Song Pan Na (modern Xishuangbanna)." It became one of the most popular tourist attractions and most sought-after residential developments in Jinghong City.[52] A decade later, the theme park rationale embodied by Gaozhuang Xishuangjing, branded "a new cultural city within Jinghong City," has been upgraded, upscaled, and applied to Nanla's long-term control zone of 200 square kilometers and Boten's 34.3-square-kilometer development area. Heavily dependent on the region's natural and cultural resources, the tourism-related real estate developments in Nanla and Boten represent a new form of frontier capitalism, a completely different approach to those developments that focused on the extraction of natural resources or enforced restrictions on agricultural land for forest protection in the border areas.[53]

A decade after the inauguration of Gaozhuang Xishuangjing, Nanla New Town and the Boten SEZ reflect Haicheng's grandiose scheme of bringing to life a Silk Road urbanism that draws upon the synergy of the projects' frontier locations and close identification with the BRI. The narratives delivered by the guides were instructive because they seamlessly metamorphosed into salespersons when introducing specific real estate projects. In the exhibition centers, immediately next to the panoramic models of the new town, 1:100 scale models of real-estate projects are displayed, showing off a variety of investment options. At both exhibition centers, the salespersons promoted these projects as "stable, high-quality assets" and "low-risk, high-yield investments" for three reasons. First, Nanla and Boten are just as well equipped with modern services and infrastructure as the older developed regions of Yunnan and other parts of China, but in addition they are blessed with an incomparable ecologically rich environment that is less disturbed and better protected thanks to their frontier location. Situated amid a lush forested landscape, a rare asset in modern urban living, the property's high appreciation rate is guaranteed. Second, Nanla and Boten, situated at the center of a region ever more integrated by the construction of the Modern Silk Roads and carefully planned to accommodate industrial and residential facilities, are bound to become logistics and tourism hubs able to handle heavy flows of freight and people. In anticipation of the opening of the China–Laos Railway in 2021, now is the best time to invest in these products, which are in high demand and likely to be sold out soon. Third, situated within the national experimental zone and transnational collaboration zone under the BRI, real estate projects in Nanla and Boten are much less likely to be exposed to policy uncertainty and market volatility than other speculative real-estate investments. Nanla and Boten form the two key nodes in a region that is guaranteed to have stable policies and politics, ensuring economic growth and a coherent and continuous path toward sustainable development.

At the macro level, the affiliation with the central government–led BRI affords security and order to the formerly "backward and lawless frontier," while special regulations that apply specifically to the "new town" and "special zone" areas maximize the potential for profit at the microlevel. Since 2010 the Chinese government has imposed restrictions to curb the national housing market, including home purchase restrictions to rein in speculative buying.[54] Despite this, Nanla New Town and Boten SEZ have been able to devise their own ways to circumvent the restrictions and expand investment, promoting "No Property Purchase Restriction, No Mortgage Lending Restriction" as a highlight of their real estate offerings. The "stand-alone guesthouse" property typology (similar to the shop house) has been instigated in Nanla New Town. Essentially a hybrid of residential and commercial property, the stand-alone guesthouse is composed of retail space on the ground and two floors of residential units above. Branded as "a high-end commercial property" product, it is legally categorized as commercial property, to which the policy of purchase restrictions does not apply, yet it has the practical advantage that property owners can rent out both the ground-floor shops and the upper-floor living units. "Designed in Dai-Thai architectural style," the salesperson explained, "the Nanla Bay project is in itself a mini–tourist attraction with long-term potential to add value." Another differentiation is applied in the Boten SEZ on the Lao side of the border. Under Lao law, foreigners are normally permitted to buy houses from Lao citizens only on 30-year leasehold agreements, but the Chinese model of 70-year property leases for residential use is applied in the Boten SEZ. In addition, the Chinese purchase restrictions do not apply in Boten because it is outside China. "Given that 90 percent of the population in the SEZ is Chinese and the Friendship Avenue project is literally

FIGURE II.1.11
Inside the Nanla New Town Planning Exhibition Center, featuring a panoramic model (1:500) of the Nanla New Town in the foreground and a rolling promotional video playing in the background, March 2019.

FIGURE II.1.12
Inside the Boten Exhibition Center, featuring a panoramic model (1:1,000) of the Boten SEZ in the foreground and a rolling promotional video playing in the background, March 2019.

FIGURE II.1.13
Inside the Nanla New Town Planning Exhibition Center, featuring a scale model (1:100) of proposed real-estate developments displaying a variety of investment options, March 2019.

FIGURE II.1.14
Inside the Boten Exhibition Center, featuring a scale model (1:100) of proposed real estate developments displaying a variety of investment options, March 2019.

only a few hundred meters away from the China-Laos border," the salesperson said, "it is an ideal foreign property investment [for the Chinese] that can be easily rented out or resold."

CONCLUDING REMARKS

Detailed examination of Silk Road urbanism reveals the increasing overlap between poverty-reduction programs and the BRI in China's southwest borderlands. This approach to urban development deploys infrastructure construction and urbanization to open previously remote border regions to domestic and international capital, turning their unique geographies, wealth of flora and fauna, and cultural and ethnic diversity into engines of profit to alleviate the "problem of poverty." China's Development-Oriented Poverty Reduction program since 1994 has had an influence on the Western Yunnan Mountainous Border Area (Dianxi Area), one of the main areas identified by the 2011–2020 Poverty Reduction and Development Plan. Mengla County, one of the twenty-two border counties of the Dianxi Area, attracted unprecedented attention after 2015, when the State Council approved the establishment of a new experimental zone within its jurisdictional boundary and positioned poverty reduction as the overarching structure that guides the socioeconomic development of Mengla County.

The recent transformation of Mengla County took place in three waves of socialist modernity visited upon the Xishuangbanna Dai Autonomous Prefecture since the establishment of the new regime in China in 1949, conceptualized as territorialization projects driven by distinct ideologies and implemented through the planning and zoning process. The first wave of socialist modernity that began in the early 1950s was driven by political ideology. Zoning was carried out based on the suitability of land for rubber plantations. The second wave in the late 1990s was driven by environmental ideology. Zoning was carried out based on the appropriateness of land for forest protection. A substantial proportion of the large impoverished population in the region was evicted from the land when it was requisitioned for rubber plantations and protected forests during the first and the second waves. The current third wave of socialist modernity is driven by economic ideology that appropriates an impoverished region and its population as a resource, with zoning based on the suitability of land for natural and cultural commodification.

The twin cities of Nanla New Town and the Boten SEZ on either side of the China-Laos border constitute the two key nodes of the Mengla Experimental Zone master plan. Situated along the Menglun-Mohan Land-Route Economic Corridor next to the ecological barrier function zone of the master plan, Nanla New Town and Boten SEZ have logistical and ecological advantages and have been strategically acquired by the Haicheng Group, in pursuit of its economic interests, including real estate, tourism, and logistics. The development of the twin cities reflects the Haicheng Group's grandiose ambition of becoming a pioneer in implementing China's BRI development strategy, enabling a Silk Road urbanism that powerfully combines the advantages of government policy and unquenchable private-sector investment. My visit to the Nanla New Town Planning Exhibition Center and the Boten Special Economic Zone Planning Exhibition Center, designed and curated by the Haicheng Group, highlights how the new town and SEZ master plans and the socioeconomic ambitions embedded in them are translated into multimedia and multiscale visual and spatial representations in the exhibition spaces.

As Michael Dwyer points out, rather than being a brand-new plan per se, the BRI is more an effort to rally a variety of existing initiatives under a single grand narrative.[55] Viewed in this way, the BRI is already a concrete reality, despite being the subject of so much speculation and debate. The overlap between the poverty-reduction program and the BRI has extended since 2013 in the upper-Mekong borderlands, a synergy driving forward the third wave of socialist modernity and affiliated territorialization projects on an unprecedented scale and at an ever-increasing speed. In the case of Mengla, the county with the longest national borderline in Yunnan Province, the BRI facilitates elevating Mengla's Development-Oriented Poverty Reduction to the next level. By invoking Mengla's historical significance on the ancient transnational trade routes, the BRI helps reconceptualize the county's borderland status from being the cause of poverty to being the remedy for poverty. Mengla is rebranded as China's gateway to South and Southeast Asia. Infrastructure projects such as the Xiaomo Highway and the China–Laos Railway are promoted as "Modern Silk Roads" channeling long-anticipated capital investment into the remote borderlands.

The new reality of Silk Road urbanism manifests in physical and discursive space. Just as the landscape is transformed by bulldozers, trucks, and construction cranes, people's perceptions of nature and culture are reshaped by maps, panoramas, and architectural models. The Haicheng Group's exhibition centers showcase the dream of Silk Road urbanism by using three main types of plan: regional, the new town, and the real-estate project. The regional plan is a 1:500,000 scale map of an imagined geography of the China-Laos-Myanmar-Thailand-Vietnam economic regional affiliation, with the twin cities of Nanla and Boten positioned at the center of the vast territory of South and Southeast Asia. The new town/SEZ plans are shown by dynamic promotional videos and 1:500/1:1,000 interactive panoramic models. They promote an idealized twenty-first-century urbanism of "human–nature harmony" that celebrates ecology and modernity and sets out a spatial order maximizing the commodification of nature and culture. The real-estate project plans are 1:100 architectural models that lay out the opportunities for unprecedented investments, unconstrained by China's home-purchase restrictions and guaranteed high appreciation rates thanks to the project's frontier position and BRI affiliation. Roadside advertisements, promotional brochures, and guides' narratives reinforce the impact of the maps, panoramas, and architectural models displayed in the exhibition centers. Together they generate a veritable symphony grandstanding the prosperous future that is fast erasing the impoverished past of the China-Laos borderlands.

NOTES

1. State Council Information Office, "The Development-Oriented Poverty Reduction Program for Rural China [中國的農村扶貧開發]," October 14, 2001, http://www.scio.gov.cn/zfbps/ndhf/2001/Document/307929/307929.htm (accessed August 4, 2019).

2. State Council Information Office, "New Progress in Development-Oriented Poverty Reduction Program for Rural China [中國農村扶貧開發的新進展]," November 16, 2011, http://www.scio.gov.cn/zfbps/ndhf/2011/Document/1048123/1048123_1.htm (accessed August 4, 2019).

3. Jesús Solé-Farràs, "Harmony in Contemporary New Confucianism and in Socialism with Chinese Characteristics," *China Media Research* 4, no. 4 (2008), 14–24.

4. State Council of the People's Republic of China, "Decision of the CPC Central Committee and the State Council on Winning the Battle against Poverty [中共中央國務院關於打贏脫貧攻堅戰的決定]," November, 29, 2015, http://www.gov.cn/gongbao/content/2015/content_2978250.htm (accessed October 15, 2019).

5. State Council of the People's Republic of China, "Outline for Development-Oriented Poverty Reduction for China's Rural Areas (2011–2020) [中國農村扶貧開發綱要(2011–2020年)]," December 1, 2011, http://www.gov.cn/gongbao/content/2011/content_2020905.htm (accessed October 16, 2019).

6. Wenxun Lin, *The Research Series on the Western Yunnan Border Counties: Mengla County* [滇西邊境縣研究書系：勐臘縣] (Kunming: Yunnan University Press, 2016), 4.

7. Lin, *The Research Series on the Western Yunnan Border Counties—Mengla County*, 8.

8. State Council of the People's Republic of China, "Outline for Development-Oriented Poverty Reduction for China's Rural Areas (2011–2020)."

9. State Council of the People's Republic of China, "Outline for Development-Oriented Poverty Reduction for China's Rural Areas (2011–2020)."

10. Ding Lu and William A. W. Neilson, *China's West Region Development: Domestic Strategies and Global Implications* (Singapore: World Scientific, 2004), 8.

11. State Council Information Office, "Decision on Major Issues concerning Comprehensively Deepening Reforms [中共中央關於全面深化改革若干重大問題的決定]," November 19, 2013, http://www.scio.gov.cn/32344/32345/32347/32756/xgzc32762/Document/1415757/1415757.htm (accessed October 18, 2019).

12. People's Government of Xishuangbanna Dai Autonomous Prefecture, "The State Council Information Office Held a Press Conference on the Establishment of the Mengla (Mohan) Key Development and Opening Up Experimental Zones [勐臘(磨憨)重點開發開放試驗區獲國務院批准設立新聞發布會召開]," October 21, 2015, https://www.xsbn.gov.cn/452.news.detail.dhtml?news_id=33911 (accessed September 14, 2019).

13. Lin, *The Research Series on the Western Yunnan Border Counties—Mengla County*, 8, 14.

14. Andrew Walker, *The Legend of the Golden Boat: Regulation, Trade and Traders in the Borderlands of Laos, Thailand, China, and Burma* (Honolulu: University of Hawaii Press, 1999), 30.

15. Chris Beyrer, *War in the Blood: Sex, Politics and AIDS in Southeast Asia* (London: Palgrave Macmillan, 1998), 106.

16. Beyrer, *War in the Blood*, 75.

17. Lin, *The Research Series on the Western Yunnan Border Counties—Mengla County*, 12.

18. Xiaolin Guo, *Towards Resolution: China in the Myanmar Issue* (Washington, DC, and Uppsala: Central Asia-Caucasus Institute & Silk Road Studies Program, Johns Hopkins University—SAIS and Uppsala University, 2007), 53.

19. People's Government of Yunnan Province, "Deciphering Master Plan for the Mengla (Mohan) Key Development and Opening Up Experimental Zones Construction [解讀《勐臘(磨憨)重點開發開放試驗區建設總體規劃》]," May 25, 2016, http://www.yn.gov.cn/zwgk/zcjd/bmjd/201904/t20190404_154908.html (accessed November 24, 2019).

20. Department of Transport of Yunnan Province, "Survey and Design of Xiaomo Highway Renovation and Upgrading Project by Yunnan Transportation Planning and Design Institute Co., Ltd. [雲南交通規劃設計研究院有限公司小磨高速改擴建工程勘察設計側記]," October 16, 2018, http://www.ynjtt.com/Item/225520.aspx (accessed November 5, 2019).

21. "Nanla New District Is Emerging at the Starting Point of Ancient Tea Horse Road [在千年茶馬古道的起點上，南臘新區崛地而起]," *Sina News*, December 24, 2018, http://news.dichan.sina.com.cn/2018/12/24/1224113.html (accessed November 10, 2019).

22. Haicheng Group, "About Haicheng [關於海誠]," http://www.yn-hc.cn/col.jsp?id=135 (accessed November 10, 2019).

23. Haicheng Group, "Gaozhuang Xishuangjing [告莊西雙景]," http://www.yn-hc.cn/nd.jsp?id=35#_jcp=1 (accessed November 10, 2019).

24. "Gaozhuang Xishuangjing: Bringing Ancient Tai Kingdom of Sip Song Pan Na Back to Life [告莊西雙景：還原你夢中的傣鄉]," *Ifeng*, September 6, 2019, https://feng.ifeng.com/c/7pkRHKkVoh2 (accessed November 25, 2019).

25. Haicheng Group, "Boten Special Economic Zone in Laos [老撾磨丁經濟區]," http://www.yn-hc.cn/nd.jsp?id=39#_jcp=1 (accessed November 10, 2019).

26. Suwatchai Songwanich, "Laos—China's Gateway to Southeast Asia," *Nation Thailand*, July 31, 2016, https://www.nationthailand.com/noname/30291836 (accessed March 7, 2019).

27. Haicheng Group, "Homepage [首頁]," http://www.yn-hc.cn (accessed November 10, 2019).

28. State Council of the People's Republic of China, "Decision on Major Issues concerning Comprehensively Deepening Reforms."

29. Wall text, "Preface [前言]," in *No One Must Be Left Behind: Witnessing the Battle against Poverty in Mengla County Exhibition* [不能沒有你：勐臘決戰脫貧攻堅紀實] (Mengla, Nanla New Town Planning Exhibition Center, 2019).

30. Lin, *The Research Series on the Western Yunnan Border Counties—Mengla County*, 3.

31. Jianchu Xu, "The Political, Social, and Ecological Transformation of a Landscape," *Mountain Research and Development* 26, no. 3 (2006), 254–262.

32. Huafang Chen, Zhuang-Fang Yi, Dietrich Schmidt-Vogt, Antje Ahrends, Philip Beckschäfer, Christoph Kleinn, Sailesh Ranjitkar, and Jianchu Xu, "Pushing the Limits: The Pattern and Dynamics of Rubber Monoculture Expansion in Xishuangbanna, SW China." *PloS One* 11, no. 2 (2016), e0150062.

33. Janet C. Sturgeon, "The Cultural Politics of Ethnic Identity in Xishuangbanna, China: Tea and Rubber as 'Cash Crops' and 'Commodities,'" *Journal of Current Chinese Affairs* 41, no. 4 (2012), 109–131.

34. Devastating flooding in 1998 affected the Yangtze, Nen, Songhua, and Pearl River basins, killing more than 3,600 people, displacing 240 million people, flooding 25 million hectares of farmland, and causing damage estimated at over US$20 billion. See Neal Lott, Tom Ross, Axel Graumann, and Mark Lackey, *Flooding in China Summer 1998* (Asheville, NC: NOAA's National Climate Data Center, 2008).

35. Graeme Lang, "Forests, Floods, and the Environmental State in China," *Organization & Environment* 15, no. 2 (2002), 109–130.

36. Yan-qiong Ye, Chen Guo-jie, and Fan Hong, "Impacts of the 'Grain for Green' Project on Rural Communities in the Upper Min River Basin, Sichuan, China," *Mountain Research and Development* 23, no. 4 (2003), 345–352.

37. Sturgeon, "The Cultural Politics of Ethnic Identity in Xishuangbanna, China."

38. Wall text, "Preface."

39. The thirteen minority nationalities in Xishuangbanna identified in the 1950s by the state research teams were further categorized into twenty-six ethnic groups in Mengla. According to the statistics from Mengla County People's Government, among the total population of 293,900 in Mengla County, Dai people made up 28.5 percent; Hani people, 23.38 percent; Yao people, 7.52 percent; Yi people, 7.08 percent; and other minorities, 4.4 percent. Statistics Bureau of Mengla County, "Statistical Communiqué of Mengla County on the 2019 National Economic and Social Development [勐臘縣2019年國民經濟和社會發展統計公報]," August 10, 2020, https://www.ynml.gov.cn/tjj/109000.news.detail.dhtml?news_id=1183070 (accessed March 4, 2021).

40. Wall text, "Preface."

41. The mounting trade tensions between China and the United States, the two largest economies in the world, are caused by the lopsided bilateral trade, with the United States running a large and growing trade deficit with China. The US trade shortfall rose from US$103.1 billion in 2002 to US$375.6 billion in 2017 before the start of the trade war in July 2018, when both the United States and China placed tariffs on hundreds of billions of dollars of each other's products.

42. Wall text, "Preface."

43. The exhibition is divided into six sections: Cordial Support [親切關懷], Genuine Collaboration [凝心聚力], Overcome Difficulties [攻堅克難], Striving Upward [自強不息], Grand Blueprints [宏偉藍圖], and Achievement Sharing [成果共享].

44. Wall text, exhibit section "Overcome Difficulties."

45. Wall text, exhibit section "Grand Blueprints."

46. Wall text, exhibit section "Achievement Sharing."

47. Peter Vandergeest and Nancy Peluso, "Territorialization and State Power in Thailand," *Theory and Society* 24, no. 3 (1995), 385–426, 387.

48. The idea of a nexus between environmental degradation and poverty can be traced to the eighteenth-century Malthusian concept of a dreadful poverty-environment spiral where the poor people regularly destroy the natural-resource system for the fulfillment of their short-term needs. The "poverty-environment nexus" has been criticized by many scholars as being unable to capture the many-patterned nexus between the environment and development.

49. People's Government of Xishuangbanna Dai Autonomous Prefecture, "Announcement

Regarding the Revision of the Outline of Mengla County Urban and Rural Master Plan (2016–2030) [關於修改勐臘縣城鄉總體規劃 (2016–2030) 綱要的通知]," November 13, 2017, https://www.xsbn.gov.cn/123.news.detail.dhtml?news_id=36628 (accessed October 17, 2019).

50. People's Government of Yunnan Province, "Deciphering Master Plan for the Mengla (Mohan) Key Development and Opening Up Experimental Zones Construction."

51. My conversations with Mrs. Wu and Mr. Liu (salesperson at Boten Special Economic Zone Planning Exhibition Center), in March 2019.

52. "Gaozhuang Xishuangjing: Bringing Ancient Tai Kingdom of Sip Song Pan Na Back to Life."

53. See, for example, Keith Barney, "Laos and the Making of a 'Relational' Resource Frontier," *Geographical Journal* 175, no. 2 (2009), 146–159; Pinkaew Laungaramsri, "Frontier Capitalism and the Expansion of Rubber Plantations in Southern Laos," *Journal of Southeast Asian Studies* 43, no. 3 (2012), 463–477; and Alice B. Kelly and Nancy Peluso, "Frontiers of Commodification: State Lands and Their Formalization," *Society & Natural Resources* 28, no. 5 (2015), 473–495.

54. Home purchase restriction [住房限購政策] was first started in Beijing in May 2010 and then progressively implemented in most major cities in China. It prohibits resident households from buying more than two homes and nonresident households from buying more than one home.

55. Michael B. Dwyer, "'They will not automatically benefit': The Politics of Infrastructure Development in Laos's Northern Economic Corridor," *Political Geography* 78 (2020), 102–118.

THE XINJIANG MODEL

Road Construction in the Kyrgyzstan–China Borderlands

Viewed from the aircraft window on a flight from Bishkek to Osh, the Bishkek–Osh Road appeared as a thin but clearly visible white line winding its way through ranges of snowcapped mountains. The original itinerary, after attending a conference in Bishkek, the capital of Kyrgyzstan, was to fly from Bishkek to Kashgar in Xinjiang in China's far west. The journey had to be rearranged after discovering that the three Air Manus flights a week from Bishkek to Kashgar (the only service between those two cities) had recently been terminated.[1] Consequently, a two-hour Bishkek to Kashgar direct flight became a three-day multimodal trek from August 15 to 17, 2018, including a flight from Bishkek to Osh and a two-day road trip from Osh to Irkeshtam on the Kyrgyzstan-China border.

Over the past two decades, key development banks, private sector stakeholders, and Kyrgyz state agencies have routinely referred to Kyrgyzstan as a landlocked country with formidable geographic barriers.[2] Bordered by Tajikistan on the southwest, Uzbekistan on the west and southwest, Kazakhstan on the north, and China on the east, Kyrgyzstan is an important strategic player in any grand vision of reinvigorating Central Asia's historical role as a land bridge between Asia and Europe. The entire republic is less than one-eighth the size of the Xinjiang Uygur Autonomous Region (XUAR) of China. Located at the western edge of the Tianshan Mountains, approximately 94 percent of its land area is mountainous terrain, with its southern border extending to the Pamir Mountains. As in most Central Asian countries, the majority of roads in Kyrgyzstan were built during the Soviet era. Roads radiating out from Moscow linked the political heart of the USSR with the capitals of the other Soviet republics. Since these former republics became independent in the early 1990s, these roads have become fragmented as new national boundaries have been established.[3]

FIGURE II.2.1
Aerial view of the Tianshan mountain range from the Bishkek to Osh flight, with the Bishkek–Osh Road is visible in the upper right, August 2018.

As the original political logic behind the old road network vanished, the degradation of the roads themselves has been compounded by lack of maintenance, presenting increasing challenges to the region's transport sectors.

The transformation of the Bishkek–Osh Road in the post-Soviet era reflects these challenges. For more than eight decades, the 620-kilometer Bishkek–Osh Road, built by the Soviet Union for military purposes before World War II, was the only direct land link between the southern and northern parts of Kyrgyzstan. The road passes through four of the seven provinces of Kyrgyzstan and links the country's two major population centers.[4] It is considered the most critical road in Kyrgyzstan, a country that is mostly dependent on road transportation for its domestic and international connectivity. During the Soviet era, Kyrgyzstan could be bypassed by going through the capital city of its neighbor Uzbekistan: Tashkent. This route was considered necessary because the Bishkek–Osh Road passes through extremely mountainous territory and is subject to snow avalanches and landslides. However, persistent border disputes between Kyrgyzstan and Uzbekistan since the collapse of the Soviet Union have resulted in the abandonment of the Bishkek-Tashkent-Osh bypass, known for its fairly flat terrain and good road conditions.[5]

In this context, following the independence of Kyrgyzstan in the early 1990s, strengthening the linkage between Bishkek and Osh within Kyrgyzstan's borders has become a top priority for the international development organizations and Kyrgyz state agencies. The Bishkek–Osh Road is at the center of laborious efforts to overcome the country's formidable topographic barriers. Projects to upgrade the Soviet-built road were kick-started by Japanese and Euro-American multilateral development organizations, in particular through the Central Asia Regional Economic Cooperation (CAREC) Program established by the Asian Development Bank (ADB) in 1997.[6] Rehabilitation of the Bishkek–Osh Road started in 1996, with the first (1996–2001), second (1998–2005), and third (2001–2007) projects funded by loans from the ADB and other development partners, including the Japan International Cooperation Agency and Islamic Development Bank.[7]

Representing one-third of the core international road corridor network in Kyrgyzstan, the Bishkek–Osh Road rehabilitation project was actively promoted by the ADB not only to connect the two major cities within Kyrgyzstan but also to help transform Kyrgyzstan "From Landlocked to Linked In" by establishing international transport corridors leading in and out of the country.[8] The ADB established the CAREC Program in 1997 to encourage economic cooperation between the countries of the Central Asian region. Six CAREC corridors consisting of 51,100 kilometers of roads and 36,800 kilometers of railways were selected to link up the region's key economic hubs and connect the landlocked CAREC countries to other Eurasian and global markets. The Bishkek–Osh Road pilot project forms part of CAREC Corridor 3, which consists of 6,900 kilometers of roadways and 4,800 kilometers of railways, running from the western and southern Siberian region of the Russian Federation through Afghanistan, Kazakhstan, Kyrgyzstan, Tajikistan, Turkmenistan, and Uzbekistan to the Middle East and South Asia.[9]

The first three Bishkek–Osh Road rehabilitation projects all experienced serious delays for various reasons. The most obvious challenge was that the road between Bishkek and Osh passes through exceptionally difficult topography with steep mountains rising over 3,000 MASL. This terrain necessitated frequent and ongoing design modifications in response to the results of geological investigations that were being continuously carried out even after construction was initiated. Rehabilitation proved impractical at several locations along the road, and completely new construction works were necessary. For example, new road construction was carried out to avoid hairpin bends and overly steep slopes. Gabion retaining structures and other additional slope stabilization measures were necessary where risks of landslides and rockfalls were identified. The unreliable supply of road construction machinery purchased from Russia further delayed construction work, as the project period overlapped with the 1998 Russian financial crisis, paralyzing material production. The situation was exacerbated by a political dispute with neighboring Uzbekistan, resulting in the closure of the Kyrgyz-Uzbek border and substantial rerouting and delay of material transportation.[10]

With the launch of the fourth Bishkek–Osh Road rehabilitation project (2014–2019), the effort to rehabilitate the Soviet-built 620-kilometer road continued. However, given that even the successful completion of rehabilitation projects cannot avoid temporary road closures due to frequent snowstorms and avalanches during

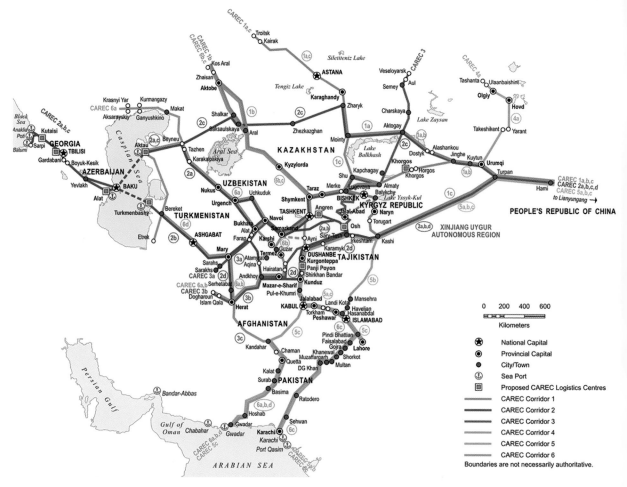

FIGURE II.2.2
Alignments of the six multimodal corridors under the Central Asia Regional Economic Cooperation (CAREC) Program. Asian Development Bank, *CAREC Transport and Trade Facilitation Strategy 2020* (Manila: Asian Development Bank, 2014), 14.

winter, an alternative route linking Bishkek and Osh is considered a necessity. One of the first plans submitted to the Kyrgyz government for the alternative Bishkek–Osh Road was made by the China Road and Bridge Corporation (CRBC) in 2010.[11] In 2014, the same year that the fourth Bishkek–Osh Road rehabilitation project was launched, the CRBC became the main contractor for the Alternative Bishkek–Osh Road, officially known as the Alternative North-South Road Project. The construction of Projects 1 and 2 of the Alternative Bishkek–Osh Road started in 2014 and 2015, respectively, with completion anticipated in 2021.[12]

Instead of traversing Uzbekistan, the Alternative Bishkek–Osh Road will pass through the town of Balykchy at the western end of Lake Issyk-Kul and the city of Jalal-Abad at the eastern edge of the Fergana Valley near the border with Uzbekistan. The 722-kilometer route proposed by the CRBC is considerably shorter than the Soviet-built 1,065-kilometer Bishkek-Tashkent-Osh bypass and is Kyrgyzstan's largest and most ambitious road project since independence.[13] With a total loan of US$850 million from the Export-Import Bank of China, this engineering feat includes two elevated bridges and a 4-kilometer-long tunnel through mountainous terrain, 1.5 times longer than the longest existing tunnel in the country.[14]

TRANSPLANTING THE XINJIANG EXPERIENCE TO KYRGYZSTAN

Chinese capital and construction companies are comparative latecomers to infrastructure development in this region. For the first few years after setting up its office in Bishkek in 2001, the CRBC worked mainly as a subcontractor for Turkish, Iranian, Spanish, and Italian companies that dominated the construction and rehabilitation projects in Kyrgyzstan, financed by funds from the ADB, the Japan International Cooperation Agency, and the World Bank.[15] The CRBC joined forces with the Bingtuan-based Xinjiang Beixin Road & Bridge Group Corporation (XBRBGC) in 2004 and started working as the main contractor on the rehabilitation of the Osh–Irkeshtam Road Project.[16] Financed to the tune of US$7.2 million in foreign aid from the Chinese government, the CRBC rehabilitated a 17.7-kilometer section of the road from Osh to Irkeshtam, one of the two main border crossings between Kyrgyzstan and Xinjiang in China.[17]

In contrast to the severely delayed Bishkek–Osh Road rehabilitation projects, this first Osh–Irkeshtam Road rehabilitation project was completed by the CRBC in the fall of 2005, more than twelve months ahead of schedule. As one of the first large-scale projects spearheaded by the CRBC in Kyrgyzstan, the project demonstrated Chinese construction companies' competitive advantages, including high efficiency, low cost, and advanced construction techniques. Since then, the CRBC has repeatedly outcompeted non-Chinese contractors, such as Yertas (Turkey), Entes (Turkey), Kayson, Inc. (Iran), and Carl Bro International (Denmark). Another US$100.6 million in aid and loans from the Chinese government supported the second and the third Osh–Irkeshtam Road rehabilitation projects, which commenced in 2008 and were completed by the CRBC in 2010 and 2011, respectively.[18]

China's road construction in Kyrgyzstan is doubtless closely tied to its goal of promoting economic growth and political stability in Xinjiang, China's westernmost province. The CRBC established its office in Bishkek in 2001, one year after the launch of China's Western Development Strategy. The rehabilitation of the Osh–Irkeshtam Road as part of CAREC Corridor 2 from 2004 to 2011 facilitated the realization of the China-Kyrgyzstan-Uzbekistan transport corridor promoted by China.[19] The efficient and successful implementation of the three projects to rehabilitate the Osh–Irkeshtam Road paved the way for the approval of the CRBC's proposed alternative Bishkek–Osh Road as well as the appointment of the CRBC as the main contractor for the project by the Kyrgyzstan Ministry of Transport and Communication in 2013.

The proposals for the alternative Bishkek–Osh Road were part of a nationwide road plan that the CRBC submitted to the Ministry of Transport and Communication and the presidential office of Kyrgyzstan in 2010.[20] This Chinese-proposed plan highlights the Osh–Irkeshtam and Alternative Bishkek–Osh Roads as two critical axes facilitating Kyrgyzstan's international trade. Construction of the Alternative Bishkek–Osh Road started in 2014, a year after the launch of China's Belt and Road Initiative. Neither the old nor the new Bishkek–Osh Road facilitated the direct connection between China's XUAR with Kyrgyzstan. However, the roads are believed to be an important instrument to ease north-south divisions in Kyrgyzstan, thereby maintaining peace and political stability along China's borderlands, which is a precondition for bringing the BRI to fruition.

Aside from the competitive advantages, such as high efficiency, low cost, and advanced construction techniques, that the CRBC and XBRBGC demonstrated through the Osh–Irkeshtam Road rehabilitation projects, a less visible motivation behind the increased Kyrgyz preference for hiring Chinese companies to plan and construct their roads relates to the close similarity between the geographical and sociopolitical conditions found in both Kyrgyzstan and Xinjiang. Running east-west through Xinjiang and Kyrgyzstan, the Tianshan mountain range divides both into distinct northern and southern districts, where opposing spheres of influence and demographics result in a division between north and south. On the Xinjiang side, Tianshan separates the Han-dominated north from the Uygur-dominated south. The southern area is further separated from eastern China by China's largest desert, the Taklamakan. On the Kyrgyz side, the ethnic Kyrgyz and Russian-dominated north has been historically influenced by Russia, while the south is home to a large ethnic Uzbek minority with its own traditions. In general, the northern regions of Kyrgyzstan and Xinjiang are less religiously devout than their southern counterparts, where traditional Islamic values prevail. The great powers (Russia in the case of Kyrgyzstan and China in Xinjiang) have historically had ready access and strongly influenced their respective northern regions.[21] The resulting economic disparity between the more urbanized north and predominately rural south only inflames ethnic and religious tensions in both cases.

The north-south divisions in Xinjiang and Kyrgyzstan have different sociopolitical histories, but in both cases strengthening road transport connections between north and south is considered a critical part of efforts to stabilize multiethnic regions and reinforce national unity. In the two decades following the establishment of Communist rule in China in 1949, the east-west road network was rapidly established across the northern half of Xinjiang. This expansion played an important role in consolidating the political and economic importance of Urumqi as a regional power center in the north to counterbalance the Uygur power center of Kashgar. The strategic importance of strengthening the north-south connection has been prioritized since the 1970s, exemplified by the construction (1974–1984) of the 560-kilometer Dushanzi–Kucha Highway across the Tianshan mountain range. This highway cut

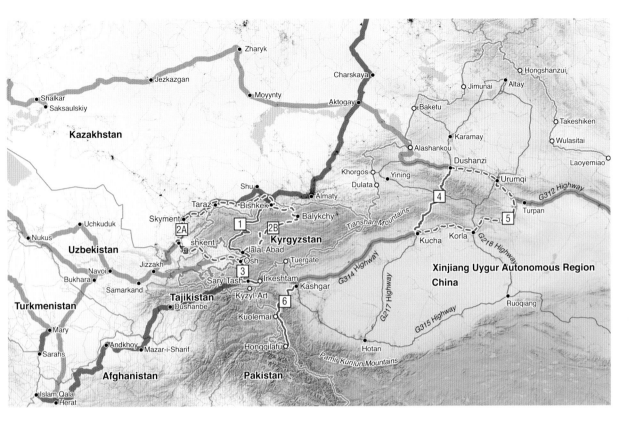

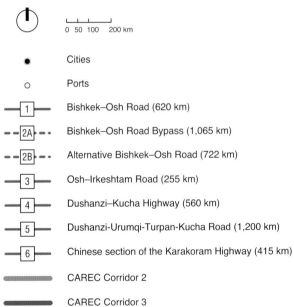

Cities ●

Ports ○

1	Bishkek–Osh Road (620 km)
2A	Bishkek–Osh Road Bypass (1,065 km)
2B	Alternative Bishkek–Osh Road (722 km)
3	Osh–Irkeshtam Road (255 km)
4	Dushanzi–Kucha Highway (560 km)
5	Dushanzi-Urumqi-Turpan-Kucha Road (1,200 km)
6	Chinese section of the Karakoram Highway (415 km)

CAREC Corridor 2

CAREC Corridor 3

FIGURE II.2.3

Map of the major roads and CAREC Corridors 2 and 3 in China's Central Asian borderlands, highlighting the transmountain arterial roads in Kyrgyzstan and in China's Xinjiang Uygur Autonomous Region.

in half the road distance between the districts north and south of the Tianshan Mountains, compared with the original route through Urumqi and Turpan. Since completion in 1984, regular maintenance and repair work has been carried out, culminating in a major rehabilitation project completed in 2014, upgrading the entire route to a high-quality tarmac road surface.[22] The 620-kilometer Bishkek–Osh Road in Kyrgyzstan was built more than four decades before its counterpart in Xinjiang, but the north-south connection was subsequently severely weakened after 1990 because of poor maintenance following the collapse of the Soviet Union.[23] This lack of connectivity was further exacerbated by the inaccessibility of the Bishkek-Tashkent-Osh bypass because of antagonism between Kyrgyzstan and Uzbekistan.

The obvious geographical and sociopolitical similarities between Kyrgyzstan and Xinjiang contribute to the former's preference for adopting the Xinjiang experience and the Chinese companies' increasing involvement in road construction projects in Kyrgyzstan. In a 2015 interview, Junwu Zhang, deputy director of the CRBC office in Kyrgyzstan, addressed the parallel geographical conditions between the Alternative North-South Road Project in Kyrgyzstan and the north-south mountainous roads in Xinjiang. In particular, he cited the recent rehabilitation of the Dushanzi–Kucha Highway and the Karakoram Highway by the CRBC as exemplars demonstrating Chinese companies' advanced construction techniques. He further advocated for Kyrgyzstan to adopt the "Chinese [Xinjiang] experience," including the planning and implementation of a nationwide road network as well as strengthening the connection between north and south, which he considered "an invaluable national security asset" as much as a generator of economic expansion. Zhang summarized the relationship between road building and national security as one that "improve[d] accessibility to secure the nation."[24]

The ideology of enhancing accessibility through road construction for national security and stability advocated by China's officials resonates with its Kyrgyz counterpart. Notably, this ideology was introduced at the end of the first decade of the new millennium, when Xinjiang and Kyrgyzstan experienced political instability. Violent attacks and riots broke out in Xinjiang between 2008 and 2012, both in the northern capital (Urumqi) and in the southern capital (Kashgar). The Kashgar attack in August 2008 resulted in the deaths of sixteen police officers four days before the beginning of the Beijing Olympics. The following year, the casualty figures for the July 2009 Urumqi riots shortly before the sixtieth anniversary of the founding of the People's Republic of China represented the worst outbreak of ethnic violence in China since the end of the Cultural Revolution. Less than a year after the August 2010 Aksu bombing, several more attacks took place in southern Xinjiang, notably in Hotan and Kashgar. These were the deadliest individual incidents in the region since the 2009 Urumqi riots. Social unrest in Kyrgyzstan and the north-south divide led to two revolutions, in 2005 and 2010. The First Kyrgyz Revolution or Tulip Revolution in Bishkek in the north of the country ousted president Askar

Akayev in 2005. The former president was blamed for causing increasing income and resource disparity between the southern and northern parts of the country. Five years later, the Second Kyrgyz Revolution or People's April Revolution unseated President Kurmanbek Bakiyev, who originated from the south of the country. This revolution sparked armed conflict between ethnic Kyrgyz and Uzbek factions in June 2010 in and around Kyrgyzstan's southern capital of Osh.

A strengthened north-south connection caters to the long-awaited objective of integrating the southern and northern parts of Kyrgyzstan. This connection has recently gained unprecedented significance in the context of constructing transnational corridors promoted by CAREC and the BRI. Kyrgyzstan is one of the first countries to support and participate in China's BRI, launched in 2013. Kyrgyzstan, with its 1,063-kilometer border with southern Xinjiang, became one of China's most important strategic partners, contributing to the implementation of the BRI in Central Asia.[25] The BRI proposes an economic corridor and key infrastructure projects through Xinjiang to strengthen east-west connectivity. One example is the 218-kilometer Kyrgyz section of the Turkmenistan-China gas pipeline, which stretches across the territory of Alay and the Chon-Alay regions of Osh.[26] It passes through the Karamyk checkpoint between Uzbekistan and Kyrgyzstan and the Irkeshtam checkpoint between Kyrgyzstan and Xinjiang. Another example is the 920-kilometer Andijan-Osh-Irkeshtam-Kashgar transport corridor, which provides the only direct connection between the Fergana Valley region of Kyrgyzstan and the southwestern portion of Xinjiang. This connection is part of CAREC Corridor 2 that passes through the Kara-Suu checkpoint between Uzbekistan and Kyrgyzstan and the Irkeshtam checkpoint between Kyrgyzstan and China.

Although these east-west linkages have been prioritized, the BRI does not overlook the importance of north-south linkages. As often quoted in the Chinese media, the "south-north connection is indispensable for the east-west connection."[27] A strong north-south connection is considered necessary to balance the improved east-west linkage of Muslim-dominated Uzbekistan, southern Kyrgyzstan, and China's XUAR. Soon after the launch of the BRI in 2013, a bilateral agreement to upgrade the China-Kyrgyzstan relationship to a strategic partnership was reached during President Xi Jinping's visit to Kyrgyzstan. To "build the China-Kyrgyzstan relationship into an example for relations between neighboring countries featuring equality, trust, cooperation, and win-win outcomes," the agreement emphasizes that both countries should "support each other in the political sphere, work closely in the security field, and cooperate for mutual benefit in the economic sector."[28]

President Almazbek Atambaev declared that Kyrgyzstan supports Xi's proposal of building the "Silk Road Economic Belt" and highlighted the importance of strengthening security cooperation with China to step up the fight against terrorism, ethnic separatism, and religious extremism, the triumvirate that Beijing calls "The Three Evil Forces." Although it does not directly link China to Kyrgyzstan, the Alternative

Bishkek–Osh Road is an important component of this strategic partnership between the two countries. Despite being committed to the BRI, Kyrgyzstan worries that an improved east-west linkage might facilitate the separation between its southern and northern halves. Kyrgyzstan has made it clear that China's involvement in the construction of the north-south corridor is a precondition for implementing projects along the west-east axis, such as the 523-kilometer China-Kyrgyzstan-Uzbekistan Railway.[29] From the Chinese perspective, tamping down Muslim influence in southern Kyrgyzstan is crucial for the stabilization and pacification of southern Xinjiang and the successful implementation of the BRI.

In addition to reinforcing the strategic partnership between China and Kyrgyzstan, the Alternative Bishkek–Osh Road is perceived by CAREC countries and multilateral institutions as a vehicle to strengthen collaboration between CAREC and the BRI. The rehabilitation of the 640-kilometer Bishkek–Osh Road, one of CAREC's pilot projects and a crucial section of CAREC Corridor 3, is chronically delayed, with construction continuing today—more than two decades after its inauguration in 1996. The 722-kilometer Alternative Bishkek–Osh Road to be built with Chinese capital, speed, and technology is viewed by CAREC as an important accompaniment to the rehabilitated road. Moreover, the collaboration between CAREC and the BRI is expected to move beyond the construction of routes connecting Bishkek and Osh, with many overlapping planning strategies and visions for the region.

Less than a year after the construction of the Alternative Bishkek–Osh Road commenced in 2014, the CAREC Institute set up a physical base in Urumqi, the capital of the XUAR, in China.[30] A memorandum of understanding was signed between the PRC and six international development banks, including the ADB, during the Belt and Road Forum for International Cooperation in May 2017. At the 16th CAREC Ministerial Conference in 2017, ministers from the eleven CAREC member countries signed the Dushanbe Declaration, an action committing the signatories to strengthening ties between CAREC and the BRI.[31] Aside from signing memoranda and declarations, CAREC senior officials have frequently signaled their intention to cooperate closely with the BRI to promote economic growth and prosperity and eliminate poverty. "The overlapping geographies of CAREC and BRI provide further impetus for close coordination to jointly build resilient and sustainable regional infrastructure, strengthen trade links, and create jobs and greater economic opportunities for all our countries," said ADB vice-president Wencai Zhang at a high-level ADB seminar in Manila in the Philippines, in May 2018.[32]

OSH AND SARY-TASH: CITIES AT CROSSROADS

As mentioned earlier, after discovering that direct Bishkek to Kashgar flights had been terminated, I adopted an alternative travel plan, including a land border crossing from Kyrgyzstan to China at Irkeshtam. The Irkeshtam checkpoint only opened on weekdays and was likely to be closed for the five-day Eid al-Adha festival from August 20 to 24, 2018, so my goal was to reach the Irkeshtam border checkpoint on Friday, August 17, before the Eid al-Adha holiday weekend.[33] A direct bus service used to run from Osh to Kashgar through Irkeshtam, but to my dismay it turned out that this service had also been suspended.

Realizing that a private taxi was now the only possible way to travel between Osh and Irkeshtam, I booked into the Chinese-owned Hotel Shanghai City (Shanghaicheng) in Osh for the night in the hope that I could negotiate a free ride or at least a reasonably priced taxi the following day. Bloggers who had previously traveled from Osh to Irkeshtam suggested that traveling the entire 255 kilometers and arriving at the border checkpoint before it closed for the day at 5 P.M. would be almost impossible due to road blockages and police inspections. Therefore, I planned to embark on a 185-kilometer road trip the morning of Thursday, August 16, from Osh to Sary-Tash, a village 70 kilometers west of Irkeshtam, staying there overnight then heading to the China-Kyrgyzstan border checkpoint on the morning of Friday, August 17.

In contrast to the Bishkek to Osh flight that only offered a view of the Bishkek–Osh Road from the air, the trip along the Osh–Irkeshtam Road gave me firsthand experience of the spatial and temporal scale of this infrastructure and the geography it negotiates. Furthermore, my overnight stays in Osh and Sary-Tash revealed the unmappable dimensions of the Osh–Irkeshtam Road, particularly the way it has catalyzed the transformation of the physical and cultural landscapes of these two cities, both at crossroads. Historically important hubs at the intersections of multiple ancient caravan routes, Osh and Sary-Tash have gained significance over the past two decades, now situated along major transportation infrastructures that have gone through several rehabilitation projects under CAREC or the BRI to accelerate regional trade flows and foster economic integration. The following section is taken from my own diary of events. It records what I heard and observed at the Hotel Shanghai City in Osh, at the Hostel Muras in Sary-Tash, and during the journey between the two cities. I explore what these exchanges and observations tell us about the social and political dynamics of the borderlands and how they influence the speed and types of traffic flow on the Osh–Irkeshtam Road.

HOTEL SHANGHAI CITY IN OSH

On Wednesday, August 15, the day before my departure toward Sary-Tash, I flew to Osh from Bishkek on the Pegasus airline around 2 P.M. After a flight of forty minutes over mountainous terrain, the airplane descended, approaching Osh at the eastern end of the Fergana Valley. Thanks to the fertile alluvial soil and rich snowmelts from the surrounding mountains, the valley floor is covered with endless agricultural fields

FIGURE II.2.4
Aerial view of the extensive agricultural fields at the eastern end of the Fergana Valley, photographed during the descent of the flight from Bishkek to Osh, August 2018.

interspersed with large and small settlements. Occupying a strategic location where the ancient Silk Road intersected with the Fergana Valley, Osh was a place where a wide variety of goods from Asia and Europe could be found and diverse cultures converged: Islamic from the west and south, Russian from the north, and Chinese to the east. Today Osh remains an important national and international transportation hub where three major highways converge. Aside from the Bishkek–Osh Road connecting Osh through the Tianshan Mountains to Kyrgyzstan's capital Bishkek and the Osh–Irkeshtam Road connecting Osh through Sary-Tash to the Irkeshtam checkpoint along the China-Kyrgyzstan border, another highway connects Osh to the Dostuk (Friendship) checkpoint along the Kyrgyzstan-Uzbekistan border.[34]

After a thirty-minute drive from Osh International Airport, the taxi stopped in front of a huge Paifang, a traditional Chinese gateway with signs for the Hotel Shanghai City in Kyrgyz, Russian, English, and Chinese. Officially opened in 2016 and located in the southern part of Osh adjacent to the Ak-Buura River, the Hotel Shanghai City is Chinese owned and operated. A media report published on October 11, 2016, described the grandiose opening ceremony of the Hotel Shanghai City, referring to the hotel and its adjacent facilities as "an integrated square with Chinese characteristics." More than 600 people attended the ceremony, including

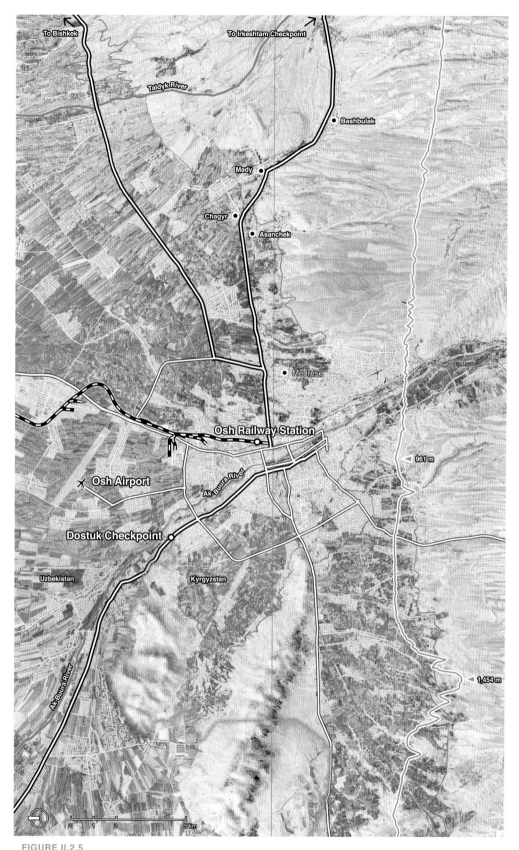

FIGURE II.2.5

Close to the Tajikistan-Uzbekistan border, Osh is an important national and international transportation hub where three major highways converge: from Kyrgyzstan's capital Bishkek; from Uzbekistan through Dostuk; and from China and Tajikistan through Sary-Tash.

FIGURE II.2.6
The Paifang-style entrance of the Hotel Shanghai City, with signs in Kyrgyz, Russian, English, and Chinese prominently displayed, August 2018.

representatives from the Chinese Consulate General in Osh, Osh city government, the Confucius Institute at Osh State University, and Chinese-funded enterprises.[35] As the largest Chinese-owned high-quality hotel in Osh, the Hotel Shanghai City is viewed as a critical facility providing accommodation, cuisine, and business facilities to the increasing numbers of Chinese business visitors to the region.

Chinese-run hotels outside China are typically known for their cheap room rates that accurately reflect the mediocre quality of the rooms and hotel facilities in general. The Hotel Shanghai City, however, is surprisingly luxurious and well equipped and has high-ranking and impressive guest reviews on the travel fare aggregator website booking.com. The hotel is celebrated for its authentic Chinese restaurant with dishes prepared by Chinese chefs, a tea-tasting room, and two luxury ballrooms. In addition to the accommodations and other facilities, numerous multilingual advertisements and signs indicate the hotel's role as an economic and cultural crossroads. Chinese-language banners advertising law firms are displayed on foldable stands beside the elevators and stairs. An advertisement for Chang An Investment Bank, a Kyrgyz bank with a commonly used Chinese name, "Chang An," which means "forever safe," is prominent in the lobby. Fixed money transfer fees for Russian, Turkish, Chinese, and European currencies are displayed at the bottom of the banner.

FIGURE II.2.7
The plaque on the pillar next to the hotel reception desk, sporting the phrase "Student Internship Basecamp" in Kyrgyz, Russian, and Chinese, August 2018.

The Kyrgyz receptionist introduced herself in flawless Chinese as *xiaoxia* (Miss Summer).[36] After paying for a single night at the Hotel Shanghai City in RMB cash, I told Miss Summer I was heading to Kashgar in Xinjiang. "I have never been to Kashgar," she said, "but I visited Urumqi two years ago as a student." She pointed at a bronze plaque on the pillar next to the reception desk, which sported the logos of Osh State University and the Confucius Institute (Kongzi Xueyuan) and the words "Student Internship Basecamp" in Chinese.[37] "I graduated from Osh State University," she said, "and I did a two-month exchange program at Xinjiang Normal University in Urumqi." Osh State University became a sister university of the Urumqi-based Xinjiang Normal University in early 2013 and was the first university in Kyrgyzstan to establish a branch of the Confucius Institute.[38] Collaboration agreements were signed between Osh State University, the Confucius Institute, and China-affiliated corporations operating in Kyrgyzstan in early 2018.[39] The collaboration aimed to promote close alliances and cooperation between the business and higher-education sectors and provide added internship and employment opportunities for Kyrgyz students and graduates. Graduating in spring 2018, Miss Summer was among the first batch of Osh State University graduates to be offered a job through such university-corporate partnerships.

I asked Miss Summer if she could help me find a taxi to take me to Sary-Tash the following morning. After calling several numbers, she confirmed that one driver was available the following day. "He is from Sary-Tash and just took someone from Irkeshtam to Osh last night," she said, "and he will pick you up from our hotel around 9 tomorrow morning." Just as Miss Summer wrote down the driver's number for me, two Chinese businessmen walked into the hotel lobby and approached the reception desk. "We are from Huarong Energy," one of them said, handing Miss Summer a business card. After finding the company's name on a prominently posted yellow sticky note on the wall, Miss Summer checked the two men in. The sticky note (with "Special Corporate Rate" written in Chinese at the very top) included a list of Chinese companies and their local contact persons written in Chinese characters and pinyin. Unsurprisingly, the companies are major construction companies (such as the CRBC and XBRBGC) or mineral- and energy-related companies (such as Full Gold Mining, China Huarong Energy, and Xinjiang Sanshanyuan Energy Development Company).

At around 9 A.M. on Thursday, August 16, a taxi driver picked me up from the Hotel Shanghai City to travel to Hostel Muras in Sary-Tash. After helping me load my luggage into the car, he said something in Kyrgyz to Google Translate on his phone. A female artificial-intelligence voice said, "We will arrive in Sary-Tash around 3 P.M." The Osh–Irkeshtam Road runs 185 kilometers from the city of Osh (963 MASL) in the Fergana Valley to Sary-Tash (3,170 MASL) in the Alay Valley, 70 kilometers west of the Irkeshtam Pass. Although Google Maps estimated that the trip between Osh and Sary-Tash by car would only take three hours, it soon became clear why the trip was going to take up to six hours as the driver predicted. Near Bashbulak, a village located half an hour's drive southeast of Osh, we were stuck in a traffic jam caused by a vast herd of horses crossing the road. Not even ten minutes after leaving Bashbulak, we were stopped again by a roadside police check. The traffic police were busy checking truck drivers' documents ahead of us. Twenty minutes passed before they checked our passports and IDs.

Via Google Translate, the driver explained to me that being held up by herds of sheep, cows, and horses crossing the road and being stopped by the traffic police several times between Osh and Sary-Tash is perfectly normal. "There was one time," he said, "I left Osh early in the morning but didn't get to Sary-Tash until 8 in the evening." The highway climbs slowly out of the fertile plain. Google Translate soon stopped working as we were driving up into the mountains, where the phone had only a sporadic signal. Nevertheless, the driver told me the names of the villages and towns and surrounding natural features as we drove past. The road to Sary-Tash is spectacular, one of the most beautiful drives in the country. Ascending to the Chyrchyk Pass (2,408 MASL), the highway runs beside the Taldyk River. It then descends to Gulcha (1,561 MASL), which nestles in a gorge at the confluence of three rivers that join to form the Kurshab River. From Gulcha, the highway follows the Alay Valley south through rugged mountains, where red sandstone cliffs loom

FIGURE II.2.8
Traffic waiting for a large herd of horses to cross the road near Bashbulak, a village in the Osh Region of Kyrgyzstan, August 2018.

above the snaking river, eventually climbing up to the Taldyk Pass (3,615 MASL) before descending to Sary-Tash.

Despite the very challenging topography, we encountered cyclists carrying surprisingly little baggage riding alone, in pairs, or in small groups. These cycle-fitness enthusiasts pit themselves against the high alpine terrain, including two mountain passes of over 2,400 MASL and 3,600 MASL between Osh and Sary-Tash, against a scenic backdrop of grand vistas, deep gorges, high snowy peaks, rural villages, and glacial rivers. We occasionally saw family cars, such as the Russian Lada, South Korean Hyundai, and Japanese Toyota, along the highway, but most of the passing vehicles were large trucks coming from or heading to China. "Chinese cars," said the driver, pointing to a truck driving toward Osh. I noticed the word "Sinotruk" emblazoned above the truck's radiator grill. The majority of these vehicles were bright yellow heavy-duty dumpster trucks produced by Sinotruk of the China National Heavy Duty Truck Group. The Kyrgyz words "Osh Pirim-Trans" printed across their wind deflectors in large type indicated that they were owned by a local joint-stock company specializing in the extraction and transportation of coal and other minerals in the Alay region of southern Kyrgyzstan.

Like Chinese road-construction contractors, Chinese mineral and energy companies are latecomers to Kyrgyzstan. The Kyrgyz mining and energy industry fell into decline after the collapse of the Soviet Union. Notwithstanding the vast confirmed reserves of precious metals, minerals, gas, and oil, resuscitation of the industry was hindered by widespread corruption, general regional instability, and an unfavorable investment climate. More recently, China's increasing involvement in Kyrgyzstan's

FIGURE II.2.9
A Sinotruk heavy-duty truck heading in the direction of Osh, bearing the name "Osh Pirim-Trans" in large letters across its wind deflector, August 2018.

FIGURE II.2.10
Cyclist heading in the direction of Osh, August 2018. The rehabilitated Osh–Irkeshtam Road has attracted increasing numbers of adventure cyclists to the region over the past decade.

mining and energy sectors, particularly in the country's impoverished yet resource-rich mountainous southern region, is a direct result of the gradually improving transport infrastructure, spurred on by a more favorable investment climate and China's BRI blueprint for steady growth in outward direct investment. The mining and energy industries are seen as opportunities to industrialize and urbanize the country's rural south, mediate the north-south economic disparity, and strengthen the country's resource and energy security.

For almost two decades after independence, Kyrgyzstan's mining sector included hardly any foreign direct-investment projects, with only a few restricted to the north of the country. The first foreign-run gold-mining project in newly independent Kyrgyzstan was inaugurated in the Kumtor deposit in the northern region of Issyk-Kul in 1997, owned and operated by the Canadian gold-mining and exploration company Centerra Gold, the biggest foreign investor and taxpayer in Kyrgyzstan, which contributes some 10 percent of the nation's GDP.[40] Almost fifteen years later, in 2011, China's Full Gold Mining launched the country's second gold-mining operation at the Ishtamberdy deposit in the southern Kyrgyz region of Jalal-Abad.[41] After independence, most of Kyrgyzstan's energy sector, especially in the south, was overwhelmingly dependent on natural gas from Uzbekistan. The Uzbek government shut off pipelines and adjusted terms of delivery on several occasions to achieve political ends.[42] To enhance Kyrgyzstan's energy security, Gazprom, Russia's state-owned gas giant, started to carry out preinvestment research into the construction of a north-south gas pipeline after it took over the Kyrgyz State Gas Firm (KyrgyzGaz) in 2014.[43] Around the same time, Kyrgyzjer Neftegaz, a non–wholly owned subsidiary of China's Huarong Energy, launched an oil and gas extraction project in the Jalal-Abad region.[44] Unlike Gazprom's inconclusive north-south gas pipeline plans, the 545-square-kilometer Kyrgyzjer Neftegaz–Huarong Energy gas extraction project is already making significant contributions to southern Kyrgyzstan's energy security.

HOSTEL MARUS IN SARY-TASH

Nearly six hours after leaving Osh, our car reached the Taldyk Pass (3,615 MASL) at about 3 P.M. on Thursday, August 16. At the side of the road I saw a white monument built to commemorate Yury Frantsevich Grushko, the engineer in charge of the design and construction of the road across the Taldyk Pass in the 1930s. Five minutes after starting our descent from the mountain pass, the road turned sharply to the east. The Alay Valley, where Sary-Tash is located, opened up before us. In sharp contrast to Osh, Kyrgyzstan's second-largest city with a population of 281,900, Sary-Tash is a small village with a population of roughly 1,500, who mostly make a living from animal husbandry, legal and illegal cross-border trading, and the income of guards stationed at the border. Despite its remoteness and high altitude, the village occupies a strategic location in the Alay Valley at the convergence of three highways leading to Osh, the Irkeshtam checkpoint along the China-Kyrgyzstan border, and the Kyzyl-Art border checkpoint along the Tajikistan-Kyrgyzstan border.

The majestic backdrop of Sary-Tash was stunning. To the south are the jagged peaks of the heavily glaciated Trans-Alay Range, a 250-kilometer-long mountain

Roadside monument at the Taldyk Pass, August 2018, built in honor of Yury Frantsevich Grushko, who was in charge of several important engineering projects in the area in the 1930s.

range separating Kyrgyzstan from Tajikistan. Located in the area where the Pamirs and the Tianshan mountain range come together, Trans-Alay is the northernmost range of the Pamir mountain system, which is often referred to as the "roof of the world." The driver wished me good luck and dropped me at the front door of Hostel Muras near the intersection of the two highways leading east to China and south to Tajikistan. A Kyrgyz woman opened the door and introduced herself in fluent English as Altynai. After dropping off luggage in my room, I went to sit on the wool carpet in the living room and chat with Altynai about my trip. I told her that I was in Bishkek for a conference and had to take this alternative route because the Air Manas direct flight from Bishkek to Kashgar had recently been discontinued. While sharing with her my observations along the road from Osh to Sary-Tash, it came as a surprise when Altynai told me that she had been hired by the CRBC for three years, from 2009 to 2012, to work on the Osh–Irkeshtam Road rehabilitation project before coming back to Sary-Tash to run this guesthouse. "I studied road economy for my undergraduate degree at Osh Technological University. The company [CRBC] hired me because of my educational background and my familiarity with this region. Sary-Tash is my hometown, and I worked for a couple of years on the road projects in Osh after college."

Altynai recalled that several projects had been carried out by Kayson, an Iranian company that upgraded various sections of the road between Osh and Sary-Tash in the late 1990s and early 2000s, before the CRBC-led rehabilitation project started. "It's not at all easy to build roads in this region, and they deteriorate really fast. The soil here freezes in winter, and there is a huge temperature difference between

FIGURE II.2.12

Located on the right bank of the Kyzyl-Suu River, Sary-Tash occupies a strategic location in the Alay Valley, where three major highways converge: from Osh, the southern capital of Kyrgyzstan; from China through Irkeshtam; and from Tajikistan through Kyzyl-Art.

FIGURE II.2.13

View over Sary-Tash, set against the spectacular backdrop of the mighty Pamir Alay mountain range, August 2018. The village consists of a hundred houses, a hospital, a school, several shops, and a gas station.

FIGURE II.2.14

The tarmac Osh–Irkeshtam Road passing through Sary-Tash, August 2018. Various sections of the road between Osh and Sary-Tash were upgraded in the late 1990s and early 2000s by an Iranian company. The current improved condition of the road is the result of the Osh–Irkeshtam Road rehabilitation project (2004–2005 and 2009–2012) carried out by the China Road and Bridge Corporation.

summer and winter." Altynai told me that a few years after the completion of the Iran-led road upgrading projects the asphalt road surface started to disintegrate, with potholes appearing. "It was a shame that the road upgraded by the Iranian company was poor quality. However, the Iranian engineers had experience in building roads in this region and set up labs in Osh to carry out various material tests related to road construction." When Altynai was working for the CRBC on the Osh–Irkeshtam Road rehabilitation project, she spent most of her time at the base camp set up midway between Sary-Tash and Irkeshtam and would travel to Osh once in a while. "One of my tasks was to coordinate between the Iranian [Kayson] engineers and the Chinese [CRBC] engineers rebuilding the road leading to the Chinese border. The Chinese engineers were using the material labs in Osh that the Iranian company had built several years previously."

When asked about her overall impression of the CRBC, Altynai replied, "The Chinese were very disciplined and so efficient. Construction was only possible from May to late October or early November every year, and they worked twenty-four hours a day during that time. One group of workers worked during the day and slept at night, while the other group worked at night and slept during the day. That was quite amazing. Everything was very well organized. There were special facilities for cooking, sleeping, and bathing. At the corner of the base camp, there was a library full of books." After Altynai completed her three-year contract on the Osh–Irkeshtam Road rehabilitation project, the CRBC came back to her in 2014 and invited her to join another project. "They wanted me to join the project upgrading the road from Sary-Tash to the Tajikistan-Kyrgyzstan border at Kyzyl-Art Pass, but it was hard for me to move there at that time because my dad passed away that spring, so I decided to come back home to take care of my mom and the guesthouse." Altynai told me she regretted having to decline the CRBC's very good offer, but she was happy spending more time with her family. "What was good about this Chinese company [CRBC] was that if you were a good worker, they really appreciated your work and tried not to let you go. A friend of mine, who also graduated from OshTU, started working with this company in 2011 and is still working with them now almost seven years later."

Altynai told me that the guesthouse had been much smaller before 2014. "My dad started to run this guesthouse around 2004 or 2005. It was quite informal at that time, and the visitors, mostly cyclists, just knocked on the door and asked to stay for one or two nights." After her father passed away, she renovated the guesthouse and expanded it from two guestrooms to six. "The number of visitors to Sary-Tash has been increasing over the past few years, and our guesthouse is quite full most of the time. I think one of the reasons is that the roads from our village to Osh, China, and Tajikistan have been upgraded. The roads are now in good condition and a dream for cyclists." Altynai described her place as an information hub. "Our guesthouse is a great place to exchange travel tips because it is at the intersection of three roads.

People you meet here might just have traveled from wherever you are heading to and can give you a lot of information." She explained that this real-time information is very important for cyclists traveling across the border to China or Tajikistan. In addition to information that the travelers exchange among themselves, most guesthouse hosts in Sary-Tash can get up-to-date information about the checkpoint working hours, which are subject to sudden and unpredictable changes owing to weather or security issues. "Most people in Sary-Tash have relatives or friends working at the checkpoints on the border with China or Tajikistan. They will let us know if anything unusual happens over there so that we can inform our guests."

Frank and Silvia, a couple from Vancouver, came back to the guesthouse after taking a walk in the village and joined Altynai and me for tea in the living room. They had come to Sary-Tash from Osh two days ago and planned to stay for another three days before departing for Murghab in Tajikistan through the Kyzyl-Art border checkpoint when it opened next Monday. "It is about 230 kilometers from Sary-Tash to Murghab, and we need to get across the 4,650-meter-high Ak-Baital Pass. It's going to be a full day's ride, so hopefully Silvia will feel better by Monday." They had originally planned to depart for Tajikistan the day before but had to change their schedule because Silvia had caught a bad cold the night before their departure. This route is not only very physically challenging but for the last few years has been considered risky in terms of security. Travelers are warned to exercise extreme caution and vigilance, especially if hiking or cycling in the Tajik countryside.[45] Two weeks before, on July 29, 2018, five terrorists in Tajikistan had rammed a car into a group of seven Western cyclists in the Danghara District outside the Tajik capital. After the crash, the attackers jumped from the car and stabbed the cyclists with knives, killing four, including two Americans, one Swiss, and one Dutch citizen.[46] Two cyclists from America had been staying at Altynai's guesthouse in Sary-Tash three days before the attack. "One evening my cousin who works at the Kyzyl-Art checkpoint called me and said the border will be closed for the rest of the week because a group of cyclists was attacked outside the Tajik capital earlier that day. I was heartbroken when I found out later that Lauren and Jay, the lovely couple who stayed at my guesthouse, were victims of that attack."

When the terrorist attack against cyclists in Tajikistan happened, Frank and Silvia were visiting Karakol Lake in northern Kyrgyzstan. "It's quite scary to realize the place where the attack happened is exactly where you are heading in two weeks. Some cyclists we encountered on the road have decided to reroute to Kashgar in Xinjiang instead of Tajikistan after that tragedy." Silvia explained her concerns about the safety of cycling in Tajikistan and asked me when I planned to leave for Kashgar. "I have to cross the border tomorrow," I said. "Eid al-Adha will start next Monday, and the border checkpoint will be closed for the entire week."

"The Irkeshtam checkpoint used to close for Eid al-Adha but not anymore," Altynai said. "My friend who works at the border checkpoint told me that Muslims in Xinjiang are not allowed to celebrate Eid al-Adha. It is no longer a public holiday on the China side, so the checkpoint will be open as usual." I told them I would not have rushed to Sary-Tash and would have preferred going from Bishkek to Osh by road rather than flying, had I known the checkpoint would still be open during Eid al-Adha. "And you could have stayed longer in Osh, it was the center of the Silk Road," Altynai said. "The Hotel Shanghai City where you stayed last night has its own travel agent who can organize good sightseeing tours for you."

The next morning Altynai kindly offered to drive me from the guesthouse to the border checkpoint herself. With the snow-capped Pamir Mountains in the distance, the tarmac road glistened in the high-altitude sunlight, a shimmering belt meandering through the rolling topography. I asked Altynai when and why the Osh to Kashgar bus service had been discontinued. She said, "There's no demand for the bus anymore because the Chinese businesspeople from Xinjiang drive their own cars to Osh and the Western travelers ride their mountain bicycles across the border to Kashgar." Although the bus service had been heavily used by the locals of southern Kyrgyzstan and southern Xinjiang in the past, it was discontinued in late 2012. The disruption of the bus service, Altynai explained, was predominantly due to the Chinese authorities' restrictions on issuing visas to Kyrgyz nationals and confiscation of passports from Chinese nationals in the western part of Xinjiang. Altynai described the Kyrgyzstan-China border as a barrier for local people: "I'm really jealous of people from other parts of the world who stay at my guesthouse. Many of them ride their motorbikes or mountain bikes all the way from Europe to Kyrgyzstan, then from Sary-Tash on to China or Tajikistan. It is so easy for foreigners to get a visa and cross the border, but we can't even visit relatives living just on the other side of it." Although she enjoyed working for the CRBC on the Osh–Irkeshtam Road rehabilitation project, Altynai expressed her dismay regarding who benefits from the road: "I was very disappointed to realize that the road was just built for big business and tourists, ignoring the locals. We Kyrgyzstanis cannot cross the border, unless you're a VIP like a manager of a company, who can apply for a business visa."

CONCLUDING REMARKS

The Bishkek–Osh Road and the Osh–Irkeshtam Road together form an exceptionally instructive case study, revealing how post-Soviet Kyrgyzstan is struggling to transform itself through road construction from "landlocked" to "land-linked," with a grand vision of reinvigorating Central Asia's historical role as a land bridge between Asia and Europe. Kyrgyzstan's transportation sector struggled in the immediate post-Soviet era, as non-Chinese foreign agencies worked to repair existing Soviet-built roads, as exemplified by the rehabilitation projects for the critical Bishkek–Osh Road, linking Kyrgyzstan's northern and southern regions. The poor structural condition of the road itself and the blocking of the alternative route through its neighbor Uzbekistan in the post-Soviet era necessitated the upgrading. It now forms part of the ADB-promoted CAREC Corridor 3. Owing to the vagaries of ground stability and the climate, economic instability, and the ongoing political dispute with neighboring Uzbekistan, the Bishkek–Osh Road reconstruction projects have experienced chronic delays that continue to this day, two decades after their commencement in 1996.

The corresponding road construction programs in Kyrgyzstan in the western part and Xinjiang in the eastern part of the Tianshan mountain range reveal the changing role of Chinese road companies from subcontractors to lead contractors in Kyrgyzstan since the early 2000s. In sharp contrast to the chronic delays suffered by the ADB/CAREC-promoted Bishkek–Osh Road rehabilitation projects, the timely completion of the Osh–Irkeshtam Road rehabilitation projects resulted in gaining approval of the CRBC-proposed Alternative Bishkek–Osh Road and the appointment of the CRBC as the main contractor. The Alternative Bishkek–Osh Road satisfies the diverse economic and sociopolitical priorities of Kyrgyzstan, China/BRI, and ADB/CAREC. For Kyrgyzstan, an improved connection between Bishkek and Osh will help integrate the southern and northern parts of the country to reinforce national unity and reduce north-south economic disparity. For China, establishing strong north-south connections in Kyrgyzstan (and Xinjiang) will help counterbalance the Muslim-dominated east-west connections along the southern side of the Tianshan mountain range, which is deemed a precondition for the successful implementation of the BRI projects. For CAREC, the China-funded alternative road is not only a reliable complement to its Corridor 3 but also a catalyst for future CAREC and BRI collaboration beyond the construction of the road itself, given the many overlapping planning strategies and visions for the region.

My unexpected detour due to the discontinuation of direct flights from Bishkek to Kashgar prompted this investigation into the Bishkek–Osh Road and the Osh–Irkeshtam Road. The three-day Bishkek–Osh–Sary-Tash–Irkeshtam itinerary from Wednesday, August 15, to Friday, August 17, 2018, was constrained by the limited transportation options between Bishkek and Kashgar and the restricted hours of the Irkeshtam checkpoint (9 A.M. to 11 A.M. and 2 P.M. to 5 P.M., Monday to Friday). In particular, my schedule was based on a belief that the checkpoint would be closed for a week for the Muslim festival Eid al-Adha, set to begin on Monday, August 20. This detour included a flight from Bishkek to Osh, the road trip from Osh to Sary-Tash, an overnight stay at the Hotel Shanghai city in Osh, and an overnight stay at the Hostel Muras in Sary-Tash. Observations and discussions recorded during the trip, interwoven with information drawn from archival documents and more recent media coverage, shed light on the mappable and unmappable dimensions of roads and the changing cultural and economic landscapes they pass through in the China-Kyrgyzstan borderlands.

Dimitris Dalakoglou and Penny Harvey argue that road construction not only "promises (or threatens) future connectivity" but also "articulates the political and material histories that often render these otherwise mundane spaces so controversial."[47] Roads can be viewed as technical systems that can facilitate political and cultural exchanges over long distances; as such, they are agents of change in human thinking, habits, and approaches to development across time and space.[48] Echoing Dalakoglou and Harvey's idea, the Bishkek–Osh Road and the Osh–Irkeshtam Road not only accommodate various local, national, and international regime interests and priorities but also showcase their struggles and conflicts. The type and speed of traffic on these roads are contingent as much on the political climate prevailing between Kyrgyzstan and its neighbors at any given time as on the geographic and climatic conditions prevalent in the Tianshan Mountains.

Encounters during the trip highlight the promise (or lack thereof) of infrastructure initiatives. Despite Kyrgyzstan's continuing efforts to expand flight connections with neighboring states, the suspension of the Bishkek to Kashgar air route two years after its first flight in 2016 underlines the enduring importance of roads to the country's domestic and international transportation system. The improvement of the condition of roads between Kyrgyzstan and its neighbors would appear to guarantee reliable travel connections for locals and travelers. However, the rerouting of cyclists after the terrorist attack in Tajikistan and the cancellation of the one-week border closure for Eid al-Adha reveal the continuing unpredictability of cross-border movement. Although the Osh–Irkeshtam Road was upgraded to improve connectivity between southern Kyrgyzstan and southern Xinjiang in China, the cancellation of the Osh to Kashgar direct bus service, resulting from the impermeability of the border to the vast majority of Kyrgyzstan citizens and Xinjiang residents, shows how this road stimulates the mobility of certain flows while limiting others.

By foregrounding discrepancies between the dreams embedded in plans and the realities on the ground, the story of the journey from Bishkek to the Irkeshtam checkpoint reveals both promise and uncertainty around the materiality and politics associated with road construction and its application in the Kyrgyzstan-China borderlands.

NOTES

1. A gushing article celebrating the launch of this new route still can be found on the Air Manas website: Air Manas, "Opening of New Regular Route Bishkek-Kashgar," September 19, 2016, https://www.airmanas.com/en/press_reliz_kashgar.html (accessed August 16, 2018).

2. See, for example, UNDP, *The Kyrgyz Republic, Human Development Report* (Bishkek, Kyrgyzstan: United Nations Development Programme, 1995); World Bank, *Kyrgyz Republic:*

Poverty Assessment (Washington, DC: World Bank, 2007); and ADB, *Kyrgyz Republic: Central Asia Regional Economic Cooperation Corridor 3 (Bishkek–Osh Road) Improvement Project, Phase 4* (Manila: Asian Development Bank, 2015).

3. David Jay Green and Armin Bauer, "The Costs of Transition in Central Asia," *Journal of Asian Economics* 9, no. 2 (1998), 345–364.

4. ADB, *Kyrgyz Republic*, 1.

5. Nobuko Shimomura, "Bishkek–Osh Road Rehabilitation Projects (I) (II)," *Japan International Cooperation Agency*, https://www2.jica.go.jp/en/evaluation/pdf/2008_KYR-P2_4_f.pdf (accessed September 25, 2019).

6. CAREC's members are Afghanistan, Azerbaijan, People's Republic of China, Georgia, Kazakhstan, Kyrgyz Republic, Mongolia, Pakistan, Tajikistan, Turkmenistan, and Uzbekistan as well as the following multilateral institutions: the European Bank for Reconstruction and Development, International Monetary Fund, Islamic Development Bank, Asian Development Bank, United Nations Development Programme, and World Bank.

7. ADB, *Kyrgyz Republic*, 2.

8. CAREC, *From Landlocked to Linked In: The Central Asia Regional Economic Cooperation Program* (Manila: Asian Development Bank, 2015).

9. ADB, *Regional Cooperation and Integration: Experiences in Asia and the Pacific* (Mandaluyong, Philippines: Asian Development Bank, 2013), 5.

10. Shimomura, "Bishkek–Osh Road Rehabilitation Projects (I) (II)"; ADB, *Kyrgyz Republic: Road Rehabilitation Project, Second Road Rehabilitation Project, and Third Road Rehabilitation Project* (Manila: Asian Development Bank, 2010), iv.

11. Yining Zhao, "China Road and Bridge Corporation: Undertaking the Tasks of Two Major Transportation Development Plans of Kyrgyzstan [中國路橋：承擔吉爾吉斯兩大交通發展規劃]," *21st Century Business Herald*, May 12, 2015, http://m.21jingji.com/article/20150512/d6d5120f9142155d67f2078929246036.html (accessed November 4, 2018).

12. Shi Hao, "China-Built Road Facilitates Transportation in Kyrgyzstan," *Xinhua Net*, June 15, 2019, http://www.xinhuanet.com/english/2019-06/15/c_138145407.htm (accessed November 12, 2019).

13. "North-South Alternate Road Corridor: Aral-Kazarman Road Opened," *AKIpress*, December 7, 2021, https://m.akipress.com/news:665658:North-South_Alternate_Road_Corridor__Aral-Kazarman_road_opened (accessed September 23, 2022).

14. Center for Strategic and International Studies, "Alternative North-South Road Aral–Kazarman (Construction)," *Reconnecting Asia*, https://reconnectingasia.csis.org/database/projects/alternative-north-south-road-aral-kazarman-construction/f1087d65-1476-48a0-a27a-76feda4e2687 (accessed March 10, 2019).

15. Zhao, "China Road and Bridge Corporation."

16. The Xinjiang Production and Construction Corps [新疆生產建設兵團], known as Bingtuan for short, was established in Xinjiang in 1954 to coordinate demobilized soldiers and early Han migrants. Major policy shifts in 1998 marked a new era for Bingtuan, which was declared to be a corporation. As one of the dozens of companies owned by Bingtuan, Xinjiang Beixin Road & Bridge Group Corporation was established in 2001 and operates transportation construction businesses.

17. Tingwen Sun and Zihao Wei, "Xinjiang Beixin Road & Bridge Group Corporation Builds a 'New Silk Road' in the Kyrgyz Republic [北新路橋在吉爾吉斯斯坦築建‘新絲綢

之路']," *Silu Xinguancha*, February 4, 2016, http://2016cn.siluxgc.com/html/C675/201602/99710486929134311368243.html (accessed October 12, 2019).

18. ADB, *Central Asia Regional Economic Cooperation Corridors 1 and 3 Connector Road Project (Phase 2)—Additional Financing: Report and Recommendation of the President* (Manila: Asian Development Bank, 2018), 2.

19. This transport corridor is also called "(Tashkent-)Andijan-Osh-Irkeshtam-Kashgar transport corridor" in CAREC documents. In addition to constructing and upgrading roads, a new long-distance railway connecting China, Kyrgyzstan, and Uzbekistan is being planned. These projects are heavily dependent on China as the key source of financing.

20. Zhao, "China Road and Bridge Corporation."

21. Neil Melvin, *Promoting a Stable and Multiethnic Kyrgyzstan: Overcoming the Causes and Legacies of Violence* (New York: Open Society Foundations, 2011); Wei Shan and Cuifen Weng, "China's New Policy in Xinjiang and Its Challenges," *East Asian Policy* 2, no. 3 (2010), 58–66.

22. Gang Li, "Delayed Opening of the Northern Reach of the Dushanzi–Kucha Highway [新疆獨庫公路北段將延期通車]," *China National Radio*, June 5, 2016, http://china.cnr.cn/ygxw/20160605/t20160605_522323281.shtml (accessed October 14, 2019).

23. ADB, *Kyrgyz Republic: Road Rehabilitation Project, Second Road Rehabilitation Project, and Third Road Rehabilitation Project* (Manila: Asian Development Bank, 2010), 5.

24. Zhao, "China Road and Bridge Corporation."

25. Catherine Wong, "Uygur Factor Keeps Kyrgyzstan on Beijing's Radar," *South China Morning Post*, August 30, 2016, https://www.scmp.com/news/china/diplomacy-defence/article/2011413/uygur-factor-keeps-kyrgyzstan-beijings-radar (accessed March 15, 2019).

26. "Gas Pipeline from Turkmenistan to China through Kyrgyzstan Will Be Built Nevertheless," *Kyrgyz National News Agency*, September 10, 2018, http://kabar.kg/eng/news/gas-pipeline-from-turkmenistan-to-prc-through-kyrgyzstan-will-be-built-after-all-kyrgyzstan-to-receive-around-60-mln-per-year (accessed February 17, 2019).

27. Shuang Wu, "South-North Connection Is Indispensable for the East-East Connection: Planning Methodologies for the Belt and Road Initiative [不通南北，難取東西：'一帶一路'規劃的方法論]," *Jinglue*, August 3, 2016, http://www.jingluecn.com/about/jlxr/yanjiuzhuli/wushuang/2016-08-03/12919.html (accessed February 12, 2019).

28. MFA, "President Xi Jinping Holds Talks with President Almazbek Atambaev of Kyrgyzstan Announcing to Upgrade China-Kyrgyzstan Relationship to Strategic Partnership," September 11, 2013, https://www.fmprc.gov.cn/web/gjhdq_676201/gj_676203/yz_676205/1206_676548/1207_676560/t1075614.shtml (accessed October 17, 2019).

29. The China-Kyrgyzstan-Uzbekistan Railway would have to traverse mountainous terrain, some sections over 3,000 MASL, with construction of approximately 213 kilometers of new lines in China, 260 kilometers in Kyrgyzstan, and 50 kilometers in Uzbekistan.

30. CAREC, *CAREC Institute Progress Report—Reference Document for the Senior Officials' Meeting* (Islamabad: Central Asia Regional Economic Cooperation, 2016), 1.

31. CAREC, *The Dushanbe Declaration* (Dushanbe, Tajikistan: Central Asia Regional Economic Cooperation, 2017).

32. ADB, "ADB Seminar Furthers Potential of Broader CAREC-BRI Collaboration," May 3, 2018, https://www.adb.org/news/adb-seminar-furthers-potential-broader-carec-bri-collaboration (accessed November 14, 2019).

33. Also known as the Feast of Sacrifice, Eid al-Adha falls on the tenth day of Dhu

al-Hijjah, the twelfth and final month in the Islamic calendar. It is the second of two Islamic holidays celebrated worldwide each year (the other being Eid al-Fitr) and is considered the holier of the two.

34. The Dostuk checkpoint was closed after deadly ethnic clashes in 2010 between local Uzbek and Kyrgyz groups in Kyrgyzstan's Osh and Jalal-Abad regions and reopened in 2017 after a deal was reached between the two countries.

35. Miao Qing, "Opening Ceremony of Hotel Shanghai City: An Integrated Square with Chinese Characteristics [奧什市中國特色綜合服務廣場'上海城'盛大開業]," *Silu Xinguancha*, October 11, 2016, http://2016cn.siluxgc.com/html/C1413/201610/6140692209581973484.shtml (accessed June 14, 2019).

36. All names used in this section are pseudonyms.

37. The Confucius Institute [孔子學院] is a nonprofit public educational organization operating at colleges and universities around the world to offer Chinese language courses and host events. The partnerships are funded and arranged in part by the Office of Chinese Language Council International [國家漢語國際推廣領導小組辦公室], known as Hanban for short, which is itself affiliated with the Chinese Ministry of Education.

38. Hanban, "Confucius Institute at Osh State University [奧什國立大學孔子學院]," http://www.hanban.org/confuciousinstitutes/node_39955_11.htm (accessed October 14, 2018).

39. Hanban, "Fostering University-Enterprise Cooperation [校企合作無縫對接]," http://www.hanban.org/article/2018-03/27/content_723826.htm (accessed October 14, 2018).

40. World Bank, *Snapshot: World Bank Program in the Kyrgyz Republic* (Bishkek, Kyrgyzstan: World Bank, 2019), 1.

41. Olga Dzyubenko, Robin Paxton, and Jason Neely, "Chinese Miner Launches Gold Plant in Kyrgyzstan," *Reuters*, September 21, 2011, https://www.reuters.com/article/gold-kyrgyzstan-idUSL5E7KL5Y020110921 (accessed October 10, 2019).

42. International Energy Agency, *Kyrgyz Republic Energy Profile* (Paris: International Energy Agency, 2021), 14.

43. Gazprom, "Gazprom Develops General Gas-Supply Plan for Kyrgyzstan," December 2, 2014, http://www.gazprom-international.com/en/news-media/articles/gazprom-develops-general-gas-supply-plan-kyrgyzstan (accessed November 14, 2019).

44. Huarong, "From China Rongsheng Heavy Industries to Huarong Energy," April 22, 2015, http://www.huarongenergy.com.hk/en/press_pop.php?id=277925&lang=en (accessed December 1, 2019).

45. Government of the United Kingdom, "Foreign Travel Advice—Tajikistan," https://www.gov.uk/foreign-travel-advice/tajikistan/terrorism (accessed August 24, 2019).

46. Larry Register, Ivan Watson, and Sol Han, "2 American Cyclists among 4 Dead in Tajikistan Hit-and-Run," *CNN*, July 30, 2018, https://edition.cnn.com/2018/07/30/asia/amiercans-killed-tajikistan-hit-and-run/index.html (accessed June 14, 2019).

47. Dimitris Dalakoglou and Penny Harvey, "Roads and Anthropology: Ethnographic Perspectives on Space, Time and (Im)mobility," *Mobilities* 7, no. 4 (2012), 459–465, 460.

48. For more on this subject, see Dimitris Dalakoglou, "The Road: An Ethnography of the Albanian–Greek Cross Border Motorway," *American Ethnologist* 37, no. 1 (2010), 132–149; Dalakoglou and Harvey, "Roads and Anthropology"; and Penny Harvey and Hannah Knox, *Roads: An Anthropology of Infrastructure and Expertise* (Ithaca, NY: Cornell University Press, 2015).

SHAN-SHUI MEMORY

Water Commodification in the China–Korea Borderlands

In the lobby of the Golden Water Crane (Jinshuihe) hot-spring resort and spa in Changbaishan National Nature Reserve, a large TV blared live footage of ice melting in Heaven Lake, a program broadcast on CCTV news entitled "Listen! This is the sound of Tianchi's thawing ice." Detailed descriptions of the structures and sounds of the thawing ice were followed by a breathless propagandistic commentary, winding up the news by declaring: "The melting ice of Heaven Lake is awesome not only because of its unique physical beauty but also because of the mighty strength and powerful optimism manifested by this magnificent natural phenomenon."

Known as Tianchi in China and Cheonji in Korea, Heaven Lake sits at 2,189 MASL in a crater straddling the Chinese–North Korean border near the summit of the highest mountain in northeastern China and the Korean Peninsula. Thanks to its year-round snow and ice cover, it is known as Mount Changbai (Changbaishan; literally, "perpetually white mountain") in China, and Mount Baekdu (Baekdusan; literally, "white head mountain") in Korea. Frozen for up to eight months from mid- or late November every year, the lake thaws in late June or early July. Live footage of the ice thawing and rivers gushing with snowmelt is broadcast widely in the Chinese, North Korean, and South Korean media. Heaven Lake and Mount Baekdu are also featured in news coverage of major political events in the two Koreas. On December 17, 2011, the day Kim Jong-il (the second Supreme Leader of North Korea) died, the North Korean news media declared that the thick ice on Heaven Lake cracked so loudly that "it seemed to shake the heavens and the earth."[1] On September 20, 2018, the last day of the inter-Korean summit, South Korean president Moon Jae-in and North Korean leader Kim Jong-un visited Mount Baekdu together. A photo of

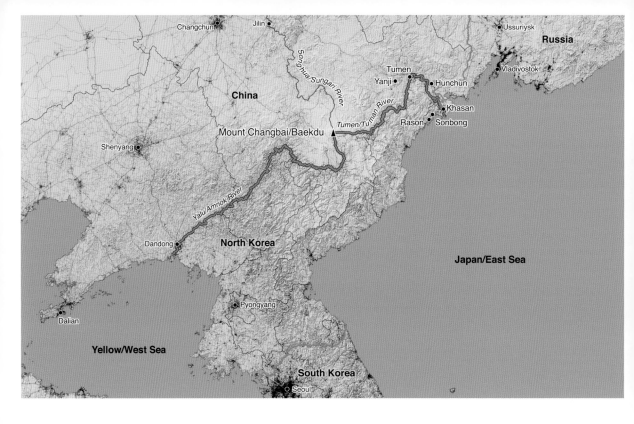

0 25 50   100 km

FIGURE II.3.1

Map of Mount Changbai/Baekdu and the China-Korea borderland. Straddling the border between China and North Korea, Mount Changbai/Baekdu gives rise to three rivers: the Songhua/Sungari, Yalu/Amnok, and Tumen/Tuman. The latter two rivers form the boundary between the Korean Peninsula and northeast China.

the two leaders and their wives posing in front of Heaven Lake and another of Moon filling a plastic bottle with water from the lake were hits on social media.

Although Mount Changbai/Baekdu is considered the ancestral provenance of the Manchus and the Qing dynasty, who ruled over imperial China from 1644 to 1912, its cultural lineage is of little relevance to the narratives of today's ethnic Han Chinese. By contrast, the mountain retains great cultural and political significance in Korea and is venerated as the cradle of ancient Korean civilization and the modern Korean state itself. The national anthems of both North Korea and South Korea make explicit reference to Mount Baekdu. The former includes a vigorous refrain: "Embracing the atmosphere of Mount Baekdu, nest for the spirit of labor, the firm will, bonded with the truth, will go forth to the entire world," while the latter trumpets "Until the day when the East Sea's waters are dry and Mount Baekdu is worn away, God protects and preserves us. Long live our nation!"[2]

Heaven Lake and Mount Changbai/Baekdu are significant not just because of their sublime, ice-white frozen beauty, captured in countless static images. A

FIGURE II.3.2
Screenshot of a news story shown on China Central Television (CCTV) Channel 13 under the headline "Listen! That's the sound of the ice melting in Heaven Lake." CCTV News, *http://news.cctv.com/2018/06/07/ARTIk6OzW9hYYtopqC2NjA7c180607.shtml* (in Chinese).

FIGURE II.3.3
Screenshot of a music video produced by the Korean Broadcasting System (KBS) of *Aegukga*, the national anthem of South Korea, with the image of Heaven Lake in the background. KBS, https://www.youtube.com/watch?v=zgozyf-nK1Q (in Korean).

dynamic hydrological process helps forge the identities of the Qing and Joseon kingdoms, later the modern Chinese and Korean states. A millennium after Heaven Lake exploded into existence during the eruption of Mount Changbai/Baekdu in the mid-ninth century, the annual cycle of the lake's freezing and melting has come to epitomize the two distinct seasonal characters of the lake and mountain. Static images featuring the lake during its eight-month annual glaciation backed by the mountain with its ever-present mantle of ice and snow are highly symbolic of endurance and perseverance. By contrast, motion pictures capturing the spring thawing of ice and rushing rivers gorged with snowmelt conjure up allusions of new beginnings, rebirth, and an exhilarating surge of vitality. If the stillness and magnificence of the frozen lake and snowcapped mountain invoke the steadfast spirit of empire or state, the gushing exuberance of the springtime snowmelt calls forth the dynamism of interstate relationships.

Heaven Lake and Mount Changbai/Baekdu set in the China-Korea borderlands lie at the crux of the Chinese and Korean *shan-shui* memories and associations. Together they represent an instructive case study of how the tangled web of history, memory, space, place, and identity continues to inform contemporary socioeconomic realities. *Shan-shui*, literally "mountain" and "water," resonates with the Latin term *genius loci*, meaning the "spirit of a place." Simultaneously natural and artificial, *shan-shui* is subject to a plurality of contested aesthetic, cultural, and political meanings. Mount Changbai/Baekdu and the Yalu/Amnok and Tumen/Tuman Rivers that flow from it have routinely been referred to as a natural border separating the Korean Peninsula from northeastern China. In fact, these natural features that historically stood at the edges of competing Eurasian polities collectively form a highly arbitrary unnatural border.[3]

The Yalu/Amnok River on the southwestern side of Mount Changbai/Baekdu became a political boundary in the fourteenth century during the Korean Goryeo dynasty (935–1392) and the Chinese Ming dynasty (1368–1644). The status of Mount Changbai/Baekdu and the Tumen/Tuman River as a boundary came to the fore in the seventeenth century during the Korean Joseon dynasty (1392–1897) and the Chinese Qing dynasty (1644–1912). Until the seventeenth century, the broad middle and lower reaches of the Tumen/Tuman River formed an obvious natural barrier.[4] The Sino-Korean border had not yet been established farther upstream around the upper reaches of the Tumen/Tuman and the areas surrounding the summit of Mount Changbai/Baekdu due to the hostile climate and impracticability of mapping the inaccessible and intricate river system. By the late seventeenth century, the urgency attached to tracing the source of the Tumen/Tuman had intensified as a result of the shifting political rivalries among the Manchu, Han, Korean, and Russian authorities.

The Manchu conquest of China and the establishment of the Qing dynasty in 1644 threw the importance of Mount Changbai/Baekdu into high relief. It was

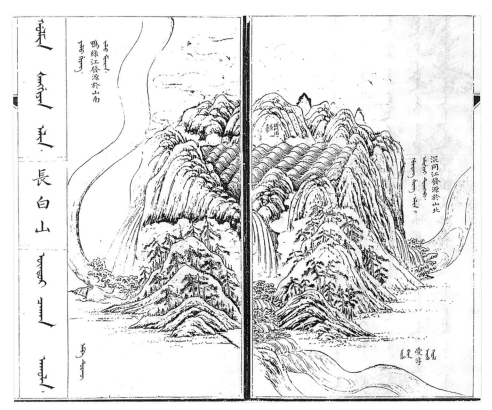

FIGURE II.3.4

An illustration entitled "Changbaishan" on the first page of the *Manzhou shilu/Manju-i yargiyan* (Manchu veritable records), which accompanies the explanation of the origin of the Manchus in Mount Changbai, showing the five peaks surrounding Heaven Lake that give rise to the region's three main rivers. *Manzhou shilu* (first volume completed in 1635) is the official history of the Manchu state under the rule of Nurhaci (1616–1626). ChinaKnowledge.de.

highly significant in terms of Manchu ethnic identity, military pride, and differentiation from Han Chinese identity.[5] An example is the often-cited ancestral legend of Bukuri Yongson, progenitor of the House of Aisin Gioro, the Manchu clan that became the imperial family of the Qing dynasty. Bukuri Yongson, son of the heavenly maiden Fekulen, who came down to earth with her sisters to bathe at a lake near Mount Changbai, united the warring Jurchen tribes and became their preeminent leader.[6] The Kangxi Emperor (1654–1722) in 1677 ennobled Mount Changbai as "the place of the rising dragon" (*longxing zhidi*), the royal ancestral mountain of the Manchu homeland, thereby dignifying it with the same ritual and ceremonial status as the Five Sacred Mountains of the Chinese Central Plains.[7] Manchu rulers also deemed their homeland of Manchuria a protected area of superior status, segregated from Han Chinese and other Tungusic peoples,[8] though the Policy of Banned Manchuria (*fengjin zhengce*; literally, "seal and prohibit policy") was as much a strategic decision to monopolize trade in lucrative local products like ginseng and sable as it

FIGURE II.3.5
Illustrations from the *Manzhou shilu/Manju-i yargiyan* (Manchu veritable records), showing three heavenly maidens bathing in Lake Bulhuri (left) and Fekulen (the youngest of them) instructing her son, Bukuri Yongson, who was to become the progenitor of the Aisin Gioro clan (right). ChinaKnowledge.de.

was a symbolic move to romanticize and glorify Manchu identity for the purposes of political legitimacy.

The area was already well known for its economically valuable natural resources and political relevance, but a clear and accurate knowledge of its geography was lacking. This deficiency delegitimized the Manchu claim of geomantic superiority over the Chinese Central Plains and undermined the authority of Qing rule in the face of increasing Russian expansion into the Heilong/Amur River region in Manchuria's northern backyard.[9] To respond to this challenge, the Kangxi Emperor launched several surveys to acquire detailed geographic information of this region, including locating Mount Changbai/Baekdu. The latest advances in cartography had become indispensable assets for the imperial powers of the seventeenth century.[10] The geographical survey of Mount Changbai/Baekdu and the Tumen/Tuman River formed part of the Kangxi Emperor's grand enterprise to map his entire empire by using surveying and cartographic techniques introduced by the Jesuits.[11]

It was a criminal case near Mount Changbai/Baekdu that drew the attention of both the Qing and Joseon courts and lent a particular urgency to conducting a survey.

Nine Koreans illegally crossed the border in late 1710 to poach ginseng roots, robbing and murdering five Qing subjects in the process.[12] The Kangxi Emperor appointed Mukedeng, a Qing official and former imperial guardsman charged with overseeing the collection of local wild products, to supervise the homicide trial in 1711.[13] A joint inspection with Joseon officials to establish the exact boundary between Qing Chinese and Joseon Korean territory was conducted in 1712. A demarcation stele, generally called the "Mukedeng stele" (Mukedengbei in Chinese), was erected the same year at the "drainage divide" (*fenshuiling*) just south of the summit of Mount Changbai/Baekdu.[14] The source of the Yalu River was west of the stele, and the source of the Tumen River was to the east. In addition to establishing a less ambiguous border along the upper reaches of the Tumen, this initiative boosted the narrative of Mount Changbai/Baekdu's preeminence among mountains and stature as the progenitor of rivers in northeast China and Korea.

The Korean Peninsula is famously mountainous. Hence the mountains themselves have a long history of inherent cultural meanings within local spiritual practices and mythologies. The ancestral Korean legend of Dangun Wanggeom, founder of the first Korean kingdom, Gojoseon, is comparable to the tale of the Manchu legendary progenitor, Bukuri Yongson. According to folklore, the heavenly prince Hwanung and his three thousand celestial followers descended from heaven onto Mount Taebaek to grant the knowledge of agriculture and medicine to the people. Hwanung married Ungnyeo (Bear Woman), who later gave birth to Dangun Wanggeom, the first king of Korea, under a sandalwood tree at Mount Baekdu. After ruling Gojoseon for 1,500 years, Dangun Wanggeom retreated to the mountains and was transmogrified into a mountain deity.[15] Earlier versions of the tale claimed that Dangun Wanggeom was born at Mount Taebaek in the central-eastern part of the Korean Peninsula. However, Mount Baekdu had been adopted as the preferred birthplace by the eighteenth century, given its increasing earthly significance.

More than half a century after the 1712 joint demarcation, Joseon king Yeongjo (1694–1776) began to worship Mount Baekdu in 1768 and dignified it with the same status as the Four Sacred Mountains of Korea and the progenitor of Korean mountains and rivers.[16] He vigorously promoted the notion that the mountain was the ruling family's birthplace and the genesis of all Korean mountains and rivers, conveniently overlooking the fact that the summit of the mountain was technically beyond the Korean border.[17] During the ninety-one years that elapsed between the Qing and the Joseon ennoblements of Mount Changbai/Baekdu, relationships among the Manchus, Hans, and Koreans changed dramatically. Joseon Korea, once subordinate to the Chinese Ming emperor, again had to yield to the political superiority of the Qing after the Manchu conquest of inner China in 1644. However, many Korean literati embraced the idea that Manchu-ruled Qing China was no longer part of true "China," leaving Joseon the true inheritor of Chinese civilization and protector of Confucian values and rituals.[18]

FIGURE II.3.6

A pictorial map of Mount Baekdu and Lake Cheonji on the fourteenth sheet of the second volume of the *Daedong yeojido* (Atlas of the Great East), showing the 1712 demarcation stele erected at the "drainage divide." Arguably the pinnacle of traditional Korean cartography, *Daedong yeojido* was published in 1861 by Kim Jeong-ho. Harvard-Yenching Library, https://nrs.lib.harvard.edu/urn-3:fhcl:3716645?n=14.

The discussion of whether Mount Baekdu is a Korean mountain emerged as a major issue in debates over Korean cultural identity. The location of the 1712 demarcation stele, approximately 5 kilometers southeast of the mountain summit, became a bone of contention among Korean literati, who held diverse opinions about the proposition that Mount Baekdu is a Korean mountain. Opponents of the idea argued that previous kings must have excluded it from state ceremonial rituals because it was located across the border. Proponents, however, held that the entire south-facing side of the mountain belonged to Korea.[19] King Yeongjo, in his lifelong mission to smooth over factional strife and secure monarchical authority, leveraged the sovereignty of Mount Baekdu as part of a strategy to strengthen his claim that he and his ancestors were indeed sons of the soil and rightful inheritors of the land of Korea. In addition to validating that the legendary ancestor Dangun Wanggeom was born at Mount Baekdu, King Yeongjo prevailed over dissenting views by citing lines from the epic *Songs of the Dragons Flying to Heaven* (*Yongbieocheonga*), which claimed that although Yi Seong-gye (1335–1408), founder and first king of the Joseon dynasty of Korea, was born near Mount Bibaek in mid-Hamgyong, his great-great-grandfather lived in Kyonghung close to Mount Baekdu.[20] It followed then that Mount Baekdu must be worshipped in compliance with the Confucian doctrine of "requiting and following one's ancestors."[21]

As indicated, unlike the contemporary discipline of geography, geographical information was collated primarily for administrative purposes in traditional Chinese and Korean geographical studies. Geography was yoked with geomancy within a nexus of imperial cosmology to demonstrate spatial evidence for the regime's legitimacy.[22] The intertwined geographic and geomantic significances of Mount Changbai/Baekdu were formed in the late seventeenth century to legitimize Qing and Joseon rule. The legitimization processes included the ennobling of Mount Changbai/Baekdu as a holy mountain and the demarcation of the border, which followed the headwaters of the rivers just below its summit. The following sections examine how the tension between the geomantic and geographical priorities has since led to contentious relationships between cultural identity and territorial sovereignty, driving contingent bordering processes under new social and political circumstances. Notably, the materiality and perceptions of Mount Changbai/Baekdu and its water play key roles in contemporary bordering processes, as revealed in the commodification of water on the Chinese side of the mountain.

The cultural and territorial significance of Mount Changbai/Baekdu instigated by the Manchu and Joseon ruling families in imperial times has been perpetuated well into the era of modern nation-states. Nationalists in both China and South Korea appropriate the residual significance of the mountain in their own ways. Given that Manchu rule was overthrown in the Chinese Revolution of 1911–1912, Chinese nationalists prioritize the territorial significance of Changbaishan and are sensitive about the extraction of natural resources by Koreans in their borderland. In contrast, given that Baekdusan stands well outside South Korean territory as a result of the partition of Korea in 1945, South Korean nationalists prioritize the cultural significance of the mountain and are sensitive about narratives applied to the mountain by Chinese companies.

A DETOUR TO THE HOLY MOUNTAIN

The summit of Mount Changbai/Baekdu and particularly Heaven Lake are known for unpredictable weather. The first page of local Chinese–Korean bilingual tourist brochures always reminds tourists about the possibility of not being able to reach the summit or see the lake due to poor weather conditions. Many people were unable to reach the top of the mountain to view the one-week thawing of the ice at Heaven Lake in 2018 due to strong winds.[23] A good number of tourists made their second or third attempts a few days later even after the end of the ice melt. The summit of Mount Changbai is packed with people on the Chinese side. Public telescopes with signs saying "Pay 10 RMB and you will be able to see North Korea" are set up at intervals along the newly constructed summit timber walkway. Over the past decade, almost half of foreign visitors to the Changbaishan Scenic Area were South Korean tourists, according to the Jilin provincial government's statistics.[24] They are easily identifiable in the melee of visitors because their tour-guide flags are in Korean and their clothes and bags frequently sport the South Korean flag.

Although the Joseon king Yeongjo did indeed include Mount Baekdu in imperial mountain worship ceremonies during the second half of the eighteenth century, the ambiguity between the mountain's sovereignty and its geomantic significance persisted for another two centuries, because the summit of Mount Baekdu was actually beyond the Korean border despite being hailed as the originator of all Korean mountains and rivers. The paradox was not resolved until the 1960s, when the summit took on a new aspirational and revivalist role in the national imagination, by redrawing the Sino-Korean border on Mount Changbai/Baekdu. For almost two decades after the division of Korea in 1945, the issue of the border had remained dormant, as China and North Korea were as close politically as "lips and teeth" (chunchi xiangyi).[25] When China started to delineate its national borders precisely in 1962, however, North Korea took the opportunity to propose redrawing the Sino-Korean border, particularly around Mount Changbai/Baekdu.[26]

Although very little is known about the negotiations surrounding the 1962 border agreement, the result is clear. China made a significant territorial concession by realigning the border to the north so that it no longer cut through the 1712 stele located south of Heaven Lake, marking the sources of the Yalu/Amnok and Tumen/Tuman Rivers. Today the mountain summit itself and approximately 54.5 percent of the surface area of Heaven Lake fall within the territory of North Korea.[27] With the signing of the Sino-Korean Border Treaty in 1962, Mount Changbai/Baekdu was officially recognized as the border mountain between the two countries. The new delineation of the border cutting across the summit of the mountain and the division and sharing of the lake were inspired by changing perceptions of the significance of Mount Changbai/Baekdu in the rising modern nation-states of China, North Korea, and South Korea.

The perception of Mount Changbai/Baekdu in Korea as a holy mountain representative of the ruling imperial lineage and therefore worthy of worship shifted in the early twentieth century to viewing it as a holy mountain representative of the nation itself and inseparable from its sovereign territory. When Mount Baekdu fell under Japanese control after the Russo-Japanese War in 1904, it started to take on an unprecedented significance as an ancestral symbol within the consciousness of Koreans. The mountain's symbolism of "Korean space" and national identity escalated with the termination of imperial Japan's 35-year rule over Korea in 1945, followed by the division of Korea between the US and Soviet spheres of influence. In contrast, after the Qing (Manchu) dynasty was overthrown in the Chinese Revolution

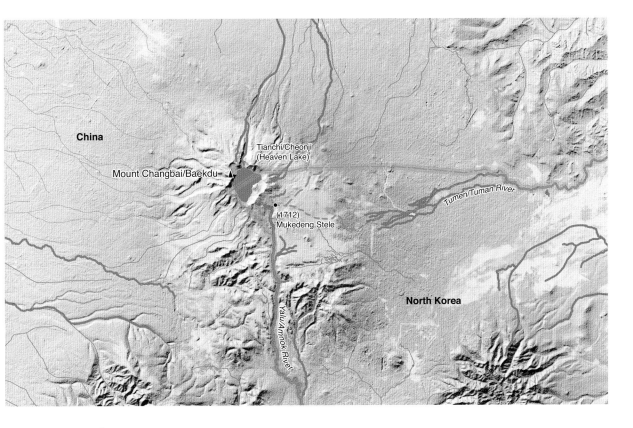

China

Tianchi/Cheonji
(Heaven Lake)

Mount Changbai/Baekdu ▲

Tumen/Tuman River

(1712)
Mukedeng Stele

Yalu/Amnok River

North Korea

0 1 2   5 km

China–North Korea border
prescribed in the 1962 Border Treaty

China-Korea border shown in the
1945 U.S. Army Map Service map (Korea, Series L751)

China-Korea border
prescribed in the 1909 Gando Convention

FIGURE II.3.7
Map showing Heaven Lake, the location of the 1712 demarcation stele, and the borders between China and Korea in 1909, 1945, and 1962.

of 1911–1912, Mount Changbai lost much of its significance as an ethnic cultural symbol and became a mere bargaining chip in territorial negotiation. China's interest in securing support from North Korea became more urgent than ever in the mid-1950s, as the Sino-Soviet relationship deteriorated and ultimately broke up in the 1960s. The sovereignty of Mount Changbai/Baekdu was the prize China could offer in return for North Korea favoring China over the Soviet Union.

While the 1962 border treaty between China and North Korea resolved the two-century anomaly of Mount Changbai/Baekdu's status as a Korean holy mountain located outside Korean sovereign territory, it compounded modern equivocal discrepancies concerning the relationship between the territorial sovereignties and cultural domains of China, North Korea, and South Korea. For nearly four decades

FIGURE II.3.8

Screenshot of an online video showing three South Korean tourists holding their national flag at the summit of the Mount Changbai/Baekdu within China. All Documentaries TV (July 13, 2012), "Flying the Taeguk Flag on Our Land, Baekdusan Mountain," https://youtu.be/L59PRv-bNjk (in Korean).

after the Korean War, people from capitalist South Korea were unable to visit Mount Changbai/Baekdu until China and South Korea formally established diplomatic relations in 1992.[28] The fact that South Koreans can access Heaven Lake and the summit of their holy mountain only from Chinese territory puts them in an awkward position, because cultural identity is so often wedded with territorial sovereignty in the modern era of nation-states. Incidents triggered by some South Korean visitors' conspicuous acts of worship at Mount Changbai/Baekdu persisted until the Changbaishan National Nature Reserve authorities imposed restrictions on any such nationalism-inspired outbursts in 2010.[29] Certain actions by South Koreans, such as ostentatiously flourishing their national flags and loudly singing their national anthem, provoked North Korean border guards nearby and dismayed visiting Han Chinese and ethnically Korean Chinese citizens, so these activities are now strictly prohibited by the local authorities.

Since then, such obtrusive acts of worship of Mount Changbai/Baekdu on the part of South Koreans who are viewed as unacceptably nationalistic by Chinese media have become much less frequent. At the same time, other diversions have been made available to cater to South Korean visitors on their quests to seek their roots. After climbing Mount Changbai/Baekdu to see Heaven Lake, tourists have a visit to a hot-spring spa as the next item on their must-do list. Hot springs in Mount Changbai/Baekdu are celebrated for their magic water imbued with high levels of hydrogen sulphide and various microelements widely believed to help treat a range of ailments, such as skin disease, high blood pressure, and heart disease. Hot-spring

FIGURE II.3.9

Tourists enjoying hot-spring therapy in the Three Treasures Pool at the five-star Golden Water Crane hot-spring resort, June 2018.

therapy is a welcome and customary way to top off a tiring day's climbing and paying respects to the great mountain. Some resorts are located on the western slopes of the mountain, but the majority of the luxurious hot-spring spas with outdoor soaking pools favored by the South Korean tourist groups are located on the northern slopes. Immersing oneself in the magical waters of the Changbai/Baekdu volcano is a less overtly patriotic but more modern consumerist way of connecting physically with the landscape and its cultural connotations.

The unique characteristics of these hot springs have been internationally recognized since the Changbaishan National Nature Reserve joined the United Nations Educational, Scientific and Cultural Organization (UNESCO) Man and the Biosphere Reserves Network in the early 1980s, but the large-scale commodification of geothermally heated water in Mount Changbai did not occur until the early 2000s. Since China and South Korea formally established diplomatic relations in 1992, the number of South Korean visitors to Mount Changbai has increased dramatically, prompting a surge in investment and the vigorous promotion of Mount Changbai to overseas tourists in the early 2000s. Mount Changbai was added to the list of China's AAAA (4A) Tourist Attractions in 2001 and to the list of China's Top Ten Famous Mountains in the following year.[30] Several infrastructure projects have now been implemented in the region, including the construction and upgrading of mountain roads and the installation of pipelines to transport natural hot-spring water from

Large *shan-shui* painting of Mount Changbai/Baekdu at the five-star Golden Water Crane Hotel, capturing the summer view of the awe-inspiring Changbai Falls, June 2018.

the upper slopes of the mountain inside the Changbaishan Scenic Area to the newly established hot-spring resorts lower in the foothills. A case in point is the construction of a 20-kilometer-long pipeline to carry water from the famous Dragon Crowd Hot Springs (Julong Wenquan) at 1,900 MASL down to newly built hot-spring resorts at 1,100 MASL, at a cost of 50 million RMB, or US$7.8 million.[31] Two five-star hot-spring resorts opened in 2009 just two years after Mount Changbai was designated as a 5A Tourist Attraction.[32] At present, five five-star hot-spring resorts with advanced medical facilities combining health care, hot-spring baths, and ecotourism are located adjacent to the Changbaishan Scenic Area.

The Golden Water Crane, one of the first five-star hot-spring resorts connected to the pipeline bringing water from the Dragon Crowd Hot Springs, has a floor area of 30,000 square meters and 400 hotel rooms capable of accommodating more than 1,000 people during the peak season. A large *shan-shui* painting of Mount Changbai/Baekdu adorns the wall along the central corridor connecting the lobby and the hot-spring pools. The painting depicts the awe-inspiring Changbai Waterfall as it gushes from Heaven Lake through a gorge at the north side of the mountain, set against the lush summer foliage of the surrounding birch forest, and draws a connection for guests between their daytime hiking experiences and evening enjoyment of the hot springs. Some pools, such as Ginseng Pool (Renshen Chi), Angelica Pool (Danggui Chi), and Gastrodia Pool (Tianma Chi), are named after the Chinese herbal medicines added to the water. Others reference the surrounding landscape, such as Sublime Mountain Pool (Qishan Chi), Beautiful Water Pool (Xiushui Chi), and Mountain Birch Pool (Yuehua Chi).

The harmonious scene of Chinese families sharing outdoor soaking pools with South Korean tourists apparently points to a new era of increasingly open and porous borders driven by consumerism and cultural globalization, an image reinforced by the culturally and politically neutral names of the soaking pools. However, as the following account reveals, more than three centuries of territorial and cultural friction between China and the Koreas cannot be so easily erased. The sensitivities of the borderland's past and the divergent *shan-shui* memories harbored by Chinese and Koreans are still alive. Borderland resources can be touchstones for cultural and political identities in China and South Korea even though they share no contemporary physical borders. The quandaries that haunt the territorial and cultural realities of today's China-Korea borderlands are the direct results of the collapse of Manchu-ruled Qing imperial China in 1912 and the division of Korea in 1945: the Manchus' ancestral mountain is firmly within a Han-dominated China, and the Koreans' ancestral mountain is far from South Korea's national border.

NONGSHIM AND EVERGRANDE: THE CONTINGENT COMMODIFICATION OF WATER

Nongshim Baeksansoo

Gaudy decorative signs advertising luxury hot-spring resorts flank both sides of the road from the Changbaishan Scenic Area to the nearby town of Erdao Baihe. The names of the spas, such as the Crown (Huangguan), Blue Landscape (Lanjing), and Purple Jade (Ziyu), are spelled out in large characters. Other low-key but clearly legible signs point to mineral-water bottling plants tucked away discreetly in the woods but operated by major beverage companies, such as China's Wahaha and Evergrande (Hengda), Taiwan's Uni-President (Tongyi), and South Korea's Nongshim (Nongxin). Owing to the local government's monopoly of the tourism sector, South Korean companies have largely been precluded from investing in Mount Changbai's hot-spring resort development. However, they have played a leading role in accelerating the exploitation and commodification of Mount Changbai/Baekdu's other great natural resource: mineral water. The large-scale extraction and commodification of mineral water in China around Mount Changbai/Baekdu began in 2011, when South Korea's largest processed food manufacturer, Nongshim, set up a large mineral-water bottling plant in Antu County in the northeastern foothills of the mountain. Soon afterward, the 195-square-kilometer Antu Drinking Water Source Water Protection Area was established in 2012, kick-starting the rapid expansion of the mineral-water industry in the region.

Advertisements for Baeksansoo, Nongshim's bottled water brand, are ubiquitous in the scenic area, along all the roads to adjacent towns, and in the lobbies of the hot-spring resorts. However, this has been the case only since 2015.[33] Before then,

FIGURE II.3.11
Advertisement for Nongshim Baeksansoo at the entrance of the Changbaishan Scenic Area, June 2018.

Baeksansoo was exported almost exclusively to South Korea along with a few other smaller markets outside mainland China, such as Hong Kong and Japan. In fact, Nongshim's decision to establish overseas extraction and bottling facilities in China was a strategy to compete with other bottled-water brands in the South Korean market. At the time, Nongshim was facing an unprecedented commercial challenge after losing its monopoly over the South Korean mineral-water brand Samdasoo. Extracted from Mount Halla (Hallasan), a volcanic mountain known for its pristine primeval forest and streams on the South Korean island of Jeju, Samdasoo has dominated the local South Korean market since its launch in 1998.[34] In 2011 the Jeju Province Development Corporation revoked Nongshim's sole right to distribute Samdasoo, secured through a trading agreement in 1998. Instead, Nongshim selected Kwangdong Pharmaceutical, a new giant in the South Korean beverage business, as Samdasoo's new distributor.[35]

Establishing a new bottled-water product to compete with the long-established Samdasoo brand was a major challenge for Nongshim. Thus, it drew on the cultural and geographical significance of water sourced from Mount Baekdu. Mount Baekdu and Mount Halla are situated at the northern and southern ends, respectively, of the Baekdu Daegan mountain range, or "spine of Korea," that runs the length of the Korean Peninsula. Mount Baekdu is referred to as the "grandfather" and Mount Halla as the "grandmother" of Korean mountains. Therefore, only water from Mount Baekdu could compare with Samdasoo from Mount Halla. Nongshim may also have been inspired by the fact that the water is highly significant for South Korean tourists visiting Mount Changbai/Baekdu in China. Many South Korean tourists used to bring bottles of water from South Korea and empty them into Heaven Lake and

Dapuchaihe

Erdaobaihe River

Jinshuihe Hotel ◁ 708 m

Erdao Baihe

Changbaishan
Biosphere Reserve

Songjianghe

Changbaishan Airport ✈

Julong Hot Springs

Changbai Waterfall

Manjiang

◁ 2,614 m

✈ Samjiyon Airport

Samjiyon

China

Baekdusan
Biosphere Reserve

Changbai Port

Hyesan

North Korea

Samsu

△   Mineral water production plants (completed)
□   Mineral water production plants (planned)
●   Townships

0   5   10   30 km

FIGURE II.3.12

Map of existing and planned hot-spring resorts and mineral-water production plants in the Mount
Changbai/Baekdu area.

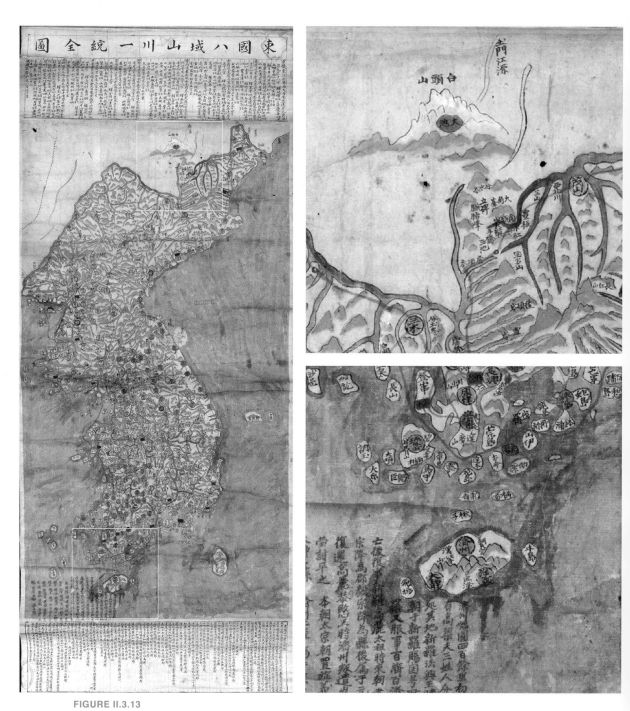

FIGURE II.3.13

Portions of *Dongguk paryeok sancheon iltong jeondo* (Complete map of mountains and streams of eight regions of the east country, circa 1869), showing Mount Baekdu (top) and Mount Halla (bottom), situated at the northern and southern ends, respectively, of the Baekdu Daegan mountain range, or "spine of Korea," that runs the length of the Korean Peninsula. Library of Congress, https://www.loc.gov/item/2011591452.

FIGURE II.3.14
Screenshot of a Jeju Samdasoo television commercial, with Seongsan Ilchulbong (Sunrise Peak) in the background and Mount Halla displayed on the product label. Jeju Samdasoo (2017), https://www.youtube.com/watch?v=O7diZnz_er4 (in Korean).

nearby streams, a gesture symbolic of their dream of Korean reunification. Despite this practice being banned by the Chinese authorities since 2010, along with waving national flags and singing national anthems, South Korean visitors still routinely fill bottles with water from streams on Mount Changbai/Baekdu to bring back home.[36] For South Koreans, no souvenir can best a bottle of water from the hallowed mountain.

Nongshim's overseas extraction of mineral water from Mount Changbai/Baekdu for its domestic market can be interpreted as a process of debordering. The fact that it is sourced from the fabled but separated Mount Changbai/Baekdu lent the water immense cultural and economic value. Baeksansoo is Nongshim's new mineral-water brand. Its image draws heavily on the cultural associations between the source of the water and ancestral Korean mythology. According to the company's official website, the name of the product "implies the symbolic meaning of Mount Baekdu" because Baeksansoo incorporates "Baeksan," the old name of Baekdusan used in the seminal geographic work *Critical Waters in the Great Eastern State* (*Daedong sugyeong*), written by the celebrated Korean thinker Dasan Jeong Yakyong.[37] By 2012, a year after the loss of the Samdasoo contract, Nongshim was already selling Baeksansoo in South Korea. By the end of 2014 it was the second-largest bottled-water brand in South Korea after Samdasoo, with a 5.4 percent market share,[38] rising to 8.6 percent today.[39]

By contrast, Nongshim's marketing of Baeksansoo in China since 2015 represents a rebordering process.[40] The rapid rise of a large, comfortably well-off middle class in China, willing to pay more for safe food and water, has driven demand for high-quality bottled-water products to unprecedented heights. Safety concerns over

China's domestic bottled-water industry escalated after the 2014 water-quality scandal surrounding Nongfu Spring, a brand that then had more than a 20 percent market share in China.[41] Nongfu Spring sales collapsed after claims came to light that it had failed national drinking water standards, including contamination by arsenic and cadmium, an eventuality that opened a window of opportunity for other brands, including Nongshim. Even so, the launch of Baeksansoo in China itself triggered Chinese nationalistic complaints, accusing the local government of selling Mount Changbai to South Korea.

Chinese netizens posted eighteenth- and nineteenth-century maps highlighting the location of the 1712 demarcation stele. Rather than emphasizing the cultural significance of Mount Changbai, a Manchu ancestral mountain, they stressed the territorial significance of the mountain by asserting that Changbaishan has always been a "Chinese mountain" and that the 1962 redrawing of the boundary to include half of Heaven Lake within North Korea was a grave sacrifice on the part of China. The economic concession in Changbaishan to a South Korean company was compared to ceding half the mountain and lake to North Korea in the 1960s. Photos and videos of South Korean visitors waving their national flags and singing their national anthem were retweeted, conflating these issues with Nongshim's production and marketing of Changbaishan's mineral water.[42]

These responses from potential Chinese consumers were predictable, but for Nongshim it was a risk worth taking, given the scale of the market opportunity in the wake of China's bottled-water scandal. In view of these sensibilities, Nongshim toned down the cultural and nationalistic narrative attached to marketing Baeksansoo in South Korea and instead now promotes a technological and cosmopolitan narrative tailored to the Chinese market. To distract from Chinese nationalists' argument that the local government is "selling Changbaishan to South Korea," the company frames its endeavor as a collaboration between local government and Nongshim, using world-class technology to produce top-quality mineral water from Changbaishan. Nongshim stresses that its bottling plant in Antu is equipped with the best packaging and bottling machinery from Krones AG of Germany and that Baeksansoo's popularity in overseas markets, including "South Korea, Japan, and Hong Kong," demonstrates its high quality. Nongshim's statement that "the smart Baeksansoo Factory in Mt. Baekdu offers healthier water for the citizens of the globe" deftly refocuses the narrative onto corporate responsibility and a global vision.[43]

Evergrande Spring

Following in Nongshim's footsteps, a number of large-scale Chinese-owned mineral-water production plants have been established in Antu County since 2012. The high quality of bottled water from Mount Changbai/Baekdu is ensured both by the purity of the water source and by the reputations of the beverage companies responsible for extraction and bottling. Only companies able to invest a minimum of 50 million RMB, or US$7.8 million, per hectare and with a production capacity of more than 300,000 tons per year are permitted to set up in Antu County.[44] Consequently, only major beverage companies with sufficient money and advanced technology can set up mineral-water bottling plants in the region. Antu County became the largest mineral-water production base in the world on completion of the largest bottling plant in the Mount Changbai/Baekdu area by Evergrande in 2014. With an annual production capacity of 15 million tons of bottled mineral water per year, Evergrande Spring (Hengda Bingquan) is over fifty times the 300,000-ton business entry criterion set by Antu County and fifteen times greater than Nongshim's Baeksansoo's 1-million-ton capacity.

Unlike the other brands run by well-established food or beverage companies, such as Wahaha, Uni-President, and Nongshim, Evergrande is a newcomer to the bottled-water industry. Like Nongshim's decision to market Baeksansoo in China, Evergrande's expansion into the mineral-water industry was also prompted by the opportunity brought about by the 2014 quality scandal concerning the domestic Nongfu Spring brand of bottled water. In addition, it fell under the umbrella of the company's business diversification strategy. Formerly Evergrande Real Estate Group, Evergrande was China's second-largest property developer by sales in 2014 and has been the largest since 2017. Based in Guangdong Province in southern China, having made its fortune by selling apartments to upper and middle-income buyers since its establishment in the mid-1990s, the company set out to diversify its portfolio in early 2010. This business diversification strategy included expansion into new territories, such as education, tourism, medical care, sports, and entertainment, and such fast-moving consumer goods as packaged foods and beverages.[45]

Evergrande's priority was to set itself apart from other domestic and foreign bottled-water brands in China. Notably, Evergrande adopted an "internationalization" marketing strategy similar to Nongshim's promotion of Baeksansoo in China, but with a different form and narrative. Soon after the launch of Evergrande Spring, the company signed cooperation agreements with distributors from thirteen European countries at a grand signing ceremony in the Great Hall of the People in Beijing in May 2014.[46] Being the first-ever Chinese mineral-water brand to export to overseas markets immediately won Evergrande Spring the confidence of its domestic consumers. According to Evergrande, its product is distinct from other Chinese domestic brands, which are increasingly at risk of contamination from nearby industrialization and urbanization. Evergrande Spring water comes from the pristine environment of Mount Changbai, "one of the three golden water sources in the world," along with the European Alps and the Russian Caucasus.[47] As Evergrande argues, it is the exceptionally high quality of Evergrande Spring's water source that inspires the confidence of its international distributors. In addition, the unprecedented success of Evergrande Spring, the first-ever Chinese mineral water to succeed in the international market, inspires national pride in domestic consumers, long used to seeing their home high-end bottled-water market dominated by foreign brands. In other words, Evergrande's export of mineral water was less about competing in overseas markets than in its home market.

Evergrande's international trade can be seen as a debordering process comparable to Nongshim's overseas extraction of mineral water to compete with Samdasoo in its domestic market. Whereas it makes sense in the Korean context for Nongshim to stress Mount Baekdu's mythical status as the origin of the Korean people, such outdated cultural mythology is irrelevant for Evergrande in the Chinese market. The high quality of water sourced from Mount Changbai, a huge resource untapped until recently, is its own advertisement. In fact, none of the Greater China region mineral-water producers in Antu County mention the Manchus and their origins in their promotional material, with the exception of Alkaqua mineral water, a product of Uni-President, the largest processed-food company in Taiwan. The Uni-President Alkaqua water official website states that "as the Manchu homeland where the dragon rises, the holy site has been well protected for over two centuries to avoid human-induced disturbances," to emphasize the high quality of water sourced from Mount Changbai.[48] Any Chinese company stressing the cultural significance of the region to the Manchus today would be considered peculiar and irrelevant, since the population has been assimilating with the Han Chinese for at least two centuries. The region is now seen more as a Korean ethnic frontier in northeast China than as anything to do with the Manchus, and it is hardly relevant to the cultural origins of the (Han) Chinese.

A rebordering process was apparent when Evergrande hired two Korean celebrities to participate in an Evergrande Spring advertisement in summer 2014, a move comparable with Nongshim's promotion of Baeksansoo in mainland China. The Evergrande Group forged constructive collaborations and encouraged the cross-pollinating of ideas across the different industries under its established brands since the company embarked on its business diversification strategy in late 2010.[49] Immediately after it was launched, Evergrande Spring became the exclusive nonalcoholic beverage provider to China's national volleyball team and the Guangzhou Evergrande Taobao Football Club, both collaborative initiatives promoting healthy lifestyles.[50] Evergrande sought to better link its entertainment and rapid-turnover consumer goods interests by commissioning a multimillion-dollar film advertisement for Evergrande Spring, directed by renowned director Chen Kaige, exclusively for its domestic market in China. Around this time, the Korean drama *My Love from the Star*, a love story between an alien and his human neighbor, met with unprecedented success in South Korea and China, drawing more than 2.7 billion views on the Chinese online platform iQiyi. Kim Soo-hyun and Jun Ji-hyun both starred in the drama and quickly became highly sought after by mass-market advertising

FIGURE II.3.15
Screenshot of an Evergrande Spring television commercial starring Korean actor Kim Soo-hyun, with Mount Changbai/Baekdu in the background. Evergrande Spring (2015), https://www.youtube.com/watch?v=JVdwLwZy61E (in Chinese).

agencies in China. For Evergrande Spring, 1 billion won (US$8.9 million) for the duo's participation in their advertisement seemed a reasonable investment because it was sure to attract unmatched attention to their brands in China.

However, the Korean stars and Evergrande Spring's advertising and marketing team were caught by surprise by the ferocious reaction from South Korean nationalists to an advertisement that was ostensibly completely culturally neutral and apolitical.[51] Nobody had any objection to K-pop idols appearing in Chinese advertisements, or Chinese food and beverage companies listing the sources of their products as Mount Changbai. From the point of view of South Korean nationalists, however, K-pop idols are expected to be ambassadors of Korean culture, so appearing in the advertisement of a Chinese product that "improperly stated" the name of the water source by using its Chinese name "Mount Changbai" (Changbaishan) rather than its Korean name "Mount Baekdu" (Baekdusan) was beyond the pale. Hence, a supposedly innocuous mineral-water endorsement became a political bear-trap. Celebrities Kim and Jun were roasted in South Korea, enduring harsh criticism for "selling out their own country for money" and betraying their homeland, despite having no particular political role or influence.

South Korean netizens and media portrayed Evergrande as pursuing a Chinese national agenda, linking the Evergrande Spring advertisement to the controversial "Northeast Project of the Chinese Academy of Social Sciences," a Chinese government-funded project to rewrite Northeast Asian history.[52] Intentionally hiring South Korean celebrities to star in an advertisement using the Chinese name for a Korean ancestral mountain was seen as asserting that Korean kingdoms were part of ancient Chinese territories. Kim and Jun temporarily backed out of the deal in June 2014 but subsequently decided to continue with the advertisement because revoking their contracts with Evergrande Spring could potentially have cost them tens of millions of won in penalties.[53] The commercial that was ultimately released features Kim Soo-hyun drinking Evergrande Spring while the Chinese narration says, "If you like me, drink Hengda Bingquan. When you drink water daily, brew tea with it, and make rice with it; the water will make you beautiful and healthy." Smiling into the camera and holding up the bottle, Kim says in Chinese, "I love only you, Evergrande Spring."[54]

CONCLUDING REMARKS

The formation of the divergent *shan-shui* memories of Chinese and Koreans since the late seventeenth century has contemporary socioeconomic implications in the context of the rapid transformation of the cultural and physical landscape of the China-Korea borderlands. Two observations can be drawn from the history of the making and remaking of the China-Korea border from the late seventeenth century to the twentieth century. First, the significance of Mount Changbai/Baekdu as a holy mountain "since time immemorial" is in fact a seventeenth-century construct to strengthen the legitimacy and authority of Qing and Joseon rule. Second, the China-Korea border at the upper reaches of the Tumen/Tuman River, including Tianchi/Cheonji, is formed by natural and human agents and is subject to physical and conceptual transformation under new social and political circumstances. In particular, water in its various forms and identities is a quintessential landscape element that lies at the very center of these constructed cultural and territorial realities and dissidences.

The contradictions embedded within the current cultural and territorial reality provide the backdrop to the contemporary commodification of borderland resources: Mount Changbai/Baekdu is identified as Korea's holy mountain, located well beyond South Korea's national border, and as the Manchus' ancestral mountain situated within the border of Han-dominated China. Since Korea was partitioned in 1945, people from South Korea were unable to visit Mount Changbai/Baekdu until China and South Korea formally established diplomatic relations in 1992. South Koreans can access Heaven Lake and the summit of their holy mountain only from Chinese territory, which is awkward because cultural identity is so often wedded with territorial sovereignty in the modern era of nation-states. These frictions are mediated by regulatory means, such as the restrictions imposed by Chinese authorities on South Koreans' obtrusive acts of worship of Mount Changbai/Baekdu, and by economic means, such as the hot-spring spas and other diversions that commodify those *shan-shui* memories.

The contingent bordering processes embedded in the commodification of mineral water are exemplified by the development of two brands of bottled water, one under South Korean and one under Chinese ownership, both extracted from the Chinese side of Mount Changbai/Baekdu. The nexus of mountain, border, and water persists within the context of increasing domestic and foreign capital flowing into this border region to invest in natural-resource commodification. On the one hand, the *shan-shui* memories can be exploited financially. While Nongshim celebrates Mount Changbai/Baekdu as "the grandfather of Korean mountains" to compete with other brands in the South Korean market, Evergrande salutes it as "one of the three golden water sources in the world" to promote its product in the Chinese market. On the other hand, these very qualities and memories can become both predictable and unforeseen economic pitfalls. While Nongshim adopted an international image to mollify anticipated Chinese nationalistic objections to its extraction of water from Mount Changbai/Baekdu, Evergrande's hiring of K-pop idols as part of its diversification and internationalization strategy prompted an unexpected nationalistic outcry in South Korea.

William John Mitchell talks about the potential of changing "landscape" from a noun to a verb: the word should be understood not only as an object to be seen or a text to be read but also as "a process by which social and subjective identities are formed."[55] Echoing and expanding on Mitchell's ideas, we can also interpret *shan-shui* as both a noun and a verb. *Shan-shui* is by default a noun, an image, or a text that we can appreciate from afar. The name "Mount Baekdu" is enunciated by North Koreans and South Koreans whenever they sing their respective national anthems. The image of Mount Baekdu stands proudly on the national emblem of North Korea together with a red star and the Sup'ung Dam, and the walls of government offices in South Korea are graced by the panoramic view of Mount Baekdu and Heaven Lake. Yet *shan-shui* can also be read as a verb, with its many cultural and emotional associations, characteristics, and processes related to particular periods in time and space. The joint survey conducted by Qing and Joseon officials in the early eighteenth century not only enabled a clear and accurate knowledge of the Sino-Korean border regions but also fostered the cultural significance and aura surrounding Mount Changbai/Baekdu. Three centuries later, South Koreans regard climbing Mount Baekdu as returning to one's roots. The place tops South Koreans' lists of "places to visit before one dies." The magic of Mount Changbai/Baekdu cannot be replicated or represented other than by physically being in its presence, experiencing the howling wind, the driving rain, the ever-shifting fog, and the rare sights and sounds of the annual ice melt on Heaven Lake.

Over the past two decades, with domestic and foreign capital flooding into the border region, the *shan-shui* characteristics of the Mount Changbai/Baekdu region are being translated into economic worth and transformed into commodities at unprecedented scales and speeds. Pipelines now connect sacred ponds on the upper slopes of the mountain to five-star hot-spring resorts in the foothills. Mineral water filtered for generations through ancient volcanic rock formations is plopped into plastic bottles in factories and whisked off to domestic or foreign markets. The might of consumerism means that Han Chinese, Korean Chinese, and South Koreans can soak together in pools filled by the hot springs of Mount Changbai/Baekdu. "The citizens of the globe" can enjoy bottled water with little pictures of Mount Changbai/Baekdu and Heaven Lake printed on the labels. A high-speed rail freight facility has been planned since early 2018 to link the recently established Mount Changbai Mineral Water Industrial Park in Antu to major regional transportation hubs, so the flows of consumable resources can be injected into new regional, national, or even transnational infrastructures. All these recent changes seem to be pointing to a new era characterized by increasingly open and porous borders enabled by consumerism and the globalization of culture. But the sensitivities of the borderlands' past and the divergent *shan-shui* memories traditionally revered by the Chinese and Koreans are still alive and kicking below the surface. The commodification of borderland resources can be a touchstone for cultural and political discord.

NOTES

1. "Kim Jong-il Death: 'Nature Mourns' N Korea Leader," *BBC News*, December 22, 2011, https://www.bbc.com/news/world-asia-16297811 (accessed August 14, 2019).

2. James B. Minahan, *The Complete Guide to National Symbols and Emblems*, 2 vols. (Santa Barbara, CA: ABC-CLIO), 82, 85.

3. For more on the making of borders between Qing China and Joseon Korea, see Ruth Rogaski, "Knowing a Sentient Mountain: Space, Science, and the Sacred in Ascents of Mount Paektu/Changbai," *Modern Asian Studies* 52, no. 2 (2018), 716–752; Menglong Ma, "Mukedeng's Borderland Patrol and the Compilation of Huang Yu Quan Lan Tu [穆克登查邊與《皇輿全覽圖》編繪]," *China's Borderland History and Geography Studies* [中國邊疆史地研究] 19, no. 3 (2009), 85–99, 148–149; and Nianshen Song, *Making Borders in Modern East Asia: The Tumen River Demarcation, 1881–1919* (Cambridge: Cambridge University Press, 2018).

4. Shuren Diao, "The Relations of Jurchens with Ming and Korea in the Early Ming Dynasty [論明前期斡朵里女真與明、朝鮮的關係]," *China's Borderland History and Geography Studies* [中國邊疆史地研究] 21, no. 1 (2002), 44–54.

5. Michael Kim, *Ginseng and Borderland: Territorial Boundaries and Political Relations between Qing China and Chosŏn Korea, 1636–1912* (Berkeley: University of California Press, 2017), 2.

6. Evelyn Rawski, *The Last Emperors: A Social History of Qing Imperial Institutions* (Berkeley: University of California Press, 1998), 73.

7. Song, *Making Borders in Modern East Asia*, 20. China's five sacred mountains are Mount Tai [泰山], Mount Hua [華山], Mount Heng [衡山], Mount Heng [恒山], and Mount Song [嵩山].

8. The Manchus are members of the southern branch of the Tungusic peoples, an ethnolinguistic group consisting of the speakers of Tungusic languages. Before the early seventeenth century, the Manchus were better known as the Jurchens.

9. Nianshen Song, "Imagined Territory: Paektusan in Late Chosŏn Maps and Writings," *Studies in the History of Gardens & Designed Landscapes* 37, no. 2 (2017), 157–173, 161. Russia entered a period of rapid expansion in the seventeenth century. In the mid-seventeenth century the riches of the Amur River valley, particularly its lucrative fur trade, drew Russian colonists into conflict with the new Qing state as they pushed farther east toward the Pacific.

10. Peter Perdue, "Boundaries, Maps, and Movement: Chinese, Russian, and Mongolian Empires in Early Modern Central Eurasia," *International History Review* 20, no. 1 (1998), 263–286.

11. Ma, "Mukedeng's Borderland Patrol and the Compilation of Huang Yu Quan Lan Tu."

12. Song, "Imagined Territory," 162.

13. Song, *Making Borders in Modern East Asia*, 3.

14. Song, *Making Borders in Modern East Asia*, 4.

15. Djun Kil Kim, *The History of Korea* (Santa Barbara, CA: ABC-CLIO, 2014), 20, 21.

16. Song, "Imagined Territory," 167. Korea's four sacred mountains are Mount Baekdu [백두산/白頭山], Mount Kumgang [금강산/金剛山], Mount Jiri [지리산/ 智異山], and Mount Myohyang [묘향산/妙香山].

17. Huazi Li, "On Chosŏn Korea's Recognition of Mount Changbai [朝鮮王朝的長白山認識]," *China's Borderland History and Geography Studies* [中國邊疆史地研究] 17, no. 2 (2007), 126–135.

18. Song, "Imagined Territory," 163.

19. Song, "Imagined Territory," 167–168.

20. *Journal of the Royal Secretariat* [승정원일기/承政院日記], vol. 1270, the ninth day of the leap seventh month, the forty-third year of King Yeongjo, cited in Song, "Imagined Territory," 167.

21. *Journal of the Royal Secretariat*, vol. 1271, the tenth day of the leap seventh month, the forty-third year of King Yeongjo, translated and quoted in Song, "Imagined Territory," 168.

22. Song, *Making Borders in Modern East Asia*, 56.

23. The personal account in this chapter is based on fieldwork conducted in June and July 2018 in Antu County and Fusong County in China's Yanbian Korean Autonomous Prefecture, in the northern and northwestern parts of the Mount Changbai/Baekdu area.

24. Changbai Mountain Management Committee, "Changbai Mountain Scenic Area Visitor Demographics [長白山景區旅遊人數情況統計]," January 10, 2017, http://changbaishan.gov.cn/shjj/tjxx/201701/t20170110_51580.html (accessed September 15, 2018).

25. The earliest record of China applying the phrase "lips and teeth" to describe its relations with North Korea was after the decision to intervene in the Korean War.

26. Zhihua Shen and Yafeng Xia, "Contested Border: A Historical Investigation into the Sino-Korean Border Issue, 1950–1964," *Asian Perspective* 37, no. 1 (2013), 1–30.

27. Zhihua Shen and Jie Dong, "Settlement of Sino-Korean Border Disputes 1950–64 [中朝邊界爭議的解決, 1950–64年]," *Twenty-First Century* [二十一世紀] 124, no. 2 (2011), 34–51.

28. Yonson Ahn, "China and the Two Koreas Clash over Mount Paekdu/Changbai: Memory Wars Threaten Regional Accommodation. *Asia-Pacific Journal—Japan Focus* 5, no. 7 (2007), 1–10, https://apjjf.org/-Yonson-Ahn/2483/article.pdf (accessed July 14, 2018).

29. Jilin Province Environmental Protection Bureau, "Management Guidelines of Changbai Mountain Natural Protected Areas [吉林長白山國家級自然保護區管理條例]," October 29, 2010, http://sthjt.jl.gov.cn/ztzl/gcjsgkgx/zcfgy/201507/t20150727_3388772.html (accessed August 12, 2018).

30. Tongqian Zou, *Innovation and Reformation of Sustainable Tourism Development at China's Heritage Sites* [中國遺產旅遊可持續發展模式創新與體制改革] (Beijing: Tourism Education Press, 2013), 156.

31. "Changbai Mountain in Jilin Province: Bathing in Hot Springs in a Snowy Landscape [吉林長白山：雪地泡溫泉，冰火兩重天]," *Huanqiu*, January 19, 2016, https://china.huanqiu.com/article/9CaKrnJTi4I (accessed September 5, 2018).

32. The Ministry of Culture and Tourism of China uses "Tourist Attraction Rating Categories of China [旅遊景區質量等級]" as a rating system to determine the quality of any given attraction in terms of safety, sanitation, and transportation. It is broken into five categories: A (1A, the lowest level), AA (2A), AAA (3A), AAAA (4A), and AAAAA (5A, the highest level).

33. My conversation with Mr. Lin, former manager of Nongshim Baeksansoo Antu bottling plant (July 2018).

34. Jeju Samdasoo, "The Birth of Samdasoo," 2016, http://www.jejusamdasoo.co.kr/samdasoo/eng/birth.htm (accessed May 14, 2019).

35. "Nongshim Loses Its Jeju Samdasoo Distribution," *Korea Joongang Daily*, November 3, 2012, http://koreajoongangdaily.joins.com/news/article/article.aspx?aid=2961743 (accessed September 5, 2018).

36. My conversation with Mr. Zhao, taxi driver at the Changbaishan Scenic Area (June 2018).

37. Nongshim, "Introduction of Product: Mt. Baekdu Baeksan Artesian Water," 2013, http://brand.nongshim.com/baeksansoo/main/index (accessed September 5, 2018).

38. "Nongshim Baeksansu Ranks No. 2 in Korea's Mineral Water Market," *Korea IT Times*, December 31, 2014, http://www.koreaittimes.com/news/articleView.html?idxno=43742 (accessed March 14, 2019).

39. "Jeju Samdasoo Losing Clout in Bottled Water market," *Korean Times*, June 7, 2019, https://www.koreatimes.co.kr/www/tech/2019/08/694_270234.html (accessed October 14, 2019).

40. "Korean Brand Baeksansoo Applies Marketing Strategy Pivoting toward the High-End Customer Market [韓國白山水發力高端礦泉水市場]," *Ta Kung Pao News*, April 9, 2015, http://finance.takungpao.com/gscy/q/2015/0409/2968269.html (accessed March 14, 2019).

41. "China's Bottled Water: The Next Health Crisis?," *China Dialogue*, July 22, 2014, https://www.chinadialogue.net/article/show/single/en/7152-China-s-bottled-water-the-next-health-crisis- (accessed October 7, 2018).

42. See, for example, All Docs TV, "Flag of South Korea Flies over Baekdusan [우리땅 백두산에 태극기 휘날리며]," July 13, 2012, https://www.youtube.com/watch?v=L59PRv-bNjk (accessed December 2, 2018); and Howan Jeong, "Baekdusan Cheonji National Anthem

[백두산 천지 애국가]," June 22, 2016, https://www.youtube.com/watch?v=SHiHVye_v0Y (accessed December 2, 2018).

43. Nongshim, "Nongshim Promotion Film," 2017, http://eng.nongshim.com/pr/promotion.html (accessed December 5, 2018).

44. "What Is the Secret Recipe behind the Increasing Exports of Mount Changbai Mineral Water? [長白山礦泉水出口增長有何"秘密武器"?]," *Xinhua News*, August 14, 2015, http://www.xinhuanet.com/food/2015-08/14/c_128127963.htm (accessed August 10, 2018).

45. Yong Zeng, *The Cultural Strategy of Real Estate* [文化地產戰略] (Beijing: Xinhua Publishing House, 2017), 85.

46. Evergrande, "Evergrande Spring Officially Announces Its Exportation to Europe [恆大冰泉宣布正式出口歐洲]," May 22, 2014, http://www.evergrandespring.com/new/index.aspx?nodeid=69&page=ContentPage&contentid=289 (accessed November 27, 2018).

47. Evergrande, "Water and Health [水与健康]," 2014, http://www.evergrandespring.com/product/index.aspx?nodeid=3 (accessed November 27, 2018). This branding strategy is not based on quantifiable information; by contrast, Evergrande most likely highlights the Alps and the Caucasus in its advertisements because bottled water from these regions is widely marketed in mainland China and is known to Chinese consumers.

48. Uni-President, "Introduction of Product: Uni-President Alkaqua Water [品牌介紹：ALKAQUA愛誇飲用天然礦泉水]," 2015, http://www.uni-president.com.cn/products-Alkaqua.asp (accessed November 27, 2018).

49. Zeng, *The Cultural Strategy of Real Estate*, 247.

50. "Extracting Huge Fortunes from Bottled-Water Industry: Evergrande Group Plans to Spend Hundreds of Millions of RMB on Its Evergrande Spring [水行業悶聲大發財：恒大欲三年砸百億打造冰泉]," *Sina Finance*, November 11, 2013, http://finance.sina.com.cn/chanjing/gsnews/20131111/073117281128.shtml (accessed May 21, 2018).

51. See, for example, "Kim Soo-hyun and Jeon Ji-hyun, Bottled Water Advertisement in China . . . 'I only love you, Hengda Bingchuan' [김수현 전지현, 中 생수 광고 . . . '너만 사랑해, 헝다빙촨']," *Dispatch*, June 27, 2014, https://www.dispatch.co.kr/104046 (accessed September 22, 2018); "Baekdusan? Changbaishan? Kim Soo-hyun's Evergrande Spring Bottled-Water Advertisement [백두산? 칭바이산? 김수현 헝다빙촨(恒大冰泉)생수광고], *ID Crew*, October 23, 2014, https://m.blog.naver.com/PostView.nhn?blogId=idcrew123&logNo=220159018922&proxyReferer=https: percent2F percent2Fwww.google.com percent2F (accessed September 22, 2018).

52. "Kim Soo-hyun and Jeon Ji-hyun Were Used in China's 'Northeast Project' . . . Baekdusan Bottled-Water Controversy [김수현-전지현 中 '동북공정'에 이용됐나 . . . '장백산 생수 논란']," *Chosun Ilbo*, June 20, 2014, https://biz.chosun.com/site/data/html_dir/2014/06/20/2014062003047.html (accessed November 27, 2018).

53. "Kim, Jun Seek to Revoke Contracts for Chinese Ad," *Straits Times*, June 23, 2014, https://www.straitstimes.com/asia/east-asia/kim-jun-seek-to-revoke-contracts-for-chinese-ad (accessed August 12, 2018).

54. Evergrande, "Kim Soo-hyun: I Love Only You, Evergrande Spring [金秀賢：我只愛你，恆大冰泉]," 2014, https://www.youtube.com/watch?v=JVdwLwZy61E (accessed November 27, 2018).

55. William John Mitchell, *Landscape and Power* (Chicago: Chicago University Press, 1994), 2.

PART III

SETTLEMENTS AND MEMORIES

CHARACTERISTICS OF CHINA'S BORDER SETTLEMENTS

In the mid-twentieth century, China, along with other newly independent states in Asia, embarked on the daunting task of redefining traditional frontiers and vaguely defined borders as recognized boundaries that could be accurately mapped and referenced in international treaties. These emerging countries considered the ability to accurately define and recognize one another's territories to be a prerequisite to their recognition as modern sovereign states.[1] China shares borders with more countries than any other state in the world and as such found itself occupying a pivotal role in the process of establishing modern national borders in Asia in a complicated geopolitical environment.[2] At the 1955 Bandung Conference, the first large-scale Asian–African Conference held to promote Afro-Asian cooperation and oppose colonialism and neocolonialism, Chinese prime minister Zhou Enlai outlined the challenging task ahead and committed China to the peaceful and cooperative resolution of boundary disputes: "China borders on twelve countries, with some of which the boundary lines remain undefined in certain sectors. . . . In defining any boundary line with our neighbors, only peaceful means can be employed and no other alternative should be allowed."[3]

At the time, a stable and defined boundary with a friendly neighbor was worth much more to the newly formed PRC than the acquisition of territory at the risk of potentially long-lasting enmities or military distractions over contested borders.[4] China resolved territorial and border disputes with most of its neighboring states relatively successfully through a peaceful and concessionary diplomatic approach. Border disputes with Vietnam, India, and the USSR, however, descended into armed conflicts over the second half of the twentieth century.

After the dissolution of French Indochina under the Geneva Accords of 1954,

China inherited borders with Vietnam demarcated in 1887 after the establishment of French Indochina and with Laos in 1895 after it was added to the French colony. The sensitive Sino-Vietnam border issue was exacerbated by the outbreak of the Vietnam War in 1955 and deteriorated further after the war ended in 1975. Tensions escalated during the Sino-Vietnam border war in 1979, with cross-border raids and skirmishes persisting throughout the 1980s.[5] China's border issues with its two biggest neighbors, India and the USSR, were even more fraught and complicated. After the Indian Independence Act and Partition of India in 1947, India continued the expansionist policies of imperial Britain, with the Sino-Indian border issue also becoming entangled with Sino-Tibetan and Indo-Tibetan relations. Border disputes mostly centered on the Aksai Chin/South Xinjiang area in the western Himalayas and Arunachal Pradesh/South Tibet in the eastern Himalayas have resulted in numerous military clashes, including the 1962 border war. Border conflicts continue to flare up periodically even today.[6] In 1922 the newly established USSR inherited the vast tracts of Chinese imperial territory annexed by tsarist Russia through the treaties of Aigun (1858) and Peking (1860). The Sino-Soviet border issue developed into an ideological and military conflict between the two countries in the 1960s. Disputes escalated in 1969, with armed clashes between China and the USSR along the eastern part of the border in Heilongjiang and in Xinjiang to the west. Violent skirmishes, a military arms race, and diplomatic squabbles continued until the collapse of the Soviet Union in the early 1990s.[7]

Whereas territorial disputes with India have persisted up to the present day, China managed to resolve border issues with Vietnam, the former Soviet republics, and Russia during the 1990s. In the case of Vietnam, work on resolving outstanding territorial issues began after the two countries officially normalized ties in November 1991, culminating with the signing of a boundary treaty on December 30, 1999. China demarcated agreed borders with Kazakhstan, Kyrgyzstan, and Tajikistan in the 1990s and signed a series of border resolutions with Russia in 1991, 1994, and 2004 to iron out their remaining territorial disputes. After a half-century of diplomatic negotiations, China entered the twenty-first century with almost all its territorial limits agreed and confirmed. China's 22,117-kilometer border abuts fourteen countries: Vietnam (1,283 kilometers), Laos (423 kilometers), Myanmar (2,185 kilometers), India (3,488 kilometers), Bhutan (470 kilometers), Nepal (1,440 kilometers), Pakistan (596 kilometers), Afghanistan (76 kilometers), Tajikistan (414 kilometers), Kyrgyzstan (858 kilometers), Kazakhstan (1,533 kilometers), Mongolia (4,677 kilometers), Russia (3,645 kilometers), and North Korea (1,416 kilometers). Border elevations range from sea level to 5,147 MASL and span diverse ecoclimatic zones, from tropical and subtropical rainforest in the southwest, to desert and semi-desert steppe in the northwest, to temperate forest, taiga, and steppe in the northeast. This immense land border also passes through culturally and ethnically diverse territories. About 19,000 kilometers, or 86 percent of China's border, run adjacent to

Chinese ethnically autonomous areas, with the 136 border counties containing thirty of the country's fifty-five ethnic minorities; 45 percent of China's total population consists of ethnic minorities.[8]

Much current research on contemporary Chinese borderlands, particularly borderland settlements, focuses on how the demarcation of accurately defined boundaries and the implementation of development projects by modern states transformed the socioeconomic patterns of traditional frontier settlements over the second half of the twentieth century.[9] In contrast, part III of this book examines the borderlands' current transformation through a wider historical perspective to reveal how past perceptions and practices continue to encourage and constrain new development to this day. Many border settlements originated in antiquity and served ancient regional trading routes. Thus, they are critical locations where the relationships between past legacies and new challenges are seen at their most intense and legible. As of 2022, sixty-four border settlements affiliated with category-one port facilities are distributed along China's land border in nine border provinces: Guangxi, Yunnan, and Tibet in the southwestern borderlands (n = 22); Xinjiang, Gansu, and Inner Mongolia in the northwestern borderlands (n = 23); and Heilongjiang, Jilin, and Liaoning in the northeastern borderlands (n = 19). This book features thirty-six border port-settlement agglomerations that clearly demonstrate the tensions and connections between past and present. The remainder of this opening essay identifies three major characteristics of port-settlement agglomerations along the border shared by China and its neighboring countries: dual directionality, multimodality, and vulnerability.

DUAL DIRECTIONALITY

One phenomenon typical of linear boundaries that follow natural features, such as rivers or mountain ranges, is the existence of twin agglomerations of border ports and settlements opposite one another. The form and operation of border ports and settlements are subject to the dual-directional flows of capital, materials, ideas, and people across the border. The dual directionality of border settlements can be traced back to the characteristics of traditional Chinese frontiers. Rather than being undeveloped wildernesses subsumed by pioneering civilization in the manner of the "American Frontierism" described by Frederick Jackson Turner, Chinese frontiers have typically been inhabited since ancient times and been subject to a long history of intercultural influences and adaptations, as argued by scholars such as Owen Lattimore.[10] Notably, despite sharing very similar geographical, ecological, cultural, and ethnic contexts, the form and operation of any given twin agglomeration are also highly influenced by the specific socioeconomic and political agendas prevailing on either side of the boundary, often resulting in markedly asymmetrical patterns of development. The dual directionality and frequently asymmetrical developmental patterns of port-settlement agglomerations are embodied in their sociodemographic composition, infrastructure specificities, and prevailing industries.

For example, the Tongjiang-Nizhneleninskoye agglomeration (No. 31) along the China–Russia border showcases how sociodemographic composition has been shaped by dual-directional influences. Tongjiang-Nizhneleninskoye is situated near the confluence of the Heilong/Amur and Songhua/Sungari Rivers. The riverbanks and adjacent broad alluvial plain had long been inhabited by the Nanai people, a seminomadic group whose livelihood relied on fishing. The entire left bank of the Amur River formerly under Qing Chinese sovereignty was ceded to tsarist Russia under the 1858 Treaty of Aigun. Major demographic changes did not take place until the 1920s, after the establishment of the Soviet Union. Soviet leader Joseph Stalin, concerned about the security of the Soviet Far Eastern border region and the historical cross-river connection, ordered the establishment of the Jewish Autonomous Oblast (JAO) immediately opposite the Chinese settlement of Tongjiang in 1928. Jews from across the USSR were resettled to the JAO, the only autonomous oblast in Russia and to this day the only official Jewish jurisdiction outside the state of Israel. On the China side of the border, Tongjiang is still inhabited by the Nanai people, many of whom live in the nearby Jiejinkou Nanai Ethnic Village established in 1984.

The transborder railway passing through the Erenhot–Zamyn-Uud agglomeration (No. 27) at the China-Mongolia border is an example of how infrastructure specificities are shaped by dual-directional influences. The three socialist states of China, Mongolia, and the Soviet Union reached an agreement after the end of World War II to develop the Trans-Mongolian Railway, following an ancient trade route connecting the cities of Jining in China, Ulaanbaatar in Mongolia, and Ulan-Ude on the Trans–Baikal (Trans-Siberian) Railway in Russia. The railway was built between 1947 and 1955, using Russia's broad gauge of 1,524 mm. During the Sino-Soviet Split of the 1960s, Mongolia aligned itself with the Soviet Union. Hence China rebuilt its section of the Trans-Mongolian Railway between Jining and Erenhot on the China-Mongolia border, changing it from Russian broad gauge to standard gauge of 1,435 mm to reduce the threat of a Soviet invasion. A gauge-changing station was set up at Erenhot in 1965. Following the gradual thaw in Sino-Mongolian relations and the resumption of cross-border trade since the late 1980s, the railway between Erenhot and Zamyn-Uud was rebuilt again, with dual-gauge tracks to allow interoperability between the two rail networks.

The Changbai-Hyesan agglomeration (No. 35) along the China–North Korea border exemplifies the way prevailing industries in the borderlands are shaped by dual-directional influences. Japan took control of the southern banks of the Yalu River after annexing Korea in 1905 and the northern banks after occupying Manchuria in 1931. Changbai-Hyesan, located in the timber-rich Mount Changbai/Baekdu region at the highest navigable point of the Yalu River, became strategically important once the Japanese developed timber and paper mills there during the 1930s. Changbai and Hyesan developed independently and differently after the defeat of the Japanese Empire in 1945. On the Chinese side of the border, the Changbaishan National Nature Reserve was established in 1960. Timber gradually gave way to industries based on nontimber forest products. The mineral-water and tourism industries took precedence in the Baishan area in the new millennium. Mount Changbai was designated a 5A Tourist Attraction in 2009. In contrast, mining superseded timber as the predominant industry on the North Korean side of the border, after a copper mine was established in the 1960s. Cross-border investment increased rapidly in the new millennium. The Hyesan-China Joint Venture Mineral Company was established in 2007 to process and sell copper, mainly to China.

MULTIMODALITY

The relationship between ports and settlements at any given location along the border is heavily influenced by its historical, geographical, and ecological contexts; the political relationship between China and the neighboring country in question; and their complementarities in terms of natural resources and economic development. Three models of contemporary port and settlement relationships can be observed along China's borderlands: Settlement-Port-Port-Settlement (SP-PS), Settlement-Port-Settlement (S-PS), and Settlement-Settlement (S-S).[11] Under the SP-PS model, port and urban functions are spatially separated on both sides of the border, with the urban settlement supporting the port as its major hinterland and the relationship between the two evolving in response to changing socioeconomic conditions and the development of transportation infrastructure. Under the S-PS model, the port in one country is an integral part of a functional urban area, while its counterpart in the other country operates separately from other urban functions. In most recent cases the former is notably more developed than the latter. Under the S-S model, ports and associated urban areas are spatially and functionally integrated on both sides of the border. In this case, cultural linkages and/or preferential trade policies facilitate frequent socioeconomic exchanges across the border.

Most examples of the SP-PS model are located in border regions at high elevations where the landscape is barren and the climate harsh. As a result, settlements are usually located some distance from their associated ports, where the natural environment is less severe and developable land more abundant. The Tuergate-Torugart agglomeration (No. 17) along the China-Kyrgyzstan border is typical of the SP-PS mode. Historically it was a caravan stop on the trade route between Kashgar and Zhetysu in Central Asia. A trade port was established at Torugart Pass (3,752 MASL) after Qing China and tsarist Russia signed the 1881 Treaty of St. Petersburg (known as the Treaty of Ili in Chinese). Due to the port's hostile high-altitude environment, it is located more than 150 kilometers away from the major hinterlands of Naryn in Zhetysu in Russia and Kashgar in Xinjiang, China. Russia built a road from Torugart to At-Bashi village and on to Naryn in the late 1890s, and China agreed to build a road between Tuergate and Kashgar in 1906 under pressure from Russia. The government of the Xinjiang Uygur Autonomous Region relocated the customs building and port facilities 110 kilometers south in the early 1990s to Tuopa Town (2,000 MASL), 50 kilometers away from Kashgar, in order to expand and upgrade Tuergate.

Port and urban functions are integrated on the China side of the border in most examples of the S-PS development model. Many of these Chinese settlements expanded rapidly in the 1960s, following the establishment of construction corps (*bingtuan*) in a number of sparsely populated frontier regions. More recent development can be credited to China's implementation of preferential policies attracting investment and domestic migration to border regions since the late 1990s. The Khorgas-Khorgos agglomeration (No. 18) along the China-Kazakhstan border is a typical example of the S-PS development model. Khorgas became a major trading pass when the Treaty of Kuldja was promulgated in 1851, regulating trade between Qing China and tsarist Russia. Chinese premier Zhou Enlai dispatched a special unit of the Xinjiang Production and Construction Corps in 1962 to establish a belt of state-run farms near the Sino-Soviet border to mitigate the impact of the 1962 Ili-Tacheng Incident: thousands of Xinjiang border inhabitants fled to the Soviet Republic of Kazakhstan, after which Khorgas evolved into a sizable *bingtuan* settlement. Since the reopening of the border in 1983, port and urban functions have been integrated at Khorgas in China, while Khorgos Port in Kazakhstan is 35 kilometers away from its nearest hinterland at Zharkent. In 2010 Kashgar and Khorgas were the first two special economic zones to be designated in Xinjiang.

Most examples of the S-S model are located in regions with moderate climates and relatively abundant natural resources, including water and land. Typically, the port and settlement agglomerations on both sides of the border are closely integrated with well-developed urban functions. The Ruili-Muse agglomeration (No. 9) along the China-Myanmar border is a typical example of the S-S model. The resource-rich Ruili/Shweli River basin was historically occupied by Mongmao, an ethnic Dai state with its capital near modern-day Ruili. The Dais found themselves divided by a border after Qing China yielded some of the territory to the south of the Ruili/Shweli River to British India under the 1894 Sino-British boundary convention. Nevertheless, Ruili and Muse maintained regular connections. During World War II, the area became a critical location on the Burma Road, enabling Western allies to send aid and supplies to support China's war effort against Japan. The strong cultural and linguistic links between Ruili and Muse have been reinforced by infrastructure development that has accelerated since the late 1980s. The Ruili Development and Experimental Zone was established in 2012. China has subsequently invested heavily in development projects on both sides of the border. Ruili-Muse also became a conduit for the China-Myanmar oil and gas pipelines that started operating in 2013 and 2017, respectively.

VULNERABILITY

Although border regions are usually under tighter control by local, regional, and national governments than other regions, border ports and settlements are often subject to both predictable and unpredictable disturbances. Some disturbances are natural disasters, such as earthquakes, landslides, and flooding, resulting from the challenging geographical settings of many border agglomerations, whereas other disturbances take the form of social unrest in these ethnically diverse regions or military attack, given the deployment of key military infrastructure, facilities, and troops at these locations. A variety of contingencies can affect the forms and operations of China's border ports and settlements, including but not limited to historic linkages and modern treaties (pre-1949), preferential policies and special zones (post-1979), military conflicts and civil unrest, cultural and religious events, infrastructure and technological advancement, geomorphology and geodynamics, and resource extraction and transportation. The constellation of thirty-six border port-settlement agglomerations featured in part III reveals the overlapping and interactive effects of multiple contingencies on any given agglomeration over time, the collaboration and competition between different agglomerations driven by past and future contingencies, and the global or regional economic and political dynamics that sometimes strengthened and sometimes impaired the form and function of border agglomerations on the local scale.

For example, the current configuration of the Irkeshtam-Erkeshtam agglomeration (No. 16) along the China-Kyrgyzstan border is the result of the overlapping and interactive effects of geodynamics and civil unrest. In October 2008 a magnitude 6.7 earthquake struck the Pamir-Tianshan area, centered near the town of Nura, 7 kilometers southwest of the Irkeshtam-Erkeshtam border port. Reconstruction on both sides of the border started soon after the earthquake. On the Kyrgyzstan side, the priority was to rebuild Nura. On the Chinese side, which experienced much less damage, the priority was to set up a new border checkpoint 136 kilometers east of the old one. This plan was not just a matter of moving a checkpoint away from an earthquake-prone location, as the Chinese authorities claimed. In reality, the move was closely related to an intense period of social unrest in southern Xinjiang in 2008, including an attack in Kashgar in August that year. With both the old and new Irkeshtam checkpoints operational, a 136-kilometer buffer zone was established to better control the flow of goods and people in this sensitive border region.

Zhangmu-Kadori (No. 11) and Gyirong-Rasuwa (No. 12) agglomerations, the only two category-one border ports on the China-Nepal border, provide examples of how interport dynamics are affected by past and future contingencies. The two ports were established in the 1960s and serve as one another's alternative crossing in case of natural disasters in this earthquake-prone region. The Gyirong-Rasuwa port, established on a major historical trading route crossing the Himalayas, was used more until the 1980s. Upgraded border facilities and the G318 highway between Lhasa and Zhangmu-Kadori resulted in Zhangmu-Kadori becoming a regional hub. After more than two decades' decline, Gyirong-Rasuwa regained its strategic importance after the launch of the BRI. While both ports were under consideration as potential sites for a future rail port on the Xi'an to Kathmandu corridor promoted by the BRI, the Sindhupalchok landslides of 2014 and the magnitude 7.8 earthquake in Nepal in 2015 severely damaged port facilities at Zhangmu-Kadori. Consequently, Gyirong-Rasuwa was seen as the more practical option for a connection to Shigatse at the southern end of the Qinghai–Tibet Railway. Now handling the majority of cross-border trade while Zhangmu-Kadori is reconstructed, Gyirong-Rasuwa is expected to become a road and rail combined port upon completion of the Shigatse–Gyirong Railway in 2022.

The sudden decline of cross-border trade at Quanhe-Wonjeong agglomeration (No. 34) along the China–North Korea border in 2017 is an example of how global economic and political dynamics can impact the form and function of a border agglomeration at a local scale. As a major border port along the Tumen River processing more than 30 percent of all trade between China and North Korea, Quanhe-Wonjeong has had its infrastructure rapidly upgraded under the BRI since 2014. A new cross-river bridge was completed in 2016. The 280,000-square-meter Quanhe International Port Joint Inspection complex was built, due to open in late 2018. As a major gateway for seafood imports from North Korea, wet markets in Quanhe and Wonjeong were upgraded between 2016 and 2017 with private Chinese investment, in anticipation of increased trade. However, initiatives intended to strengthen cross-border trade through infrastructure development experienced an unexpected hiatus when the UN imposed sanctions on North Korea because of its missile test in August 2017. China then had to ban imports of North Korean iron, coal, and seafood to comply with UN obligations. Construction on the inspection complex has slowed down since then, and the wet markets on both sides of the border stand idle.

Dual directionality, multimodality, and vulnerability are lenses through which to understand the diversity and dynamics of China's borderland settlements and how they are constantly shaped by interrelated forces that traverse borders, socio-ideological divides, and histories. Part III constitutes an atlas of thirty-six examples of port-settlement agglomerations along China's land border. Of these, thirteen agglomerations are located in the southwest borderlands, including the boundaries between China's Guangxi Zhuang Autonomous Region and Vietnam (n = 2); China's Yunnan Province and Vietnam, Laos, and Myanmar (n = 7); and China's Tibet Autonomous Region and India and Nepal (n = 4). Ten agglomerations are located

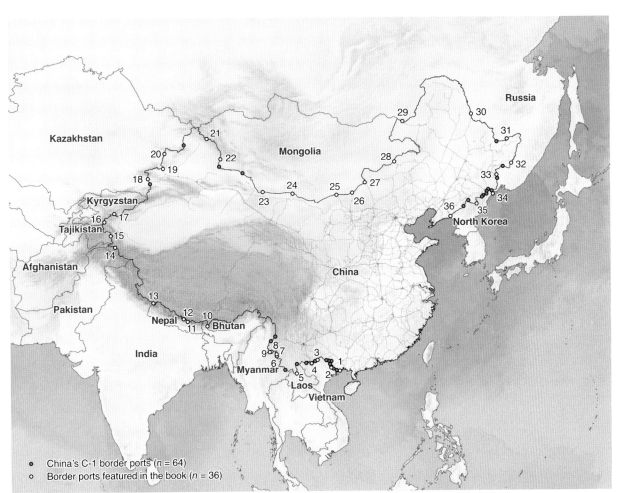

- China's C-1 border ports (*n* = 64)
- Border ports featured in the book (*n* = 36)

Southwestern Borderlands		Northwestern Borderlands		Northeastern Borderlands	
1	Dongxing–Mong Cai	14	Khunjerab Pass–Sost	24	Ceke–Shivee Khuren
2	Pingxiang–Dong Dang	15	Karasu-Kulma	25	Ganqimaodu–Gashuun Sukhait
3	Tianbao–Thanh Thuy	16	Irkeshtam-Erkeshtam	26	Mandula-Khangi
4	Hekou–Lao Cai	17	Tuergate-Torugart	27	Erenhot–Zamyn-Uud
5	Mohan-Boten	18	Khorgas-Khorgos	28	Zuun Khatavch–Bichigt
6	Qingshuihe-Chinshwehaw	19	Alashankou-Dostyk	29	Manzhouli-Zabaykalsk
7	Nansan-Laukkai	20	Baketu-Bakhty	30	Heihe-Blagoveshchensk
8	Wanding–Pang Hseng	21	Hongshanzui-Dayan	31	Tongjiang-Nizhneleninskoye
9	Ruili-Muse	22	Takeshiken-Bulgan	32	Hulin-Markovo
10	Nathula-Sherathang	23	Mazongshan-Narinsebestei	33	Suifenhe-Grodekovo
11	Zhangmu-Kadori			34	Quanhe-Wonjeong
12	Gyirong-Rasuwa			35	Changbai-Hyesan
13	Purang–Lipulekh Pass			36	Dandong-Sinuiju

in the northwest borderlands, including the boundaries between China's Xinjiang Uygur Autonomous Region and Pakistan, Tajikistan, Kyrgyzstan, and Mongolia ($n = 9$) and China's Gansu Province and Mongolia ($n = 1$). Thirteen agglomerations are located in the northeast borderlands, including the boundaries between China's Inner Mongolia Autonomous Region and Mongolia and Russia ($n = 6$), China's Heilongjiang Province and Russia ($n = 4$), and China's Jilin Province and North Korea ($n = 3$).

Each agglomeration is documented with a map and a narrative. Each 1:175,000 scale map includes three layers: major settlements (villages, towns, and cities), key infrastructure (roads, railways, land or river ports, and other supporting facilities), and geo-ecological conditions (natural features, land cover, geographic locations, and elevations). Drawn in the same style and at the same scale, these maps facilitate easy cross-referencing and comparison. The accompanying narrative covers a time frame from the mid-nineteenth century to the present day and describes critical transformations and developments on both sides of the border under review. Special attention is paid to the evolution of infrastructure projects in the borderlands, especially how their inauguration, adaptation, or destruction has been determined by diverse parties driven by a wide range of political, military, and economic motives.

NOTES

1. Neville Maxwell, "Settlements and Disputes: China's Approach to Territorial Issues," *Economic and Political Weekly* (2006), 3873–3881, 3873.

2. Hongyi Nie, "Explaining Chinese Solutions to Territorial Disputes with Neighbour States," *Chinese Journal of International Politics* 2, no. 4 (2009), 487–523, 487.

3. Excerpt from Zhou Enlai's speech at the Bandung Conference, held in Bandung, Indonesia, in April 1955, translated and quoted in Maxwell, "Settlements and Disputes," 3874.

4. Maxwell, "Settlements and Disputes," 3874.

5. For more on the Sino-Vietnam relations and border conflicts, see Victor C. Funnell, "Vietnam and the Sino-Soviet Conflict, 1965–1976," *Studies in Comparative Communism* 11, no. 1/2 (1978), 142–169; Ramses Amer, "Sino-Vietnamese Normalization in the Light of the Crisis of the Late 1970s," *Pacific Affairs* 67, no. 3 (1994), 357–383; and Gu Xiaosong and Brantly Womack, "Border Cooperation between China and Vietnam in the 1990s," *Asian Survey* 40, no. 6 (2000), 1042–1058.

6. For more on Sino-Indian relations and border conflicts, see Steven A. Hoffmann, *India and the China Crisis* (Berkeley: University of California Press, 1990); Dibyesh Anand, "Revisiting the China-India Border Dispute: An Introduction," *China Report* 47, no. 2 (2011), 65–69; and M. Taylor Fravel, "Stability in a Secondary Strategic Direction: China and the Border Dispute with India after 1962," in *Routledge Handbook of China-India Relations* (New York: Routledge, 2020), 169–179.

7. For more on Sino-Soviet relations and border conflicts, see Thomas W. Robinson, "The Sino-Soviet Border Dispute: Background, Development, and the March 1969 Clashes,"

American Political Science Review 66, no. 4 (1972), 1175–1202; Yang Kuisong, "The Sino-Soviet Border Clash of 1969: From Zhenbao Island to Sino-American Rapprochement," *Cold War History* 1, no. 1 (2000), 21–52; and Sergey Radchenko, *Two Suns in the Heavens: The Sino-Soviet Struggle for Supremacy, 1962–1967* (Washington, DC: Woodrow Wilson Center Press, 2009).

8. Daquan Huang, Yue Lang, and Tao Liu, "Evolving Population Distribution in China's Border Regions: Spatial Differences, Driving Forces and Policy Implications," *PLOS One* 15, no. 10 (2020), 1–21, 5.

9. See, for example, Prasenjit Duara, "Local Worlds: The Poetics and Politics of the Native Place in Modern China," in Thomas Lahusen (ed.), *Harbin and Manchuria: Place, Space and Identity* (Durham, NC: Duke University Press, 2001), 13–45; Byung Ho Lee, "Forging the Imperial Nation: Imperialism, Nationalism, and Ethnic Boundaries in China's Longue Durée" (PhD dissertation, University of Michigan, 2011); and Sarah Turner, Christine Bonnin, and Jean Michaud, *Frontier Livelihoods: Hmong in the Sino-Vietnamese Borderlands* (Seattle: University of Washington Press, 2015).

10. Owen Lattimore, *Inner Asian Frontiers of China* (New York: American Geographical Society, 1940).

11. These three models are based on and revised from four modes of border ports and border cities identified in Jiaoe Wang, Yang Cheng, and Huihui Mo, "The Spatio-temporal Distribution and Development Modes of Border Ports in China," *Sustainability* 6, no. 10 (2014), 7089–7106.

SOUTHWESTERN
BORDERLANDS

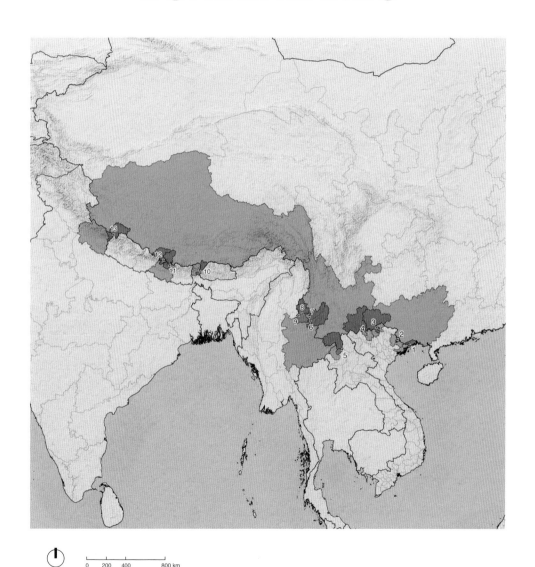

1. DONGXING–MONG CAI

The French exerted an overwhelming presence in Lower Cochinchina (southern Vietnam) in the 1860s, helping Nguyen Anh unify Vietnam under the Nguyen dynasty, the last monarchy in Vietnamese history. The French then took control of Cochinchina in 1867 but did not secure control over Annam (central Vietnam) and Tonkin (northern Vietnam) until the early 1880s. During the Sino-French War of 1884–1885, the French fought for control over Tonkin, a tributary state of Qing China with potentially profitable trade links with southern China. Under the terms of the Treaty of Tianjin, signed in June 1885, China was obliged to recognize Annam and Tonkin as French protectorates and open its borders to Sino-French trade.

Soon after the establishment of French Indochina in 1887, thirty-three border steles were erected along the 200-kilometer border between the Qing Empire's Qinzhou (now Fangchenggang City) and Tonkin under French administration. The border mainly followed the Beilun/Ka Long River, which empties into the Gulf of Tonkin (known in Chinese as Beibuwan). The French established a consular station at Dongxing in 1895, located on the northwest shores of the Gulf of Tonkin. Three years later, the French began construction of a steel bridge crossing the Beilun/Ka Long River between Dongxing in Qinzhou and Mong Cai in Tonkin, which was completed in 1900.

Beginning in the early 1930s, France started to accelerate the exploitation of Indochina's natural resources to diversify the colonial government's revenue base. According to French economic projections, the pillars of Tonkin's economy were to be gold, silver, and tin as well as rice, corn, and tea. Industrialization included the establishment of textile factories exporting products to China and throughout the French Empire. Japan invaded parts of French Indochina in September 1940, extending full control over the area in July 1941, while allowing the French administration to act as a puppet government. Dongxing Port was established in 1955 after the founding of the People's Republic of China in 1949. China and Vietnam jointly replaced the steel bridge built by the French with the reinforced concrete China-Vietnam Friendship Bridge in 1958. Dongxing became part of the newly designated Fangcheng Various Nationalities Autonomous County in 1978. The following year, Dongxing Port was closed and the China-Vietnam Friendship Bridge destroyed during the brief but intense Chinese-Vietnamese border war.

It took until 1991, twelve years after the 1979 border war, before normal relations were restored between China and Vietnam. The Dongxing Border Economic Cooperation Zone was established in 1992. Dongxing became part of Fangchenggang City in 1993. Dongxing Port was reopened a year later, and the cross-river bridge was rebuilt and renamed the Beilun River Bridge. The Dongxing Key Development and Opening Pilot Zone was established in 2010. Two years later, the Vietnamese prime minister approved the establishment of the Mong Cai Border Gate Economic Zone to kick-start the development of the entire northeastern region of Vietnam and to catch up with the surge in development on the Chinese side of the border. This new economic zone was also identified as a future development hub for the

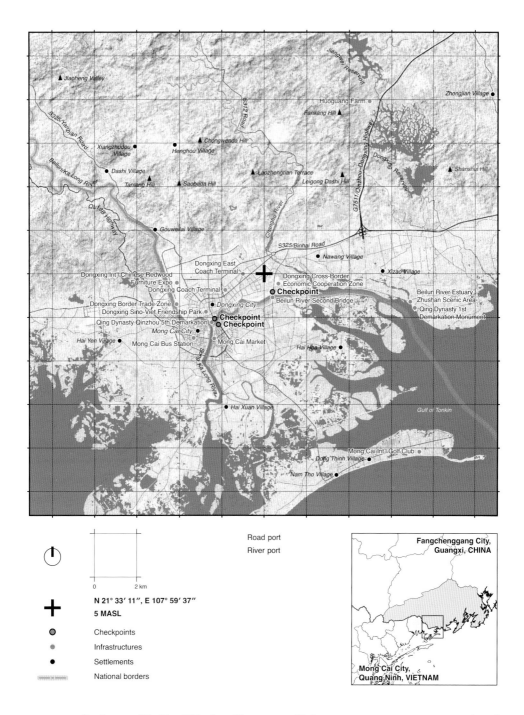

Road port
River port

N 21° 33′ 11″, E 107° 59′ 37″
5 MASL

⊙ Checkpoints
• Infrastructures
● Settlements
⬚ National borders

Fangchenggang City,
Guangxi, CHINA

Mong Cai City,
Quang Ninh, VIETNAM

Beibuwan/Gulf of Tonkin Economic Belt, an important international and regional economic cooperation area under the Chinese government's Western Development Strategy. China subsequently invested heavily in Mong Cai, particularly in textile-related industries. The Beilun River Bridge II was built 3 kilometers downstream from Beilun River Bridge I in 2019, to accommodate the increasing cross-border flow of people and goods.

2. PINGXIANG–DONG DANG

Pingxiang has long been a strategic location on China's southern frontier. During the Qing dynasty, several forts were built to guard the long, narrow Zhennanguan (literally, "south-suppressing") Pass between the Zuobi and Youfu Mountains. A major conflict erupted between Qing and Vietnamese forces at Zhennanguan Pass in 1789. Despite winning the battle, Vietnamese king Quang Trung sought to repair his tributary relationship with the Qing rulers and restore cross-border trade, in order to deter the threat of a joint Qing-Siamese pincer attack. Qing forts at the Zhennanguan Pass were destroyed during the Sino-French War of 1884–1885, which was ended by the Treaty of Tianjin in 1885. In accordance with the treaty, the Qing government opened the border for Sino-French trade and signed a contract for the construction of the Longzhou–Nanguan Railway with a French engineering firm, La Compagnie de Fives-Lille. However, the project was suspended due to disagreements over the proposed gauge of the railway.

Su Yuanchun, the Qing admiral of Guangxi in charge of defense of the frontier, took control of the strategic Zhennanguan Pass in 1890. He constructed 130 forts connected by trails and served by one of the earliest roads in China, the Longzhou–Nanguan Road, for transporting artillery and ammunition. The Huali Motor Company launched a shuttle-bus service between Longzhou in Guangxi and Lang Son in French Annam via Zhennanguan in 1916. Simultaneously, the Nationalist government embarked on the construction of the Nanning–Nanguan Road, completed in 1921.

The Japanese Imperial Naval Air Force bombed Zhennanguan in 1926, and the Japanese army invaded Pingxiang three times: in 1928, 1929, and 1933. The Chinese Nationalist government started construction of the Nanning to Pingxiang section of the Hunan–Guangxi Railway in 1937 in the hope of establishing a transport corridor that would enable Western allies to send supplies to aid China's anti-Japanese war efforts. Construction of the Hunan–Guangxi Railway was suspended and Pingxiang Station destroyed in 1939 after the Japanese army burned down the fort at Zhennanguan. As a result, foreign aid entered China via the Nanning–Nanguan Road.

Construction of the Hunan–Guangxi Railway resumed after the founding of the People's Republic of China. The Nanning to Pingxiang section opened to traffic in 1951. Zhennanguan was renamed Munanguan (literally, "south-harmonizing") Pass in 1953. Munanguan Port was opened the following year. The Hunan–Guangxi Railway was completed in its entirety in 1955 and the transnational Pingxiang–Hanoi Railway opened to traffic. During the Vietnam War, China helped North Vietnam by transporting major supplies through Munanguan, later renamed Youyiguan (literally "friendship") Pass in 1965. Sino-Vietnamese relations deteriorated after the end of the Vietnam War in 1975. Youyiguan Port was closed due to the brief but intense Chinese-Vietnamese border war of 1979.

China and Vietnam formally normalized relations in 1991. The Pingxiang (Youyiguan) Road Port was reopened the following year. The Pingxiang Railway Port was opened in 1996 and Sino-Vietnamese railway transport

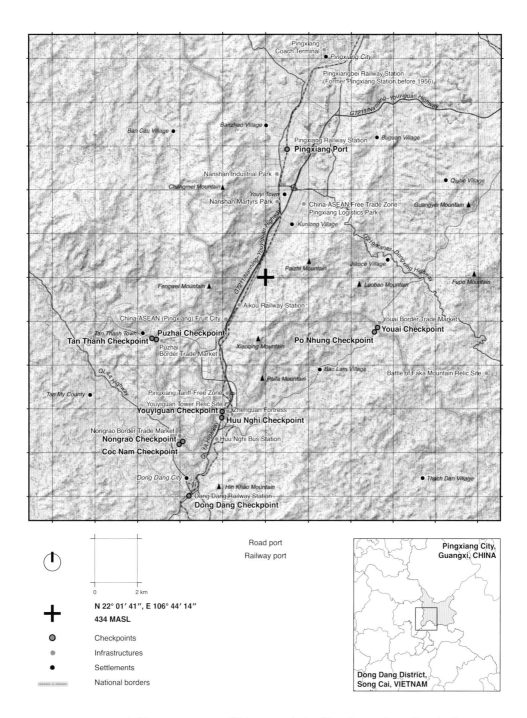

Pingxiang
Coach Terminal
● Pingxiang City

Pingxiangbei Railway Station
(Former Pingxiang Station before 1956)

G7211 Nanning–Youyiguan Highway

Ban Cau Village ●   Banzhao Village ●

Pingxiang Railway Station   ● Buguan Village
○ **Pingxiang Port**

Nanshan Industrial Park
Changmei Mountain ▲   ● Qiube Village
Youyi Town
Nanshan Martyrs Park   China-ASEAN Free Trade Zone   Guangyin Mountain ▲
Pingxiang Logistics Park
● Kunlong Village

G7211 Nanning–Youyiguan Highway

G219 Kanas–Dongxing Highway
Paizhi Mountain   Jiaoce Village ●
Fengwei Mountain ▲   ▲ Luobao Mountain   Fupo Mountain ▲
Aikou Railway Station

China-ASEAN (Pingxiang) Fruit City
Tan Thanh Town   ○ **Puzhai Checkpoint**   Youai Border Trade Market
Tan Thanh Checkpoint ○   ○ **Youai Checkpoint**
Puzhai
Border Trade Market   ▲ Xiaoqing Mountain   **Po Nhung Checkpoint**

QL 4A Highway   ▲ Paifa Mountain   ● Bao Lam Village
Tan My County ●   Battle of Faka Mountain Relic Site

Pingxiang Tariff-Free Zone
Youyiguan Tower Relic Site
Youyiguan Checkpoint ○   Zhenguan Fortress
Huu Nghi Checkpoint
Nongrao Border Trade Market   ● Huu Nghi Bus Station
Nongrao Checkpoint ○
Coc Nam Checkpoint   QL 1A Highway

Dong Dang City ●   ● Thach Dan Village
▲ Hin Khao Mountain
○ Dong Dang Railway Station
Dong Dang Checkpoint

Road port
Railway port

N 22° 01′ 41″, E 106° 44′ 14″
434 MASL

○ Checkpoints
● Infrastructures
● Settlements
National borders

**Pingxiang City,
Guangxi, CHINA**

**Dong Dang District,
Song Cai, VIETNAM**

resumed. That same year, China rated the Youyiguan Pass Scenic Spot as a national 4A-level scenic destination. Construction of a New Pingxiang Railway Station and joint inspection building began in 2004, which commenced operations in 2006. The Pingxiang Key Development and Open Pilot Zone was established in 2016. Today the port of Pingxiang in the Guangxi Autonomous Region is China's largest overland port for fruit imports and exports.

3. TIANBAO–THANH THUY

Situated along the Panlong/Lo River, a tributary of the Red River, Tianbao (literally, "naturally protected") had long been a major hub on the historic Southern Silk Road for trading goods such as cotton and silk from China and yarn and sea salt from Vietnam by river and horse-drawn caravans. It was officially opened for trade with Annam in 1796. The French fought for control of Tonkin and its potentially profitable trade route to southern China during the Sino–French War of 1884–1885. The war ended with the signing of the Treaty of Tianjin in June 1885, and French Indochina was established in 1887. During the 1890s, the Qing court and French colonial government established several joint military posts (*duixun* in Chinese) at important border-crossings, including the one at Tianbao. The French planned to establish a navigable route along the Panlong/Lo River. This proved impossible, however, after expeditions found that several sections of the river were either too narrow or unpassable because of treacherous shoals.

Administrative reforms were carried out in 1912 with the establishment of the Republic of China. Tianbao became part of the Malipo Duixun Supervision District, under the direct control of Yunnan Province. Border trade through Tianbao was suspended after Japan stationed troops in northern Indochina in September 1940 to secure a base for prosecuting the Second Sino-Japanese War (1937–1945). China regained control of the area after the end of the war. In 1950 the Communist Party of China appointed General Chen Geng to lead troops via Tianbao to support the Vietnamese against the French army, at the request of North Vietnamese president Ho Chi Minh. Trade resumed across the Sino-Vietnamese border at Tianbao in 1952, and Tianbao Port was officially established in 1954. Wenshan Zhuang and Miao Autonomous Prefecture was established in 1958, occupying a strategic location at the intersection between Vietnam and three border provinces of China: Yunnan, Guangxi, and Guizhou.

A road connecting Malipo Town and Tianbao Port was completed in 1959. China helped North Vietnam's struggle against South Vietnam and the United States during the Vietnam War. Tianbao was one of the key points through which Chinese supplies entered Vietnam between 1965 and 1968. Sino-Vietnamese relations deteriorated after the end of the Vietnam War in 1975, and Tianbao Port was closed due to the border war between China and Vietnam in 1979. A series of border clashes continued between China and Vietnam after the 1979 Sino-Vietnamese War, peaking in 1984–1985. The 1984 Battle of Laoshan in Malipo was one of the deadliest conflicts during this time, with hundreds of thousands of landmines laid by both sides.

China and Vietnam formally normalized ties in 1991. China has launched three major rounds of mine-clearance operations along the border with Vietnam since then. The river-based connection between Tianbao and Thanh Thuy resumed in 1991, with Tianbao Port officially reopened and the cross-border land-based connection restored in 1992. Construction began in 2002 on Stage I of the Malutang Dam on the Panlong River, which started to generate

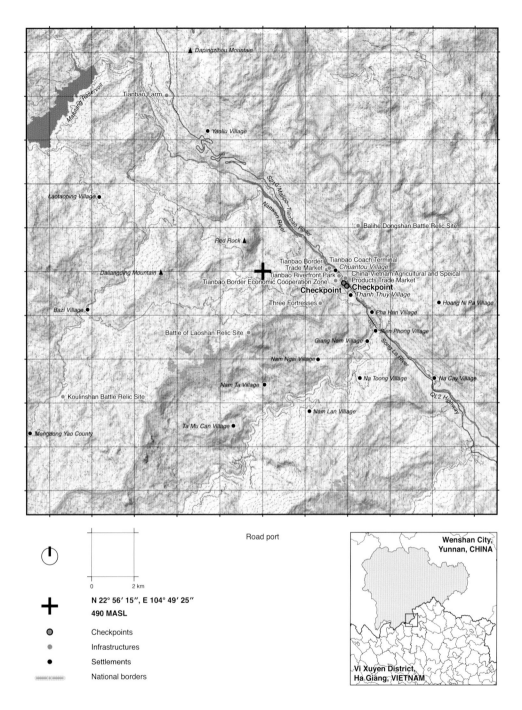

Road port

N 22° 56′ 15″, E 104° 49′ 25″
490 MASL

⬤ Checkpoints
● Infrastructures
● Settlements
▬▬▬ National borders

Wenshan City,
Yunnan, CHINA

Vi Xuyen District,
Ha Giang, VIETNAM

electricity in late 2004. The China Southern Power Grid began exporting electricity into Vietnam via Tianbao Port in 2005. Construction of Stage II of the Malutang Dam began the same year and was completed in 2010. Tianbao Port was upgraded to a national-level port in 2011. Construction of the core area of Tianbao Port's new supporting zone started in 2018.

4. HEKOU–LAO CAI

Hekou–Lao Cai along the Red River had been a major hub of the Yunnan opium trade since the early nineteenth century and became a stronghold of the Black Flags, a group of armed bandits under Commander Liu Yongfu in the late 1860s. The French colonized Cochinchina (southern Vietnam) in 1867 but did not secure control over Annam (central Vietnam) and Tonkin (northern Vietnam) until the early 1880s. The Black Flags represented the main obstacle to the French administration's plan to establish a profitable trade route with China along the Red River. The French fought for control over Tonkin and the potentially profitable trade route to Southern China during the Sino-French War of 1884–1885. The war ended with the signing of the Treaty of Tianjin in June 1885, and French Indochina was established in 1887.

A number of treaties and conventions were established as a result of French territorial aggression in 1885. Hekou was established as a treaty port in 1896, with a customs station opened there a year later. The Indochina section (Lao Cai to Hai Phong) of the Kunming–Hai Phong Railway was completed in 1906. Hekou, situated opposite Lao Cai, allowed the railway to be extended into China. The border crossing was temporarily closed in 1908 during the United League's eighth anti-Qing uprising in Hekou, planned by Sun Yat-sen. The entire Kunming–Hai Phong Railway line was completed in 1910, and commercial operations began. Japan stationed troops in northern Indochina during the Second Sino-Japanese War. The Hekou–Lao Cai Railway Bridge and 177 kilometers of railway north of Hekou were destroyed in 1941 on the orders of the Nationalist government in Nanjing to prevent Japanese forces from invading China via the Kunming–Hai Phong Railway.

Hekou Port was established in 1952 after the founding of the People's Republic of China. The Chinese section of the Kunming–Hai Phong Railway between Kunming and Hekou was renovated and reopened in 1957. That same year, Hekou Town became part of the newly designated Hekou Yao Autonomous County. In 1979, during the brief but intense Chinese-Vietnamese border war, Hekou Port was closed and the Hekou–Lao Cai Railway Bridge destroyed.

The Hekou Border Economic Cooperation Zone was established in 1992, a year after China and Vietnam formally renormalized ties in 1991. Hekou Port was reopened the following year, and the Hekou–Lao Cai Railway Bridge was rebuilt. The Kunming–Hai Phong Railway resumed international freight services in 1996 and passenger services the following year. The Nanxi River Bridge, 150 meters downstream from the railway bridge, was built in 2000 to accommodate the ever-increasing cross-border freight traffic. The Hekou–Lao Cai power transmission project was completed in 2004, and the China Southern Power Grid began exporting electricity to Vietnam. Construction of the Honghe River Bridge, located 4 kilometers upstream from the Nanxi River Bridge, started in 2006 and was completed in 2009. Checkpoint facilities were constructed at both ends of the bridge. A memorandum of understanding on the construction of the Lao Cai–Yunnan Cross-Border Economic Cooperation

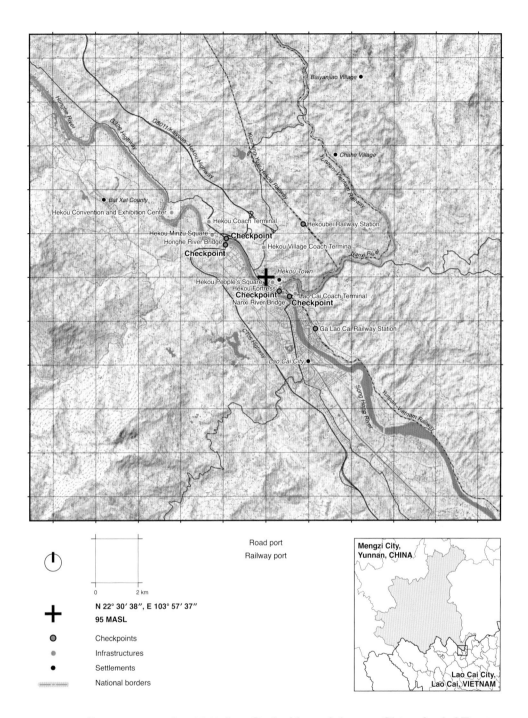

Road port

Railway port

0   2 km

N 22° 30′ 38″, E 103° 57′ 37″

95 MASL

Checkpoints

Infrastructures

Settlements

National borders

Mengzi City,
Yunnan, CHINA

Lao Cai City,
Lao Cai, VIETNAM

Zone was signed in 2010. Lao Cai had hosted thirteen China-funded Foreign Direct Investment projects by 2015, including the Hekou–Lao Cai power transmission project, Seng Chung Ho hydropower plant, and Lao Cai Iron and Steel Factory.

5. MOHAN-BOTEN

Prior to French intervention in the late nineteenth century, the Lao Kingdom of Lan Na was under the suzerainty of Siam (now Thailand). As part of the historic Southern Silk Road, various caravan and river-based routes along the upper Mekong River linked Southern Yunnan's Sip Song Pan Na with Lan Na in northern Siam. After the establishment of French Indochina in 1887, the French planned further expansion toward the Mekong River, viewing it as a potential trade route to China. The Franco-Siamese War of 1893 ended with the Treaty of Bangkok, under which Siam was obliged to cede its Lao principalities on the eastern bank of the Mekong to the French, which led to significant expansion of French Indochina.

Soon after securing France's western colonial boundary with Siam, the French authorities embarked on negotiations with China to demarcate their border. Known for its numerous salt wells, Boten was an important supplier of salt and a well-established stopping place along a major trade route plied by caravans. Qing China, preoccupied with Japanese aggression during the First Sino-Japanese War, signed an agreement with France in 1895, ceding control of Boten and granting preferential terms for French goods entering Yunnan. In 1913, a year after the establishment of the Republic of China, the Yunnan provincial government sent troops to oust local rebels in Sip Song Pan Na. Zhenyue (literally, "pacifying Indochina") County, later renamed Mengla County, was established along the southernmost border of China with French Indochina in 1927.

Sip Song Pan Na experienced a boom in rubber production when the central government of the PRC designated natural rubber as a strategic industrial product during the Korean War in response to US trade embargos. The local chieftain system was abolished in 1953, and the Xishuangbanna Dai Autonomous Prefecture was established. Meanwhile, the Kingdom of Laos proclaimed independence in 1953. The French signed a peace accord to that effect at the Geneva Conference of 1954. Regional tensions resulted in the China-Laos border remaining relatively closed until the early 1990s. The Greater Mekong Subregion Economic Cooperation Program was established in 1992. An agreement was reached between China and Laos to establish Mohan Port in Mengla County, China, and Boten Port in Luang Namtha Province, Laos.

Boten, located just inside the Laos border, experienced a casino-driven boom in the early 2000s. It was dominated by a 2007 land concession leased by a Hong Kong–registered company, called Golden Boten City, which rapidly declined after a Chinese crackdown on cross-border gambling. Boten was promoted to the status of a strategic location in 2010, when a memorandum of understanding was signed between Laos and China to build a 414-kilometer railway linking the Laos capital Vientiane with Boten on the China-Laos border and then with Kunming, the capital of Yunnan Province. China and Laos signed an agreement on the development of the Mohan-Boten Economic Cooperation Area in 2015. Boten experienced a rapid transformation after Golden Boten City was acquired from its original owners by a Yunnan-based

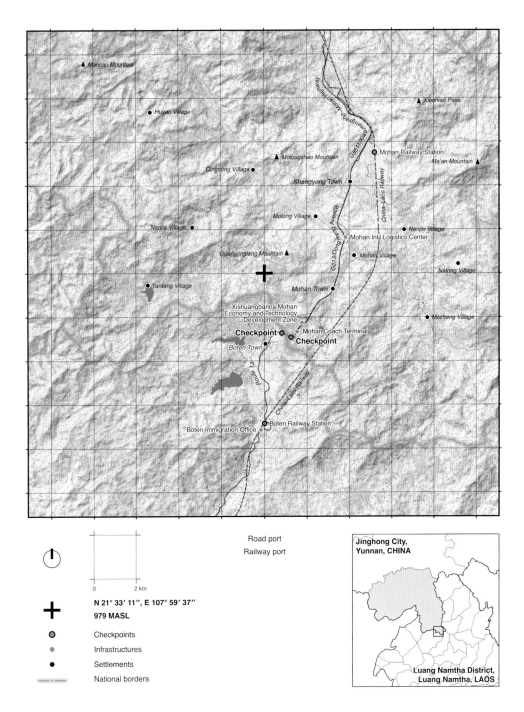

▲ Maocao Mountain

● Huyao Village

Zhengyang-Mohan Highway

▲ Xiaomiao Pass

▲ Molongzhao Mountain

Qingsong Village ●

G8511 Xiao

Shangyong Town ●

● Mohan Railway Station

Ma'an Mountain ▲

China–Laos Railway

Molong Village ●

Nanlie Village ●

G213/Dongmeng Avenue

● Mohan Intl Logistics Center

● Nanpo Village

Guangjingtang Mountain ▲

● Mohan Village

Nalong Village ●

✚

● Yantang Village

Mohan Town

Xishuangbanna Mohan
Economy and Technology
Development Zone

Checkpoint ⊙

● Mohan Coach Terminal

● Mozheng Village

Checkpoint

Boten Town ●

Route 13

China–Laos Railway

⊙ Boten Railway Station

Boten Immigration Office ●

Road port

Railway port

Jinghong City,
Yunnan, CHINA

Luang Namtha District,
Luang Namtha, LAOS

company in 2016. The Boten SEZ was established under a 90-year lease agreement. Construction of the China–Laos Railway formally began in 2016, and the Chinese section of the Kunming–Bangkok Expressway from Kunming to Mohan was completed in 2017. Chinese president Xi Jinping and his Lao counterpart, Thongloun Sisoulith, attended a virtual ceremony to jointly inaugurate the China–Laos Railway on December 3, 2021.

6. QINGSHUIHE-CHINSHWEHAW

The mineral-rich Nanting River basin had long been under the control of the Gengma chieftain, recognized as a vassal of the Ming Dynasty. The Gengma clan became increasingly influential during the Qing dynasty after being granted the management rights of an imperial silver-processing factory in 1783. British influence reached the mountainous frontier regions by the early nineteenth century. Upper Burma was annexed after the Third Anglo-Burmese War in 1885. The province of Burma was created in 1886 as part of British India. With the combined threats of British authority in Burma and French rule in Indochina, the poorly demarcated nature of China's southern boundaries became a source of anxiety for Chinese authorities. The Chinese and British delineated the southern section of the Sino-Burmese boundary in 1899, ending at the confluence of the Qingshuihe/Nanpa River and Nanting River, a tributary of the Nu/Salween River. In the late nineteenth century the British and French both planned railways connecting Yunnan with their respective spheres of influence. Unlike the French Kunming–Hai Phong Railway, which was completed in 1910, the British Yunnan–Burma Railway was shelved because it was not financially viable.

After the establishment of the Republic of China in 1912, the Gengma chieftainship was changed to a district administration, and Mengding Town was established. After the outbreak of the Second Sino-Japanese War, the Burma Road linking Kunming in Yunnan and Lashio in Burma through Wanding was constructed and completed in 1938, in order to transport supplies from the Western allies to China. The Yunnan–Burma Railway project originally envisioned by the British in the late nineteenth century was resurrected. The railway, which entered China at Qingshuihe village in Mengding, was intended to strengthen the connection established by the Burma Road. The Japanese Imperial Army occupied Lashio in 1942 and advanced toward Yunnan to prevent Allied forces transporting supplies from Burma to China. As a result, construction of the railway was abandoned, the Chinese Expeditionary Force dynamited the finished section of the Yunnan–Burma Railway to prevent enemy advances, and construction was never resumed.

The Mengding border trade market was opened to local residents in 1950, after the founding of the People's Republic of China. Gengma County was established in 1952 as part of the Mianning Prefecture (approximating today's Lincang City) by the PRC and renamed Gengma Dai and Va Autonomous County in 1955. The border trade market opened intermittently through the 1960s. China-Burma trade slowed during the Cultural Revolution. The Qingshuihe checkpoint closed in 1966. Cross-border trade did not resume until the early 1980s. Construction of the Qingshuihe border passageway began in 1980, the Qingshuihe border trade market opened in 1988, and Qingshuihe Port was officially opened in 1991.

Qingshuihe Port was upgraded to a national-level port in 2004. Construction of the Yunnan–Burma Railway Heritage Park in Lincang City started in 2009 and opened to the public in 2013. The park commemorates more than 300,000 people, mostly ethnic minorities, who worked on the construction of

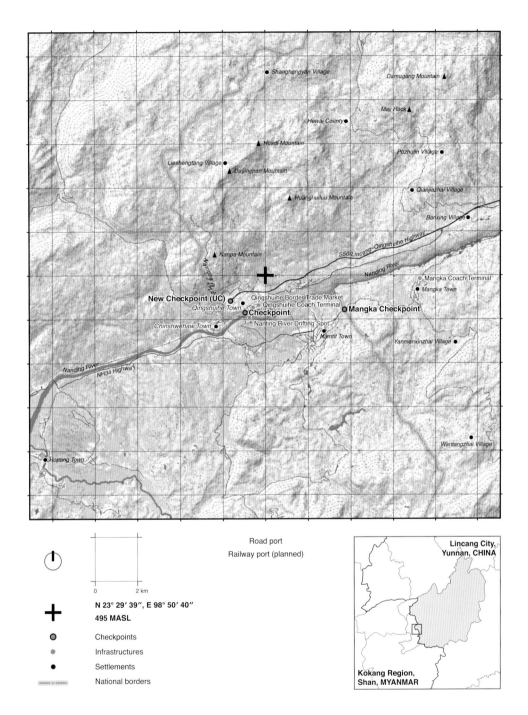

Road port
Railway port (planned)

N 23° 29′ 39″, E 98° 50′ 40″
495 MASL

Checkpoints
Infrastructures
Settlements
National borders

Lincang City,
Yunnan, CHINA

Kokang Region,
Shan, MYANMAR

the Chinese section of the railway from 1938 to 1942. The Lincang Border Economic Cooperation Zone was established in Mengding in 2011. Infrastructure construction in the area has accelerated since then. The Mending section of the Lincang–Qingshuihe Highway opened to traffic in 2018. The Dali–Lincang Railway opened to traffic in 2020, with plans to extend it to Qingshuihe Port to connect with railways in Myanmar.

7. NANSAN-LAUKKAI

The Kokang region, located east of the Salween River (known in China as the Nu River), was settled in the mid-seventeenth century by the exiled Han royal family at the end of the Ming dynasty. The Qing dynasty recognized Kokang as a vassal state in 1840, along with its leader's hereditary rights. Upper Burma was annexed by the British after the Third Anglo-Burmese War in 1885. The province of Burma was established as part of British India the following year. Han Chinese–dominated Kokang was initially included in Qing China under the 1894 Sino-British boundary convention but was later ceded to the British under a supplementary agreement in 1897 to become part of Hsenwi State in Burma's northern Shan States. The rapid increase in the use and production of opium in Burma is linked to the international opium trade condoned by the British colonial government since the 1820s. Kokang became a major opium producer and an important transit point for opium exported to China from Burma's trans-Salween area. Approximately 40,000 pounds of opium were produced annually in Kokang at the beginning of the twentieth century.

Trade between Kokang and Yunnan was formalized after the establishment of Zhenkang County by the Qing administration in 1908. This major trade route followed the river valley via Nansan in Zhenkang and Laukkai in Kokang. During the Japanese occupation of Burma (1942–1945), Kokang armed factions fought with China's Nationalist (Kuomintang: KMT) forces against the Japanese and border trade between Nansan and Laukkai was suspended. Shortly after the end of World War II, China's Civil War flared up again. In the early 1950s almost the entire Kokang region was taken over by KMT forces fleeing the newly established People's Republic of China.

Mianning Prefecture (approximating to today's Lincang City) was established by the PRC in 1952. The PLA stationed troops in Nansan on the border with Kokang, where the KMT had taken sanctuary, and trade between Nansan and Laukkai resumed. Nansan Town and Lincang County were established in 1988, followed by Nansan Port in 1991. Myanmar (formerly Burma) entered a relatively stable period in the late 1980s after four decades of internal conflict since independence in 1948. Laukkai developed rapidly after the ceasefire of 1989, and Kokang was designated the autonomous First Special Region of the northern Shan State of Burma. Laukkai has witnessed a boom in casino-related development since an opium ban was enforced in Kokang region in 2003, with casinos providing alternative employment and income in the context of the region's intensifying drug eradication programs.

The Lincang Border Economic Cooperation Zone was established on the China side of the border in 2011. Despite efforts to boost economic development through cross-border cooperation, unrest in Myanmar's Kokang region remains the main obstacle to peace and economic growth. A series of clashes between the Myanmar army and the Kokang resistance broke out in late August 2009. As many as 30,000 refugees fled through Nansan into China's Yunnan Province. From February to June 2015 another series of clashes

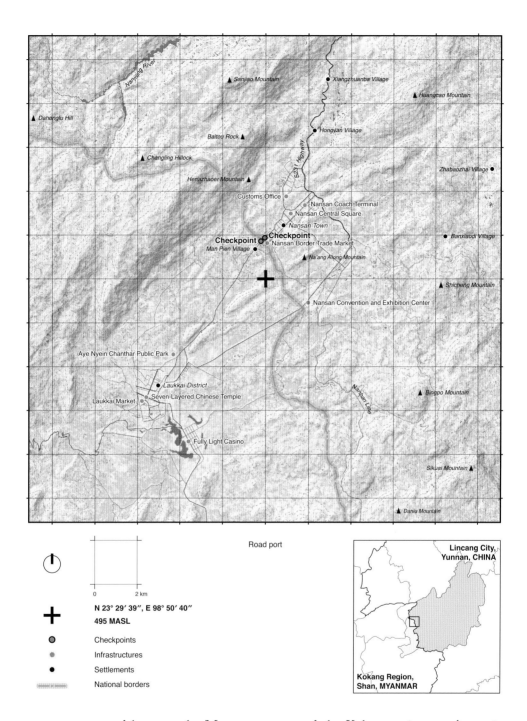

N 23° 29′ 39″, E 98° 50′ 40″
495 MASL

○ Checkpoints

● Infrastructures

● Settlements

━━━ National borders

Road port

Lincang City,
Yunnan, CHINA

Kokang Region,
Shan, MYANMAR

erupted between the Myanmar army and the Kokang resistance. Approximately 70,000 civilians sought shelter on the Chinese side of the border, and the newly constructed Nanshan International Convention Center was used as a temporary refugee camp.

8. WANDING–PANG HSENG

The ancient trade route along the Ruili/Shweli River saw a boom in jade trading in the late eighteenth century because of the growing interest in Burmese jade of the Qianlong Emperor (1735–1796). In one of his Ten Great Campaigns, he declared war on Burma after the Burmese king refused to pay him tribute. The Sino-Burmese War of 1765–1769 was ended by treaty in 1770, under which the Burmese king allowed jade exports to China. British influence reached the mountainous frontier regions in the early nineteenth century and continued with the Anglo-Burmese Wars (1824–1885), resulting in British control over most of Burma. Upper Burma was annexed after the Third Anglo-Burmese War in 1885, and Burma was declared a province of British India the following year. Under the 1894 boundary convention and supplementary agreement of 1897, which delineated the border between British Burma and Qing China, the Ruili River and its tributary the Wanding River form the boundary between Burma's Shan State and China's Yunnan Province.

Wanding, a small but long-established caravan stop on the trade route between Yunnan and Burma, with a wooden bridge across the Wanding River, was designated a town in 1932 by China's Nationalist government. During the Second Sino-Japanese War, the old trade route between Yunnan and Burma played a new and decisive role. The 1,154-kilometer Burma Road linking Kunming in Yunnan and Lashio in Burma through Wanding was completed in 1938 to enable Western allies to send supplies and aid to China in its war with Japan. The Wanding wooden bridge was replaced with a stone bridge as part of the Burma Road project. The 1,726-kilometer Ledo Road linking Ledo in India and Kunming in Yunnan through the Kachin State of Burma was constructed in 1942 as an alternative supply road after the Japanese cut off the Burma Road. The Wanding stone bridge was destroyed in 1944 and rebuilt by China's American allies as a Bailey bridge in 1945.

Wanding Port was established in 1952. Wanding Town became part of the Dehong Dai and Jingpo Autonomous Prefecture designated in 1953. The China-Burma Joint Demarcation Meeting was held in Wanding in 1960, and the China-Burma Boundary Treaty was signed in Beijing on October 1 of that year. China-Burma trade slowed after the 1967 anti-Chinese riots and expulsion of Chinese communities from Burma. Relations improved significantly in the 1970s, and a bilateral preferential trade agreement was signed in 1971.

The Wanding Border Economic Cooperation Zone was established in 1992. A reinforced concrete bridge was built in 1993 next to the old Bailey bridge, now preserved as a historical monument with national-level protection. With the completion of the Mangman to Myanmar secondary highway in 2013, the Mangman Passage of Wanding Port was officially opened 10 kilometers downstream from the town center of Wanding. While jade, rubber, and timber accounted for the majority of Chinese imports from Myanmar, oil and gas have become important strategic imports since the early 2000s to fuel

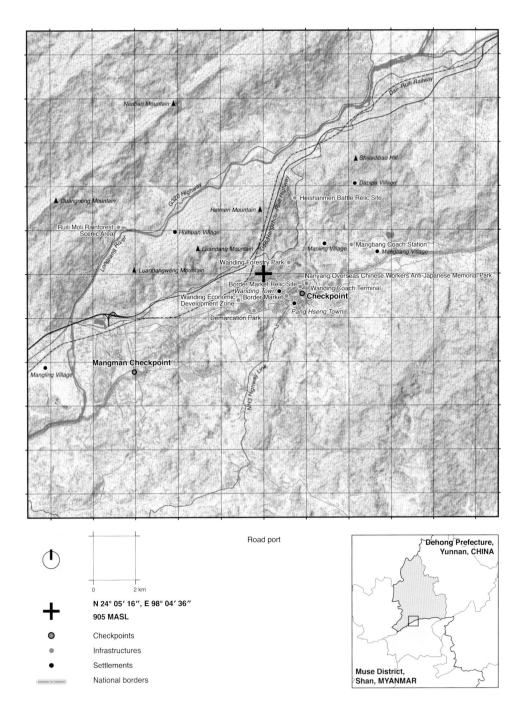

Road port

N 24° 05′ 16″, E 98° 04′ 36″
905 MASL

- ● Checkpoints
- ● Infrastructures
- ● Settlements
- ⸺ National borders

Dehong Prefecture,
Yunnan, CHINA

Muse District,
Shan, MYANMAR

urbanization and development in southwestern China. Talks regarding the
feasibility of the China-Myanmar oil and gas pipeline project from Kyaukpyu
to Kunming through Ruili and Wanding began in 2004. Gas and oil pipelines
became operational in 2013 and 2017, respectively.

9. RUILI-MUSE

The jade-rich Ruili/Shweli River basin for a long time was under the control of Mongmao (also known as Luchuan in Chinese literature), an ethnic Dai state with its capital near modern-day Ruili. Mongmao was recognized as a vassal of the Ming dynasty. A fortress called Pinglucheng (literally, "pacification of Luchuan") was built there in 1596. Pinglucheng evolved into an important trading center for jade and the ancient horse-drawn caravan route along the Ruili/Shweli River experienced a surge in trade in the late eighteenth century. Increasing British influence extended to the mountainous frontier regions in the early nineteenth century. Upper Burma was annexed after the Third Anglo-Burmese War in 1885, and Burma became a province of British India the following year. According to the Anglo-Chinese Agreement Modifying the 1894 Convention (1897), the British were to "perpetually lease" the Chinese territory situated at the junction of the Ruili/Shweli and Namwan Rivers, known as Namwan Assigned Tract or Mongmao Triangular Area.

After the outbreak of the Second Sino-Japanese War in 1937, the Burma Road was completed in 1938, enabling Western allies to supply aid to China. The road linked Kunming in Yunnan and Lashio in Burma, crossing the China-Burma border at Wanding to the east of Ruili. During the war, the Central Aircraft Manufacturing Company (CAMCO) retreated from Hangzhou, the capital of Zhejiang Province in eastern China, and established a new factory at Loiwing in Ruili near the China-Burma frontier in 1939. CAMCO also built Nanshan Airport near Loiwing, the second largest airport in Yunnan at that time. Nanshan Airport became an important base for the American Volunteer Group (AVG) set up by the US government to aid the Nationalist government of China against Japan. CAMCO also established a facility at Mingaladon Airport near Rangoon, producing ground-attack aircraft for the AVG. After the Japanese occupied Burma and advanced toward Yunnan, CAMCO retreated from the frontier and burned down the Loiwing factory.

Nanshan Airport was abandoned after the founding of the People's Republic of China. The land was later reclaimed for agriculture. Ruili became part of the newly designated Dehong Dai and Jingpo Autonomous Prefecture in 1953. The China-Burma Boundary Treaty was signed in Beijing in October 1960, and the Namwan Assigned Tract became Burmese territory the following year. The Ruili Jiegao Bridge was built in 1989, connecting the road in Myanmar's Shan State with China National Highway 320 (G320), a 3,695-kilometer highway running between Shanghai on the coast and Ruili at the Sino-Burmese border.

Ruili became a Tourism Open County in 1990, and Ruili Port was opened. Two years later, Ruili became a Border Open City and the Ruili Border Economic Cooperation Zone was established. The jade trading and processing industry expanded rapidly after 1992. Ruili became one of the four major jade trading centers in China. Tourism also boomed after Ruili was designated as one of the first batch of China Excellent Tourist Cities by the National Tourism Administration in 1999. Ruili Port was upgraded to a national-level port in 2000. Development accelerated further after the Yunnan Ruili Key

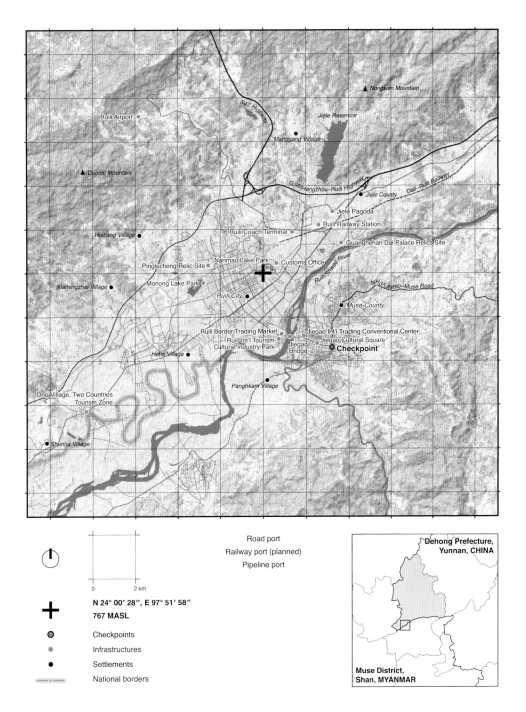

Road port
Railway port (planned)
Pipeline port

Dehong Prefecture,
Yunnan, CHINA

Muse District,
Shan, MYANMAR

N 24° 00′ 28″, E 97° 51′ 58″
767 MASL

Checkpoints

Infrastructures

Settlements

National borders

Development and Opening Up Experimental Zones were established in 2012. The China-Myanmar oil and gas pipeline from Kyaukpyu to Kunming started operations through Ruili in 2013 and Wanding in 2017. Ruili became part of the Dehong Area of China (Yunnan) Pilot Free Trade Zone established in 2019, positioning it as a portal hub for the China-Myanmar Economic Corridor.

10. NATHULA-SHERATHANG

Sikkim began as a hereditary monarchy in the eastern Himalayas in the mid-seventeenth century. The Dromo Valley runs south from the Tibetan plateau, connecting with Sikkim and Bhutan via the Nathula and Jelepla mountain passes. It had long been strategically important for trans-Himalayan trade and military activity. Nepal invaded Sikkim and advanced into southern Tibet in 1788 in the hope of taking control of the formal trade route established through the Dromo Valley in 1784. Qing China made Sikkim a protectorate after the Sino-Nepalese War of 1788–1792, stationing a governor in the Dromo region (known in Chinese as Yadong), while the Dromo Valley was annexed by Tibet.

The British in India wanted to establish trade with Tibet on their northern frontier to keep Russia at bay. Sikkim was a perfect corridor for this purpose, given its close kinship and religious affiliations with Tibet. After the Anglo-Nepalese War of 1814–1816, Sikkim and British India signed the 1817 Treaty of Titalia, under which the British took control of Sikkim's internal and external affairs. After the Treaty of Tumlong (1861), Sikkim became a de facto British protectorate. Topographical and geographical surveys were conducted with a view to opening up trade routes and building roads between India and Tibet. Meanwhile, Qing authority over Tibet weakened in the latter half of the nineteenth century, given the Qing dynasty's domestic and foreign-relations burdens, particularly the Opium Wars of 1839–1842 and 1856–1860 and the Taiping Civil War of 1850–1864.

The British and Qing China signed the Chefoo Convention in 1876, known in Chinese as the Yantai Treaty, which specified the extraterritorial privileges of British subjects in China, including the right to open up trade between India and Tibet. Britain and Qing China signed the Convention of Calcutta in 1890, which recognized Sikkim as a British protectorate and demarcated the Sikkim-Tibet border. A protocol was added to the 1890 convention in 1893, opening the market at Yadong/Dromo to British India. The Convention between the British and Qing China respecting Tibet was signed in 1906, after which a British trade-agent was stationed at Yadong/Dromo. After the Qing Empire was overthrown in the 1911 Chinese Revolution, Tibet became a de facto independent state. The Yadong/Dromo region fell under full British control.

Following Indian independence, Sikkim retained its protectorate status with the Union of India after 1947 and the Republic of India after 1950. The People's Republic of China annexed Tibet in 1951 and regained control over the Yadong/Dromo region under the Agreement on Trade and Intercourse between the Tibet Region of China and India of 1954. Border trade was interrupted because of skirmishes at the Nathula Pass during the 1962 Sino-Indian Border War and in 1967, when further clashes broke out at Nathula and Chola on the Sikkim border. Sikkim became a state of India in 1975.

China and India signed a joint declaration on border issues in 2003 under which India recognized Tibet as Chinese territory and China recognized Sikkim as part of India. Sino-Indian trade across the border at the Nathula Pass

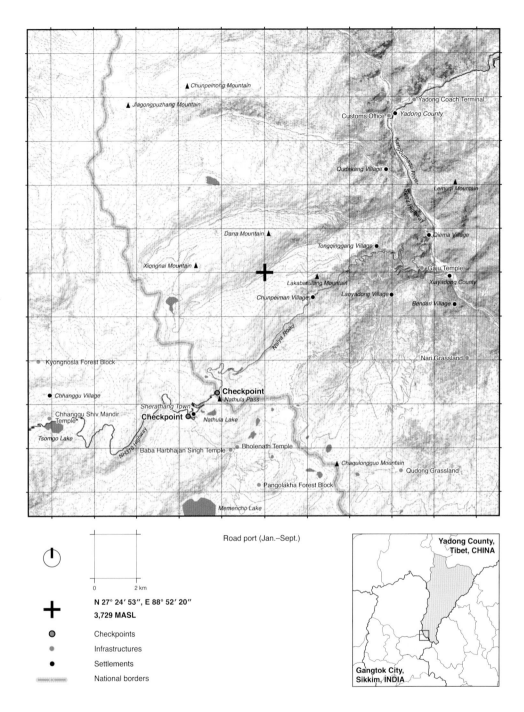

Road port (Jan.–Sept.)

0   2 km

N 27° 24′ 53″, E 88° 52′ 20″
3,729 MASL

● Checkpoints
● Infrastructures
● Settlements
▬▬▬ National borders

Yadong County,
Tibet, CHINA

Gangtok City,
Sikkim, INDIA

was revived in 2006, when the Xining to Lhasa section of the Qinghai–Tibet Railway entered service. Three railways extending from Lhasa have been proposed, including a Lhasa-Shigatse-Yadong Railway. China opened a second land crossing into Tibet in 2015 via Nathula to allow Indians to undertake the Kailash-Manasarovar Yatra (pilgrimage), after the old route via the Lipulekh Pass was badly damaged by flooding in 2013.

11. ZHANGMU-KADORI

The Tibetan Ganden Phodrang regime became a protectorate of Qing China in the mid-eighteenth century. Nyalam Town, on the western bank of the Poiqu River (known as the Bhotekoshi River in Nepal), had long been strategically important for trans-Himalayan trade and security. Nepal attempted to invade Tibet through Nyalam in 1788 but had to renounce its claims to Tibet after losing the Sino-Nepalese War of 1788–1792. Russian and British rivalry for control of Central Asia prompted the Tibetan government to ban all foreigners and close its borders in 1850. During the Nepalese-Tibetan War of 1855–1856, the Nepalese army occupied Burang, Gyirong, Nyalam, and Rongshar. The war ended with the Treaty of Thapathali (1856), under which Nepal recognized Qing China's suzerainty over Tibet and the Tibet government agreed not to impose customs duties on Nepali products.

Qing authority over Tibet weakened in the latter half of the nineteenth century due to the Qing dynasty's domestic and foreign-relations burdens, including the Opium Wars of 1839–1842 and 1856–1860 and the Taiping Civil War of 1850–1864. Britain began discreetly mapping Tibet in the 1860s for military and commercial purposes. The entire southern flank of Tibet was under British control by the 1890s. Following their military expedition to Tibet (1903–1904), the British forced Tibet into a trade agreement in 1904 to forestall any Russian overtures. Qing China reasserted its authority shortly after the British military expedition to Tibet. Britain and Russia acknowledged Qing suzerainty over Tibet in 1907. After the Qing Empire was overthrown during the 1911 Chinese Revolution, Tibet became a de facto independent state, consisting of the western half of the Tibetan Plateau.

Soon after its establishment, the People's Republic of China enforced its long-held claim to Tibet, embarking on a military campaign in 1950 after months of failed negotiations, capturing the Chamdo region, and annexing Tibet in its entirety in 1951. Nepal restored diplomatic relations with China in 1955, after which the two nations signed a new treaty. Nepal recognized Tibet as part of China under the 1956 treaty that superseded the 1856 Treaty of Thapathali. Several border ports were established after the Sino-Nepalese Border Treaty and Sino-Nepalese Treaty of Peace and Friendship were signed, in March and April 1960, respectively. Zhangmu Port (2,300 MASL) was opened 35 kilometers downstream from Nyalam Town (3,750 MASL) in 1965.

Construction of the China-Nepal Friendship Highway began in 1963. Opened to traffic in 1967, the highway runs from Lhasa, the capital of Tibet, to Zhangmu–Kadori on the Sino-Nepalese border linking to the Araniko Highway and Kathmandu, the capital of Nepal. It is also the westernmost part of the China National Highway 318 (G318), connecting Tibet with Shanghai on the east coast. The Zhangmu-Kadori port was expanded following the upgrading of the Friendship Highway in the early 1980s, soon outcompeting the China-Nepal border port of Gyirong-Rasuwa to become the primary trading post between Tibet and Nepal. The Zhangmu-Kadori

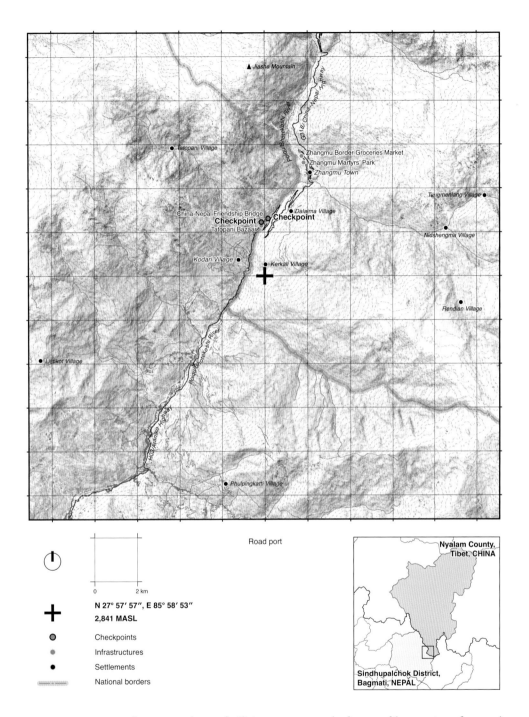

Road port

N 27° 57' 57", E 85° 58' 53"
2,841 MASL

○ Checkpoints

● Infrastructures

● Settlements

━━ National borders

Nyalam County,
Tibet, CHINA

Sindhupalchok District,
Bagmati, NEPAL

route and associated port facilities were severely damaged by a series of natural disasters, including the 2014 Sindhupalchok landslides and 2015 magnitude 7.8 Nepal earthquake. After four years of reconstruction, Zhangmu Port resumed limited operations for goods and vehicles in May 2019.

12. GYIRONG-RASUWA

Situated on the eastern bank of the Gyirong River, a tributary of the Trishuli River, Gyirong is a long-established caravan stop on the Tubo to Nepal trade route, forming the Himalayan branch of the ancient Silk Road connecting the Tibetan Tubo Kingdom and Nepal. Russian and British rivalry for control of Central Asia prompted the Tibetan government to ban all foreigners and close its borders in 1850. During the Nepalese–Tibetan War of 1855–1856, the Nepalese army invaded Gyirong and built a fort at Rasuwa. The war was ended with the Treaty of Thapathali. Following its military expedition to Tibet in 1903–1904, Britain forced Tibet to sign a trade agreement in order to forestall any Russian overtures. After the Qing dynasty was overthrown in 1911, Tibet became a de facto independent state.

After months of failed negotiations with Lhasa, the newly established People's Republic of China embarked on a military campaign in 1950 and annexed Tibet in 1951. Nepal recognized Tibet as part of China under a 1956 treaty that superseded the 1856 Treaty of Thapathali. Gyirong Port (1,837 MASL), 25 kilometers downstream from Gyirong Town (2,700 MASL), was established in 1961, a year after ratification of the Sino-Nepalese Border Treaty and Sino-Nepalese Treaty of Peace and Friendship. China and Nepal jointly built a wooden suspension bridge (Rasuwa Bridge 1) across the Gyirong River in 1972, connecting Gyirong and Rasuwa. The road between Gyirong Town and Gyirong Port was completed in 1979, and a steel suspension bridge (Rasuwa Bridge 2) was opened to traffic.

Gyirong-Rasuwa Port was well used for two decades until the mid-1980s, when the bulk of China-Nepal cross-border trade shifted to Zhangmu-Kadori Port after that port's border facility upgrades and completion of the China–Nepal Friendship Highway connecting Zhangmu and Lhasa. Customs officers were withdrawn from the Gyirong Port in 1985. The port mainly catered to local barter trade until it started to gain geopolitical significance in the new millennium. After social unrest in Tibet in 2008, several development initiatives were launched by the Chinese government in the region, notably the plan to construct the South Asia Trade Corridor. China considered improving links between Tibet and Nepal to be a precondition for strengthening ties with the South Asian Association for Regional Cooperation. Preparatory work for the expansion of Gyirong Port began in 2009, leading to its reopening in 2014 with a new stone bridge (Rasuwa Bridge 3) connecting Gyirong and Rasuwa.

Gyirong-Rasuwa played a minor role as a China-Nepal cross-border trade route until after the 2015 Nepal earthquake, which severely damaged the Zhangmu-Kodari cross-border route. China and Nepal signed a treaty in 2016 on trade and transit, including a plan to build a 515.8-kilometer railway from Kathmandu, the capital of Nepal, to Shigatse at the southern end of the Qinghai–Tibet Railway in China. The railway supports China's objectives to further develop and secure Tibet, while simultaneously enabling Nepal to reduce its overdependence on India, which currently accounts for 60 percent

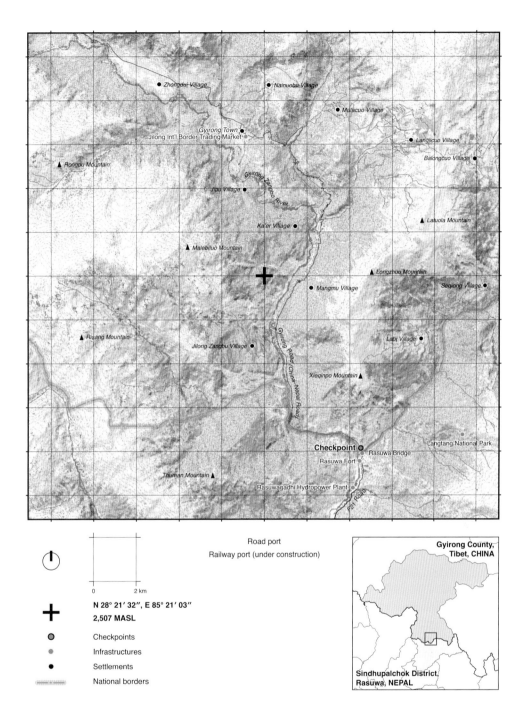

Road port

Railway port (under construction)

0   2 km

N 28° 21′ 32″, E 85° 21′ 03″

2,507 MASL

Checkpoints

Infrastructures

Settlements

National borders

Gyirong County,
Tibet, CHINA

Sindhupalchok District,
Rasuwa, NEPAL

of Nepal's foreign trade. The two countries had agreed on the technical details of the railway by 2018. Gyirong-Rasuwa was selected as its preferred border crossing. Survey work in preparation for the construction of the 443.8-kilometer Shigatse to Gyirong section of the China–Nepal Railway began in 2020, scheduled for completion in 2022.

13. PURANG–LIPULEKH PASS

Purang has long been subjected to multiple religious and cultural influences, being located south of the Mount Kailash–Lake Manasarovar complex, which is sacred to the Bön, Buddhist, Hindu, and Jain religions. Purang was once the capital of the Purang-Guge Kingdom, which was conquered by Tibet under the Fifth Dalai Lama in 1679–1680. By the late eighteenth century, British influence was increasingly affecting the region. Competing interests over the Himalayan region led to the Anglo-Nepalese War of 1814–1816, resulting in the Treaty of Sugauli (1816). The treaty established a territorial boundary along the Kali River, a tributary of the Ganges originating at Kalapani in the Himalayas. The valley of Kalapani, topped by the Lipulekh Pass, had long formed an Indian pilgrimage route to Kailash-Manasarovar.

Russian and British rivalry for control of Central Asia prompted the Tibetan government to ban all foreigners and shut its borders in 1850. This did little to stop European explorers from crossing the frontier illicitly, with British teams discreetly mapping Tibet from the 1860s. Many expeditions were sent to western Tibet, including the sacred Kailash-Manasarovar region, source of three of Asia's mightiest rivers: the Indus, Ganges, and Brahmaputra. Following the British military expedition to Tibet of 1903–1904, three ports were opened up to British trade according to the Convention of Lhasa (1904), including Yadong and Gyantse in southern Tibet and Gartok, which was Lhasa's administrative headquarters for western Tibet as well as its principal trade market.

Following Nepali and Indian independence in 1923 and 1947, respectively, the Indo-Nepal Treaty of Peace and Friendship was signed in 1950. After Tibet's annexation by the People's Republic of China in 1951, India increased its security presence along the northern border, including the valley of Kalapani at the trijunction of the Indian, Chinese, and Nepali borders. Purang Port was established in 1954 to facilitate the Kailash-Manasarovar Yatra and facilitate trade among border residents. Purang Port is connected to India via the Lipulekh Pass and to Nepal via the Tinkar Pass. Lipulekh Pass and Purang Port closed after the outbreak of the Sino-Indian Border War in 1962 and were not reopened until 1992. Disputes arose between Nepal and India in 1998 over the Kali River and consequently over Kalapani territory and the strategic Lipulekh Pass. While India claimed that the Kali River begins only after the Kalapani River is joined by other streams, Nepal laid claim to all the areas east of the Kalapani River, one of the headwaters of the Kali River.

China and India reached a settlement over their border disputes in 2003 and signed the Declaration on Principles for Relations and Comprehensive Cooperation. After Tibetan unrest in 2008, several development initiatives were launched in the region. The government of the Tibet Autonomous Region formulated a ten-year development plan for the Purang–Lipulekh Pass on the Sino-Indian border in 2012. After the pilgrimage route to Kailash-Manasarovar via the Lipulekh Pass was badly damaged in the floods of 2013, China opened a second land crossing in Tibet at Nathula to allow access for Indian pilgrims undertaking the Kailash-Manasarovar Yatra in 2015. That

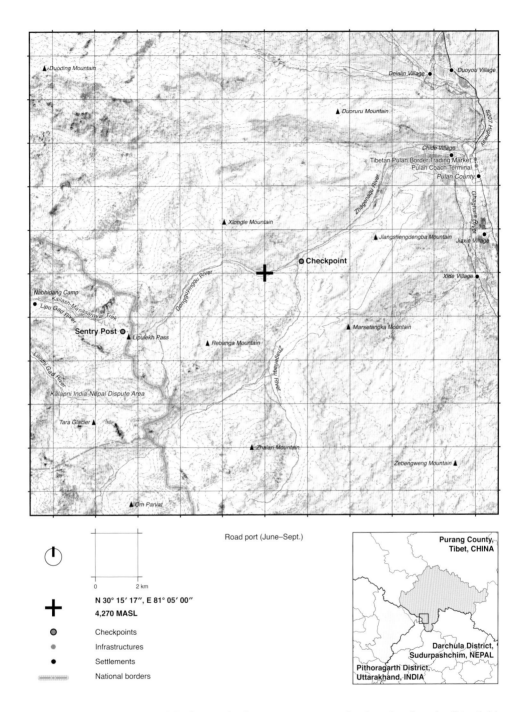

Road port (June–Sept.)

N 30° 15′ 17″, E 81° 05′ 00″
4,270 MASL

- ◉ Checkpoints
- ● Infrastructures
- ● Settlements
- National borders

Purang County, Tibet, CHINA

Darchula District, Sudurpashchim, NEPAL

Pithoragarth District, Uttarakhand, INDIA

year, China and India reached an agreement to further develop the Lipulekh Pass as a bilateral trade gateway. However, the Sino-Indian agreement caused dissatisfaction in Kathmandu, given the ongoing dispute between Nepal and India over the Kalapani territory. Nepal protested against India's unilateral inauguration of a metalled road through Kalapani connecting Dharchula in Uttarakhand with the Lipulekh Pass on the Chinese border in 2020.

NORTHWESTERN
BORDERLANDS

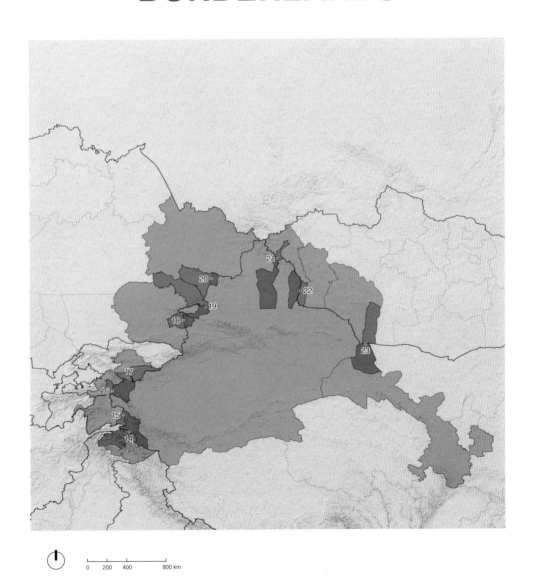

14. KHUNJERAB PASS–SOST

Despite the barriers posed by its inhospitable terrain and mighty mountain ranges, Kashmir was a major trading junction for Indo–Central Asian commerce. The southern branch of the ancient Silk Road followed the Yarkand River, a tributary of the Tarim River, connecting Aksu, Yarkand, and Tashkurgan. It then crossed the Karakoram Mountains via the western passes of Kilik, Mintaka, and Khunjerab, following the Gilgit River, a tributary of the Indus River, to Gilgit in northern Kashmir. The Sikh Empire ceded Kashmir to the British East India Company after being defeated in the Anglo-Sikh War of 1845–1846. The territory was sold to the influential noble Gulab Singh, and a Muslim-majority state was formed under a Hindu Dogra ruler.

The Pamir and Hindu-Kush mountains had been on the front line of the Great Game since the mid-nineteenth century. Multiple boundaries had been drawn to mark the extents of the Russian, British, and Chinese spheres of influence. Russia and Britain agreed on the demarcation of the northern border of Afghanistan (then a British protectorate) in 1884. That same year, Russia and China signed a protocol to the Treaty of Saint Petersburg/Ili, which effectively left much of the Pamirs in a no-man's land. The British proposed a new boundary between China and British India in 1899, broadly following the main ridgeline of the Karakoram mountain range that divides the watersheds of the Indus and Tarim Rivers.

The 1947 Partition of India resulted in the formation of the newly independent Hindu-majority India and Muslim-majority Pakistan. Kashmir has been the subject of dispute between the two countries ever since. Following the Indo-Pakistani War of 1947–1948, a cease-fire line in Kashmir was established under the Karachi Agreement of 1949, later designated as the Line of Control in 1972. Gilgit-Baltistan, which constitutes the northern portion of the Kashmir region bordering China, is administered by Pakistan. After the establishment of the People's Republic of China, the Tashkurgan Tajik Autonomous County was established on the Chinese side of the border with Kashmir in 1954.

Pakistan initiated the Indus Valley Road project in 1959 to strengthen its territorial control in the highly contested region and decided to extend the road to the Chinese border after the 1965 Indo-Pakistani War. China and Pakistan reached an agreement in 1966 to build the Karakoram Highway (KKH), also known as the China-Pakistan Friendship Highway. The highway connects Kashgar in Xinjiang, China, and Gilgit in Pakistan, crossing the border at the Khunjerab Pass. Work on the KKH was abruptly interrupted in 1971 by the Indo-Pakistani War but resumed in 1974. The KKH was completed in 1979, twenty years after its inauguration, and was officially opened to traffic in 1986.

China's Ministry of Foreign Trade approved the establishment of customs facilities at the border checkpoint (5,100 MASL) in 1974. The port was established at Khunjerab Pass in 1982. Due to the extreme climate, Chinese customs moved to Pilale (4,200 MASL) in 1982 and again to Tashkurgan Town (3,100 MASL) in 1993. The reconstructed and upgraded Pakistani portion of the KKH became part of the China-Pakistan Economic Corridor,

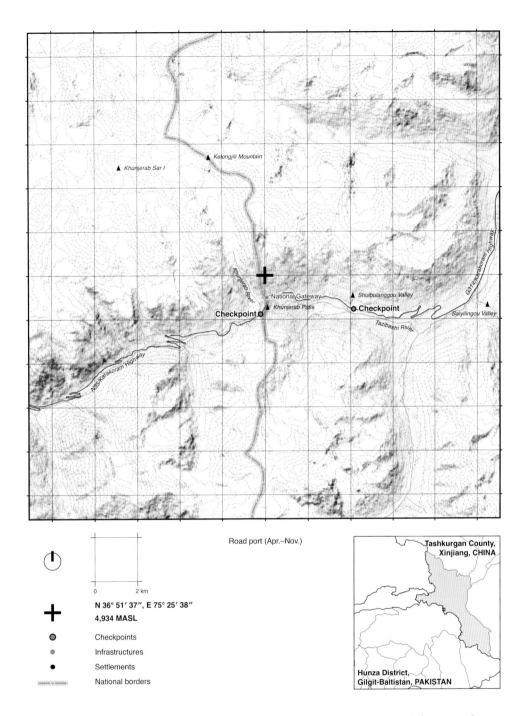

Khunjerab Sar I ▲

Kelongjili Mountain ▲

Khunjerab River

National Gateway ●

Khunjerab Pass ▲

Checkpoint ◉

Shuibulanggou Valley ▲

Checkpoint ◉

Tazibashi River

Saiyilingou Valley ▲

G314 Karakoram Highway

N35 Karakoram Highway

Road port (Apr.–Nov.)

N 36° 51′ 37″, E 75° 25′ 38″
4,934 MASL

0   2 km

◉ Checkpoints

● Infrastructures

● Settlements

National borders

Tashkurgan County,
Xinjiang, CHINA

Hunza District,
Gilgit-Baltistan, PAKISTAN

which was launched in 2013. The KKH is prone to natural disasters due to the extremely challenging terrain and climate. The KKH was blocked by a 20-kilometer-long lake that formed after massive landslides in Gilgit-Baltistan in 2010. The China Road and Bridge Corporation reinstated the KKH in 2015 by completing four large tunnels along the south shore of the barrier lake.

15. KARASU-KULMA

The historic region of Badakhshan in the Pamir Mountains was an important trading center on the ancient Silk Road. Badakhshan, then ruled by the Khanate of Kokand, became a vassal of Qing China in 1759 after the Qing Qianlong Emperor wrested control of Xinjiang from the Dzungar Khanate. Russia gradually took control of the entire territory of what would come to be known as Russian Turkestan between 1864 and 1885, with the Khanate of Kokand becoming a Russian vassal state in 1868. The kingdom of Kashgaria was established in Xinjiang in 1865 by the Muslim adventurer Yaqub Beg, who had fled from the Khanate of Kokand after losing Tashkent to the Russians. General Zuo Zongtang defeated Yakub Beg in 1877, restoring control of Xinjiang to Qing China.

Russia and China signed a protocol in 1884 to the Treaty of Saint Petersburg/Ili, declaring that the Russian boundary would run southwest from the Uzbel Pass and the Chinese boundary due south from the same point. This protocol effectively created a wedge of unclaimed land, including much of the Pamir mountain range. Russia subsequently sent forces into the Pamirs to secure its control over this area south of the Uzbel Pass, claiming the Sarikol Range to be the Sino-Russian boundary. Sino-Russian talks on the Pamirs began in 1892, but the issue was shelved in 1894 when China and Russia joined forces to resist Japan's advance into Northeast Asia.

The Pamirsky Post, one of Russia's most advanced military outposts in Central Asia, was established in 1893 at Murghab in Russian-controlled Badakhshan. Murghab became part of the Gorno-Badakhshan Autonomous Oblast in eastern Tajikistan after Tajikistan became an autonomous Soviet socialist republic in 1924 and a separate constituent republic in 1929. Work was carried out in the late nineteenth century to extend the road between Osh and Sary-Tash farther south toward Murghab, later known as the Pamir Highway. Much of the Pamir Highway linking the Pamir Mountains to the rest of the Soviet Union was constructed in the 1930s. On the other side of the border, following the founding of the People's Republic of China, the Tashkurgan Tajik Autonomous County was established in Xinjiang in 1954 and put under control of the Kashgar authorities in 1956. Construction of the Chinese portion of the Karakoram Highway between Kashgar and the Khunjerab Pass through Tashkurgan started in 1965.

After the collapse of the Soviet Union, the Tajikistani Civil War (1992–1997) broke out, with Gorno-Badakhshan declaring its independence. Although Gorno-Badakhshan remains an autonomous region within Tajikistan, the area continues to be politically unstable. China and Tajikistan delineated their border to the north of the Uzbel Pass in 1999. The road connecting Murghab to the Kulma Pass on the China-Tajikistan border was completed in 2001, and the Pamir Highway was thereby connected to China and the Karakoram Highway. Karasu Port, the only border port between China and Tajikistan, was established in 2004 and began year-round service in 2010. Sino-Tajikistani relations further improved when Tajikistan ceded the northeastern slopes of

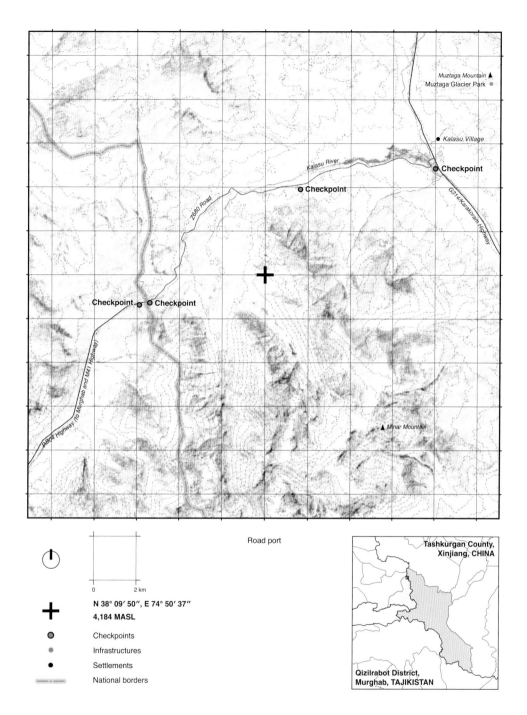

Muztaga Mountain ▲
Muztaga Glacier Park ●

● *Kalasu Village*

Kalasu River

○ **Checkpoint**

○ **Checkpoint**

G314 Karakoram Highway

Z580 Road

Checkpoint ○─○ **Checkpoint**

Rabot Highway (To Murghab and M41 Highway)

▲ *Minar Mountain*

Road port

⊕ ↑

0 ___ 2 km

✚ **N 38° 09′ 50″, E 74° 50′ 37″**
4,184 MASL

● Checkpoints
· Infrastructures
● Settlements
▬▬ National borders

Tashkurgan County,
Xinjiang, CHINA

Qizilrabot District,
Murghab, TAJIKISTAN

the Sarikol Range to the south of the Uzbel Pass to China in 2011, ending a 130-year-old dispute. China and Tajikistan signed a number of technical, economic, and cultural exchange agreements in 2015. Technical studies were completed by 2017 for the Five Nations Railway Corridor Project, a railway linking China with Iran via Kyrgyzstan, Tajikistan, and Afghanistan.

16. IRKESHTAM-ERKESHTAM

The 1864 Protocol of Chuguchak (known as the Protocol of Tacheng in Chinese) was signed between Qing China and tsarist Russia to clarify the border between the Altai Mountains to the north and the Tianshan Mountains to the south. Irkeshtam was a long-established caravan stop on a major trade route running along the southern foot of the Tianshan Mountains. The Irkeshtam border trade port was established in 1884 after the second Kashgar treaty, an auxiliary treaty of the 1881 Treaty of Saint Petersburg/Ili, defined the southernmost section of the Chinese-Russian boundary. As tsarist Russia gradually extended its control across Central Asia over the second half of the nineteenth century, a horse trade route was established in 1893 between Irkeshtam in Xinjiang and Osh in Russian Turkestan.

Irkeshtam became a major node on the postal and telecommunications network between Russia and Xinjiang in China in 1895, when Russia set up a telegraph station in Kashgar to communicate with the Russian Telegraph Bureau in Andijan via Irkeshtam. After the establishment of the Republic of China in 1912, the Chinese republican government started to invest in transport and telecommunications infrastructure in Xinjiang with a telegraph line between Kashgar and Irkeshtam established in 1917. During the Second Sino-Japanese War, a 214-kilometer road between Irkeshtam and Kashgar was completed in 1944 by the Nationalist government to facilitate transportation of supplies from Western allies.

The People's Republic of China prioritized the maintenance of the road between Irkeshtam and Kashgar. Soon after its formation in 1951, the government of Ulugqat County in Xinjiang embarked on the repair of four major river crossings along the route. Irkeshtam's role as a major node on the postal and telecommunications network between the Soviet Union and Xinjiang in China was superseded in 1952 by Tuergate, 100 kilometers northeast on the Sino-Soviet border. The Irkeshtam border crossing was then closed for more than three decades, from the late 1950s until the early 1990s, due to the hostile political relations between the Soviet Union and China during that time.

After the 1991 collapse of the Soviet Union, Kyrgyzstan and China delineated their agreed border in 1996. Irkeshtam Port was opened on a trial basis in July 1997, officially becoming fully operational in May 2002. The China Road and Bridge Corporation (CRBC) joined forces with the Xinjiang Beixin Road & Bridge Group Corporation in 2004 to work on the rehabilitation of the Osh–Irkeshtam Road Project in Kyrgyzstan. In response to a magnitude 6.7 earthquake that struck the region in October 2008 and an intensification of social unrest in southern Xinjiang, Chinese authorities constructed a new border port complex in Ulugqat Town, which started operation in 2011, 136 kilometers east of the old Irkeshtam Port. The launch of the Belt and Road Initiative in 2013 led to the rapid development of a number of transportation projects. The CRBC commenced work on upgrading the road between Osh (Kyrgyzstan) and Kashgar (Xinjiang) in 2013 and carried out a feasibility

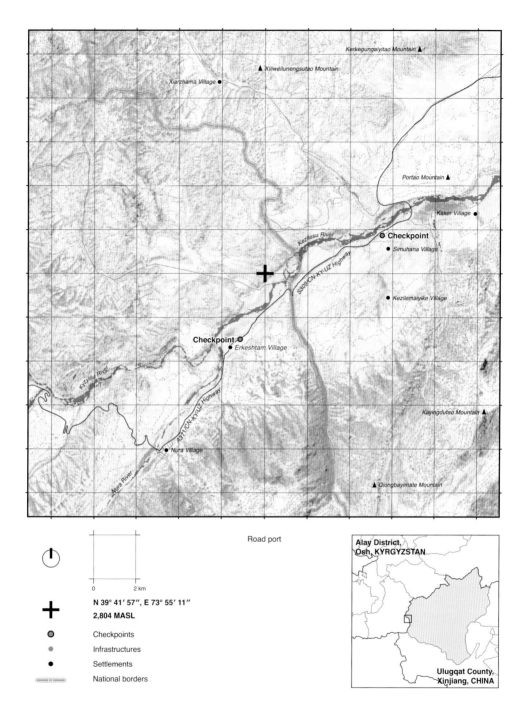

Kerkegungaiyitao Mountain ▲

▲ Xiliweilunengsutao Mountain

Xiarzhama Village ●

Portao Mountain ▲

Kaker Village ●

Kezilesu River

○ Checkpoint

● Simuhana Village

S309/CN-KY-UZ Highway

● Kezilemaiyike Village

Checkpoint ○

● Erkeshtam Village

KYZ-visu River

A371/CN-KY-UZ Highway

Kayingdutao Mountain ▲

● Nura Village

Nura River

▲ Qiongbayimate Mountain

Road port

0   2 km

N 39° 41′ 57″, E 73° 55′ 11″

2,804 MASL

◉ Checkpoints

● Infrastructures

● Settlements

National borders

Alay District,
Osh, KYRGYZSTAN

Ulugqat County,
Xinjiang, CHINA

study for the China-Kyrgyzstan-Uzbekistan (CKU) Railway project. The Kashgar–Irkeshtam Railway railway is part of the western sector of the CKU Railway. The CKU transportation corridor officially opened in October 2017 and became fully operational by February 2018.

17. TUERGATE-TORUGART

Tsarist Russia gradually extended its control across Central Asia over the second half of the nineteenth century. The Sino-Russia border was clarified under the Protocol of Chuguchak/Tacheng ratified by Qing China and tsarist Russia in 1864. In 1868, at the direction of the first governor-general of Russian Turkestan, a fortress was built in Naryn on the major caravan route between Kashgar under Qing administration and Zhetysu (Semirechye), which had been annexed by tsarist Russia.

Qing China and tsarist Russia signed the Treaty of Saint Petersburg/Ili in 1881, after which a border trade port was established at Torugart, midway between Kashgar and Naryn on the caravan route through the Tianshan Mountains. Russia built a 150-kilometer road between Torugart and At-Bashi village in the late 1890s, which was later extended to Naryn. Under Russian pressure, the Qing government agreed to build a 170-kilometer road between Tuergate and Kashgar. Russia's Sino-Russian Transport Bank loaned 20 million rubles toward the construction of the road, and Russian merchants were given a trade monopoly on the route.

The newly established People's Republic of China designated the route between Kashgar and Tuergate as the primary land link between Xinjiang and then Soviet Kyrgyzstan. Irkeshtam, a border town located 100 kilometers southwest of Tuergate, was a major node of the postal and telecommunications networks between the Soviet Union and Xinjiang in China until it was replaced by Tuergate in 1952. The Army Corps of Engineers of the PLA (Xinjiang Garrison) renovated the road between Tuergate and Kashgar in 1953. Tuergate Port was a major importer of petroleum, fertilizer, and mineral products from the Soviet Union and Eastern Europe from the 1950s until 1969, when the port was closed due to the Sino-Soviet border conflict. The early 1980s saw a thaw in Sino-Soviet relations. Tuergate Port reopened in December 1983. The border dispute between Kyrgyzstan and China was resolved in 1992 after the dissolution of the Soviet Union, although some restrictions and regulations still remain. Russian border guards patrolled the Kyrgyzstan side of the border until 1999, after which they were replaced with Kyrgyz personnel.

Before the official opening of Irkeshtam Port in 2002, Tuergate Port remained the only significant port on the border between China and Kyrgyzstan. Given Torugart Pass's very high altitude (3,752 MASL), with freezing temperatures, extreme winds, and an oxygen-deficient atmosphere, the national and Xinjiang Uygur Autonomous Region governments decided in 1992 to relocate the customs buildings and port facilities 110 kilometers south to Tuopa Town (2,000 MASL). The new Tuergate Port complex located midway between Kashgar and Ulugqat became operational in late 1995. Following the launch of China's Belt and Road Initiative in 2013, the China Road and Bridge Corporation (CRBC) has taken on a leading role in the development of transport-related projects throughout the region. The 168-kilometer Kashgar–Tuergate Highway in Xinjiang was upgraded by the CRBC in 2014. The CRBC completed the upgrading of the 539-kilometer Bishkek-Naryn-Torugart Highway in

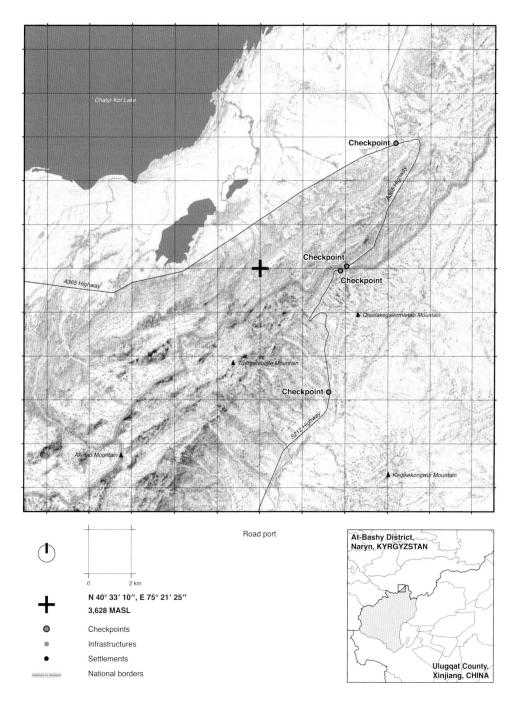

Chatyr Kol Lake

Checkpoint

A365 Highway

Checkpoint
Checkpoint

A365 Highway

▲ Qiaolakegalermietao Mountain

▲ Tuergatebiele Mountain

Checkpoint

S212 Highway

Aketao Mountain ▲

▲ Keqikekongwur Mountain

Road port

N
0   2 km

N 40° 33′ 10″, E 75° 21′ 25″
3,628 MASL

⬤ Checkpoints
● Infrastructures
• Settlements
▬▬ National borders

**At-Bashy District,
Naryn, KYRGYZSTAN**

**Ulugqat County,
Xinjiang, CHINA**

2019, one of the eight major regional highways in Kyrgyzstan. The CRBC also carried out a feasibility study for the Kashgar–Tuergate Railway in 2013, which is part of the northern sector of the China-Kyrgyzstan-Ukraine Railway. By 2021, despite almost twenty-five years of negotiations among the three countries, agreement over the construction of the China-Kyrgyzstan-Ukraine Railway remained elusive.

18. KHORGAS-KHORGOS

In competition with the surge in British trade with China after the First Opium War (1839–1842), Russia pushed hard to increase Sino-Russian trade in China's northwest. Cross-border trade began in Kuldja (Ili in Chinese) in the late 1840s. The 1851 Treaty of Kuldja further regularized trade and allowed for Russian settlements in Kuldja and Chuguchak (Tacheng in Chinese). The 1864 Protocol of Chuguchak/Tacheng signed by Qing China and tsarist Russia clarified their border from the Altai Mountains in the north to the Tianshan Mountains in the south. A border post was established on the eastern bank of a tributary of the Ili River at Nikan (now Khorgas), a long-established caravan stop on the major traditional trade route running just north of the Tianshan Mountains.

During the Dungan Revolt (1862–1877, a Muslim rebellion in northwestern China, including Xinjiang), Russian troops seized the opportunity to occupy the Ili region in 1871. Although the 1881 Treaty of Saint Petersburg/Ili restored Qing sovereignty in the Ili region, it also granted Russia the right to trade in six towns in Mongolia, Gansu, and Xinjiang, including Khorgas. Khorgas continued to be a major trade port between Russia and the Republic of China after 1912, although it was temporarily closed during the Russian Civil War (1917–1922). It was reopened in 1920 when the ROC and the Russian Soviet Republic signed the Ili Protocol to reestablish and develop trade between Xinjiang and the Soviet Union's Central Asian territories.

During the Second Sino-Japanese War, road networks were expanded rapidly in the region to provide logistical support for the Chinese armed forces. Supplies entered Xinjiang from Soviet Russia through Khorgas and then moved on to Urumqi and Lanzhou. Khorgas continued to serve as the primary trade port between the Soviet Union and China's northwest after the establishment of the People's Republic of China, although relations between the Soviet Union and China deteriorated in the late 1950s. Hostilities were triggered by the Ili-Tacheng Incident in spring 1962, when more than 67,000 mostly ethnic Kazakhs from Xinjiang fled to the Soviet Republic of Kazakhstan via Khorgas and Baketu. The port at Khorgas remained closed after this incident until 1983, when political relations thawed. The Yining Border Economic Cooperation Zone was established in 1992.

The new millennium witnessed the rapid development of transnational infrastructure and cross-border cooperation zones in the region. Construction of the Central Asia–China Gas Pipeline began in 2007, with stage one becoming operational in December 2009. Pipelines A, B, and C enter China at Khorgas and Alashankou, where they connect to the second West-East Gas Pipeline of China. Construction of the Khorgas/Khorgos International Center for Cross-Border Cooperation began in 2004. The center was opened in April 2012, and railway tracks from the Chinese and Kazakh sides of the border were finally connected in December 2012. The port at Khorgas was also connected to Lianyungang Port in Jiangsu Province on China's east coast by highway and railway. The Khorgos Eastern Gates SEZ opened in 2015,

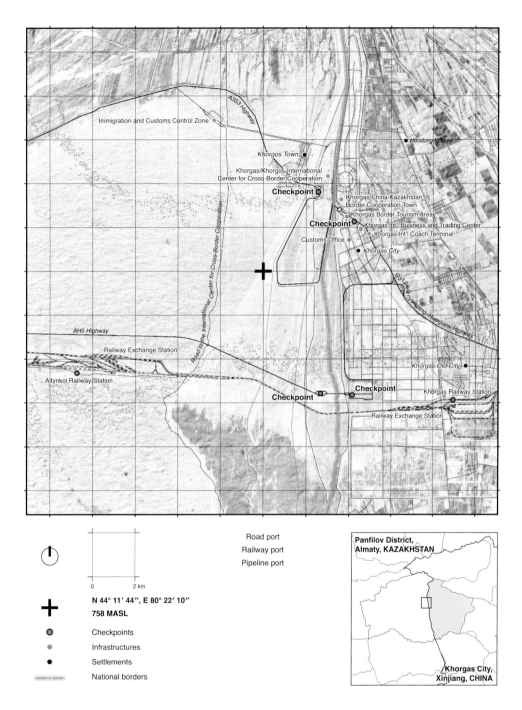

Road port
Railway port
Pipeline port

Panfilov District, Almaty, KAZAKHSTAN

Khorgas City, Xinjiang, CHINA

N 44° 11′ 44″, E 80° 22′ 10″

758 MASL

Checkpoints

Infrastructures

Settlements

National borders

jointly developed by the Kazakhstan's national railway company and China's Lianyungang Port Holdings Group (LPH). China's COSCO Shipping and the LPH were granted a 49 percent stake in the Khorgos Eastern Gates project in 2017, the same year the western route of the China Railway Express through Khorgas/Khorgos started operating.

19. ALASHANKOU-DOSTYK

Qing China and tsarist Russia defined their western border from the Altai Mountains in the north to the Tianshan Mountains in the south under the 1864 Protocol of Chuguchak/Tacheng. The border cut across Dzungarian Gate (now Alashankou-Dostyk), a geographically and historically significant mountain pass between China and Central Asia. As early as 1886, Russian engineers proposed a railway between Siberia and Russian Turkestan, part of a larger plan to enhance Russia's military and economic presence at the border with China. A Russian commission was established in 1896 to assess the feasibility of the Turkestan–Siberia Railway, and work on it started in 1906.

By the early twentieth century, Qing China and tsarist Russia were aware of the potential of petroleum resources in the Dzungarian Basin. In 1905, Russian geologist Vladimir Obruchev confirmed the vast potential of Dushanzi, at the southwestern edge of the Dzungarian Basin. The Qing Xinjiang regional government established a joint public-private enterprise at Dushanzi in 1909, which drilled its first oil well after importing a rig and refining cauldron from Russia. The Dushanzi operation ceased in 1911 because of the Chinese Revolution and was not fully restored until 1936, when the Dushanzi oil refinery was established with Sino-Soviet collaboration.

Construction of the Turkestan–Siberian Railway was suspended for a decade following the outbreak of the Russian Civil War in 1917. Work resumed in the late 1920s, and the railroad was mostly built during the USSR's first Five-Year Plan (1928–1932). A Sino-Soviet alliance was formed after the establishment of the People's Republic of China. The signing of a Sino-Soviet agreement in 1954 laid the institutional foundations for construction of a new railway joining the existing lines on both sides of the border, thereby enabling goods to be transported from China's Pacific coast to the Baltic ports. The railway line was planned to connect Alashankou with Aktogay on the Turkestan–Siberian Railway in Soviet Kazakhstan and Alashankou with Lanzhou on the Lanzhou–Lianyungang Railway in China.

Due to a breakdown in Sino-Soviet relations, construction of the Aktogay–Lanzhou Railway was suspended in 1961. Work on the section between Urumqi and Alashankou only resumed in 1985. It was completed and linked to the Aktogay to Dostyk section in 1990. Alashankou Port was established the same year, opening to international freight on a temporary basis in July 1991. After the dissolution of the Soviet Union, Alashankou Port was officially opened.

Energy projects have dominated the region's development since the late 1990s. The Kazakhstan-China Oil Pipeline enters China at Alashankou. The pipeline became operational in December 2005 and first delivered oil to the Dushanzi refinery in June 2006. Stage one of the Central Asia–China Gas Pipeline, which also entered China at Alashankou, became operational in 2009. Construction of the China Guodian Corporation's million-kilowatt Alashankou wind farm began the same year to harness the power of the area's strong winds. Over the past two decades, Alashankou has witnessed the rapid development of its transport infrastructure, making it a major node on the

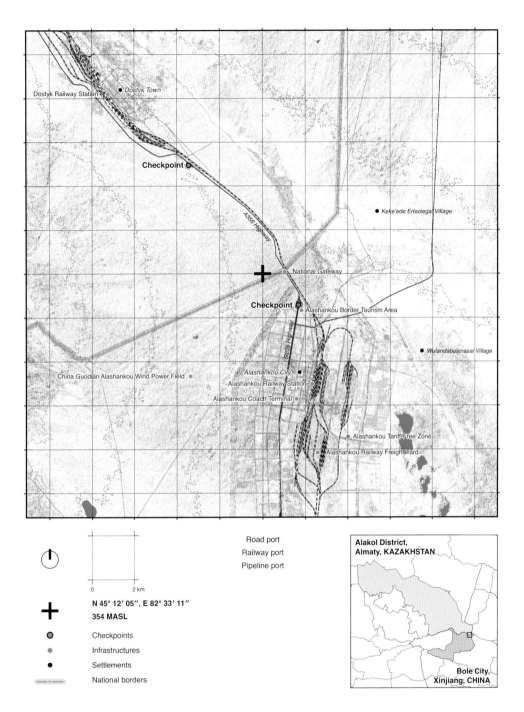

Road port
Railway port
Pipeline port

**Alakol District,
Almaty, KAZAKHSTAN**

N 45° 12′ 05″, E 82° 33′ 11″

354 MASL

Checkpoints

Infrastructures

Settlements

National borders

**Bole City,
Xinjiang, CHINA**

China Railway Express (CR Express) network connecting China and Europe. Asia's largest indoor container transfer station was completed at Alashankou in 2009 to protect container loading and unloading from the extreme local climate. CR Express services began operating through Alashankou-Dostyk in 2011. The number of CR Express freight trains passing through the port surpassed 10,000 for the first time in 2019.

20. BAKETU-BAKHTY

The steppes of Dzungaria, bounded by the Tianshan Mountains to the south and the Altai Mountains to the north, have long been inhabited by nomadic peoples. The territory came under the control of Qing China in 1759 after the Qianlong Emperor wrested control of Xinjiang from the Dzungar Khanate. A Qing fort was built on the banks of the Ujar River in 1764. It was relocated to Chuguchak/Tacheng in 1766 and named Suijingcheng (literally, "city to establish tranquillity"). Qing Chinese and Russian territorial claims in Central Asia edged ever closer by the late eighteenth century, as the Russian Empire gradually integrated the Kazakh steppes under its control. Russia defeated three leading Kazakh khans between 1822 and 1848 and built a number of forts to subdue its newly conquered territories.

To compete with the surge in British trade with China following the First Opium War, Russia pressed to increase its Chinese trade through China's northwest. Chuguchak/Tacheng and Kuldja/Ili were considered the most important commercial centers in western China. The 1851 Treaty of Kuldja regularized trade and permitted Russian settlement in both Chuguchak and Kuldja. The Convention of Peking (1860) was signed between Qing China and tsarist Russia, assigning the basin of the Naryn River and Lake Issyk-Kul in the Tianshan Mountains to Russia. The 1864 Protocol of Chuguchak/Tacheng further defined the Sino-Russian border. The entire region between Lake Balkhash and the Tianshan Mountains, including the western part of Chuguchak Mountain, was assigned to Russia. Suijingcheng was destroyed in 1865 during the Dungan Revolt and was rebuilt by 1888 after Qing forces reconquered Xinjiang in 1877.

Tacheng County was established in 1913 after the Republic of China took power in 1912. The port in Tacheng was closed in 1917 at the outbreak of the Russian Civil War and reopened in 1920. After Japan took control of China's coast during the Second Sino-Japanese War, Dzungaria became a logistical lifeline through which vital supplies were imported to China via Kuldja or Tacheng. Baketu Port in Tacheng was established in 1953 by the People's Republic of China. It was closed following the Ili-Tacheng Incident in the spring of 1962, when more than 67,000 mostly ethnic Kazakhs fled Xinjiang to the Soviet Republic of Kazakhstan through Khorgas and Baketu. The Chinese central government sent a special team of the Xinjiang Production and Construction Corps to establish a belt of state-run farms near the Sino-Soviet border in order to counter the impact of the Ili-Tacheng Incident and stabilize the region. Sino-Soviet border hostilities erupted in 1969, with one of the most violent clashes occurring in August that year at Tielieketi in Tacheng.

As relations between China and the Soviet Union thawed, trade across the Sino-Soviet border had resumed by the early 1980s. Baketu Port officially opened in 1992. That same year, Tacheng was designated as an open border city, and the Tacheng Border Economic Cooperation Zone was established. The Chinese central government launched a national plan in 2020 to mobilize the resources of nineteen prosperous provinces and municipalities to assist in Xinjiang's economic development. Liaoning, a coastal province in

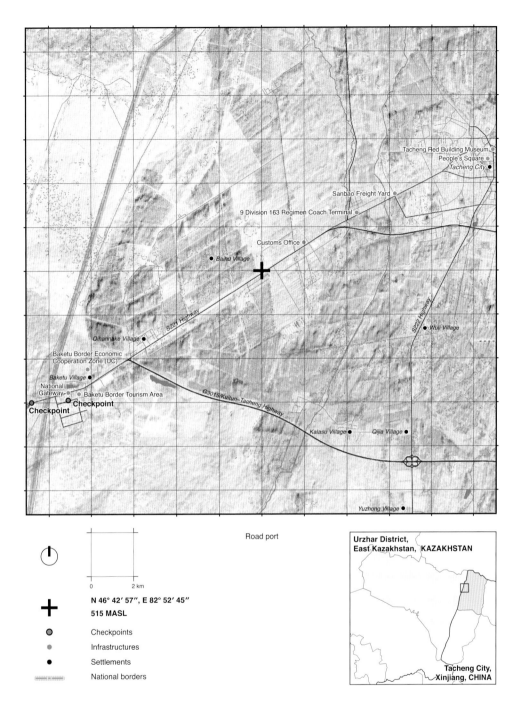

Road port

N 46° 42′ 57″, E 82° 52′ 45″
515 MASL

⊙ Checkpoints
• Infrastructures
● Settlements
▭▭▭ National borders

Urzhar District,
East Kazakhstan, KAZAKHSTAN

Tacheng City,
Xinjiang, CHINA

northeastern China, was assigned to be the supporting partner for Tacheng Prefecture. The national-level Baketu Border Economic Cooperation Zone (also known as the Liaoning-Tacheng New District) was established in 2011. Transportation infrastructure was rapidly developed in the region, with the Karamay–Tacheng Expressway completed in 2014 and the Karamay–Tacheng Railway in 2019.

21. HONGSHANZUI-DAYAN

Russian and Qing territorial interests started to clash over the Irtysh basin and its Altai Mountain catchment in the early eighteenth century. Historically referred to as Jinshan (literally, "gold mountain") in Chinese literature, the Altai Mountains are rich in forest and mineral resources. The Qianlong Emperor's defeat of the Dzungar Khanate (1758–1759) and his annexation of Xinjiang prompted Russian concerns about the possibility of Chinese fleets entering the Irtysh basin and western Siberia from Lake Zaysan. The Convention of Peking (1860) and Protocol of Chuguchak/Tacheng (1864) defined the border between the Russian and Qing Empires in the Irtysh basin. Lake Zaysan was assigned to Russia in its entirety.

During the Dungan Revolt, a Muslim rebellion in northwestern China, the Tibetan monk Bla Ma Dkar Po led a Mongolian volunteer army to defend Tibetan Buddhism in the region. Qing authorities built a Buddhist temple with the name "Chenghuasi" (literally, "spreading civilization") in 1871 northeast of Ulungur Lake (Buluntuohai in Chinese) and celebrated the Tibetan monk as a great defender of Qing territory. The area around the Altai Mountains had long been the homeland of the Mongol tribe of Altai Uriankhai, which had been organized into several banners under the authority of Qing ambans (high officials) since the 1759 Qing conquest of Xinjiang. In the aftermath of the Dungan Revolt, Kazakhs also migrated into Altai Uriankhai territory, and the Chenghuasi area developed into a sizable settlement.

Russian expansion into Mongolia became feasible when Saint Petersburg came to terms with Britain and later Japan to delimit their respective spheres of interest in China in the late nineteenth century. On the eve of the collapse of the Qing dynasty, the region of Outer Mongolia declared its independence in 1911, but this was not recognized by the newly established Republic of China. The Altai region was divided between Outer Mongolia and Xinjiang in 1913. Chenghuasi County (now Altai City) and Buluntuohai County (now Fuhai County) were established in 1919 within the Altai Special District in Xinjiang, China. Outer Mongolia's independence was recognized by the ROC in 1946. A number of Sino-Mongolian border conflicts flared up in the 1950s. Mongolian forces entered China by the Hongshanzui Pass in 1956 and occupied approximately 720 square kilometers in the Altai Special District. The Sino-Mongolian Border Treaty was signed in 1962 in Mongolia's favor to appease Mongolia at the height of the Sino-Soviet split (1956–1966).

The region developed visibly in the early 1990s. Hongshanzui Port was established and a border trade market built in 1992. Discussions promoting economic and cultural exchanges among Russia, Kazakhstan, China, and Mongolia, which share the Altai Mountain region, started in 2002 when a transboundary coordination mechanism was adopted, advocating international recognition of the ecological and cultural importance of the Altai Mountains. The Russian Altai was included on UNESCO's World Heritage List in 1998, and the Chinese Altai was added to the UNESCO World Heritage tentative list in 2010. A proposal to establish the Trans-Altai International Tourism

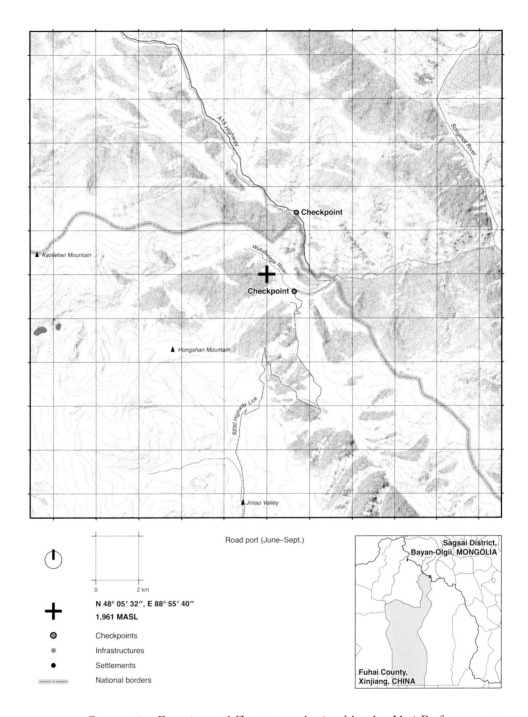

Road port (June–Sept.)

N 48° 05' 32", E 88° 55' 40"
1,961 MASL

○ Checkpoints
· Infrastructures
● Settlements
▭▭▭ National borders

Sagsai District,
Bayan-Olgii, MONGOLIA

Fuhai County,
Xinjiang, CHINA

Cooperative Experimental Zone was submitted by the Altai Prefecture government to the Chinese central government for approval in 2015. Work began in 2017 on the extension of the Xinjiang–Tibet Highway (G216) from Altai City to Hongshanzui Port on the Sino-Mongolian border.

22. TAKESHIKEN-BULGAN

After Qing forces conquered Dzungaria in 1759, the Office of the Governor of Khovd, a Qing government unit responsible for all of western Mongolia, was established in 1761. Russian pressure to increase Sino-Russian trade through China's northwestern regions grew during the nineteenth century, as Russia sought to compete with Britain's surge in trade with China after the First Opium War. After the 1851 Treaty of Kuldja, trade in livestock and fur boomed in the valley of the Bulgan River, a tributary of the Ulungur River that flows from the Altai Mountains. Sino-Russian trade further expanded after the 1881 Treaty of Saint Petersburg/Ili, when six towns in Mongolia, Gansu, and Xinjiang were opened to Russian consulates and traders, including Khovd in Mongolia.

In 1911, on the eve of the collapse of the Qing dynasty, Outer Mongolia declared its independence. It was not recognized by the Republic of China, established in 1912. The ROC government established Bulgan County in 1924, straddling the Xinjiang–Outer Mongolian border. When the ROC recognized the independence of Outer Mongolia in 1946, the eastern half of Bulgan became part of Khovd Province in Mongolia and the western half became part of the Altai Special District in Xinjiang, China. The Chinese portion of Bulgan County was incorporated into Qinghe County in 1947, named after the Qinggil River, another tributary of the Ulungur River originating in the Altai Mountains.

The Sino-Mongolian relationship improved after the establishment of the People's Republic of China. Several agreements involving Chinese aid and economic and technical assistance were signed between the two countries during the second half of the 1950s. To appease Mongolia within the context of the Sino-Soviet split (1956–1966), a Sino-Mongolian Border Treaty was signed in 1962 in favor of Mongolia's territorial claims, so that the international boundary of the Khovd region now follows the boundary between the catchments of the Qinggil and Bulgan Rivers. The Sino-Mongolian relationship deteriorated once again after Mongolia and the Soviet Union signed a mutual assistance agreement in 1966. Mongolia requested deployment of Soviet forces on its territory, leading to Chinese security concerns and the suspension of Sino-Mongolian border trade.

The Sino-Mongolian relationship improved in the late 1980s. The two countries signed a treaty on border control in 1988. Takeshiken Port was established the following year, 15.5 kilometers west of the Sino-Mongolian border. Rapid port development resulted in the development of Takeshiken Town by 1998. Efforts have been made to promote transnational tourism in the Altai Mountains region since the early 2000s. China and Mongolia signed a memorandum of understanding in 2005 on the Implementation Plan for Chinese Tour Groups visiting Mongolia. The following year, the Takeshiken Port Tourism Development and Cooperation Colloquium was held in Qinghe County. Both China and Mongolia have taken various measures over the past decade to enhance environmental protection in the region and seek international recognition of the ecological and cultural importance of the Altai

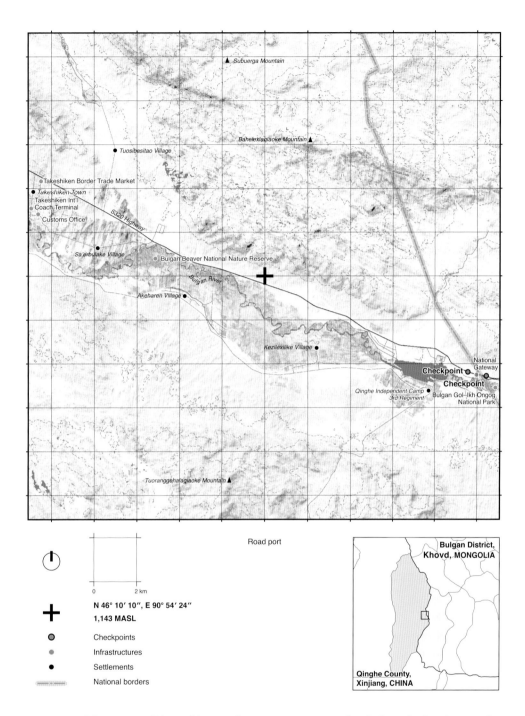

Road port

N 46° 10′ 10″, E 90° 54′ 24″

1,143 MASL

⦿ Checkpoints

● Infrastructures

● Settlements

▬▬▬ National borders

Bulgan District,
Khovd, MONGOLIA

Qinghe County,
Xinjiang, CHINA

Mountains. China Altai, with its nature reserves (including the headwaters for the Irtysh and Ulungur Rivers), was added to the UNESCO World Heritage tentative list in 2010. Bulgan Gol–Ikh Ongog National Park was established on the Mongolian side of the border in 2011. Transnational conservation efforts focus particularly on protecting the Sino-Mongolian beaver, an endangered species found only in the Ulungur River basin.

23. MAZONGSHAN-NARINSEBESTEI

The Mazongshan area is located at the northwestern end of the Hexi (or Gansu) Corridor of the Northern Silk Road. During the Qianlong period (1735–1796), a north-south trade route across the Qilian Mountains and the Hexi Corridor connecting Tibet, Qinghai, Mongolia, and Russia was set up. Natural springs, notably the Gongpoquan Spring near Mount Mazongshan and the Sebestei Spring near Mount Baitag Bogd, were critical to water the camel caravans that trekked through the Black Gobi Desert to the north of the Qilian Mountains. General Zuo Zongtang was victorious in 1873 at Suzhou, the last rebel stronghold in the Hexi Corridor in west Gansu during the Dungan Revolt. Zuo executed or resettled thousands of Muslims in the Hexi Corridor to prevent future collusion among the Muslims of Gansu, Shaanxi, and Xinjiang.

Outer Mongolia declared independence after the collapse of the Qing dynasty in 1911, but this was not recognized by the new Republic of China. The ROC government supported the Sino-Swedish Expedition (1927–1935) led by Sven Hedin and Xu Xusheng. This expedition included scientific missions and grand schemes to map an air route from Berlin to Peking and plan roads and railways from Peking to Kashgar. In the early stage of the expedition, Hedin suffered from gallstones while traveling through the Black Gobi Desert and had to rest at the Sebestei Spring for nearly a month. At the outbreak of the Second Sino-Japanese War in 1937, the ROC government established the Governance Bureau of Mazongshan, later the Governance Bureau of Subei (literally, "north of Suzhou"). The ROC recognized Outer Mongolia's independence in 1946.

The People's Republic of China founded the Subei Autonomous District in 1950, which was upgraded to Subei Mongol Autonomous County in 1955. Construction of the 1,892-kilometer Lanzhou–Xinjiang Railway began in 1952, running along the Hexi Corridor and entering Xinjiang near the Hongliu River. The project was completed in 1962. When China and Mongolia signed a treaty delineating their common frontier in 1962, text and maps from Sven Hedin's report on the Sino-Swedish Expedition (1927–1935) were used by Chinese premier Zhou Enlai to bolster Chinese territorial claims to the area around the Sebestei Spring. On the Mongolian side of the border, Great Gobi A and Great Gobi B both became part of the Greater Gobi Strictly Protected Area (SPA) established in 1975, designated by the United Nations as an international Biosphere Reserve in 1991.

Mazongshan Port was established in 1992, and the port highway on the Chinese side of the border was completed in March 1993. However, the Mongolian checkpoint was unilaterally closed in August 1993 under pressure from the United Nations, because the planned port highway in Mongolia would pass through the Great Gobi A SPA. Since then, both countries have pursued bilateral negotiations seeking an alternative route for the port highway in Mongolia, with the object of resuming border port operations. Infrastructure development on the Chinese side of the border proceeds despite uncertainty over the reopening of the Mazongshan Port. Construction of

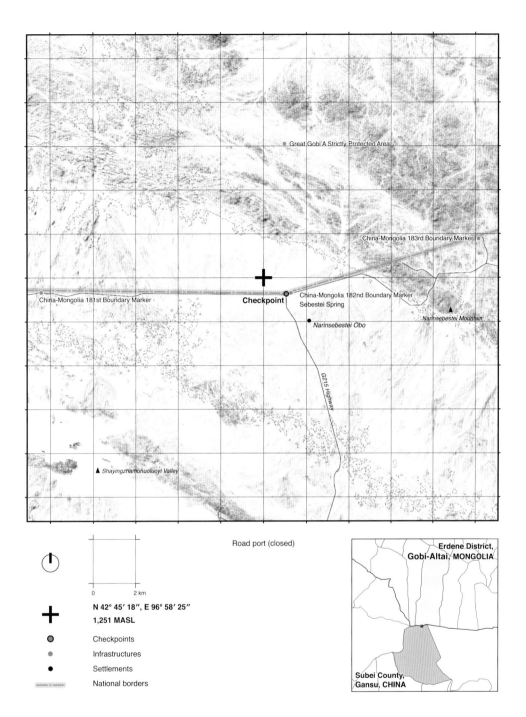

Road port (closed)

N 42° 45′ 18″, E 96° 58′ 25″
1,251 MASL

● Checkpoints

● Infrastructures

● Settlements

National borders

the 2,822-kilometer Beijing–Urumqi Expressway (G7) started in September 2012. It opened to traffic in April 2019. Originally envisioned during the Sino-Swedish Expedition, the G7 Expressway passes through several deserts in northwestern China, including the Black Gobi in Gansu. The G215 Highway, which runs from Pu'er City in Yunnan to Mazongshan Town in Gansu, was extended to Mazongshan Port in 2018.

NORTHEASTERN
BORDERLANDS

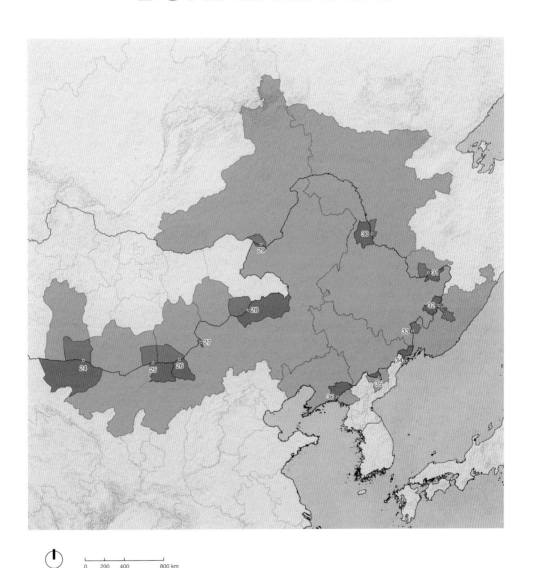

24. CEKE–SHIVEE KHUREN

Increasing Russian influence in Mongolia beginning in the mid-nineteenth century threatened the interests of the Qing Empire, which had exerted control over the area since the seventeenth century. Separated by the Gobi Desert, one of the world's largest tracts of arid sand dunes and gravel plains, Inner Mongolia in the south was closely tied to the Qing administrative system, while Outer Mongolia in the north was viewed militarily by China as a buffer area until the early 1900s. Russia and Britain delineated their respective spheres of interest in China in 1895: Russia agreed to refrain from new railway construction in the Yangtze Basin, while Britain promised to do likewise in Chinese territories north of the Great Wall.

After the Russo-Japanese War, Russia and Japan signed a treaty in 1907 dividing Manchuria and Mongolia into two separate spheres of interest, with Outer Mongolia being recognized by Japan as part of the Russian sphere. During the first decade of the twentieth century, the Qing authorities accelerated Han migration to Inner Mongolia in the belief that Russia would find it difficult to absorb territories with significant Han populations. On the eve of the collapse of the Qing dynasty in 1911, Outer Mongolia declared its independence, but this was not recognized by the newly established Republic of China until 1946.

Chu-yen (or Juyan) is a unique wetland located in the Gobi Desert in Inner Mongolia and historically part of the Hexi (or Gansu) Corridor of the Northern Silk Road. It was investigated by Russian explorer Pyotr Kozlov and British explorer Aurel Stein in the early twentieth century and by the Sino-Swedish Expedition in 1930. The last group led by Swedish explorer Sven Hedin acquired several thousand Han dynasty wooden slips. A strategic garrison site with military and agricultural colonies established since the second century BC, Chu-yen included two lakes fed by the Etsin-gol/Heihe River that flowed from the Hexi Corridor in the southwest. Given its strategic frontier location, the Chu-yen region witnessed the establishment of air-defense projects and rapid agricultural reclamation of arid land over the three decades after the establishment of the People's Republic of China. These projects, however, led to acute environmental degradation. The region was reduced to a dustbowl for the rest of the twentieth century. West Chu-yen Lake dried up in 1961, and East Chu-yen Lake dried up in 1992.

Ceke (meaning "river bay" in Mongolian) opened in 1992 as a seasonal port. Water reallocation projects had been planned and implemented within the Etsin-gol/Heihe River basin since 2001, and the East Chu-yen Lake reappeared in 2003. The demarcation of the Sino-Mongolian border was completed in 2005. Ceke Port was officially established and began year-round service. The same year, Mongolia's Naryn Sukhait Coal Mine, 56 kilometers north of the border port, began operating. Since then, several infrastructure projects have been put in place to facilitate the production and transportation of coal, notably the export of electricity from China to Mongolia since 2007 and the completion of the Jiayuguan–Ceke Railway in 2006 and the

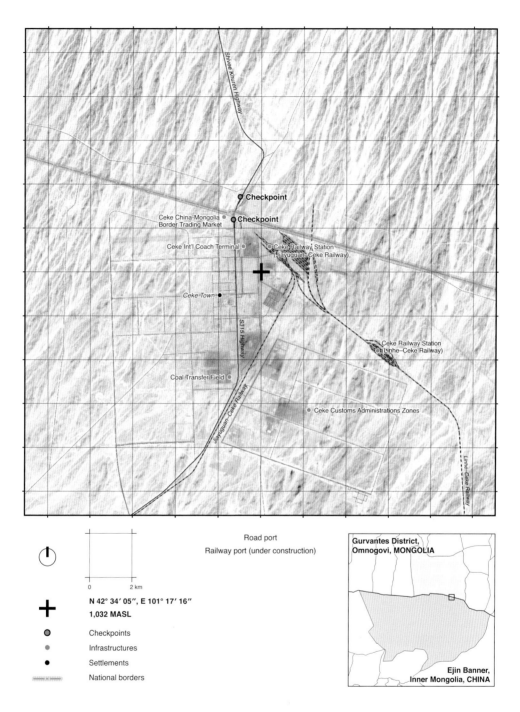

Checkpoint

Checkpoint

Ceke China–Mongolia
Border Trading Market

Ceke Int'l Coach Terminal

Ceke Railway Station
(Jiayuguan–Ceke Railway)

Ceke Town

Ceke Railway Station
(Linhe–Ceke Railway)

Coal Transfer Field

Ceke Customs Administrations Zones

Shivee Khuren Highway

S315 Highway

Jiayuguan–Ceke Railway

Linhe–Ceke Railway

Road port
Railway port (under construction)

0   2 km

N 42° 34′ 05″, E 101° 17′ 16″
1,032 MASL

Checkpoints
Infrastructures
Settlements
National borders

Gurvantes District,
Omnogovi, MONGOLIA

Ejin Banner,
Inner Mongolia, CHINA

Linhe–Ceke Railway in 2010. Work began in 2016 to extend the Linhe–Ceke Railway to the Naryn Sukhait Coal Mine via Ceke–Shivee Khuren. The railway is planned to connect with the Trans-Siberian Railway as part of the fourth Eurasian Landbridge in the long run.

25. GANQIMAODU–GASHUUN SUKHAIT

Shortly after its defeat in the Crimean War (1854–1855), tsarist Russia energetically set about expanding its influence in the Far East. The Amur Committee of the Russian Ministry of Foreign Affairs concluded that Russia's goal should be to form an independent protectorate in Mongolia and Manchuria if Qing China were ever to collapse. Russian expansion into Mongolia became feasible when Saint Petersburg made agreements with Britain and later Japan on their respective spheres of influence in China. Russia agreed to terms with Britain in 1895 then made diplomatic arrangements with Japan after the Russo-Japanese War (1904–1905). A secret treaty signed in 1907 allotted Manchuria to Japan and Mongolia to Russia.

In 1911, on the eve of the collapse of the Qing dynasty, Chinese authorities opened a colonization bureau in Urga (now Ulaanbaatar) to facilitate Han immigration into Mongolia. Outer Mongolia declared its independence in 1911, but this was not recognized by the newly established Republic of China until 1946. Rapid Han colonization of Mongolia was intended to resist Russian influence but in fact only served to exacerbate regional tensions. The ROC government designated Suiyuan, Chahar, and Jehol, three special Inner Mongolian regions bordering Outer Mongolia and Manchuria, as provinces in 1928. Yan Xishan, a Chinese warlord and governor of Shanxi, forcibly occupied Suiyuan, an arid plateau between the Gobi Desert and the Yellow River, in the early 1930s. Under the direction of retired officers from Yan's army, farmer-soldiers from Shanxi undertook iron mining and began reclaiming the region's steppe lands for agriculture.

The Japanese-backed Mongolian army invaded mineral-rich Suiyuan in November 1936. The Japanese Empire formed the puppet state of Mengjiang in 1939, consisting of the former Chinese provinces of Suiyuan and Chahar in Inner Mongolia. Mengjiang was also known as Mengkukuo, in analogy to Manchukuo, another Japanese puppet state in Manchuria, established in 1932. After the Japanese Empire was defeated in 1945, the territory of Mengjiang was returned to Chinese control. A Soviet exploration team discovered one of the world's largest untapped coking and thermal coal deposits at Tavan Tolgoi in southern Mongolia in the 1940s and undertook exploratory drilling and feasibility studies. In 1954, after the founding of the People's Republic of China, the Urad Middle Banner was incorporated into Suiyuan in the Inner Mongolia Autonomous Region.

Ganqimaodu (*gants mod* means "tree" in Mongolian) in the northern part of the Urad Middle Banner was approved in 1989 as a temporary transit point for Sino-Mongolian border trade. Ganqimaodu Port was established and opened seasonally in 1992. After the upgrading of Ganqimaodu Port in 2005, including the construction of a joint inspection building, the port became operational all year round. Rapid development of the port led to the establishment of Ganqimaodu Town in 2012. Several infrastructure projects, including a plan to supply electricity from China to Mongolia and the Wanshuiquannan–Ganqimaodu Railway, were completed around the same time. This facilitated the production and transportation of coal from Mongolia's Tavan Tolgoi Coal

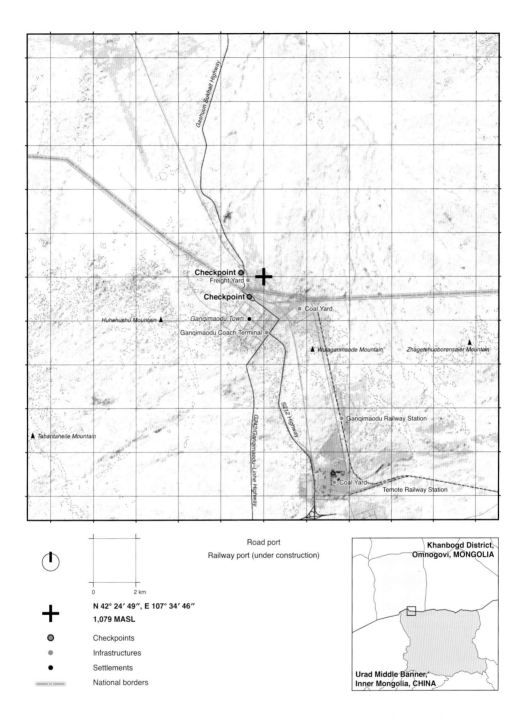

Checkpoint
Freight Yard
Checkpoint
Huhehushu Mountain ▲
Ganqimaodu Town
Ganqimaodu Coach Terminal
Coal Yard
▲ Wulaganmaode Mountain
Zhagetehuoborensaier Mountain ▲
Gashuun Sukhait Highway
G242/Ganqimaodu–Linhe Highway
S212 Highway
▲ Tabantaheile Mountain
Ganqimaodu Railway Station
Coal Yard
Temote Railway Station

Road port
Railway port (under construction)

0   2 km

N 42° 24′ 49″, E 107° 34′ 46″
1,079 MASL

⊙ Checkpoints
· Infrastructures
● Settlements
National borders

Khanbogd District,
Omnogovi, MONGOLIA

Urad Middle Banner,
Inner Mongolia, CHINA

Mine, located 240 kilometers north of the border port. China and Mongolia signed an agreement in 2013 to extend the Wanshuiquannan–Ganqimaodu Railway to the Tavan Tolgoi Mine through Ganqimaodu–Gashuun Sukhait. The Linhe–Ganqimaodu Highway (G242) was opened to traffic in 2018. Construction began on the Tavan Tolgoi–Ganqimaodu Railway, scheduled to be completed in 2022.

26. MANDULA-KHANGI

In response to increasing colonial interference in China, the Guangxu Emperor issued an imperial edict in 1895 kick-starting national reforms, including the prioritization of railway construction. The emperor approved the construction of China's first railway designed and built solely by the Chinese in 1905. The Beijing–Kalgan Railway was completed in 1909, connecting Beijing and Kalgan (now Zhangjiakou), capital of Chahar and a long-established trading post south of the Great Wall. In 1916 the railway was incorporated into the Beijing–Suiyuan Railway. It was extended westward to Suiyuan's capital, Guisui (now Hohhot), in 1921 and to Baotou in 1923. Situated in an arable region of the Yellow River's Great Bend, Baotou had developed into a growing industrial center and an important railhead since the early 1920s, transporting wool and hides brought down the Yellow River from Qinghai and Gansu to Beijing and Tianjin. The ROC government designated Suiyuan, Chahar, and Jehol (three special regions within Inner Mongolia) as provinces in 1928.

From the late 1920s through the 1930s, Germany arguably exerted the greatest influence among the ROC governing elite. The two countries negotiated a set of barter agreements under which China would exchange raw materials for German military and industrial equipment. During the Sino-Swedish expedition (1927–1935), a group of geologists, who focused on identifying iron ore deposits to serve German, Soviet, and nascent Chinese industry, discovered rare-earth deposits at Bayan Obo, a sacred Mongolian site 120 kilometers north of Baotou. A German-Chinese joint venture constructed Baotou Airport in 1934 and opened a weekly air service to Baotou in Suiyuan, Yinchuan in Ningxia, and Lanzhou in Gansu.

The Japanese-backed Mongolian army invaded Suiyuan in November 1936, determined to control its mineral wealth under the guise of incorporating the territory into an independent Mongolian state. The ROC government, however, retained control of Bayan Obo. Mengjiang, also known as Mengkukuo, was formed in 1939 as a puppet state of the Empire of Japan, consisting of the former Chinese Inner Mongolian provinces of Suiyuan and Chahar. Mengjiang returned to Chinese control after the defeat of the Japanese Empire in 1945. After the founding of the People's Republic of China, construction of the Baotou–Baiyun Obo Railway started in 1956. The railway opened two years later. The Baiyun Obo Mine in the Darhan Muminggan United Banner of the Inner Mongolia Autonomous Region was officially established in 1957 in the world's largest known deposit of rare-earth metals.

Mandula, in the northern part of the Darhan Muminggan United Banner, opened as a port on a temporary basis in 1992 and was officially designated Mandula Port in 2002. The Baotou–Baiyun Obo Railway's northern extension to Mandula was completed in 2010. After the upgrading of Mandula Port and construction of Khangi Port across the border in Mongolia in 2015, Mandula Port opened for year-round service. Transportation infrastructure has developed rapidly in the region recently, with construction of the Baotou–Mandula Highway (G210) starting in 2017. Several railway projects serving various

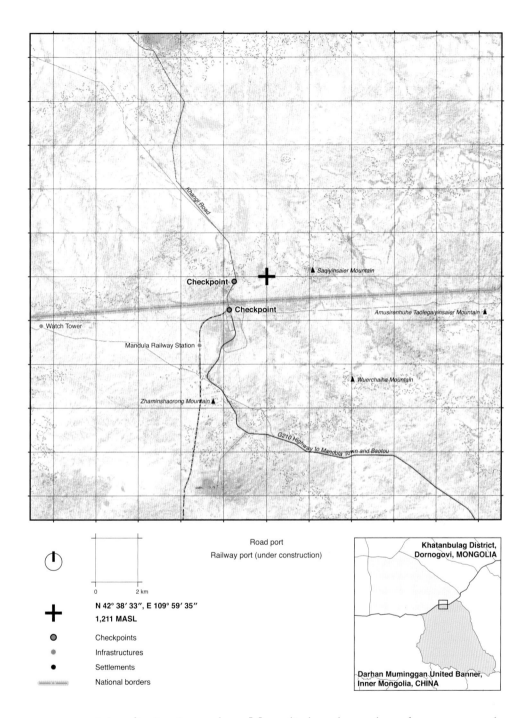

Road port
Railway port (under construction)

N 42° 38′ 33″, E 109° 59′ 35″
1,211 MASL

Checkpoints
Infrastructures
Settlements
National borders

Khatanbulag District,
Dornogovi, MONGOLIA

Darhan Muminggan United Banner,
Inner Mongolia, CHINA

mining districts in southern Mongolia have been planned or are currently under construction. Work began on the 414.6-kilometer Tavan Tolgoi–Zuun Bayan Railway in May 2019. The planning phase of the 281-kilometer railway connecting Zuun Bayan to the China-Mongolia border at Khangi-Mandula commenced in 2020.

27. ERENHOT–ZAMYN-UUD

The Treaty of Nerchinsk (1689) and the Treaty of Kyakhta (1727) defined relations between Imperial Russia and the Qing Empire of China until the mid-nineteenth century. The town of Kyakhta, south of Lake Baikal, was opened to the caravan trade between Russia and China in 1727. Caravans ran south to Urga (now Ulaanbaatar), southeast across the Gobi Desert to Kalgan (now Zhangjiakou), and then southeast over the mountains to Peking (now Beijing). Yilin (from the Mongolian "Ereen," meaning "multicolored") was established as a post in the Gobi Desert between Urga and Kalgan in 1820. The name refers to the landscape of the Dabusan Nur salt lake north of the post. The Qing government established a telegraph line between Urga and Kalgan in 1899 and set up a telegraph station at Yilin, called Erlian on contemporary maps.

The Beijing–Kalgan Railway (later part of the Beijing–Baotou Railway) was completed in 1909, connecting the national capital, Beijing, and Chahar's regional capital, Kalgan. Outer Mongolia declared its independence in 1911 on the eve of the collapse of the Qing dynasty, but this was not recognized by the newly established Republic of China until 1946. A road between Urga and Kalgan was completed in 1918, and Erlian became one of its major stops. American explorer Roy Chapman Andrews led several expeditions into the Gobi Desert and Mongolia between 1922 and 1928 and discovered various dinosaur fossils around the Dabusan Nur. Suiyuan and Chahar in Inner Mongolia became part of Mengkukuo (the puppet state of the Empire of Japan) in 1939. They were returned to Chinese control after Japan's defeat in 1945.

Through the joint efforts of China, Russia, and Mongolia, the Trans-Mongolian Railway, following the trade route from Urga to Kalgan, was built between 1947 and 1955, using the Russian broad gauge. The northern section between Ulan-Ude on the Trans-Siberian Railway in Russia and Ulaanbaatar in Mongolia was completed in 1950 and extended to the Chinese border in 1955. The southern section between Jining on the Beijing–Baotou Railway and Erlian was built between 1953 and 1955. The Trans-Mongolian Railway was opened in 1956, and Erlian Town (now Erenhot) was formally established. During the Sino-Soviet split (1956–1966), China changed the entire southern section of the railway from Russian broad gauge to standard gauge to prevent Soviet invasion through the Trans-Mongolian Railway. A gauge-changing station was set up at Erenhot in 1965.

Sino-Mongolian relations improved in the late 1980s. The Erenhot Road Port opened in 1992, and the railway track from Erenhot to Zamyn-Uud was rebuilt with dual-gauge tracks to facilitate railway interoperability. The Dabusan Nur salt lake has provided an economic boom to Erenhot's chemical industry since the late 1990s and has become a tourist attraction because of its wealth of dinosaur fossils. The Dinosaur Museum of Erenhot, first built in the late 1980s, was expanded in 2009. The Erlian Basin Cretaceous Dinosaur National Geopark was established in the same year. The new millennium saw several rounds of infrastructure and border port upgrading at Erenhot. The Erenhot Road Port was expanded in 2000. Mongolia's Zamyn-Uud Free Trade

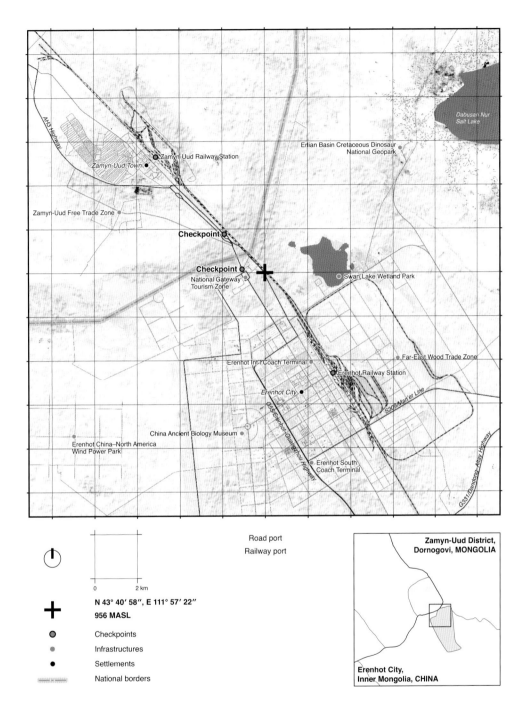

National gateway
Tourism Zone

N 43° 40′ 58″, E 111° 57′ 22″

956 MASL

Road port
Railway port

Checkpoints

Infrastructures

Settlements

National borders

**Zamyn-Uud District,
Dornogovi, MONGOLIA**

**Erenhot City,
Inner Mongolia, CHINA**

Zone was established in 2004. The Erenhot Road Port was further expanded in 2011, and the Erenhot National Key Development and Open Pilot Zone was established in 2014. A plan to develop a China-Mongolia-Russia Economic Corridor was jointly announced by the leaders of the three countries in 2016. China and Mongolia signed a collaboration agreement on the Erenhot–Zamyn-Uud Economic Cooperation Zone in 2019.

28. ZUUN KHATAVCH–BICHIGT

The Greater Khingan Range separates the flat lowlands of the Northeast (Manchurian) Plain to the east from the high Mongolian Plateau to the west. After the Manchus took control of Inner Mongolia in the seventeenth century, the Chahar Mongols moved into the Xilingol (meaning "foothill river" in Mongolian) grasslands west of Bogd Mountain, a subrange of the Greater Khingan Range. Bogd Mountain is the source of several rivers, including the Ulagol, which flows northwest into the Ulagol Marsh, the largest endorheic wetland in Inner Mongolia. A post was established at Uliastai, northwest of the Ulagol Marsh, in 1750. The Russian government sent a research and trading mission (1874–1875) to China seeking new overland routes to the Chinese market. The expedition team visited Chahar in 1874.

After the Russo-Japanese War, Russia and Japan signed a secret treaty in 1907, allotting Manchuria to the Japanese and Mongolia to the Russian sphere of interest. In 1911, on the eve of the collapse of the Qing dynasty, Outer Mongolia declared its independence. It was not recognized by the newly established Republic of China until 1946. Japan occupied all of northeastern China in late 1931 and established the puppet state of Manchukuo in 1932. Mengjiang (Mengkukuo), also a puppet state of the Empire of Japan, was established west of the Greater Khingan Range in 1939, consisting of the former Chinese provinces of Suiyuan and Chahar in Inner Mongolia. Both Manchukuo and Mengjiang returned to Chinese sovereignty after the defeat of the Japanese Empire in 1945.

After the founding of the People's Republic of China, Chahar province was abolished and divided between Inner Mongolia, Beijing, and Hebei. The East United Banner was established in 1952 and divided into East and West Ujimqin Banner in 1956. As part of a national policy of frontier development and consolidation, grassland was rapidly converted to arable land in the Ulagol basin starting in the late 1950s. This process accelerated after the establishment of the Inner Mongolia Production and Construction Corps in 1969. The Ulagol Reservoir was built between 1977 and 1980 to provide water for the increasing demand for irrigation. Uliastai Town was established in 1984 as the administrative center of the East Ujimqin Banner.

Zuun Khatavch ("Zuun" meaning "eastern" and "Khatavch" meaning "threshold" in Mongolian), 65 kilometers northwest of Uliastai, was established as a temporary Mongolia-China transit point in 1989. Zuun Khatavch opened as a seasonal port in 1992, and the Ulagol Development Zone was set up. Khatavch/Gadabuqi Town was established in 2004. The Ulagol Reservoir, destroyed in flooding in 1998, was rebuilt to provide water to the Ulagol Development Zone. Zuun Khatavch Port began year-round service in 2008 and was identified in 2009 as serving one of the three key corridors connecting the Liaoning Coastal Economic Belt in northeastern China with Russia and Mongolia. The Ulagol wetland dried up in 2010 due to the overexploitation of water resources by the Ulagol Development Zone and the region's burgeoning coal mines. A 300-kilometer railway was built in 2014 between Zuun Khatavch

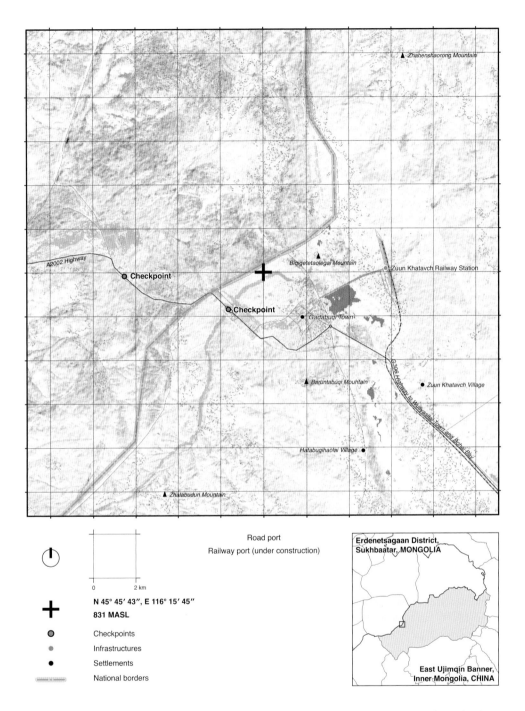

Road port
Railway port (under construction)

N 45° 45′ 43″, E 116° 15′ 45″
831 MASL

Checkpoints
Infrastructures
Settlements
National borders

Erdenetsagaan District,
Sukhbaatar, MONGOLIA

East Ujimqin Banner,
Inner Mongolia, CHINA

0   2 km

Zhahenshaorong Mountain

A2002 Highway

Checkpoint

Biqigetetaolegai Mountain

Zuun Khatavch Railway Station

Checkpoint

Gadabuqi Town

Baruntabuqi Mountain

Zuun Khatavch Village

G306 Highway to Uliyasutai Town and Bohai Bay

Hatabuqihaolai Village

Zhalabudun Mountain

Port and Zhusihua, where it linked up with an existing major railway built to transport coal between Xilingol and Tongliao. China and Mongolia agreed to build a cross-border extension of the Zhusihua–Zuun Khatavch Railway to Mongolia's Khuut Coal Mine in 2016. The Uliastai to Zuun Khatavch section of the Bohai Bay–Zuun Khatavch Highway (G306) was completed in 2020.

29. MANZHOULI-ZABAYKALSK

Greater Manchuria, homeland of the Manchus, had become the center of imperial competition in Northeast Asia by the late seventeenth century. The 1858 Treaty of Aigun specified the Aigun River as the Sino-Russian border, reversing the 1689 Treaty of Nerchinsk, thereby transferring the area between the Stanovoy Range and the Amur River from Qing Chinese to tsarist Russian sovereignty. After Qing China and tsarist Russia signed the 1881 Treaty of Saint Petersburg/Ili, Russia extended its influence further into Manchuria in an attempt to counter increasing Japanese influence in the region. Tsar Nicholas II negotiated an agreement with the Qing court in 1896, obtaining permission to construct a branch of the Trans-Siberian Railway through Manchuria, known as the Chinese Eastern Railway. The T-shaped CER ran from Manzhouli to Suifenhe and from Harbin to Port Arthur (Port Lüshun) at the tip of the Liaodong Peninsula.

Manzhouli became the western terminus of the CER in 1901 and soon developed into a busy cargo transit point. The 2,500-kilometer CER was quickly built over five years and was completed in 1902. Despite signing a convention confirming Chinese authority in Manchuria, Russia continued to increase its territorial and commercial dominance in the region until its defeat in the Russo-Japanese War, which formally ended with the signing of the Treaty of Portsmouth in September 1905. Three months later, Japan and China signed a treaty, recognizing the arrangements made under the Treaty of Portsmouth. In addition, Japan required China to open sixteen of its northeastern towns and cities for international trade, including Manzhouli.

In 1911, on the eve of the collapse of the Qing dynasty, Outer Mongolia declared its independence and occupied Manzhouli. Its independence was not recognized by the newly established Republic of China. Chinese control over Manzhouli was restored in 1914. Local Mongolians rebelled in 1920 and Manzhouli attained some measure of local autonomy after the 1921 Mongolian Revolution. Manzhouli fell under Japanese control in the 1930s as part of the Empire of Manchuria (Manchukuo, 1932–1945), a puppet state of the Empire of Japan. After the end of the Second Sino-Japanese War, the Sino-Soviet Treaty of Friendship and Alliance was signed in 1946. According to the treaty, the ROC agreed to recognize Outer Mongolia's independence and Manzhouli became part of Inner Mongolia. The Civil War flared up in China shortly after the end of World War II. Manzhouli served as a major point of entry for Soviet supplies to the Communist Party of China.

After the founding of the People's Republic of China, Manzhouli Port continued its role as a major port through which Soviet aid was supplied to China, until the aid ceased in 1960, due to the Sino-Soviet split. Manzhouli Port was open only for trains between Moscow and Beijing by 1966. As relations between China and the Soviet Union thawed in the late 1980s, trade across their border resumed. Manzhouli Port reopened in 1988 and was designated an experimental zone in China's Reform and Opening Up policy. The Manzhouli Border Economic Cooperation Zone was established in 1992 and was designated a national 4A-level scenic spot by the China

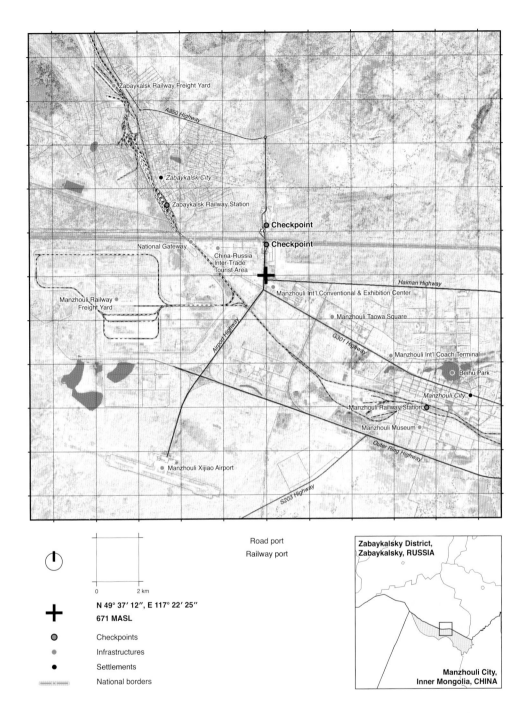

Road port
Railway port

Zabaykalsky District,
Zabaykalsky, RUSSIA

N 49° 37′ 12″, E 117° 22′ 25″
671 MASL

⊙ Checkpoints
• Infrastructures
• Settlements
▪▪▪ National borders

0   2 km

Manzhouli City,
Inner Mongolia, CHINA

National Tourism Administration. Manzhouli Xijiao International Airport opened in 2005 after two years of construction. The Manzhouli Key Development and Open Pilot Zone was established in 2012, and the eastern route of the China Railway Express (CR Express) through Manzhouli-Zabaykalsk began operations the following year. The number of CR Express freight trains passing the port surpassed 10,000 for the first time in 2021.

30. HEIHE-BLAGOVESHCHENSK

The Amur or Heilong River valley became the focus of confrontation between Qing China and tsarist Russia when Russia's territorial expansion and foreign trade reached the Far East in the seventeenth century. Aigun became the seat of the Qing military governor of Heilongjiang in 1683. Qing and Russia signed the Treaty of Nerchinsk in 1689, which recognized Chinese sovereignty over both sides of the Amur River. In 1858, distracted by the Taiping Civil War and the Second Opium War, China signed the Treaty of Aigun, which superseded the Treaty of Nerchinsk, granting the entire left bank of the Amur River to Russia. Under this arrangement, Hailanpao, situated at the confluence of the Amur and the Zeya River, fell within Russian territory. The settlement was renamed Blagoveshchensk (literally, "city of good news") and designated the Russian seat of government for the Amur region.

The old town of Aigun was raided and destroyed by Russian Cossacks and bandits in 1900. Chinese merchants fled 30 kilometers upstream to Heihe, immediately opposite the Russian settlement of Blagoveshchensk. In the aftermath of the Russo-Japanese War, China and Japan signed the Japanese Treaty relating to Manchuria in 1905, which required China to open sixteen towns and cities to international trade in the northeast, including Aigun (Heihe). Construction began in 1907 on the Amur Railway, the last section of the Trans-Siberian Railway to be built in Russia, including a branch line to Blagoveshchensk. Aigun Port opened in 1921, closed temporarily during the 1929 Sino-Soviet conflict over the administration of the Northern Chinese Eastern Railway, then reopened in 1930.

The Japanese army occupied Heihe and took control of Aigun Port in 1933, soon after the establishment of the Manchukuo puppet state in 1932. The Manchukuo National Railway started work on the Bei'an–Heihe Railway, which was completed and opened in 1935. During the 1945 Soviet-Japanese War, the Soviet Red Army seized the Bei'an–Heihe Railway and built a temporary railway across the frozen Amur River that winter to transport its spoils of war. Soviet forces then dismantled the entire Bei'an–Heihe Railway as they withdrew from China in April 1946. Reconstruction of the Bei'an–Heihe Railway began in 1963 under the People's Republic of China but was put on hold again in 1966 due to the outbreak of the Cultural Revolution and the deterioration of Sino-Soviet relations.

Sino-Soviet relations had thawed sufficiently by the early 1980s for the two countries to reach an agreement to reopen Heihe Port. The port officially opened in 1986. Reconstruction of the Bei'an–Heihe Railway resumed that year, and it opened to traffic in 1989. Heihe City was designated as a Border Open City in 1992. That same year, the Heihe Border Economic Cooperation Zone was established, and Heihe Port began year-round service with motor transport, using the frozen river in winter. China and Russia signed an agreement in 1995 to build the Blagoveshchensk-Heihe Bridge, which had first been proposed by the Soviet Union in 1988. After a decade of feasibility studies, construction finally started in December 2016. Transnational energy projects were also transforming the region, as a thirty-year gas deal had been

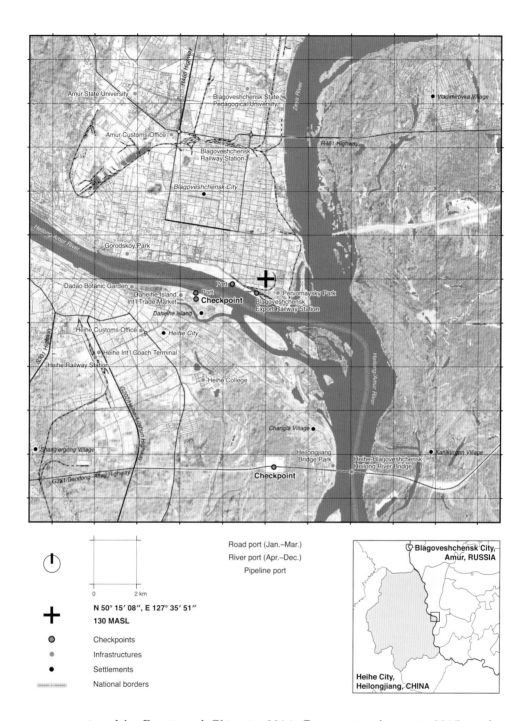

Road port (Jan.–Mar.)
River port (Apr.–Dec.)
Pipeline port

N 50° 15′ 08″, E 127° 35′ 51″
130 MASL

⊙ Checkpoints
• Infrastructures
• Settlements
〜〜〜 National borders

⦵ **Blagoveshchensk City,**
Amur, RUSSIA

Heihe City,
Heilongjiang, CHINA

signed by Russia and China in 2014. Construction began in 2015 on the pipeline connecting Blagoveshchensk and Heihe, a branch of the Power of Siberia pipeline transporting natural gas from Yakutia to Primorsky Krai in eastern Siberia. The Power of Siberia pipeline started delivering gas to China in December 2019.

31. TONGJIANG-NIZHNELENINSKOYE

The Three River Plain at the confluence of the Heilong/Amur River, the Wusuli/Ussuri River, and the Songhua/Sungari River was historically the range of the Nanais, a seminomadic group that surrendered to the Manchus in 1631. Qing China and tsarist Russia signed the Treaty of Aigun in 1858, which reversed the 1689 Treaty of Nerchinsk by transferring sovereignty of the entire left bank of the Amur River from China to Russia. The Qing authorities established the garrison of Lahasusu (meaning "old home" in the Nanai language) in 1882 at the confluence of the Sungari and Amur as a base for their campaign against Russian influence in the region.

In response to increasing Japanese influence in the region, Tsar Nicholas II negotiated an agreement with the Qing court to construct the Chinese Eastern Railway, a branch of the Trans-Siberian Railway, through Manchuria. Russia occupied Lahasusu from 1898 to 1900 on the pretext of storing materials brought via the Sungari River for construction of the CER. The Qing Chinese–Russian agreement concerning the CER ignited the Boxer Rebellion (1899–1901), an uprising against the spread of Western and Japanese influence in northern China. After its failed attempt to put down the uprising, Qing China signed the multinational Boxer Protocol with the Eight-Nation Alliance, obliging it to set up foreign-managed customhouses near the treaty ports. Accordingly, three customhouses were established in the Heilongjiang region, with the Lahasusu customs established in spring 1910 under British control.

After the founding of the Republic of China, Lahasusu became the administrative center of Tongjiang (literally, "joining rivers") County, established in 1913. Soviet leader Joseph Stalin ordered the establishment of the Jewish Autonomous Oblast (JAO) immediately opposite Tongjiang in 1928, in an effort to strengthen Soviet control of its Far Eastern border regions. During the 1929 Sino-Soviet conflict over the administration of the Northern CER, the Soviet army attacked Lahasusu from the Sungari River and temporarily closed down the Lahasusu customhouse. Japan took control of the Lahasusu customs after invading northeastern China in 1931 and setting up the puppet state of Manchukuo in 1932. At the outbreak of the Soviet-Japanese War in 1945, the Soviet Red Army took over Tongjiang. Tongjiang Port was established in 1958 under the People's Republic of China and hosted a boom in Sino-Soviet trade until its closure in 1966 due to the Cultural Revolution and deteriorating Sino-Soviet relations.

The Jiejinkou Nanai Ethnic Village was established in 1984 on the right bank of the Amur River, 38 kilometers downstream from Tongjiang Town and opposite the Russian settlement of Nizhneleninskoye in the JAO. Tongjiang Port was reopened in 1986 with two operational areas: the western operational area located along the Sungari River 3.5 kilometers upstream from Tongjiang Town and the eastern operational area located along the Amur River at Hayudao Island in Jiejinkou. Work on the Xiangyangchuan–Hayudao Railway connecting Tongjiang and settlements in the middle and lower reaches of the Sungari River began in 2003 and was completed in 2007. In the face

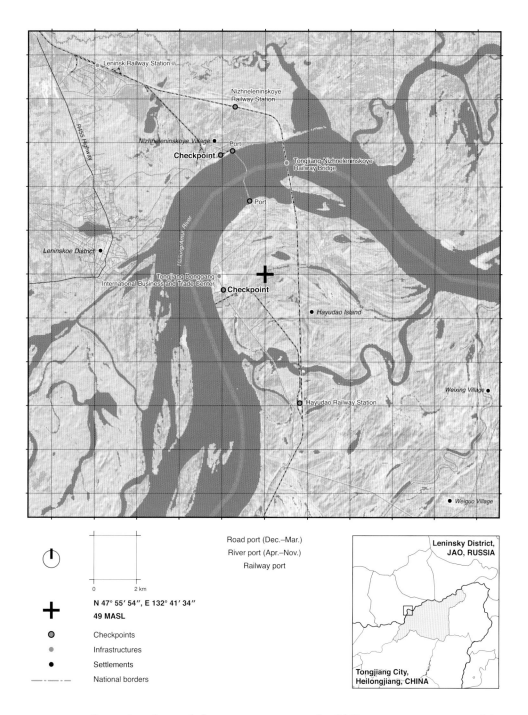

Road port (Dec.–Mar.)
River port (Apr.–Nov.)
Railway port

0   2 km

N 47° 55′ 54″, E 132° 41′ 34″

49 MASL

Checkpoints

Infrastructures

Settlements

National borders

Leninsky District,
JAO, RUSSIA

Tongjiang City,
Heilongjiang, CHINA

of growing demand for cargo transport, the JAO government proposed in 2007 to build a railway bridge between Hayudao in Tongjiang and Nizhnele-ninskoye. A bilateral agreement between China and Russia was reached in 2008. Construction work began in 2014 on the Tongjiang-Nizhneleninskoye Railway Bridge, completed in 2019. It was the first border crossing railway bridge between China and Russia.

32. HULIN-MARKOVO

The Treaty of Aigun (1858) between Qing China and tsarist Russia delineated the boundary between Chinese and Russian far eastern possessions. The 1860 Convention of Peking confirmed the Treaty of Aigun, recognizing Russian sovereignty over the left bank of the Amur River and the area between the Ussuri River and the Pacific Ocean. This set the scene for Russia to establish its major Pacific port city of Vladivostok, where construction of the Trans-Siberian Railway (TSR) was inaugurated in 1891, including Lesozavodsk Station on the Ussuri Line. The settlement of Nema Ting established in Mishan Prefecture by the Qing authorities in 1909 was renamed Hulin the following year in recognition of its location on the right bank of the Qihulin River, a tributary of the Ussuri River.

Russian settlements started to congregate around Lesozavodsk Station after the opening of a sawmill in 1924. Japan invaded northeastern China in 1931 and established its puppet state of Manchukuo in 1932. The Manchukuo National Railway started work on the Linkou–Hulin Railway (Linhu Railway) in 1934 for better transportation of coal and timber from Manchuria to Japan. Completed and opened to traffic in 1937, it ran from Hulin and Mishan to Linkou on the Tumen–Jiamusi Railway. The Japanese army completed an extensive fortification in 1939 at Hutou, strategically located 70 kilometers downstream from the confluence of the Sungacha and Ussuri Rivers with commanding views over the TSR. The Soviet Red Army established a machine-gun artillery division at Lesozavodsk the same year.

Japanese forces at Hutou Fortress battled Soviet troops for eleven days after the end of World War II and were eventually defeated. As it withdrew from China in late 1946, the Soviet Red Army demolished the Mishan to Hutou section of the Linhu Railway, together with all the barracks, fortifications, and communications facilities built by the Japanese within 100 kilometers of the Sino-Soviet border. The Bureau of Reclamation of the Railway Corps of the People's Liberation Army embarked on a program of establishing farms in Mishan and Hulin in 1955 as part of a national policy of frontier development and consolidation. The Mishan–Hutou Railway was repaired in 1956 to serve as a special line for the No. 858 Farm. During the Sino-Soviet border conflict in 1969, Zhenbao/Damansky Island, on the Ussuri River 130 kilometers downstream from the confluence of the Sungacha and Ussuri Rivers, was the scene of major hostilities.

Hulin Port was established in 1988 along the China-Russia border, 58 kilometers southeast of Hulin Town. The Soviet-China eastern sector border agreement was signed in May 1991, allocating 167 Ussuri River islands to Russia and 153 to China, including Zhenbao/Damansky Island. Hulin Port was opened on a temporary basis, and an iron plate pontoon bridge was built. Hulin Port officially opened the following year, and the Songacha River Bridge was completed. A tarmac road between Hulin town and Hulin Port in China was opened to traffic in 2004. The Markovo Port checkpoint building on the Russian side of the border was also completed that year. China and Russia

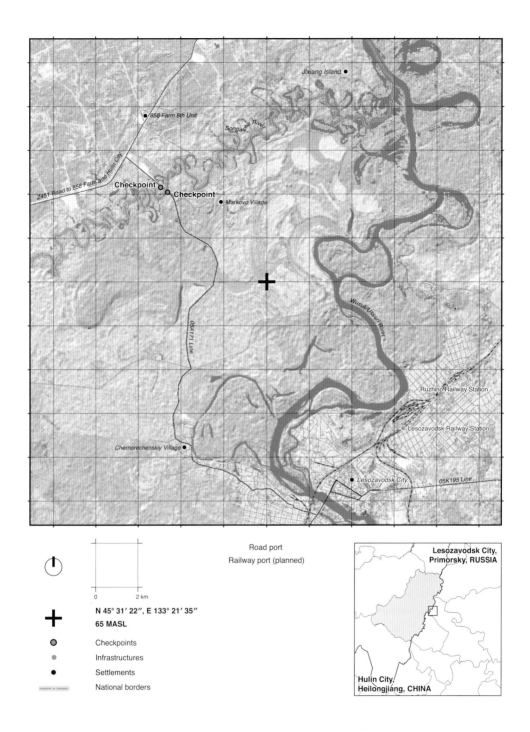

Road port

Railway port (planned)

N 45° 31′ 22″, E 133° 21′ 35″

65 MASL

⊙   Checkpoints

•   Infrastructures

●   Settlements

National borders

Lesozavodsk City, Primorsky, RUSSIA

Hulin City, Heilongjiáng, CHINA

reached an agreement in 2015 to build a 57.1-kilometer cross-border railway between Hulin Station on the Midong Railway (formerly the Linhu Railway) in China and Lesozavodsk Station on the TSR in Russia, to give the landlocked northeastern regions of China better access to Vladivostok on the Pacific.

33. SUIFENHE-GRODEKOVO

The area around Suifenhe, a river flowing into the Amur Bay through the Khanka Lowlands, was subject to increasing Russian influence after 1860, when the Sino-Russian Treaty of the Convention of Peking recognized the area between the Ussuri River and the Pacific Ocean as Russian territory. Russia won a concession from the Qing dynasty in 1897 to construct the Chinese Eastern Railway, a branch of the Trans-Siberian Railway, through Manchuria. The Grodekovo Station in Russia was established in 1898 and a border station in China in 1899, 10 kilometers from one another along the Suifenhe River. The CER was officially opened in 1903, with the Chinese border station renamed Suifenhe Station. Settlements soon grew rapidly around the Suifenhe Station, which was nicknamed "the window of East Asia."

After the Russian Civil War (1917–1922), the USSR and China jointly administered the Northern CER. During the 1929 Sino-Soviet conflict over the administration of the Northern CER, Suifenhe Station was destroyed then quickly rebuilt in late 1929 after the cessation of hostilities. Japan established its puppet state of Manchukuo in northeastern China in 1932 and took control of Suifenhe City in 1933. The city fell into a steep decline after the Japanese army set up a blockade, closing the cross-border railway and stifling Sino-Soviet trade and commerce. The USSR sold its rights to the CER to the Manchukuo government in 1935, and the railway was changed from Russian broad gauge to standard gauge. Japanese control of Manchukuo ended after the 1945 Soviet-Japanese War. The railway soon reopened, and cross-border trade resumed at Suifenhe.

Suifenhe experienced a significant resurgence after the founding of the People's Republic of China and became a primary entrepôt for Sino-Soviet trade and commerce throughout the 1950s. The Suifenhe Railway Port was established in 1953. The Suifenhe Sino-Soviet Friendship People's Commune was established on the Chinese side of the border in 1958, and the settlement around Grodekovo Station on the Russian side was given its present name, Pogranichny, meaning "border." In 1964, in the midst of the Sino-Soviet split, the Suifenhe Friendship Commune was disbanded and Suifenhe Port closed. In the aftermath of the 1969 Zhenbao/Damansky Island incident, all toponyms of Chinese origin in Primorsky Krai were replaced with Russian names. The Suifenhe River was renamed the Razdolnaya (meaning "widely flowing") by the Russian authorities in 1972.

Sino-Soviet relations improved in the 1980s. After the Suifenhe and Pogranichny governments signed a bilateral collaboration agreement in 1987, local cross-border trade resumed. The new national gateway at Suifenhe was completed in 1991. Suifenhe was designated a Border Open City in 1992. It was the scene of rapid development after the launch of the Northeast China Revitalization Strategy in 2003. Upgrading and electrification started on the Harbin–Suifenhe Railway, the former eastern branch of the CER, in 2010. The Heilongjiang section of the Suiman Expressway was opened to traffic that same year. When complete, the Suiman Expressway will connect two cities on the Sino-Russian border: Suifenhe in Heilongjiang and Manzhouli

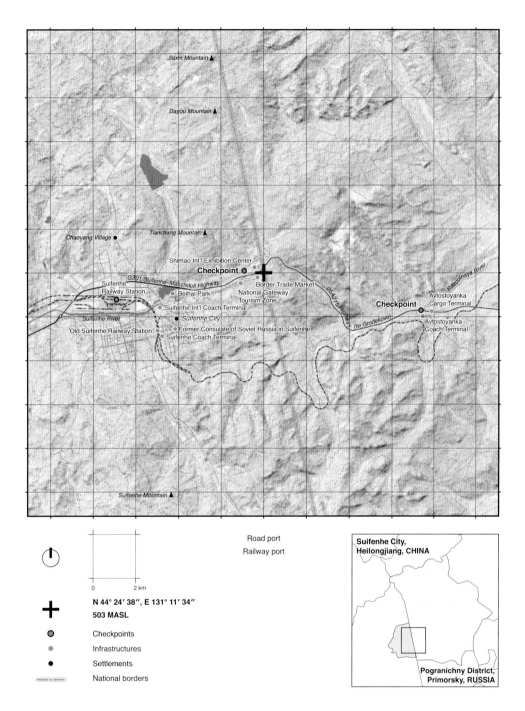

Road port
Railway port

Suifenhe City,
Heilongjiang, CHINA

N 44° 24′ 38″, E 131° 11′ 34″
503 MASL

⊙   Checkpoints

•   Infrastructures

●   Settlements

▪▪▪▪▪   National borders

Pogranichny District,
Primorsky, RUSSIA

in Inner Mongolia. Construction began on the new Suifenhe Station in 2013, and the old Russian-built station was repurposed as the Chinese Eastern Railway Museum. The Suifenhe Area was designated part of the Heilongjiang Pilot Free Trade Zone in September 2019. Timber has become the backbone of Suifenhe's economy, with Gorodekovo-Suifenhe now being a major center for the export of Russian timber.

34. QUANHE-WONJEONG

The Tumen River region was a strategic location on the ancient maritime trading and cultural exchange route from China to Korea and Japan. Russian influence in the region had increased since the early nineteenth century. After the 1858 Treaty of Aigun and 1860 Convention of Peking, tsarist Russia successfully made its territorial claim over the Tumen River Estuary, formerly under Qing Chinese control, so that the last 15 kilometers of the Tumen River formed the border between tsarist Russia and Joseon Korea. The Qing official Wu Dacheng observed in the early 1880s that Russia had extended its territory approximately 50 kilometers upstream from the mouth of the river. Following a joint demarcation exercise carried out at Wu's insistence, a new border treaty between China and Russia was signed in 1886, confirming the relevant terms of the 1860 Convention of Peking and affirming China's navigation rights along the final stretch of the Tumen River to the sea.

After the Russo-Japanese War, Japan and China signed an agreement in 1905 recognizing the arrangements made in the Treaty of Portsmouth that formally ended the war. In addition, Japan required China to open sixteen towns and cities in the northeast, including Hunchun in the lower Tumen region, for international trade. Japan annexed Korea in 1910 and established its puppet state of Manchukuo in northeastern China in 1932. That same year, an agreement to construct six highway bridges over the Yalu and Tumen Rivers by 1939 was signed by Japanese officials of its annexed Korea and officials of Manchukuo. A bridge connecting Hunchun Quanhe (literally, "circular river") and Wonjeong was completed in 1936, 36 kilometers upstream from the mouth of the Tumen River.

Ethnic Koreans in the Tumen region were granted their own autonomous region in 1952, which was upgraded to the Yanbian Korean Autonomous Prefecture in 1955. During the Korean War, the Soviet Union built a wooden bridge 500 meters downstream from the China-Korea-Russia boundary tripoint to carry armaments and supplies to support the Korean People's Army. The Soviet Union upgraded the wooden bridge to a railway bridge in 1959 with 11 meters of clearance, effectively blocking shipping access along the final stretch of the Tumen River. Many refugees crossed the river into North Korea in the 1950s and 1960s to escape economic hardship and famine in China. The flow of refugees had reversed by the late 1970s, and a bilateral agreement was reached by China and North Korea in late 1981 to close the port and bridge at Hunchun Quanhe on January 1, 1982.

The Hunchun Quanhe Port was reopened to diplomatic and commodity services in September 1995. Quanhe-Rajin-Busan intermodal freight transport connecting northeastern China and North and South Korea began operations in November that same year. The land route between Quanhe and Rajin Port along North Korea's coast is of critical importance to China's land-locked Yanbian Prefecture, and Quanhe-Wonjeong's infrastructure has been dramatically upgraded since 2014 under the BRI. This port is a major gateway for seafood imports from North Korea, so wet markets in Quanhe and

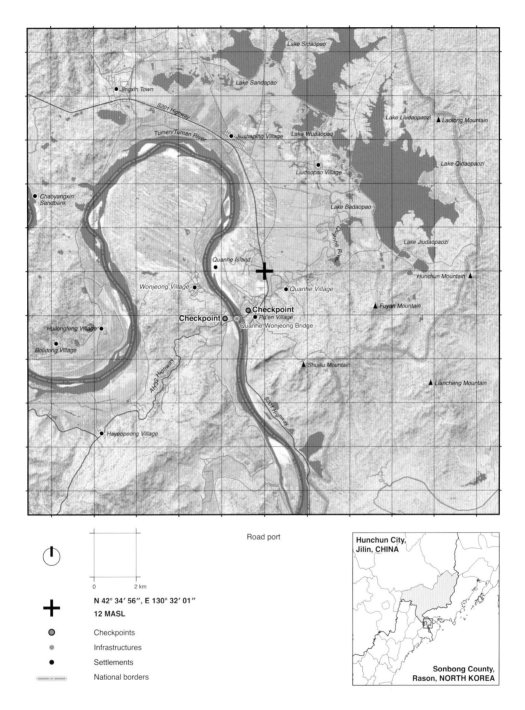

Road port

N 42° 34′ 56″, E 130° 32′ 01″

12 MASL

- ◉ Checkpoints
- • Infrastructures
- • Settlements
- ⚏ National borders

Hunchun City, Jilin, CHINA

Sonbong County, Rason, NORTH KOREA

Wonjeong were upgraded with private Chinese investment in anticipation of increased trade. Works on the New Quanhe-Wonjeong Bridge started in 2014 and were completed in late 2016. A year later, however, cross-border trade fell significantly when the UN imposed sanctions on North Korea because of its missile testing in August 2017.

35. CHANGBAI-HYESAN

Mount Changbai/Baekdu was ennobled as an ancestral mountain by Qing China in the seventeenth century and by Joseon Korea in the eighteenth century. A joint border demarcation was carried out in 1712 at Mount Changbai/Baekdu, the source of both the Yalu River and Tumen River, which formed the boundary between northeastern China and the Korean Peninsula. The Qing-Joseon border area was deliberately depopulated by the Qing authorities until the 1858 Treaty of Aigun and 1860 Convention of Peking codified the tsarist Russian presence in the region. Russia recruited Korean immigrants to reclaim the wildlands to reinforce its control over the newly established Primorskaya Oblast in the Far East region. In response, the Qing authorities recruited Han Chinese to settle and farm the border region.

After the Russo-Japanese War, the Korean Empire became a protectorate of Imperial Japan in 1905. The Qing authorities established an administrative office in Changbai in the upper reaches of the Yalu River in 1908. Qing China and Japan signed the Jiandao/Kando Convention in 1909, under which Japan affirmed China's territorial rights over Kando on the north bank of the Tumen River in exchange for Chinese recognition of Japan's special economic and political influence in Manchuria. Japan took control of Changbai in 1931, which then became part of the puppet state of Manchukuo in 1932. The Japanese developed timber and paper mills at Changbai-Hyesan at the highest navigable point on the Yalu River. As part of the Japan-Manchukuo joint program to construct six river/border-crossing bridges from 1932 to 1939, the Changbai-Hyesan Bridge across the Yalu River was completed in 1936. It was destroyed by floods in 1943, then reconstructed.

After the founding of the People's Republic of China, Changbai County was established in 1949 and designated as Changbai Korean Autonomous County in 1958. During the Korean War, the Changbai-Hyesan Bridge was blown up by the US military to prevent Chinese and Soviet armaments and supplies from reaching North Korea. It was restored after the war in late 1953. The Changbaishan National Nature Reserve was set up in 1960, after which industries related to nontimber forest products, such as ginseng, superseded timber extraction on the Chinese side of the border. Hyesan in North Korea was the scene of a mining boom after copper ore deposits were discovered in the 1960s. The Changbai-Hyesan Bridge was again destroyed by floods in 1964. During China's Cultural Revolution, China–North Korea relations deteriorated and cross-border trade came to a standstill.

It was not until 1985 that China and North Korea reached an agreement to reconstruct the Changbai-Hyesan Bridge. After the bridge reopened in late 1985, cross-border trade resumed. On the North Korean side of the border, mining and hydropower have developed rapidly since the early 2000s. The Samsu Reservoir in Hyesan, completed in 2005, serves North Korea's largest hydroelectric project. The Hyesan-China Joint Venture Mineral Company was established in 2007 to produce and sell copper, mainly to China. The mineral-water industry boomed on the Chinese side of the border in the early

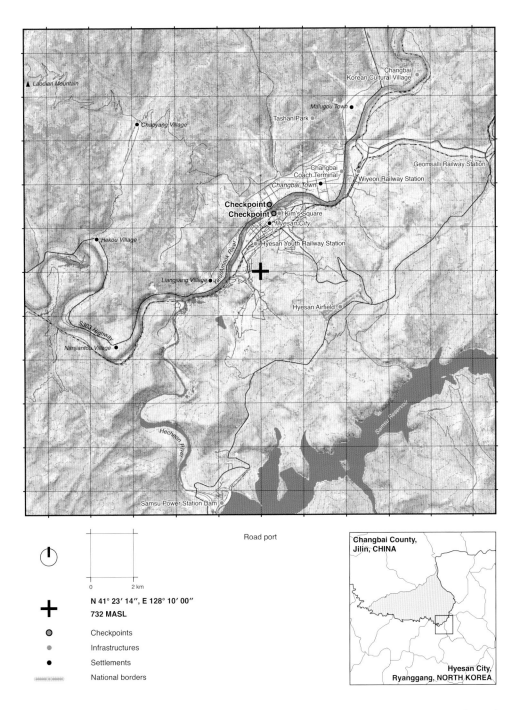

Laodian Mountain

Chaoyang Village

Changbai
Korean Cultural Village

Malugou Town
Tashan Park

Changbai
Coach Terminal
Changbai Town
Wiyeon Railway Station
Geomsalli Railway Station

Checkpoint
Checkpoint
Kim's Square
Hyesan City

Hekou Village

Hyesan Youth Railway Station

Liangjiang Village

Yalu/Amrok River

Hyesan Airfield

S303 Highway

Nanjiantou Village

Hecheon River

Samsu Reservoir

Samsu Power Station Dam

Road port

0   2 km

N 41° 23′ 14″, E 128° 10′ 00″
732 MASL

⊙ Checkpoints
• Infrastructures
• Settlements
⌇⌇ National borders

**Changbai County,
Jilin, CHINA**

**Hyesan City,
Ryanggang, NORTH KOREA**

2000s. Baishan was granted the official title of China International Mineral Water City in 2004. There was also a surge in tourism in Baishan in the new millennium, with Mount Changbai designated one of China's 4A Tourist Attractions in 2001 and further upgraded to a 5A Tourist Attraction in 2009. The Changbai Port Scenic Area was established and opened in 2017.

36. DANDONG-SINUIJU

Situated on the north bank of the Yalu River, which demarcates the western portion of the boundary between northeastern China and the Korean Peninsula, Antung (literally, "pacifying the east") was established by Qing China in 1876. Tsar Nicholas II obtained permission from Qing China in 1896 to construct the Chinese Eastern Railway, a branch of the Trans-Siberian Railway, through Manchuria. Japan and the United States were wary of Russia's increasing influence in Manchuria. They each signed treaties with China in October 1903 to expand commerce. Antung was designated as a port city under the Sino-American treaty, but its opening was prevented by the outbreak of the Russo-Japanese War in 1904.

During the Russo-Japanese War, Japan built a 300-kilometer railway line from Antung to Mukden (now Shenyang), the center of Manchuria's road and rail networks. The southern branch of the CER was transferred to Japanese control and became the South Manchuria Railway (SMR) after the war, and the Mukden–Antung Line (now Shenyang–Dandong Railway) was connected to the SMR. The Korean Empire became a protectorate of Imperial Japan in 1905. Antung was opened as a port city, with a customs station established in 1907. The steel-structure First Yalu River Bridge linking Antung and Sinuiju was completed on the eve of the collapse of the Qing dynasty in 1911, connecting the Mukden–Antung Line in Manchuria and the Shintetsu–Gyeongui Line in Korea at Sinuiju.

The Yalu River hinterland was richly forested. Timber was one of the main drivers of Antung's rapid growth. Antung became one of the largest timber ports in the world by the early 1920s, thanks to modern Japanese machinery. Japanese forces occupied all of northeastern China in late 1931 and established the puppet state of Manchukuo in 1932. Construction of the Second Yalu River Bridge began in 1937. After its completion and opening in 1943, the First Yalu River Bridge was repurposed as a road bridge. During the Korean War, both cross-river bridges were blown up by the US military to prevent China and the Soviet Union from supplying armaments and other goods to North Korea. Only the Second Yalu River Bridge was rebuilt after the war and renamed the Sino-Korean Friendship Bridge. International freight services linking Beijing, Pyongyang, and Moscow via Antung Railway Station became operational in 1955.

Antung was renamed Dandong Port in 1965 but closed soon afterward, in 1966, when China–North Korea relations deteriorated during China's Cultural Revolution. Following the 1978 launch of China's Reform and Opening Up policy, cross-border trade between China and North Korea resumed. Dandong Port was reopened in 1981. The Dandong Border Economic Cooperation Zone was established in 1992. The First Yalu River Bridge, destroyed during the Korean War, was renamed the Yalu River Broken Bridge and designated a national historic monument in 2006. China's premier Wen Jiabao signed an economic cooperation agreement with North Korean leader Kim Jong-il in 2009, with a New Yalu River Road Bridge featuring prominently in the cooperation package. Construction of the New Yalu River Road Bridge began

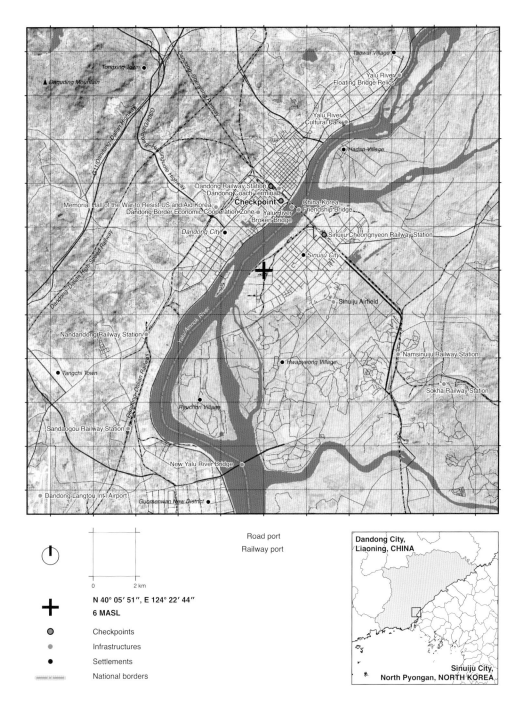

Road port
Railway port

0   2 km

N 40° 05′ 51″, E 124° 22′ 44″
6 MASL

⬤ Checkpoints
• Infrastructures
● Settlements
     National borders

Dandong City,
Liaoning, CHINA

Sinuiju City,
North Pyongan, NORTH KOREA

in 2010, and the main structure was installed across the river in 2013. Completion of the project was originally scheduled for 2014 but was postponed due to construction delays in North Korea. The North Korean section was finally completed in 2021, but the opening of the bridge has been delayed indefinitely because of North Korean demands that China pay the construction costs of the North Korean road links to the bridge.

EPILOGUE

On the morning of June 12, 2018, I took a taxi from China's Hunchun City to the Quanhe-Wonjeong border crossing on the China–North Korea border. As we approached the border, I watched on my mobile phone a live broadcast of the historic summit between the leaders of the United States and North Korea, the first time a sitting American president and a North Korean leader had ever met. The summit was under way at the Capella Hotel on a resort island in Singapore that once housed a Japanese prisoner-of-war camp during World War II but is now called Sentosa (meaning "peace and tranquillity"). After outlining the summit schedule for the day, the announcer enthusiastically listed the working-lunch menu items, featuring a mix of Eastern and Western cuisines, including prawn cocktails, beef short ribs, Korean braised cod, and Chinese-style Yangzhou fried rice.

At about 11:50, just as Donald Trump and Kim Jong-un concluded their two-hour meeting and were about to start lunch, I got out of the cab and walked to the border inspection building. I stowed my laptop, phone, and camera in a locker on the Chinese side before proceeding to the North Korean checkpoint. I handed my passport to a young border guard who appeared to be in his early twenties and explained that I was heading to the Rason Special Economic Zone for a three-day visit. Ignoring anything to do with my visit, he just asked me what I majored in at college. "Landscape architecture," I said. "Oh, landscape . . . so you must be good in geography as well," he commented, stamping my passport and handing it back to me.

Crossing the border at Quanhe-Wonjeong to enter North Korea was easier than I expected and, surprisingly, a lot smoother than most border crossings I had experienced before. At 12:30 I stepped out of the inspection building to wait for the car scheduled to pick me up. A few minutes later, a voice behind me quietly asked, "Do you know where Singapore is?" I turned around to find the border guard who had just stamped my passport taking a cigarette break. "Singapore is in Southeast Asia, at the southern tip of the Malayan Peninsula," I replied. "Is Singapore a city or a country?" "Well, it's both, it's a city-state." "Have you ever visited Singapore? How big is it? Is it bigger than Hong Kong?" Having visited Singapore four times, I told him that

Hong Kong is about one and a half times the size of Singapore. I showed him a Merlion charm purchased in Singapore the previous summer and explained that the mythical half-lion, half-fish is the official mascot of the country. We continued the question-and-answer session for the next few minutes until my car arrived, talking about Singapore, an island some 5,000 km away where a historical event affecting the future of North Korea and potentially the whole Korean Peninsula was in progress. Neither of us mentioned the US–North Korea summit directly. I was not sure how much he knew or was supposed to know about the event or whether it was proper for me to bring it up all since he had not asked.

I did not realize until two days later that most people in North Korea were entirely unaware of the summit until June 14, 2018, when the event was broadcast live there for the first time. I was buying some souvenirs and books at the Rason Foreign Language Bookstore that morning when all of a sudden the saleswomen left their counters and rushed to the far end of the bookstore and gathered in front of a wall-mounted TV. The Korea Central TV program started with a few minutes' footage of major attractions in Singapore, such as the Merlion statue and Marina Bay, before shifting to the Capella Hotel summit venue. A stage bedecked with the US and North Korean flags appeared. The moment the two leaders strode toward each other and shook hands, the saleswomen jumped and cheered and then started hugging together, sobbing and crying. A middle-aged saleswoman spoke to her colleagues in a quiet and quavering voice: "After six long decades, we can finally stand on the same stage with the Americans." As an outsider, I could not comprehend everything, but I was moved by the emotional reactions of these ordinary people who had lived their whole lives under the clouds of political tension and the threat of war between the United States and North Korea. Their families may well have been split by the fortified border in the unresolved aftermath of the Korean War in the 1950s, and many suffered severe hardship after North Korea lost its Eastern Bloc trading partners in the 1990s.

It was a coincidence that my research trip and the 2018 US–North Korea summit in Singaporetook took place simultaneously. The experiences of chatting with the North Korean border guard about Singapore at the border crossing on June 12 and watching the "live" broadcast on June 14 with the saleswomen in a bookstore just fifty minutes away from the border opened my eyes to the disorienting time lapse in terms of the dissemination of information and the intensity of emotion felt by ordinary people in relation to a geopolitical event with global significance. Unlike the saleswomen in Rason, the young border guard could well have overheard something about the summit from Chinese businesspeople a few days earlier, so he would have been eager to know more about it on the actual day. Reflecting on our discussion about Singapore, during which the summit was never mentioned, I think he might either have intentionally restrained himself from asking directly about the summit since he was not supposed to know about it at the time or simply been curious about

Singapore and wanted to know more about it from a landscape architect who must by definition be "good in geography." The border guard might, like myself, be curious about far-flung places that he could never visit and be keen to construct an imagined geography based on what he heard or overheard from travelers he encountered at the border crossing.

I treasure encounters such as this one at the China–North Korea borderland. They are crucial for my borderland research and can be obtained only through experience on the ground in specific places and times. Transnational frontiers are often poor in data. Information about them is fragmentary and often conflicting, thanks to their perplexing histories, complex circumstances, and rapid pace of change. I consider this kind of direct-on-the-ground experience indispensable, as it permits me to reconcile abstract geographical information with the real site conditions that are rich in texture, narrative, and often dissension. Moreover, such grounded experiences help me devise more nuanced and timely research questions than if I relied only on desktop research and structured or semistructured interviews. This book is rooted in and inspired by these grounded experiences. The protracted process of contextualizing and historicizing them enables me to define China's borderlands at multiple scales and from a variety of perspectives. Inevitably, despite a methodologically rigorous process of gathering, projecting, organizing, and narrating information, what you read here is more closely aligned with my imagined geography than it is with the reality of China's borderlands. Just as the North Korean border guard's geographical imagination of Singapore is constrained by the fact that he has never set foot there, my experiences in China's borderlands and my interpretations of those experiences are constrained by my ethnic, national, and professional identities and are thus unavoidably biased and subjective to some extent.

The significance of China's borderlands, the timeliness of the issue, and the academic lacuna that this work aims to fill all serve to justify the existence of this book, as set out in the introduction. On a more personal level, my motivation for writing it is simple. Telling anecdotes such as my encounters with the North Korean border guard and bookstore saleswomen is a convenient way of explaining what I do as a landscape architect and researcher. These anecdotes illustrate how the role of a landscape architect is not limited to transforming physical space by planting trees or designing gardens, streetscapes, and parks. It can also extend to providing a critical understanding of the multifaceted interrelationships of landscape, society, and individuals that extends beyond spatial definitions well into the sociopolitical realm. Though this book resonates with the excitement of personal anecdotes in casual conversation, at the same time it affords me the space and time to decipher how these personal experiences are shaped by, respond to, and reveal the past and present perceptions and practices that are remaking material spaces at and near borders, reprogramming border processes, and transforming social relations and patterns of movement. Naturally, writing a book with length and image limitations involves being selective with information, making categories where none exist, eliminating certain details, and reducing complexity to cater to target audiences. As a result, this book does not claim to be a complete representation of China's borderlands. Rather, it is a transect sliced through the vastness of the subject matter, which may intersect with many others and is available to be expanded, deepened, and adjusted over time.

INDEX

Note: page numbers in *italics* refer to figures or maps; page numbers in **bold** indicate primary entries for port-settlement conglomerations.

Development-Oriented Poverty Reduction
program, 115–116, 118, 126, 128, 141–143
Dianxi Area (Western Yunnan Mountainous
Border Area), 116–119, *117*
Dong Dang. *See* Pingxiang–Dong Dang
Dongxing–Mong Cai, **222–223**
Dostyk. *See* Alashankou-Dostyk
Dragon Crowd Hot Springs, 190
dual directionality, 211–213
Dungan Revolt, 18, 258, 262
Dushanzi–Kucha Highway, 152–154, *153*
Dushanzi-Urumqi-Turpan-Kucha Road, *153*
Dwyer, Michael, 142
Dzungaria, 260, 262, 266

E10 Ethanol Mandate Plan (Implementation
Plan concerning the Expansion of Ethanol
Production and Promotion for Transportation
Fuel), 92
economic cooperation zones: Baketu Border
Economic Cooperation Zone (Liaon-
ing-Tacheng New District), 263; Dandong
Border Economic Cooperation Zone, 296;
Dongxing Border Economic Cooperation
Zone, 222–223; Erenhot–Zamyn-Uud
Economic Cooperation Zone, 279; Heihe
Border Economic Cooperation Zone, 284;
Lincang Border Economic Cooperation
Zone, 233, 234; Manzhouli Border Economic
Cooperation Zone, 282–283; Ruili Border
Economic Cooperation Zone, 238; Suifenhe
Border Economic Cooperation Zone, 290;
Tacheng Border Economic Cooperation
Zone, 262–263; Trans-Altai International
Tourism Cooperative Experimental Zone,
264–265; Wanding Border Economic
Cooperation Zone, 236. *See also* special
economic zones
Eid al-Adha, 157, 170–171, 175n33
Eight-Nation Alliance, 25
Erenhot–Zamyn-Uud, 68, 212, **278–279**
Erkeshtam. *See* Irkeshtam-Erkeshtam
ethnic minorities. *See* minority nationalities
Eurasian Riverway (Russian), *11*
Evergrande Spring, 196–200, *199*, 205n47
exports of plants, 69–71, *73–74*

First Ministry of Machine Industry, 77
Five-Year Plans: First (1953–1957), 43, 77; Tenth
(2001–2005), 65; Eleventh (2006–2010),
91; Twelfth (2011–2015), 66; Thirteenth
(2016–2020), 92
foreign aid programs, 44–45, 80–83
Franco-Siamese War, 230
French colonialism: Boten, acquisition of, 15;
Indochina, 12–16, *17*, 222, 228, 230; Mekong
Expedition, 10–12; Pavie Mission, 12
frontiers, Inner Asian. *See* Silk Roads and Inner
Asian frontiers

Ganqimaodu–Gashuun Sukhait, **274–275**
Gaozhuang Xishuangjing project, 122, 137
Gashuun Sukhait. *See* Ganqimaodu–Gashuun
Sukhait
geomancy, 182, 185, 186
Germany, 19–22, 41, 47–48
Gezhouba Water Control Project, 81
Glukhovskoy, A. I., 18
Go Out policy (*zouchuqu*), 47, 78–80, 84
Golden Boten City, 230–231
Golden Water Crane, 190
Gong Zizhen, 5
Gorno-Badakhshan, 252
Grain for Green or Returning Farmland to
Forest Program, 125
Grand Eurasia Roadway, 22–23, *23*
Great Eurasian Waterway (Russian), 18
Great Stone Industrial Park (GSIP), Belarus,
84–87
Great Yangtze Riverway (British), 18
Greater East Asia Co-Prosperity Sphere
(GEACPS), 24, 28
Greater Mekong Subregion (GMS) Economic
Cooperation, 105–107
Greater Southeast China Subregion (GSCS),
104
Greater Tumen Initiative (GTI), 109–111
Greater Tumen Subregion (GTS), 109–111
Greece, 57–59
Grodekovo. *See* Suifenhe-Grodekovo
Grushko, Yury Frantsevich, 165, *166*
Guangxi Zhuang Autonomous Region, 95, 98
Guangxu Emperor, 276
Gyirong-Rasuwa, 215–216, **244–245**

Han ethnicity, 7, 32n15
Hankou, 103
Harvey, Penny, 173
Heaven Lake (Jianchi/Cheonji), 177–180, *179*,
185–186, 190